The WILD WOODS GUIDE

to tim: for exploring . . .
love annie: spring 2007

D1484223

HarperResource

An Imprint of HarperCollins*Publishers*

The WILD WOODS GUIDE

From
Minnesota to Maine, the Nature and Lore of the Great North Woods

Doug Bennet & Tim Tiner

Illustrations by Marta Lynne Scythes

FIRST EDITION

Printed on acid-free paper

Designed by Nicola Ferguson
Illustrations by Marta Lynne Scythes
Diagrams and charts by Lisa Rebnord

Library of Congress Cataloging-in-Publication Data

Bennet, Doug.
    The wild woods guide : from Minnesota to Maine, the nature and lore of the great north woods / [by Doug Bennet, Tim Tiner ; illustrations by Marta Lynne Scythes].—1st ed.
      p. cm.
    ISBN 0-06-093601-0
    1. Natural history—Northeastern States.   2. Natural history—Canada, Eastern. 3. Forest ecology—Northeastern States.   4. Forest ecology—Canada, Eastern.   I. Tiner, Tim. II. Title.

QH104.5.N58 B46 2003
508.3152'0974—dc21

                                                         2002027566

03 04 05 06 07 WBC/RRD 10 9 8 7 6 5 4 3 2 1

Contents

Contents

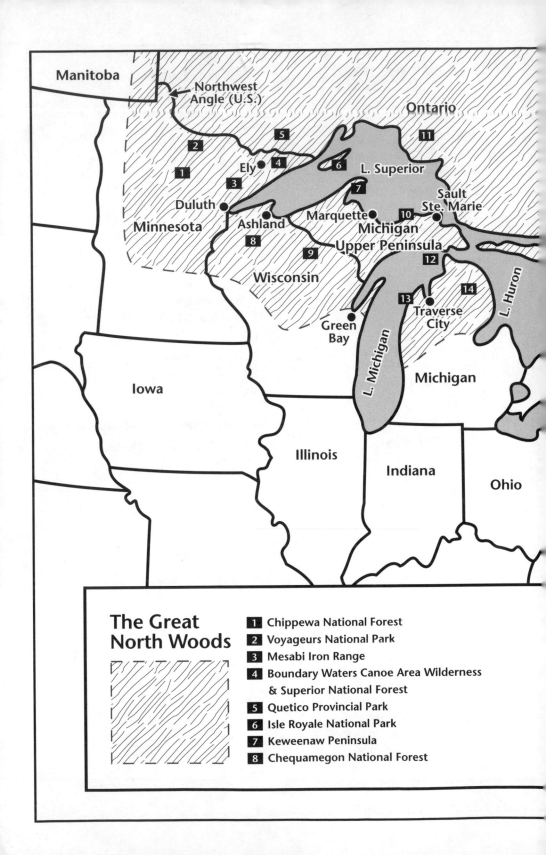

Manitoba

Northwest
Angle (U.S.)

Ontario

2

5

11

1

Ely **4**

6

L. Superior

3

7

Sault
Ste. Marie

Duluth

Marquette

10

Ashland

Michigan

8

Upper Peninsula

Minnesota

9

12

Wisconsin

13

14

L. Huron

Green
Bay

Traverse
City

L. Michigan

Iowa

Michigan

Illinois

Indiana

Ohio

**The Great
North Woods**

1 Chippewa National Forest
2 Voyageurs National Park
3 Mesabi Iron Range
4 Boundary Waters Canoe Area Wilderness
   & Superior National Forest
5 Quetico Provincial Park
6 Isle Royale National Park
7 Keweenaw Peninsula
8 Chequamegon National Forest

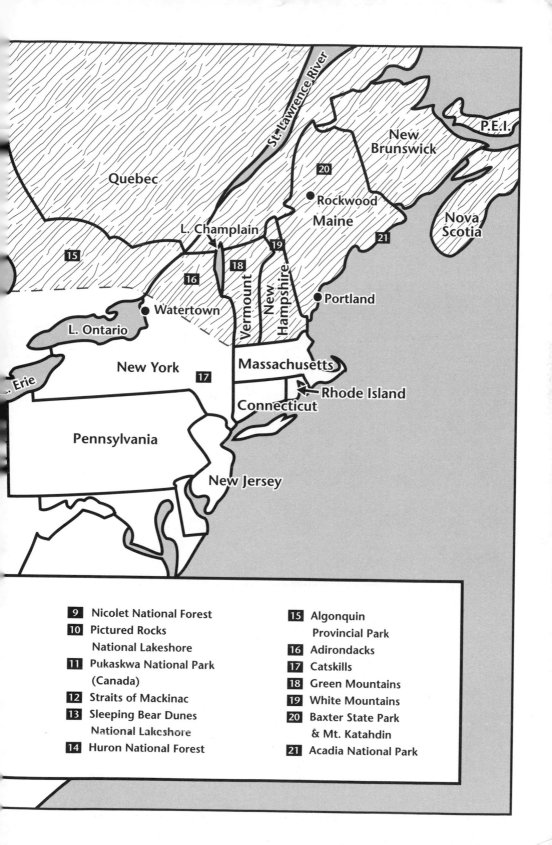

9 Nicolet National Forest
10 Pictured Rocks
    National Lakeshore
11 Pukaskwa National Park
    (Canada)
12 Straits of Mackinac
13 Sleeping Bear Dunes
    National Lakeshore
14 Huron National Forest

15 Algonquin
    Provincial Park
16 Adirondacks
17 Catskills
18 Green Mountains
19 White Mountains
20 Baxter State Park
    & Mt. Katahdin
21 Acadia National Park

Introduction

From the time we are children, there are hundreds of questions swirling around in our minds prompted by experiences in the woods and wilderness. Such experiences make fresh the sense of wonder with which the pretechnological human mind must have viewed the natural world, with all of its sublime and spectacular phenomena. The intent of this book is to answer, from that sense of wonder, a good number of those common questions regarding the "great north woods" and to relate some of the amusing bits of stories, history, and ideas that surround them.

As much as possible, *The Wild Woods Guide* aims to incorporate the whole outdoor experience—the bugs that pester, the wind that scatters them, the trees the wind sways, the life within the soil beneath the trees, the birds in the air, the animals in the night, and the stars, moon, and northern lights that dance across the night sky. We have concentrated on the most commonly seen or experienced species and things in the north, as they are what occupy one's attention most of the time when camping, canoeing, hiking, or visiting cottage, cabin, or camp.

By the "north woods," we refer to the vast, mixed-forest hinterland that sweeps from Minnesota and Wisconsin through the densely treed northern reaches of Michigan, the Canadian Shield of central Ontario, New York's Adirondacks, Vermont and southern Quebec, the Maritimes and the mountains of New Hampshire, to Maine. It is a rocky realm of lakes and streams, mountains and hillsides, to which generations have been drawn for revitalization and reconnection with nature, and is best exemplified by world-famous preserves such as the Boundary Waters Canoe Area Wilderness, Baxter State Park, the Adirondacks, and White Mountain National Forest.

Although there are many forest types within the region, with far northern Minnesota and parts of the Appalachians taking on a more boreal evergreen character, a similar range exists throughout. The north woods is commonly considered a distinct bioregion characterized by the species of trees, plants, and animals covered in this book. Many of these species may also be found in other parts of the country, but we have sought, by concentrating on this specific region, to give as complete a picture as possible within the space of the book. The timings of migrations, mating seasons, and other phenological events accounted for each species are based on their occurrences specifically within the region, though they may differ somewhat from north to south, with elevation, and from season to season.

We have arranged the entries in a way that we hope is useful to readers. There are four parts: "Animal Kingdom," "Plant Kingdom," "The Heavens," and "Mother Earth." The sections within the parts are arranged alphabetically; thus, "Fish" comes before "Mammals" in the part titled "Animal Kingdom." Finally, within each section, the individual entries are arranged alphabetically by common name. An index is also included, complete with references to species not featured but nonetheless appearing within these pages.

Being journalists, rather than biologists, ourselves, we have endeavored to be accurate while straying from a strict scientific or academic tone in the book. Our intent is to answer the many questions of campers and cottagers in the same spirit in which they are asked. If we anthropomorphize, it is because that is indeed what campers and others naturally tend to do when they talk about and relate to the natural world around them. We have striven, however, to ensure that a sense of fun does not distort the true nature of the subject.

ANIMAL
KINGDOM

BIRDS

Birds are the most conspicuous variety of wildlife in the wilderness. Some 650 species of birds nest regularly in North America north of Mexico. Most fly primarily during the day, adding music and bright splashes of color to the forest and waterfront.

The majority of birds—more than 75 percent of all species on the continent—are migratory. An estimated five billion fly south from the northern states and Canada every fall. Hardy chickadees, ravens, barred owls, and ruffed grouse remain behind to tough it out through the winter. But before the snows are even melted, a parade of migrants begins, heralding the return of spring, and reaching a crescendo with waves of wood warblers in mid-May. Some come all the way from South America to raise a new generation on the bugs, berries, and seeds of a north woods summer.

BARRED OWL

Voice in the Night on Silent Wings

"Who cooks for you?" is probably the most persistent question of the night in the north woods. The phrase, when hooted through cupped hands, is the approximate sound of the barred owl's call, which may be heard throughout the year. Though infrequently seen, the barred owl is one of the loudest and noisiest of northern hooters. Its March-to-April mating season is known as the months of madness, for hoots, screams, whistles, barks, and cackles are all part of the owl's courtship repertoire. Later, when they are nesting and their eggs or young are vulnerable to predators, barred owls enter their quietest period.

Though a separate species, barred owls are essentially the eastern version of the

CALLS: Slightly muffled, but resonant, hollow, rapid hoots that sound like "Who cooks for you, who cooks for you all?" or "hoohoo-hoohoo, hoohoo-hoohooaw," with the first hoot sounding like a dog bark and the last uttered in a drawn-out, fading gargle that is not always audible from afar; also screams, barks

NAME ORIGIN: Old English *ule,* meaning "howler"

NAME FOR A GROUP: A parliament of owls

LENGTH: 17–20 in (43–51 cm)

WINGSPAN: 3.3–4 ft (1–1.2 m)

WEIGHT: Males 1–1.8 lb (470–810 g); females 1.3–2.2 lb (610–1,000 g)

MARKINGS: Both sexes gray-brown; vertical light and dark bars on whitish chest, white spots on back; round, puffy, ghostly-looking head with gray facial disk around dark brown eyes; feathered legs

ALIAS: Northern barred owl, wood owl, crazy owl, *Strix varia*

PREFERRED HABITAT: Mature, dense, moist coniferous and mixed forests, especially in swamps and near marshes, rivers, or lakes

HOME RANGE: 0.3–1 sq mi (0.9–2.3 km²)

FOOD: Mice; voles; squirrels; chipmunks; young hares; shrews; frogs; snakes; salamanders; grouse, smaller owls, and other birds; crayfish; fish; insects; spiders

closely related, controversial spotted owl of the Pacific Northwest. The endangered spotted owl's very specific habitat requirements have been a lightning rod for conflict over the preservation of ancient forests from logging. Though the barred owl also needs dense woodlands, it is not quite as dependent on large tracts of old growth and is thankfully secure and abundant in most of the northeast.

To many eastern woodland peoples, the owl represented the female moon spirit. It was thought to have beneficial, healing powers and to be a messenger between living and dead relatives. Owl feathers were hung from tobacco pipes as prayer offerings to the Earth and moon. Owls were similarly associated with the moon and with female deities in the Old World. Athena, the Greek goddess of wisdom and war, was usually depicted with an owl at her side. Sometimes, though, the owl's persona was more ambiguous. To the Chinese, it was both a thunderbird and a stealer of souls. It was a symbol of death in ancient Rome and an evil night hag, a witch in bird form, in the Christian world. When her husband bumps off the king of Scotland, Shakespeare's Lady Macbeth hears an owl call and says:

NEST: Usually in a tree cavity with an opening 20–28 in (50–70 cm) wide and 16–33 ft (5–10 m) above the ground; sometimes in an old crow's or hawk's nest

AVERAGE CLUTCH: 2–3 white eggs, about the size of chicken eggs but spherical

INCUBATION PERIOD: 28–33 days

FLEDGING AGE: About 6 weeks

LIFE SPAN: More than 10 years in wild; up to 23 years in captivity

PREDATORS: Great horned owls. Crows and hawks may eat young.

DROPPINGS: Resemble melted candle wax

RANGE: Throughout eastern United States to eastern prairies, north to boreal forest across Canada to Rockies

WINTER WHEREABOUTS: Stays on breeding range; flies further south in winters when food is scarce

FIRST APPEARANCE OF OWLS: Up to 65 million years ago

NUMBER OF OWL SPECIES NESTING IN NORTH WOODS REGION: 10

NUMBER OF OWL SPECIES WORLDWIDE: About 130

ALSO SEE: Deer Mouse

It was the owl that shriek'd, the fatal bellman,
Which gives the stern'st good-night.

But to be as wise as an owl is an axiom that has survived from ancient Greek times. The image was probably fostered by the bird's huge, serious eyes, with lids that close downward like a human's, rather than with the bottom lids rising up, as with most birds. Owl's eyes are also set flat on their faces like humans', giving them binocular vision—each eye's view overlaps to enhance depth perception and faraway details. A large number of light-sensitive retinal rods at the back of their eyes make owls see small objects in the dark up to six times more clearly than do humans. Their eyes are so large that owls can barely move them up, down, or sideways in their sockets, while their broad faces narrow their view to 110 degrees, compared with 180 degrees for humans. They make up for it by being able to turn their necks 270 degrees, sometimes so quickly that their heads appear to completely rotate.

Despite their sharp, long-range sight, owls do not see as well close up. They don't give a hoot about farsightedness because highly specialized hearing allows them to pinpoint small prey exactly. In experiments conducted in absolute darkness, they have no trouble catching mice.

An owl's ear openings are long slits even bigger than its eyes, hidden by large flaps of skin and feathers at the sides of its head. The ear slits are at the edge of rings of feathers spreading from around the eyes, forming a facial disk that acts like a radar dish in picking up sounds. The disk feathers move to help direct the sound, and the skin flaps over the ears can be raised to deflect noise coming from behind the head. Each ear slit is in a slightly different position, enabling the owl's brain to detect noises at two different angles at the same time—high-tech stereophonics. The two sound lines target the prey precisely, with the owl snatching it up where the lines meet. Owls can hear and locate prey even beneath the snow. Deep or crusted snow makes hunting difficult, leading to good times and population explosions for mice.

Even while it is using noise as its meal ticket, the owl itself is silent, swooping down without warning, on fluffy, serrated-edged wing feathers that make no sound. Their puffy feathers always make owls look bigger than their actual size. A light body, in relation to their large wings, makes them particularly buoyant, with less need of flapping. Owls usually hunt from perches on dead trees. Since they eat small animals whole, pellets of regurgitated bones, fur, feathers, claws, and beaks often mark the spot beneath a regular perch or nest.

Though they are mainly nocturnal, barred owls sometimes hunt during the day, like moonlighting humans, when they're raising families. They're a settled lot, and from one generation to the next often use the same nest for one or two decades.

Unlike smaller birds, the downy white young hatch separately, a couple of days apart, because their mother starts incubating each egg as she lays it, around early April, rather than waiting until all are together. If food is in short supply, only the oldest—the biggest and first to eat—will survive. When they are four or five weeks old, usually in June, the young begin hanging around on branches outside the nest, though it's a week or two more before they fledge. They continue to live off the folks until the autumn, when they set out into the world to establish their own territories and make something of themselves.

BLACK DUCK

Smitten by Shotguns and Mallards

Once reputed the most common quacker in the east, the darkly mottled black duck has been in a state of flux for more than fifty years. Though still the fowl most likely to turn up in weedy backwaters through much of the north woods, it has been significantly diminished by hunting, habitat loss, and even sex and assimilation.

Blackies are the most wary of ducks, flying straight up out of the water at the slightest whiff of trouble. It's in the air that they must have earned their name, appearing very dark against the sky, save for the flashing white undersides of their wings. Both the challenge of their fast, elusive flight and the fact that they are a large, tasty eating duck have long made them an autumn shotgun favorite. They fell from the sky in numbers approaching a million birds up to the early 1980s. Perhaps pushed by the hunting pressure, black ducks expanded their range westward from Lake Erie, reaching Minnesota between the

TOP FLYING SPEED: More than 25 mph (40 km/hr)

LENGTH: 21–25 in (53–63 cm)

WINGSPAN: 33–37 in (84–94 cm)

WEIGHT: Females 2.2–2.7 lb (1–1.2 kg); males 2.5–3.3 lb (1.1–1.5 kg)

MARKINGS: Mostly dark brown, with sandy face and neck, violet-blue wing patch, white inner-wing undersides, and orange-red or olive feet; bills yellowish on males, greenish and often mottled on females

ALIAS: American black duck, dusky duck, blackie, black mallard, brown duck, Labrador duck, blackjack, redleg, velvet duck, blue-winged duck, *Anas rubripes*

SCIENTIFIC NAME MEANING: In Latin, *anas* is "duck," *ruber* is "red," and *pes* is "foot."

NAME FOR A GROUP: A paddling of ducks

CALLS: Females quack like mallards, males make a low croak.

1950s and '70s. Overall, however, their population dropped by half over the same period, prompting a lawsuit by the U.S. Humane Society and other groups that forced the introduction of a one-black-duck-per-day bag limit on hunters in 1983 and a shortening of the shooting season to one month. The population has since increased slightly.

Blackies are the most wary of ducks, flying straight up out of the water at the slightest whiff of trouble

---

Compounding the problems faced by black ducks is an apparently irresistible green-headed waddler well known to most city dwellers: the ever-popular mallard. Native to both North America and Eurasia, mallards are the ancestors of most domestic ducks and are genetically almost identical to black ducks. The two probably separated only during the past ice age, with black ducks becoming camouflaged for a wooded setting. With the clearing of forests, however, western mallards moved east. Some 1.7 million have also been released from game farms in the northeast since 1940, creating large population pools that expand into northern waters wherever black duck numbers are falling. Under such conditions, the two species interbreed, with the brightly colored mallard drakes seeming to win out over the less glamorous local males. Their hybrid descendants, which invariably tend to look like mallards, are fortified with black duck genes

PREFERRED HABITAT: Beaver ponds; sluggish alder-lined streams; shallow, weedy lakes; marshes; swamps; bogs
DENSITY IN PRIME HABITAT: Up to 5 nests per acre (0.4 ha)
HOME RANGE: Up to 5 sq mi (13 km²)
FOOD: Pondweed, water shield, water lily, sedges, wild rice, and other grasses and aquatic vegetation; seeds; berries; acorns; mussels; crayfish; frogs; toads. Ducklings, and less so adults, eat insect larvae, snails, worms, other aquatic invertebrates, and tadpoles.
NEST: Depression in grassy vegetation, filled with leaves and stems, lined by down, hidden in a brushy stand of sweet gale or other shrubs or sedge along a shoreline or an island; sometimes on a muskrat lodge or further from shore
AVERAGE CLUTCH: 8–10 creamy-white or greenish eggs, about the size of large chicken eggs
INCUBATION PERIOD: 26–29 days
FLEDGING AGE: 58–63 days
AGE OF FIRST-TIME BREEDERS: 1 year
LIFE SPAN: Up to 19 years
PREDATORS: Skunks, raccoons, and mink take eggs; snapping turtles, pike, and muskies prey on ducklings.
INTERSPECIES BREEDING PARTNERS: Mallards, pintails, and wigeons
PORTION OF NORTH AMERICAN BIRDS THAT HYBRIDIZE WITH OTHER SPECIES: About 10%
AGE OF OLDEST WATERFOWL FOSSILS: 80 million years
DATE OF FIRST DOMESTICATION OF MALLARDS: At least 1st century A.D.

that make them fairly resistant to a blood parasite, known as avian malaria, spread by north woods black flies. The parasite normally causes mallards to go duck up.

One reason blackies and mallards mate so readily with each other is that their courting customs are virtually the same. Either species will respond to the overtures of the other. These consist of a variety of posturings, including drakes cruising by females shaking their heads and tails and holding their chests high. On their wintering grounds, small groups of males often circle around hens whistling catcalls, making nasal quacking small talk, and flicking water at the ducks that take their fancy. For their part, females may goad the drakes they are entertaining into attacking interloping rivals to test their mettle. Just before finally mating, pairs get in the mood by facing each other and rapidly raising and lowering their heads in tandem.

When not courting, mating, or building nests, females spend most of their time in eating overdrive, concentrating on protein-rich invertebrates, before laying their eggs. Black ducks are "dabblers," gleaning their food from the surface of the water or dipping their heads down to forage off shallow bottoms, seeming to moon observers in the process. Once mother ducks begin laying eggs, their mates begin to loosen the strings of their attachment. Within one to three weeks, they usually paddle off to hang out with the boys in the middle of larger lakes to molt, rendering them flightless for about ten days. Their single-parented offspring emerge from their shells between mid-May and early June. Females escort the downy ducklings out of the nest usually within a day of hatching, and tend them up to a week or two before they fledge in midsummer, when the mothers seclude themselves to molt. Later, everyone joins the groups of dads out on the big lakes, where pairing off for the following spring's mating season begins.

DUCKISMS: Lame duck, sitting duck, dead duck, odd duck, just ducky, "Don't forget to duck."
RANGE: Throughout north woods region to North Carolina; southern Great Lake hinterlands, north to Labrador, Hudson Bay, and northern Saskatchewan
SPRING MIGRATION IN NORTH WOODS REGION: Late March to early May
FALL MIGRATION IN NORTH WOODS REGION: October to late November
WINTER WHEREABOUTS: Northeastern Maine, Great Lakes, southeastern Minnesota, to northern Florida and eastern Texas; almost two-thirds between Long Island and North Carolina
NUMBER SHOT BY HUNTERS IN UNITED STATES IN AUTUMN: 180,000
ESTIMATED POPULATION ON WINTERING GROUNDS: 260,000
NUMBER OF DABBLING DUCK SPECIES NESTING IN NORTH WOODS REGION: 9
NUMBER OF DUCK FAMILY SPECIES WORLDWIDE: 148
ALSO SEE: Common Merganser, Beaver

BLACK-CAPPED CHICKADEE

Big Vocabulary and Expanding Mind

atrolling the woods in their gray, black, and white uniforms, tame chickadee troops communicate with a kind of rudimentary language, one of the first to be discovered among wildlife. Their namesake, a buzzing "chick-a-dee-dee" call, which is uttered in innumerable different combinations, key shifts, and repetitions that some researchers liken to human sentence structure, carries a wide variety of distinct messages, allowing flock members to keep in contact, announce food discoveries, and warn of danger. They also have a wide repertoire of tweets, twitters, gargles, and hisses—fifteen types of vocalizations in all—used in love, war, and other social interactions.

The chickadee phrase humans most long to hear comes on sunny midwinter days, when males start laying claim to breeding territories by whistling their high, lingering mating song. Though the song may be heard into early summer, its first echo through the cold, still woods is taken

AVERAGE TERRITORIAL FLOCK: 6–8 birds

BODY TEMPERATURE: 108°F (42°C), dropping to 41–45°F (5–7°C) during regulated hypothermia to conserve energy on cold winter nights

APPROXIMATE NUMBER OF FEATHERS: 2,000

FLYING SPEED: Average 12 mph (20 km/h). (Dense plumage yields warmth but slow flight.)

WING BEATS PER SECOND: 30

HEARTBEATS PER MINUTE: 500–1,000

LENGTH: 4.5–6 in (12–15 cm)

WINGSPAN: 6–8.5 in (15–22 cm)

WEIGHT: $\frac{1}{3}$–$\frac{1}{2}$ oz (10–14 g)

MARKINGS: Black cap and beard, white cheeks and belly; gray wings, back, and tail; rusty-buff wash on lower sides; deep black eyes

ALIAS: Common chickadee, black-capped titmouse, long-tailed chickadee, *Parus atricapillus*

CALLS: Nasal, buzzing "chic-a-dee-dee," simple, whistled song with

as a promise of spring. After spending the early winter in small foraging flocks, chickadees disperse over a wider area in March. The top one or two males of the flock take territories in the winter-foraging area, often pairing up with their previous year's mate. The other, usually younger chickadees are pushed out to less favorable sites. On average, only one couple per flock survives from one breeding season to the next, most often the dominant pairs with the best feeding and sheltering sites.

In place of chocolates, courting male chickadees offer females large insects, which have lots of protein to help in egg production. If they can't find an unoccupied woodpecker hole or other tree cavity to call their own, they spend a week or two pecking one out, usually three to thirteen feet (one to four meters) above the ground. Lower-ranking female chickadees sometimes fly to the territory of a dominant male for an illicit liaison, then return to their nests on the wrong side of the tracks to have their cuckolded husbands help raise their blue-blooded brood.

From the time the eggs are laid, usually one a day, until the young are fledged, chickadee parents become quiet and secretive. Fathers bring food while mothers incubate. Like most songbirds, chickadee chicks hatch helpless and blind. But stoked with a superrich protein diet of insects, they increase their weight by 50 to 75 percent in the first twenty-four hours. They are ten times their birth weight after ten days and fledge when two to three weeks old. Families fly together for another three or four weeks before the young disperse.

In late summer and fall, chickadees form small, inquisitive flocks again, often

the first note much higher than the second, commonly written as "fee-bee" or "fee-bee-ee"

PREFERRED HABITAT: Mixed and deciduous woods with paper birch or alder, especially near forest edge; swamps

FOOD: Mostly caterpillars, spiders, beetles, katydids, plant lice, insect eggs and pupae, carrion; in fall and winter, about 50% hemlock and other conifer seeds, berries, cherries, acorns, maple sap

FLOCK TERRITORY: 20–56 acres (8–23 ha)

AVERAGE BREEDING TERRITORY: 3–18 acres (1.2–7.3 ha)

NEST: Cavity in tree or stump, especially birch, lined with moss, fur, grass, pine needles, and feathers, with an opening about 1 in (2.5 cm) wide

AVERAGE CLUTCH: 6–8 reddish-brown-spotted, dull white eggs, about the size of pistachio-nut shells

INCUBATION PERIOD: 11–13 days

FLEDGING AGE: About 16 days

AGE OF FIRST-TIME BREEDERS: Most 1 year

AVERAGE ANNUAL ADULT MORTALITY: 40%

AVERAGE ADULT LIFE SPAN: Average 2.5 years; up to 12 years

PREDATORS: Sharp-shinned hawks, saw-whet owls, northern shrikes. Nests raided by red squirrels, raccoons, weasels, snakes.

ACCOLADES: State bird of Maine and Massachusetts

OFTEN SEEN WITH: Nuthatches, brown creepers, downy and hairy woodpeckers in winter flocks; plus kinglets, warblers, and vireos in autumn flocks accompanied by migrating species also for-aging for seeds, insects, and bug eggs. Chickadees specialize in searching through the bark crevices of low outer branches, hanging upside down from the tips or hov-ering under leaves. Young-of-the-year chickadees that join the flock are usually from other areas, not the offspring of the resident dominant pairs, ensuring the gene pool is mixed.

RANGE: Northern United States to New Jersey, Appalachians to North Carolina, Indiana, Kansas, Colorado, and northern California; north to Alaska and northern boreal region of Canada

WINTER WHEREABOUTS: Most stay put. Flocks of young birds sometimes migrate to southern portions of breeding range mid-September to November, especially in years of food shortage; return April–May.

NUMBER OF U.S. CHICKADEE AND TITMOUSE SPECIES: 12

NUMBER OF CHICKADEE AND TITMOUSE SPECIES WORLDWIDE: 65

Each troop maintains and defends its borders from neighboring chickadee bands. The stakes can be high, since each chick-adee may hide hundreds of seeds, berries, and insect bodies daily in autumn, stashing them under bark and inside knotholes or tufts of pine needles and curled dried leaves. Researchers from Rockefeller University at a field station in upstate New York found that to handle all the data on the locations of these winter food stores, chickadees do something humans cannot: They expand their memory banks, growing new neurons in the hippocampus, the part of the brain that deals with spatial recollection.

They also have a wide repertoire of tweets, twitters, gargles, and hisses—fifteen types of vocalizations in all—used in love, war, and other social interactions

Their brains actually become bigger. Quick access to the food is essential because the tiny birds burn up all of their body fat to stay warm on most winter nights and must replenish it anew every day, requiring far more food than they do in the summer.

BLUE JAY

Smart, Loud, Bold, and Brash

Among other birds, blue jays are not nearly the favorites they are of humans. Jays have a nasty habit of eating birds' eggs and even their nestlings. Nest robbing is really only a rare treat for them, making up less than 1 percent of their diet, but it's enough to make them terrors. Small birds often gang up and mob a jay to drive it away, noisily diving at and sometimes striking it in the air. For their part, jays frequently mob hawks, owls, crows, weasels, and foxes, which can threaten them or their offspring. The jay's loud, harsh alarm call also commonly warns other birds and animals that a potential predator is entering the area.

Blue jays in general are considered bold, brash, alert, and intelligent. They can adapt quickly to a wide variety of habitats, though they favor evergreen trees for nesting and roosting, and oak and beech trees

LENGTH: 10–12 in (26–30 cm)
WINGSPAN: 16–17 in (41–42 cm)
WEIGHT: 2.3–3.9 oz (65–110 g)
MARKINGS: Blue back, white undersides, black necklace, blue crest
ALIAS: Bluecoat, common jay, jay-bird, nest robber, northern jay, corn-thief, *Cyanocitta cristata*
NAME ORIGIN: Old German *gahi*, meaning "quick"
NAME FOR A GROUP: A party of jays
CALLS: Wide variety, including short, loud, harsh screams, a "queedle" sound like a squeaky clothesline, and whistles
PREFERRED HABITAT: Mixed and deciduous forest edges, especially stands with oak or beech
FOOD: About 80% acorns, beech- and hazelnuts, pine seeds, berries; the rest caterpillars,

for feasting on acorns and nuts. When oaks have a major acorn crop, once every four to ten years, blue jay populations increase significantly.

A single jay can hide or bury up to 5,000 nuts and acorns in a single autumn, retrieving them later through the winter. Many commonly fly a mile (1.6 kilometers), sometimes up to 3 miles (4.8 kilometers), to a fruitful stand, cram their throats and beaks with up to five acorns or fifteen beechnuts, and then return to their territories to hide the loot. Those they forget about often germinate, making the birds important agents of long-distance nut dispersal. Experts studying buried pollen records believe blue jays may have played a big part in the rapid advance of oaks into New England and the upper Midwest after the glaciers retreated 10,000 years ago.

In early spring, loose winter-feeding parties of jays begin to break up. Males fight, establish territories, and, despite their reputations as raucous brigands, sing softly to their mates. By late April or May, they become unusually quiet and inconspicuous as they begin nesting, quite the opposite of most male songbirds. Females do most of the building of their well-hidden nests over the period of about a week. As with many species, her mate concentrates on fetching food and feeding her like a nestling. This "baby" behavior helps bond the pair and provides the required energy and protein for developing eggs.

Blue jay young, like many other birds, hatch featherless, blind, and unable to generate enough heat to warm their blood to normal survival temperatures. For their first two or three days, they are closely brooded and not fed, instead living off the

beetles, grasshoppers, and other insects, their eggs and cocoons, spiders, frogs, minnows, bird eggs, and nestlings

NEST: Bulky construction of sticks, grasses, bark, and mud, lined with moss, feathers, and rootlets, wedged between a forked branch, usually 6–50 ft (2–15 m) above the ground

AVERAGE CLUTCH: 4–6 cherry-tomato-sized light green, blue, or buff eggs, with brown specks

INCUBATION PERIOD: 17–18 days

FLEDGING AGE: 17–21 days

AGE OF FIRST–TIME BREEDERS: 2 years

NEST FAILURE RATE: 34–90%

ANNUAL ADULT MORTALITY: About 50%

LIFE SPAN: Up to 18 years in wild, 26 years in captivity

PREDATORS: Hawks, owls. Nests raided by crows, squirrels, rat snakes, and probably raccoons.

FLYING SPEED: Average 20 mph (33 km/hr); 32–40 mph (51–64 km/h) in migration

MIGRATION ALTITUDE: Usually 570–660 ft (175–200 m); up to 1,000 ft (300 m)

RANGE: All eastern United States to Rockies and eastern Texas, north across southern boreal region of Canada

SPRING MIGRATION IN NORTH WOODS REGION: Late April to June

FALL MIGRATION IN NORTH WOODS REGION: September to October

WINTER WHEREABOUTS: Most remain in north and probably less than 20% fly to southern portion of summer range

NUMBER OF U.S. JAY SPECIES: 5

ALSO SEE: Black-Capped Chickadee, Red Oak

yoke absorbed from their eggs. After those first critical days, their circulatory systems rev up, their blood warms, and they acquire downy insulation. Their bright red, opened mouths trigger an automatic feeding response in their parents, who nourish them with a rich soup of regurgitated caterpillars and other juicy insects. By June, four-week-old fledglings accompany their parents in regrouping flocks of foraging jays.

A single jay can hide or bury up to 5,000 nuts

and acorns in a single autumn

In the fall, especially September, blue jays gather in larger flocks, sometimes in the hundreds, and migrate south. Up to 30,000 a day, spread out in long, loose lines, have been counted in steady flights past some hawk watches. While many stay in the north to tough it out all winter, they sometimes all but vanish from some areas, possibly because of poor nut and seed crops.

A close relative, the gray jay, generally stays in the north all winter, rarely traveling farther south than northern Wisconsin and the Adirondacks. Gray jays survive by building up winter food stores starting in June, chewing seeds to coat them with saliva, which acts as a preservative, and then sticking them beneath bark and moss. Their diligent endeavors allow 83 percent of territorial gray jays to live through winter, a much higher rate than migrant species enjoy. The uncrested gray birds, also called whiskyjacks, are renowned for their friendliness, often taking food from campers, especially in late summer and early fall. Their tame demeanor may have led to an old superstition that gray jays were the ghosts of dead lumberjacks.

BROAD-WINGED HAWK

Secretive Midstory Sentinel

As birds of prey, hawks have the advantages of size, deadly striking power, and remarkable eyesight. They peer downward with eyes that can make out long-distance details far smaller than anything human beings could distinguish. On their breeding grounds, crow-sized broad-winged hawks use their powers of vision to detect minute moving prey from midcanopy hunting perches above small clearings, beaver ponds, stream sides, and other forest edges. Transparent, side-closing lids let them moisten their eyes without blinking so they won't miss a thing.

On the fresh, breezy days of mid-September, eagle-eyed hawk watchers at strategic locations such as Putney Mountain in Vermont and Hawk Ridge above Duluth, Minnesota, scan billowy white clouds and

MIGRATION ALTITUDE: Most at 1,000–2,600 ft (300–800 m), up to 8,200 ft (2,500 m)

AVERAGE GLIDE PERFORMANCE: 11 ft (or 11 m) forward for every 1 ft (or 1 m) drop

AVERAGE DAILY MIGRATION DISTANCE: 60–300 mi (100–500 km), covered in 6 hours

TOTAL MIGRATION DISTANCE: 2,800–6,200 mi (4,500–10,000 km), undertaken over average of 40 days

FLYING OR GLIDING SPEED: 20–40 mph (33–67 km/h)

LENGTH: Males 13–17 in (33–44 cm); females 15–19 in (38–48 cm)

WINGSPAN: 2.6–3 ft (80–94 cm)

WEIGHT: Males 11–14 oz (310–400 g); females 14–20 oz (390–560 g)

deep blue skies for large flights of migrating broad-wings. The raptors they admire so much face a daunting task when migration time comes around. Their winter homes are in the dense rain forests of Central and South America. Broad-wings must conserve their energy as much as possible because their bodies are heavier in proportion to their wings than smaller migrants'. They also don't get a lot to eat along the way.

To make it, broad-wings harness the energy of the sun on clear days, soaring upward in tight circles on rising columns of warm air, called thermals. Because patches of open ground and rock faces heat up more quickly than the atmosphere, the air just above them expands and rises like a bubble as it warms. Broad-wings rise as high as 8,000 feet (2,440 meters) before the thermal weakens, its moisture condensing into droplets and forming small cumulus clouds. Then, launching off on air currents, the hawks may glide for up to almost 4 miles (6 kilometers), losing altitude slowly until reaching the next thermal, marked by groups of other hawks drifting upward. The amount of flapping required throughout is kept to a bare minimum.

Because they have farther to migrate than most other hawks, broad-wings return to the north later and head south earlier, when the sun is high and yields six or seven hours of good thermals. The cold-blooded prey that makes up a big portion of their grub is abundant only during the year's three or four warmest months, anyway. Draining from forests across the northeastern United States and Canada, they bunch up along the shores of the Great Lakes, which they can't cross for lack of thermals over water. Cold fronts of northwest winds

MARKINGS: Adults have black-edged white underwings, mottled reddish bars on breast, wide black and white tail bands, and brown backs; young birds are more streaked, less distinct.

ALIAS: Broad-wing, broad-winged buzzard, *Buteo platypterus*

NAME ORIGIN: Old English *haf*, meaning "seize"

CALL: Very high, thin, 2-note whistle, 2–4 seconds long

PREFERRED HABITAT: Near streams, beaver meadows, bogs, and other openings in dense deciduous or mixed woods

FOOD: Toads, frogs, snakes, chipmunks, mice, voles, squirrels, baby hares, shrews, small birds, salamanders, grasshoppers, dragonflies, crickets, caterpillars, earthworms, crayfish

DAILY FOOD HELPING: 0.5–0.8 oz (14–23 g)

NEST: Loose sticks lined with leaves, moss, and bark, usually 6–12 m (20–40 ft) up in the crotch of a deciduous tree, especially birch or aspen, sometimes in an old crow's, hawk's, or squirrel's nest

AVERAGE TIME REQUIRED TO BUILD A NEST: 3–5 weeks

AVERAGE CLUTCH: 2–4 spotted white eggs, about the size of small chicken eggs

INCUBATION PERIOD: 31 days

FLEDGING AGE: 35–42 days

AVERAGE NUMBER OF NESTLINGS THAT FLEDGE: 1.5

MORTALITY RATE IN FIRST 6 MONTHS: 50–75%

LIFE SPAN: Up to 18 years

PREDATORS: Great horned owls, raccoons, and crows raid nests.

in mid- to late September can pepper the skies with huge, rising kettles, or "boils," of broad-wings over choice north-shore sites such as Hawk Ridge, where up to 110,000 have been counted passing above in a single season.

In April, the returning hawks are detoured along the southern edges of the big water bodies. Many thousands are again spotted over other watches, including Whitefish Point, near the east end of Michigan's Upper Peninsula, and Braddock Bay, on the New York Lake Ontario shore, which tallied more than 100,000 broadwings one spring, headed for the Adirondacks and points north. Up into the 1930s, such well-known migration spots were scenes of slaughter, with large numbers of hawks shot from the sky because they were considered vermin, or at least good target practice. Roger Tory Peterson, originator of the classic Peterson series of nature guides, counted 254 southbound raptors brought down by gunners in a single morning in 1935 at Cape May, New Jersey.

POPULATION DENSITY IN SUITABLE HABITAT: 1 pair per 1–2 sq mi (0.4 km²)

ESTIMATED NORTH AMERICAN POPULATION: More than 1 million

RANGE: All eastern United States to edge of prairies, south to eastern Texas and northern Florida, north to southern Canada

SPRING MIGRATION IN NORTH WOODS REGION: Early April to mid-May; peak, late April

WINTER WHEREABOUTS: Southern Florida, Cuba, Central America to Amazon and Bolivia

AVERAGE LAST DEPARTURE FROM NORTH WOODS REGION: Mid-August to late October; peak, mid-September.

NUMBER OF DAY-HUNTING BIRD-OF-PREY SPECIES NESTING IN NORTH WOODS REGION: 11

NUMBER OF DAY-HUNTING BIRD-OF-PREY SPECIES WORLDWIDE: About 292

ALSO SEE: Barred Owl, Sun, Thunder and Lightning, Turkey Vulture

Although broad-wings appear to migrate in flocks, they are really traveling as individuals following the same highway. Even mates, which may return to the same nest site every year, journey separately and remain single in their winter resorts. Their lifelong relationship is purely seasonal, bound by a common nesting site. Some ornithologists believe that they may not even recognize each other in the spring. They engage in courtship flights and mating calls as soon as they return.

COMMON MERGANSER

Tree-Nesting Northern Duck

Compared to the weedy waters to the south and west, much of the north woods can be a rather duckless place. Despite the wealth of lakes across most of the region, many are too deep, rocky, and sterile to support the abundant aquatic plants eaten by mallards and other dabbling ducks. One duck that actually prefers such clear water, the diving, fish-eating common merganser, has been pushed back from southern areas by cottage development, powerboats, overfishing, and water pollution. Though not considered tasty hunting prizes, mergansers were once persecuted by cottagers who, after fishing out and polluting lakes, concluded the longtime-resident mergansers must be responsible for the disappearance of fish.

In truth, mergansers are usually too thinly spread out to have a significant impact on fish populations. They concentrate on slow-moving species rather than sport fish.

TOP FLYING SPEED: 42–51 mph (70–85 km/h)

TOP MIGRATING SPEED OF ANY BIRD: 69 mph (113 km/h), by canvasback ducks

WING BEATS PER SECOND: 4.6

LENGTH: 1.8–2.2 ft (55–68 cm)

WINGSPAN: 2.8–3 ft (86–91 cm)

WEIGHT: Males 2.7–5 lb (1.2–2.2 kg); females 2–4 lb (0.9–1.8 kg)

MARKINGS: Reddish-brown head and crest, gray back, white breast, throat, and square wing patches flashing in flight on female; green-black head, black back, white breast, neck, and sides on males; orange-red feet and saw-edged bills on both

ALIAS: Goosander, saw-bill, fish duck, American merganser, flapper, sheldrake, *Mergus merganser*

NAME ORIGIN: Latin *mergus anser*, meaning "diving goose"

CALLS: Though usually silent, males make low, raspy croaks, females a guttural call.

PREFERRED HABITAT: Forest lakes, ponds, rivers

USUAL DEPTH OF HUNTING GROUNDS: 1.5–6 ft (0.5–1.8 m)

DEEPEST DIVES: 20 ft (6 m)

LENGTH OF DIVES: Usually less than 30 sec; up to 2 min.

FOOD: Minnows, suckers, sculpin, stickleback, and other slow-moving fish, most 4–12 in (10–30 cm) long; aquatic insects; fish eggs

In April, mergansers gather in big flocks in large rivers and on sheltered bays along the Great Lakes as they wait for the ice to break up on smaller inland lakes. They often begin their air-and-water courtship chases at those sites and are already paired up when they arrive at breeding grounds. Male mergansers, along with other ducks, geese, and swans, have the distinction of being among the few birds with penises. Most birds merely have cloacas, orifices combining all excretory functions, which are rubbed together during mating in what's known as a "cloacal kiss." Male ducks, however, inflate a fold of skin from the cloaca for the job.

Male usefulness in the continuance of the species does not extend far beyond their penises. Though they defend nesting territories for a time, soon after the last eggs are laid, males drift away.

Soon after hatching, usually in June, merganser ducklings bail out like tiny paratroopers one after another from tree-cavity nests up to fifty feet (fifteen meters) high, their light bodies fluttering to the ground without injury. Hatchlings waddle behind their mothers to the water and swim and dive immediately. They also hitch rides on their mothers' backs. But the most common summer merganser sight is a hen with a long line of paddling ducklings behind her, tracing the indentations of the shore. Often there may be twenty ducklings or more in tow. The large broods are often the result of other mothers laying their eggs in the temporarily unoccupied nests of other birds when nesting cavities are in short supply. Broods also often become amalgamated as the ducklings grow, especially after about thirty to sixty days, when mothers drift off to molt, leaving them alone for good.

NEST: Usually a down-lined tree cavity with an opening 5 in (13 cm) wide; sometimes in a crevice or beneath rocks, a stump, roots, or bushes; within 200 yd (183 m) of a shoreline

AVERAGE CLUTCH: 8–12 light brown eggs, about the size of large chicken eggs

INCUBATION PERIOD: 28–35 days

FLEDGING AGE: 60–75 days

AVERAGE ANNUAL ADULT SURVIVAL: 50–70%

PREDATORS: Mink, martens, raccoons, skunks. Snakes eat eggs; barred owls, pike, muskies, and pickerel prey on young.

RANGE: Throughout most of north woods region, restricted to northern rim of Michigan's Lower Peninsula, scattered along Appalachians south to Pennsylvania; in all states from Black Hills and Rockies, west; north to Alaska and across forested regions of Canada

SPRING MIGRATION IN NORTH WOODS REGION: Late March to early May

FALL MIGRATION FROM NORTH WOODS REGION: Mid-September to early December

WINTER WHEREABOUTS: Southern New England and Great Lakes to northern Mexico

OTHER TREE-CAVITY-NESTING DUCKS: Wood ducks, common goldeneyes, buffleheads, hooded mergansers

NUMBER OF DIVING DUCK SPECIES NESTING IN NORTH WOODS REGION: 8

GREAT BLUE HERON

Motionless Giant in the Shallows

LENGTH: 3.3–4.5 ft (1–1.4 m)
WINGSPAN: 5.6–6.6 ft (1.7–2 m)
HEIGHT: Up to 4 ft (1.2 m)
WEIGHT: 4.6–5.5 lb (2.1–2.5 kg)
FLYING SPEED: 19–29 mph (30–46 km/h)
WING BEATS PER SECOND: 2.3–3.2
MARKINGS: Gray back (with bluish hue in the right light), white head and front of neck, long black head plume, bright yellow eyes
ALIAS: Blue heron, blue crane, gray crane, big cranky, *Ardea herodias*
CALLS: Loud shrieks, harsh squawks, deep croaks
PREFERRED HABITAT: Marshes, swamps, beaver ponds, shallows, weedy lakeshores; up to 2,000 ft (610 m) in Vermont mountains
AVERAGE FEEDING TERRITORY: About 140 yd (128 m) of shore, or 1.5 acres (0.6 ha) of marsh
FOOD: Fish, frogs, crayfish, mollusks, snakes, mice, young muskrats, small birds, insects
AVERAGE DAILY FOOD INTAKE: 1.1 lb (0.5 kg)
DISTANCE BETWEEN NESTING AND FEEDING SITES: Average 1.5–4 mi (2.4–6.5 km); up to 19 mi (30 km)
NEST: Loose platform tangle of sticks, 1.6–3.3 ft (0.5–1 m) wide, usually 30–50 ft (9–15 m) up in a deciduous tree
AVERAGE CLUTCH: 3–5 light

L ike a *Flintstones* airbus rising out of the primordial past, a great blue heron lifts high into the air with just a few slow, heavy flaps of its huge pinions. With long legs dangling and neck folded back in an S, herons in flight do evoke images of extinct pterodactyls. It is widely accepted, in fact, that birds evolved directly from dinosaurs, though pterodactyls were not dinosaurs and the first birds probably did not fly. Feathers are thought to be modified scales that first evolved for insulation rather than flight. In recent years, a number of dinosaur fossils have been found with primitive downy fluff, suggesting to many paleontologists that the ancient beasts were, like birds, warm-blooded.

Herons are a tad more subtle than the dinosaurs of popular conception, but they are every bit as terrifying to just about anything that moves and will fit down their throats. Patience is everything to hunting herons. Starting early in the morning, they wade along the edges of marshes and streams and wait statue-still until a fish or frog comes within range of their lightning-quick bills. After spearing a fish, they may flip it into the air to catch and eat it headfirst. The heavy, muscle-bound neck must be doubled back when the bird is in flight, unlike cranes, geese, and swans, who employ their relatively lithe, long necks to leisurely gobble plants and insects. Given the chance, blue herons will also snap up small shorebirds, rodents, and snakes, sometimes hunting on land or fishing at night if the light is good.

Though they hunt alone and defend fishing holes from each other—sometimes in aerial combat—herons congregate in colonies in their off-hours. Heron rookeries are generally densely packed, noisy, foul-smelling places in remote, hard-to-reach swamps, marshes, islands, or uplands. Some are known to be at least 60 years old. White, acidic bird droppings cover the trunks and lower branches of nesting trees, often killing them after years of use. Huge stick nests teeter on flimsy branches, helping to keep raccoons away but making landing difficult. Sometimes eggs or chicks are even flung to the ground.

blue-green eggs, a little larger than chicken eggs

INCUBATION PERIOD: 28 days

FLEDGING AGE: 56–60 days

AGE OF FIRST-TIME BREEDERS: 3–4 years

ANNUAL MORTALITY: About 70% in 1st year, 35% in 2nd year, 20% afterward

ADULT LIFE SPAN: Average 6–8 years, up to 23 years

PREDATORS: Ravens, crows, herring gulls, hawks, owls, eagles, blue jays, raccoons, and bears raid nests.

LARGEST COLONY IN NORTH WOODS REGION: 670 nests in Lake Champlain

BIRD SPECIES THAT NEST IN COLONIES: About 12%

RANGE: Throughout north woods region and parts of every state to southern Alaska and Canadian mid-boreal region

SPRING MIGRATION IN NORTH WOODS REGION: Mid-March to mid-May; peak, early April

FALL MIGRATION IN NORTH WOODS REGION: Late July to late November; peak, August and early September

WINTER WHEREABOUTS: Atlantic seaboard, Great Lakes, southern Minnesota to Venezuela

AGE OF OLDEST BIRD FOSSILS: 140 million years

AGE OF LONG-NECKED ANCESTOR OF HERONS, STORKS, AND FLAMINGOS: 40–50 MILLION YEARS

NUMBER OF HERON SPECIES NESTING IN NORTH WOODS REGION: 3

NUMBER OF HERON AND RELATED BITTERN SPECIES WORLDWIDE: 60

ALSO SEE: Osprey, Wetlands

After laying their eggs in late April or May, at least one parent remains at the nest until the little ones are about a month old. Baby herons look like gawky little punk rockers with frizzy Mohawk hairdos. Life is not easy, with all the commotion in the nest, and even after they fledge, the odds are stacked against them. Many do not learn the skill and patience needed for hunting and end up starving. Two-thirds of fledglings die in their first year and only about 10 percent survive to mate.

Patience is everything to hunting herons

Before migrating, large numbers of herons gather in on large lakes and wetlands, starting in August. Flocks of up to 100 file out over several weeks, though a few stragglers may linger into late November.

Herons have been hurt by development, water pollution, acid rain, wetland drainage, woodlot cutting, and nest-site disturbance. The long, dark plume jutting from the back of the great bird's head was highly prized for ladies' hats 100 years ago, spelling the demise of many a heron. Protection efforts, however, have resulted in populations stabilizing in most areas of the north woods and even increasing in Michigan and New York. The return of beavers to many areas also probably helped by creating innumerable small ponds, ideal heron hunting habitat.

HERMIT THRUSH

Reputed Finest of Songsters

Testosterone, the hormone that fuels machismo among humans, cues birds to start singing. In the springtime, lengthening daylight stimulates testosterone production in male birds, putting them into breeding serenading mode. Of all the avian melodies, the hermit thrush's fluted, resonant tones, carrying far through the forest, are considered by many to be the most beautiful. The spotted songster, in fact, is a close relative of the celebrated European nightingale, long a favorite of poets and writers. For a grieving Walt Whitman, the call of the hermit thrush embodied his deepest emotions in "When Lilacs Last in the Door-yard Bloom'd," his requiem for the assassinated Abraham Lincoln and a war-shattered nation:

CALLS: Resonant, ringing, melodious song that sounds like a flute, often consisting of several phrases repeated in a row, each 1–2 seconds long, varying in pitch and style, with a clear, deep opening note followed by higher, rapid, fluttering couplets, fading at the end; also low call notes of "tuk" or "chuk"

LENGTH: 6.25–7 in (16–18 cm)

WINGSPAN: 11–12 in (28–30 cm)

WEIGHT: 0.9–1.3 oz (26–37 g)

MARKINGS: Black-spotted white breast, brown back, rusty brown tail, and distinct white eye ring

ALIAS: Swamp angel, *Catharus guttatus*

NAME FOR A GROUP: A mutation of thrushes

. . . *(Victorious song, death's outlet song,*
yet varying, ever-altering song,
As low and wailing, yet clear the notes,
rising and falling, flooding the night,
Sadly sinking and fainting, as warning
and warning, and yet again bursting
with joy,
Covering the earth, and filling the spread
of the heaven,
As that powerful psalm in the night I
heard from recesses,) . . .

Distinctive of northern woodlands and mountains in the east, the hermit's ringing tunes have earned it the status of Vermont's official state bird. Singing most actively at dusk and dawn, the thrush achieves its virtuosity by using its bronchial tubes, which branch off from the windpipe into the lungs, to sing two notes at the same time. Unlike a human, whose voice box is located at the top of the windpipe, or trachea, a bird produces sounds from the bottom of its trachea. The more muscles attached to the voice box, the greater the range of sounds it can produce.

The hermit thrush is like a much-loved pop star that seeks anonymity

---

For all its echoing, mellifluous beauty, the hermit thrush, as its name suggests, is like a much-loved pop star that seeks anonymity. Unlike the treetop-singing robin, the most familiar of thrushes, the smaller hermit remains well hidden as it flutes, often on the forest floor, where it both

PREFERRED HABITAT: Large tracts of dense, young, upland woods; often closer to forest edge than other thrushes

FOOD: Mostly beetles, grubs, caterpillars, ants, spiders; some worms, snails, salamanders, blueberries, blackberries. In fall and winter, eat more berries, of elder, dogwood, pokeweed, and poison ivy; cherries; wild grapes; seeds; and buds.

NEST: Neat cup, 4–6 in (10–15 cm) wide, of twigs, leaves, bark strips, and an outer layer of moss and ferns; lined inside with rootlets, pine needles, grass, and willow catkins; usually in a dip in the ground hidden beneath branches of a small evergreen, ferns, or low shrubs; sometimes up to 10 ft (3 m) in a small tree or shrub

AVERAGE CLUTCH: 4 olive-sized light blue or pale turquoise eggs

INCUBATION PERIOD: 11–13 days

FLEDGING AGE: 10–15 days

NEST FAILURE RATE: Average about 37%

NESTS PARASITIZED BY COWBIRDS: 5–22%

LIFE SPAN: Up to 8 years in wild

PREDATORS: Sharp-shinned hawks. Nests raided by red squirrels and weasels.

NUMBER OF PAIRS OF MUSCLES ATTACHED TO THE VOICE BOXES OF SONGBIRDS: 5–9

NUMBER OF PAIRS OF MUSCLES ATTACHED TO THE VOICE BOXES OF GEESE: 1

NUMBER OF PAIRS OF MUSCLES ATTACHED TO THE VOICE BOXES OF TURKEY VULTURES: 0

RANGE: Throughout north woods region south to Pennsylvania, West

nests and forages. It habitually seems nervous, cocking its tail and then slowly dropping it down. If spotted, the little bird usually plunges silently into dense shrubbery before the observer has a chance to identify its fleeting visage. Remaining unseen is vitally important for the male thrush so that he can regularly steal away to the well-hidden nest where he feeds his mate while she incubates their future family.

Even after the breeding season, retiring hermit thrushes keep to themselves, seldom joining in flocks. Some may begin leaving their nesting grounds in August, but most migrate in October, following the coast or inland river valleys and highland corridors south. The rugged individualists also winter much further north than most of their tropical thrush brethren. While some sun-seeking hermits retreat to Mexico, many are content to live off the fruit of the land in Dixie, subsisting on berries, seeds, and buds.

Virginia, and Ohio; also most of western United States to Rockies, north to Alaska and most of forested region of Canada

SPRING MIGRATION IN NORTH WOODS REGION: Mid-April to mid-May; peak, late April to early May

FALL MIGRATION IN NORTH WOODS REGION: Late August to late October; peak, early to mid-October

WINTER WHEREABOUTS: New Jersey, southern Ohio, and Illinois, Oklahoma, and southwestern United States south to Guatemala; to southern Maine, New York, and Vermont in mild winters

NUMBER OF THRUSH SPECIES NESTING IN NORTH WOODS REGION: 7

NUMBER OF THRUSH SPECIES WORLDWIDE: 175

ALSO SEE: Red-Eyed Vireo, Yellow-Rumped Warbler

The northern woods host a bevy of other ground-feeding thrushes as well, all of them accomplished songsters. Haunting the deep interior of moist, mature deciduous and mixed forests, the wood thrush is slightly larger than the hermit and closely resembles it in both looks and sound. The woody, however, lacks any red tint in its tail, and the first note of its song is more twittered than clear and low. The veery, on the other hand, has a solidly russet-brown back and wings and faded brown breast spots. It calls out its own name in a spiral of descending notes from the thick understories of damp, low-lying young broadleaf and mixed forests and swamps. In damp coniferous woods, though, the fluted songs ripple upward and are performed by the gray-olive-backed Swainson's thrush. Finally, around forest edges and clearings everywhere, is the state bird of both Wisconsin and Michigan, the loquacious robin. Northern robins, though, seem a breed apart from those of the city, being far more shy and secretive, like the other thrushes of the forest.

HERRING GULL

Sublime Flight over Northern Lakes

Herring gulls and humans have similar relationships with the north woods: While nowadays there are fewer opportunities for individuals to support themselves, those fortunate enough to live there enjoy a serenity away from the rat race to the south. For the gull, life in large colonies on the Atlantic and Great Lakes shores and in urban areas can be brutal and vicious, with constant fighting over food and territory, violation of spouses, and cannibalistic neighbors eating unattended nestlings.

In contrast, the less abundant food sources in interior forest lakes usually support only colonies of a few or single nesting pairs. Though they also flock with many other gull species on the coasts, north woods herring gulls seem a different breed, beautiful and serene as they fly above wilderness

LIFE SPAN: Average 10–15 years, up to 31 years in wild, 50 years in captivity
NAME ORIGIN: Cornish *gullan*, meaning "wailer"
LENGTH: Males 2–2.2 ft (60–66 cm); females 1.8–2.1 ft (56–63 cm)
WINGSPAN: 4.3–5 ft (1.3–1.5 m)
WEIGHT: Males 2.2–2.6 lb (1–1.2 kg); females 1.8–2.2 lb (0.8–1 kg)
MARKINGS: White head, tail, and undersides; black-tipped gray wings; pink legs; red spot on lower yellow bill; immatures brownish
ALIAS: Seagull, common gull, lake gull, winter gull, harbor gull, *Larus argentatus*
CALLS: Wide variety of loud squeals, wails, and clucks

lakes. The less alluring, spotty, immature gulls also tend not to return to inland lakes until they are four or five years old and attired in smart breeding plumage.

Herring gulls frequent many different habitats because they are generalists—not specially adapted for any one thing but taking advantage of opportunities wherever they find them. Despite their seemingly effortless wide-winged glides, they are not the strongest fliers, depending instead on updrafts and thermals. But few other birds are as well rounded, walking, swimming, and flying with equal ability. Gulls can eat just about anything but are mainly scavengers of dead fish, preferring to scoop them from the surface in their bills rather than dive. When the eating's good, herring gulls can wolf down equal to one-third their own weight in a single gorging. They will also eat the eggs and young of other birds, making the herring gull unpopular with feathered peers.

> *When the eating's good, herring gulls can wolf down equal to one-third their own weight in a single gorging*

When they return in early spring, herring gulls embark on one of the most complex and prolonged courtships in the bird world. Over a period of two months or more, males strut, call out, stretch their necks, and offer gifts to passive debutantes to prove they'll be good providers. Among couples going steady, there is prolonged

PREFERRED HABITAT: Lakes, rivers, wetlands

HOME RANGE: 10–15 sq mi (26–39 km²)

FOOD: Omnivorous, preferring small fish, mollusks, crayfish; also mice, insects, wild berries, carrion, and Kentucky Fried Chicken bones

NEST: Grass and other vegetation often laid in a bare rock depression, 14–36 in (35–90 cm) wide, at least 6.5 ft (2 m) from any other nests, usually on a small, rocky island or an inaccessible point

AVERAGE CLUTCH: 3 spotted olive-colored eggs, a little larger than chicken eggs

INCUBATION PERIOD: 30–32 days

FLEDGING AGE: 45–50 days

AGE OF FIRST-TIME BREEDERS: Males 4 years; females 5 years

ANNUAL MORTALITY: Eggs 20–30%; chicks 30–50%; 1st years 50%; adults 10–20%

PREDATORS: Mink, foxes, hawks, falcons, eagles, and coyotes eat adults; raccoons, skunks, snakes, and other gulls raid nests.

FLYING SPEED: 16–49 mph (25–67 km/h)

RANGE: Most of north woods region, but mainly along shores of Great Lakes in Wisconsin and Michigan's Lower Peninsula, and of Lake Champlain in Vermont; also around rest of Great Lakes and Atlantic Coast to North Carolina, north through Canada to Alaska and high Arctic

SPRING MIGRATION IN NORTH WOODS REGION: Mid-March to late May

FALL MIGRATION IN NORTH WOODS REGION: Early September to December

rubbing of bills, contorting of bodies, and mutual preening.

Both females and males make and aggressively defend the nests. Males also feed their mates and help incubate the eggs. For the first few crucial days after they hatch, the downy young live mainly off their egg yolks, while their parents concentrate on guarding them. Chicks can walk within a few days and begin venturing outside the nest two or three days after hatching. Mortality is high among the young, but with each passing year, survival becomes easier.

Gull numbers have increased greatly since the beginning of the twentieth century, when egg collecting as well as feather plucking for women's hats reduced the American population to a mere 8,000 nesting pairs in Maine. They became protected by law in 1916 and got another boost when DDT, which caused thin eggshells, deformities, and hormone imbalances, was banned in the 1970s.

WINTER WHEREABOUTS: Great Lakes, Mississippi Valley, Atlantic Coast, and Gulf of Mexico, younger birds flying farther south than breeders

ESTIMATED WINTER POPULATION ON ATLANTIC COAST: 1 million

AGE OF OLDEST GULL-LIKE ICHTHYORNIS FOSSILS: 85 million years

FAMOUS INDIVIDUALS: Jonathan Livingston Seagull; Gertrude and Heathcliff; the slain gull of Chekhov's *The Sea Gull,* symbol of the destructive force of human whims

NUMBER OF GULL SPECIES NESTING IN NORTH WOODS REGION: 2

NUMBER OF GULL SPECIES WORLDWIDE: 45

ALSO SEE: Lakes, Osprey, Minnows

HUMMINGBIRD

Tiny Bird of Amazing Feats

Though hummingbirds are usually seen at cabin sugar-water feeders throughout the north woods, they are a lot more common in the wilderness than most people imagine. In the wild, they're usually heard before they're seen, a whirring hum too deep a sound for a bee or other insect to produce. Ever on the lookout for nectar meals in colorful flowers, hummingbirds are often attracted by bright nylon tents or orange and red plastic tarps. Zipping through on wings moving too quickly to be seen, they may at first appear to be large dragonflies, but when hovering, they hold their tiny bodies vertically in the air. Their wings actually move in curving figure eights, allowing hummingbirds to fly straight up, down, backward, and even upside down.

WING BEATS PER SECOND: Average 40–80. Males in courtship dives reach up to 200.

FLYING SPEED: Average 27 mph (45 km/h); up to 60 mph (97 km/h) in a dive

HEARTBEATS PER MINUTE: Almost 500 at rest (50–180 in torpor); up to 1,260 in flight. (Hummingbird species have fastest rate of all birds and mammals.)

RESPIRATORY RATE: 250 breaths a minute

DAYTIME BODY TEMPERATURE: About 104°F (40°C)

NUMBER OF CALORIES EXPENDED PER MINUTE OF HOVERING: 11

LENGTH: 2.8–3.5 in (7–9 cm)

They can veer sideways on a dime or stop instantly, to hover while feeding.

One thing hummingbirds can't do is glide. To stay aloft, these smallest of all birds must keep their wings in perpetual hyperflap. The feat takes incredible strength and energy. A hummingbird's Herculean chest muscles—comprising 30 percent of its body—and its atomic-speed heart are both proportionally larger than those of any other bird. Nectar provides sugar that can be burned immediately as energy in the hummingbird's high-octane engine. Insects lapped up with the nectar or caught separately offer protein for building body tissue. Still, to keep going, hummers refill their bellies about every seven to twelve minutes. They may consume and burn food equal to half their weight every day. To sustain their metabolic rate, a 175-pound (80-kilogram) man would have to pack away about 100 pounds (45 kilograms) of Hershey's bars a day and drink 120 cans of beer to keep his skin from catching fire.

Hummingbirds are especially active just before dusk and after dawn, storing up or replenishing vital fuel. On most nights, they conserve energy by slowing down their heart and breathing rates by 90 percent, dropping their body temperature to half the daytime average. In the cold highlands of their wintering grounds in Mexico, and points south, hummingbirds go into a prolonged torpor. Their ability to revive from this deathlike state made them sacred to the Aztecs, who considered hummingbirds to be the spirits of dead warriors. Inca women roused the tiny hummers from their deep sleep by warming them between their breasts. In the Pacific Northwest,

WINGSPAN: 4–5.2 in (10–13 cm)

WEIGHT: 1/8 oz (3–4 g)

MARKINGS: Iridescent green back, gray-white belly. Male has bright iridescent red throat and a forked tail.

APPROXIMATE NUMBER OF FEATHERS: 940

NAME OF A HUMMINGBIRD AVIARY: Jewel room

ALIAS: Ruby-throated hummingbird, common hummingbird, *Archilochus colubris*

CALLS: High-pitched, twittering squeaks

BODY TEMPERATURE: 105–109°F (41–43°C)

PREFERRED HABITAT: Mixed and deciduous forest edges, clearings, river- and lakeshores, islands, swamps, bearer pond fringes; up to 3,500 ft (1,067 m) in Adirondacks

FOOD: Nectar, sap, mosquitoes, spiders, flies, bees, gnats, aphids, caterpillars, insect eggs. Insects may make up to 60% of diet.

HUMMINGBIRD-POLLINATED FLOWERS: Jewelweed, columbine, cardinal flower, honeysuckle, fireweed, thistles, wild bergamot, willow catkins, and some 20 other known flowers

NUMBER OF LICKS PER SECOND: 13

NEST: Neat, deep, thick-walled cup of moss, lichens, grass, bud scales, and plant down, bound tightly together with spider silk, about 1.5–2 in (4–5 cm) wide

AVERAGE CLUTCH: 2 pea-sized oblong white eggs

INCUBATION PERIOD: 12–14 days

FLEDGING AGE: 18–22 days

LIFE SPAN: Up to 9 years in wild, 12 years in captivity

hummingbirds were depicted on totem poles as messengers of the dead.

One quite erroneous belief people once held was that hummers and other small birds migrated by hitching rides on the backs of larger birds such as geese. In truth, ruby-throats, the one hummingbird species to summer in eastern North America, can fly 500 miles (800 kilometers) nonstop across the Gulf of Mexico in twenty-six hours, fueled on 0.07 ounce (2 grams) of fat, which makes up about half their body weight before starting out. Ruby-throats spend a couple of days rebuilding their fat supplies between each 100- to 200-mile (160- to 320-kilometer) leg of their journey overland. They migrate during the day, close to the ground.

Hummingbirds fly straight up, down, backward, and even upside down

When hummingbirds arrive in the north woods in May, most of the flowers they depend on are not yet open, while rain and bad weather limit access to others. For about a month, they turn instead to the plentiful sweet sap oozing from rows of holes drilled into tree trunks by yellow-bellied sapsuckers, which return north a few weeks earlier than their tiny associates. One study found that mother hummers always built their nests within a quick dash of regularly tapped sapsucker trees and relied solely on sap during incubation. It is unlikely hummingbirds could breed in the north woods without the presence of their tree-boring benefactors.

As the weather warms, hummingbirds are especially attracted to red

PREDATORS: Sharp-shinned hawks, kestrels, bullfrogs, bass and other large fish sometimes capture adults; weasels, chipmunks, crows, snakes, praying mantises, and yellow jackets eat eggs or young.
NUMBER OF HUMMINGBIRDS KILLED ANNUALLY IN TROPICS FOR FASHION ACCESSORIES IN LATE 1800s: About 5 million
RANGE: All eastern United States to Texas and central Florida, north to southeast Canada and prairie provinces
SPRING MIGRATION IN NORTH WOODS REGION: Early May to early June; peak, late May
FALL MIGRATION IN NORTH WOODS REGION: Early August to early October; peak, late August or early September
WINTER WHEREABOUTS: Southern Florida and Texas coast to Costa Rica
NUMBER OF HUMMINGBIRD SPECIES NESTING IN UNITED STATES: 15
NUMBER OF HUMMINGBIRD SPECIES IN THE AMERICAS: 319–338
NUMBER OF HUMMERS ELSEWHERE IN THE WORLD: 0
LOOK-ALIKES: 3 species of large clearwing sphinx moths hover at flowers in daytime like hummingbirds
ALSO SEE: Jewelweed, Speckled Alder, Yellow-Bellied Sapsucker

flowers, which often have no scent but more nectar than others. Some long, tubular blossoms, such as cardinal flowers, can be fertilized only by the hummingbird, which picks up pollen on its head while probing each bloom with its needlelike bill and lapping nectar from the bottom of the flower cup with its long, brushy tongue.

The north woods' abundance of summer flowers provides a rich breeding ground for hummers, but the birds don't stick around for long. Males arrive first, establish territories in dense forests and wetlands, and defend them against each other, calling out in high squeaks. Females also establish territories, and both sexes will aggressively fend off much larger brutes, from chickadees to turkey vultures, using their darting speed to advantage. Males impress potential mates by flying in wide, exact arcs, about 4 yards (3.7 meters) in diameter, as if suspended on a string. Actual mating lasts for three to five seconds, then couples split for good.

Mothers spend six to ten days building their neat, tiny nests before looking for swinging bachelors to father their broods. Nests are well camouflaged, ten to twenty feet (three to six meters) above the ground on the outer horizontal branches of small deciduous trees and shrubs, often alder, in meadows or near stream edges. Bee-sized, blind, naked chicks usually hatch in early summer and are fed regurgitated nectar and insects. When they fledge, they are good fliers right off the mark, their wings buzzing away like wind-up toys. After flying with their mothers for another four to seven days, young hummers are sent off on their own, or are abandoned by mothers setting off for their tropical retreats.

KINGFISHER

Author of the Riverside Rattle

In Greek mythology, the gods turned the sea-tossed queen Alcyone and her husband into kingfishers and afterward stilled the winds for two weeks around the winter solstice each year—a time still known as the halcyon days—so that they could build a floating nest of fish bones. Though the belted kingfisher's scientific name, *alcyon*, pays tribute to the story, the pigeon-sized bird actually nests, amazingly enough, in burrows dug into high banks on or near shorelines. Both cartoonlike mates, with their great long beaks and tiny feet, spend one to three weeks chiseling into the banks and kicking out sand. Kingfishers' bills make them so top-heavy that sailors and fishermen used to hang their bodies on boats to serve as weather vanes. Their

LENGTH: 11–15 in (28–37 cm)

WINGSPAN: 22–23 in (56–58 cm)

WEIGHT: 4.5–6.2 oz (127–175 g)

MARKINGS: Gray-blue bushy crest, breast band, and back; white undersides; red stomach band on females

ALIAS: Belted kingfisher, lazy bird, alcyon, *Megaceryle alcyon*

CALL: Loud, harsh rattle

PREFERRED HABITAT: Lakeshores, streams, and marshes with eroded banks

FOOD: Minnows, perch, other small or young fish, frogs, tadpoles, crayfish, salamanders, insects, mice

AVERAGE BREEDING TERRITORY: 880–1,320 yd (800–1,200 m) of shoreline

AVERAGE NON-BREEDING TERRITORY: 330–550 yd (300–500 m) of shoreline

NEST: Burrow, 3–6 ft (0.9–1.8 m) long and about 10 in (25 cm) wide, in side of sand, clay, or gravel bank

AVERAGE CLUTCH: 6–7 glossy white eggs, about the size of large chestnuts

INCUBATION PERIOD: 22–24 days

FLEDGING AGE: 27–29 days

PREDATORS: Sharp-shinned and Cooper's hawks. Skunks, mink, raccoons, and snakes raid nests.

FLYING SPEED: Up to 36 mph (60 km/hr)

RANGE: All United States except small part of southwest, north to

oversized headgear is designed to take the impact of hitting the water beakfirst as they dive for fish.

The availability of shoreline territory and nest sites limits kingfisher numbers. They hunt over shallow, clear water from a favorite perch, often on dead trees in standing water. Flying with a distinctive rattling call and uneven wing beats, they may hover briefly before dropping straight down with their wings fixed, like little fighter jets. Captured fish are brought back to the perch, stabbed, flipped in the air, and swallowed. If one is too big, it may stick out of a kingfisher's mouth while the bird's digestive juices go to work on the swallowed end. A pile of regurgitated bones and scales on the ground usually marks a regular kingfisher hunting perch.

Alaska and across Canadian boreal region
SPRING MIGRATION IN NORTH WOODS REGION: Late March to early May
FALL MIGRATION IN NORTH WOODS REGION: Mid-September to late November
WINTER WHEREABOUTS: Southern edge of north woods region to Panama and West Indies
NUMBER OF U.S. KINGFISHER SPECIES: 3
NUMBER OF KINGFISHER SPECIES WORLDWIDE: 87
ALSO SEE: Crayfish, Minnows

Kingfishers nest in burrows dug into high banks on or near shorelines

---

Males arrive in April, about a month before their spouses, and pick the nest sites. They stake out closely guarded territories along shorelines, keeping out other kingfishers and even escorting canoes along their length. Females later join in shore patrols. The availability of territory and nest sites limits their numbers.

After laying their eggs in May or early June, females do most of the incubating. The young hatch featherless, and about a week later they sprout tiny pinfeathers in sheaths, making them look more like porcupines than birds. Full feathers explode from the sheaths all at once about two weeks later. Parents teach their fledglings to hunt by dropping fish into the water for them when they are hungry. Families break up when the young are about six weeks old. Many kingfishers remain in autumn as long as the fishing's good and the water hasn't iced over.

LOON

Spirit of the North Woods

Evoking the essence of the north woods, the spine-tingling cry of the loon has stirred the imagination of countless generations. Human reverence for the bird is documented by 5,000-year-old loon pictographs on cliffs scattered around the Great Lakes region. The native peoples of northern New England said Kwee-moo, the loon, was the messenger of the deity Gluskabe. Loons, in fact, are sacred birds bridging the material and spiritual worlds in a continuum of ancient lore from eastern North America all the way to central Siberia. In many remarkably similar versions of the creation story on both continents, it is the loon that retrieves mud from the bottom of primordial seas to form the Earth.

In addition to the loon's ability to journey both in the sky and in the watery depths, the almost human quality of its long, soulful call probably earned the awe of northern peoples. The familiar, modulating wail, sometimes heard in choruses

AVERAGE TIME UNDERWATER: 40–45 sec

MAXIMUM TIME UNDERWATER: More than 3 min

AVERAGE DEPTH OF HUNTING GROUNDS: 7–15 ft (2.1–4.6 m)

DEEPEST DIVES: 230 ft (70 m)

FLYING SPEED: Average 75 mph (120 km/hr); up to 100 mph (160 km/hr) in a dive

WING BEATS PER SECOND: 3.8–4.4

MIGRATION ALTITUDE: 5,000–9,000 ft (1,500–2,740 m)

LENGTH: 2.3–3 ft (70–90 cm)

WINGSPAN: 3.6–5 ft (1.3–1.5 m)

WEIGHT: Males 5.5–14 lb (2.5–6.3 kg); females 3.5–10 lb (1.6–4.6 kg)

LOON WEIGHT PER SQ IN (6.5 CM²) OF WING: 0.6 oz (17 g)

MALLARD DUCK WEIGHT PER SQ IN OF WING: 0.3 oz (8.5 g)

MARKINGS: Iridescent black head and neck; white necklace around neck; checkered black-and-white back; white breast and belly; long, pointy black bill; red eyes.

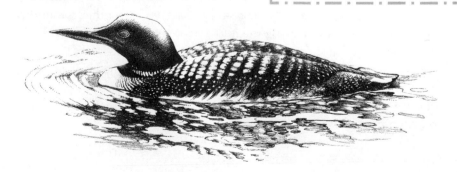

on still nights or after a rain, is actually just one of four distinct types of loon calls, each rising in pitch according to the intensity of emotion. The wail is used to summon mates and offspring, or as a territorial declaration to neighbors.

Each male also has his own distinctive yodel for territorial defense, most often heard early in the season. Neighboring loons can recognize each other's yodels from those of interlopers. Males sometimes yodel at low-flying planes. When they sense danger, loons blurt out a tremolo phrase like the laugh of a mad scientist, perhaps inspiring the goofy laughter of Daffy Duck, himself a confused amalgam of black duck and loon. A fourth type of call consists of hoots made by pairs, families, or groups of loons as a kind of random small talk.

Most of the communication between loons, however, is actually by body language. Biologist William Barklow studied Maine loons up close for fifteen years, infiltrating their ranks by snorkeling among them with a goose decoy painted to look like a loon on top of his head. He noted more than twenty-five regular communication body postures. Among them, loons greet each other by gracefully stretching out their wings, show submission by hunching low, and indicate peaceful or amorous intentions by pointing their beaks downward.

Normally, a breeding pair of loons maintains an entire lake, or a bay in a large lake, as their exclusive territory. In the rush to secure the best waters, loons return to their breeding grounds within days, sometimes even hours, of ice breakup. Capable

Juveniles younger than 3 years old, and adults in fall and winter, have dark gray backs and white bellies.
ALIAS: Common loon, great northern diver, *Gavia immer*
PREFERRED HABITAT: Deep, clear lakes; large rivers
BREEDING TERRITORY: Average 12–425 acres (5–170 ha)
FOOD: Perch, young bass, sunfish, minnows, and other fish weighing 0.35–2.5 oz (10–70 g), caught only during day; also some crayfish, frogs, mollusks, leeches, aquatic insects, water lily roots and other aquatic plants
AVERAGE DAILY FOOD HELPING: 2.2 lb (1 kg), or about 30 small fish
PORTION OF POPULATION THAT SWITCHES MATES ANNUALLY: About 20%
NEST: Simple low pile of vegetation, often on the lee side of a small island or point, on an old muskrat lodge, or in a cove, just above the waterline
AVERAGE CLUTCH: 2 olive-colored eggs with dark spots, about as big as a midsized potato
INCUBATION PERIOD: 28–29 days
ANNUAL LOONLING MORTALITY: 15–30%
FLEDGING AGE: 11–12 weeks
AGE OF FIRST-TIME BREEDERS: 4–7 years
LIFE SPAN: Average 7–10 years; oldest known 18 years; may live up to 30 years
PREDATORS: Ravens, gulls, crows, eagles, raccoons, skunks, snapping turtles, and large fish such as pike eat chicks and eggs.
GREATEST PESTS: Blackflies

of covering hundreds of miles in a single flight, they often make scouting missions from ice-free staging areas on the Atlantic Coast, Great Lakes, or Mississippi River to check the progress of the thaw on inland lakes. Males usually arrive first. Though mates overwinter separately, a happily nesting pair usually renews its bond with an elegant, quiet, diving courtship waltz when they return to their original honeymoon lake each spring. Competition from a rival, however, sometimes forces one of the former mates to hit the road and look for a new partner. Couples having little reproductive success may also break up and move on to other lakes.

Loons mate and nest on land, within a few feet of shore. That's about as far as they ever venture on dry ground, because their legs are placed so far back under their bodies that they can walk only by using their wings as crutches, though flapping enables them to run. The word *loon* itself comes from the Scandinavian *lom,* which in English means "lame." Their torpedo-like bodies are built more for swimming and diving than flying. Many of their bones are solid, rather than honeycombed with air spaces like those of most birds. Depending on the wind, they need 20- to 440-yard- (17- to 400-meter-) long takeoffs on the water to gain enough lift from their relatively small thrashing wings to fly. Takeoffs are impossible from land, and confused loons that have accidentally landed on frozen, black-ice lakes or parking lots have had to be rescued. Beneath the water, though, loons pivot like otters and outswim many fish.

LOON POPULATIONS: Minnesota, 12,000; Maine, 4,300; Wisconsin, 3,000; Michigan, 800; New York, 400; New Hampshire, 300; Vermont, 100

POPULATION DENSITY IN PRIME HABITAT: Up to 1 pair per sq mi (2.6 km²)

ACCOLADES: Official bird of Minnesota and Ontario

ESTIMATES OF LOON POPULATION WITH HARMFUL LEVELS OF MERCURY: 70% in New England, 22% in Minnesota

RANGE: Throughout north woods region, plus northern Massachusetts, northeastern North Dakota, western Montana, and nearby bits of Wyoming and Washington; north to Alaska and Arctic

SPRING MIGRATION IN NORTH WOODS REGION: First arrivals late March in south, peaking early May as first arrive in northern Minnesota

FALL MIGRATION IN NORTH WOODS REGION: September to late November

WINTER WHEREABOUTS: Eastern loons go to Atlantic and Gulf Coasts, and a few to Great Lakes

AGE OF OLDEST LOON FOSSILS: 40–50 million years

NUMBER OF LOON SPECIES WORLDWIDE: 5

CLOSEST RELATIVES TO LOONS: Probably penguins, gulls, and albatrosses

ALSO SEE: Blackflies, Painted Turtle, Common Merganser, Lakes, Perch

Even baby loons are in the water swimming within hours of hatching, usually between June and mid-July. They paddle very close behind their parents, often riding on their backs during the first two or three weeks of their

lives when they are tired, cold, or in potential danger from underwater predators. Both parents take turns attending the loonlings, starting to teach them
to fish when they are about four weeks old. In August, parents begin spending a few hours each day with growing groups of younger, nonmating loons
for ritualized social gatherings on larger lakes, leaving their unfledged young
at home. The visits grow longer until the young are fledged and can totally
feed themselves, by September or early October, when parents leave them
for good, flying south in loose migratory flocks forming long lines of up to
hundreds, each bird spaced up to a quarter of a mile (400 meters) apart.
Fledglings soon form their own flocks and follow their elders south one to
three weeks later. The last loons leave shortly before freeze-up. Young loons
spend their second summer along the ocean coast; their flightless molting
period, lasting several weeks, occurs too late for them to join the migration.

Their heavy dependence on fish, and their need of clear, undisturbed
water to find them, has imperiled loons in areas under pressure from development. They once bred as far south as Pennsylvania, Ohio, and Iowa. Summer
water-level fluctuations from dams and motorboat wakes can flood out nests.
But in lakes with heavy recreational angling, the biggest cause of death
among adult loons is usually poisoning from swallowing lead sinkers and jigs
(New Hampshire has become the first state to ban them). Acid rain has also
cut down the fish supply in some lakes, while fish contaminated with mercury, aluminum, chlorinated hydrocarbons, and other pollutants cause reproductive failure and nervous system dysfunctions among loons. Thousands of
wintering loons have washed up on Florida beaches some years, starved
because they can no longer coordinate their muscles while trying to catch
fish.

Designated as threatened in Michigan, Vermont, and New Hampshire
and as a species of special concern in New York and Massachusetts, the common loon has become the object of intense protection efforts. Project Loon-
watch and other programs in several states have organized corps of Loon
Ranger volunteers to help monitor breeding grounds, build artificial nest
platforms, and raise public awareness. Their efforts have helped to boost loon
numbers by 80 percent in Wisconsin and 95 percent in New Hampshire
since the 1970s.

OSPREY

Crooked-Winged Fishing Master

Back in the twentieth century, the banning of DDT may have come just in time for the osprey. At the top of the aquatic food chain, ospreys are the ultimate recipients of pesticides flushed by rain from farm fields and lawns into rivers and lakes and collected in the fish they eat. DDT interferes with estrogen, the hormone that regulates calcium, leading to thin eggshells and nesting failure. Breeding ospreys nearly disappeared in the lower forty-eight states in the 1960s. After DDT was banned in 1972, offspring survival rates increased and osprey populations rose severalfold. The provision of artificial nesting platforms on top of utility poles and towers also helped out and are now used by two-thirds of Wisconsin's 360-plus osprey couples. Northern Minnesota, Michigan,

LENGTH: 1.7–2.2 ft (53–66 cm)
WINGSPAN: 4.6–6 ft (1.4–1.8 m)
WEIGHT: Males 2.6–3.5 lb (1.2–1.6 kg); females 3.5–4.4 lb (1.6–2 kg)
MARKINGS: Black mask, white head and undersides, dark brown back, brown patches at front "elbow" of white underwing, short fan-shaped tail with light and dark bars. Females usually have a dark, streaky necklace.
ALIAS: Fish hawk, *Pandion haliaetus*
CALL: Short, sharp, repeated whistle
PREFERRED HABITAT: Shallow lakes, rivers, marshes, swamps, bogs
AVERAGE DEFENDED TERRITORY: 1.2–3.7 acres (0.5–1.5 ha) of shallow water

and Maine also each welcome hundreds of the fabled fish hawks returning from South American wintering grounds each breeding season.

Ospreys are the most widespread birds of prey in the world. They fly over every continent except Antarctica. They're also one of the north's largest raptors, and the only one, save for the bald eagle, that catches fish. The black-masked birds of prey usually hover 30 to 100 feet (9 to 30 meters) above shallow water, heads hanging as they look for fish. When they see one, they tuck in their wings and drop straight down, braking as they snatch up their hapless prey. Their talons have sharp spines and a reversible toe to hold slippery dinners.

Unlike many hawks, ospreys can cross over large bodies of water in migration. Rather than having to depend on warm air rising from sun-baked clearings to give them lift, they have more wing relative to their bodies than do other hawks, allowing them to flap long and hard instead of needing to glide to conserve energy. Sometimes they migrate carrying a fish; hawk watchers call this "packing a lunch." Radar has picked up migrants at more than 3,000 feet (900 meters) above the ground, far beyond binocular range. Most north woods ospreys migrate south in early to mid-September, following the Mississippi Valley, Appalachian Mountains, or Atlantic Coast. They return in April, traveling alone, but following the same routes until they spread out on their breeding territories.

For about two weeks in spring, males swoop and dive in courtship flights, calling out loudly. Mates return to the same nest,

AVERAGE DEPTH OF FISHING GROUNDS: 3–7 ft (0.9–2.1 m)

FOOD: 99% catfish, sunfish, bass, perch, pike, sucker, and other fish; occasionally frogs, crayfish, snakes, rodents

NEST: Usually 3.3 ft (1 m) wide and 1 ft (30 cm) deep, of woven sticks, cattails, and other aquatic plants, 30–66 ft (9–19 m) above wetlands or a shoreline in the crown of a dead, broken-topped tree

AVERAGE CLUTCH: 3 mottled white or tan eggs, the size of large chicken eggs

INCUBATION PERIOD: 35–42 days

FLEDGING AGE: 49–61 days

AGE OF FIRST-TIME BREEDERS: 3–5 years

ANNUAL MORTALITY: 40–60% for fledglings; 10–15% for adults

LIFE SPAN: Average 6–10 years; up to 35 years

PREDATORS: Raccoons, ravens, and crows raid nests; great horned owls may kill adults or young.

FISHING SUCCESS RATE: 20–25% of all dives

RANGE: Most of north woods region except most of Vermont and New Hampshire; also along Atlantic Coast and Gulf of Mexico, Rockies to the Pacific, except for southwest; Alaska and most of forest region of Canada

SPRING MIGRATION IN NORTH WOODS REGION: Late March to late May; peak, mid-April

FALL MIGRATION IN NORTH WOODS REGION: Mid-August to early November, peak, mid-September

WINTER WHEREABOUTS: Southern Mexico and Caribbean to central

or aerie, every year, repairing and adding to it, sometimes for generations. Nests can weigh up to hundreds of pounds. Occasionally, ospreys nest in the middle of heron colonies, which may prompt the herons to abandon the site. If they stay or return, however, the osprey presence ultimately benefits herons by keeping away nest raiders, such as great horned owls.

Chile, most in northern South America

POPULATION IN LOWER 48 STATES: More than 14,000 pairs

HIGHEST FALL COUNT AT HAWK RIDGE, DULUTH, MINNESOTA: 575, in 1998

ALSO SEE: Smallmouth Bass, Broad-Winged Hawk, Great Blue Heron

Females lay their clutch in late April or in May and are fed by their partners while they incubate. After the eggs hatch, fathers must provide enough fish, about 6 pounds (2.7 kilograms) a day, to double the weight of their offspring each week or so. Mothers stay with the young constantly for their first month. Parents continue to feed them for up to several weeks after they fledge. Then they're on their own, though they remain in the area for a while. After they migrate, young ospreys enjoy a tropical adolescence, hanging out in the jungle and not returning to the north until they are two years old.

Ospreys are sometimes mistaken for bald eagles because of their large size and white heads. Eagles, though, hold their wings straight, rather than in the crooked elbowlike pose of the osprey. The national bird is also considerably more stocky, weighing three times as much as an osprey. There are many accounts of bald eagles, which are generally more scavengers than hunters, accosting ospreys in the air and forcing them to drop their catch, which the eagle retrieves.

Bald eagles also suffered serious declines from DDT poisoning, but have tripled their numbers in some areas over the past twenty years. They occur along major rivers and large lakes over much of the north woods region, though in lower numbers than ospreys. Chippewa National Forest in Minnesota boasts the highest breeding density of bald eagles in the lower forty-eight states, with more than 200 nesting pairs.

OVENBIRD

An Echo of the Jungle

Evoking an exotic, tropical jungle atmosphere in the heart of the north woods, the ovenbird's sudden, penetrating "teacher-teacher-teacher-teacher-teacher" rises to an echoing crescendo quite unlike the more delicate melodic airs of most of its fellow warblers. That the sparrow-sized operatic sprite should sound so tropical is appropriate, since it spends its winters beneath steamy forest canopies as far south as Colombia. Migrating songbirds, in fact, probably evolved from tropical species that gradually extended their ranges northward. For them, coming from a region much more packed with an incredible abundance and variety of life-forms, the springtime explosion of insects and vast nesting opportunities of the north woods are ideal for raising a family, even if they are forced south again with the advance of each winter. Longer northern days also afford more hunting time and faster nestling growth.

CALLS: Song a very loud, rapid, rising "teacher-teacher-teacher," repeated about 8–10 times, building to a crescendo; also loud, sharp call notes "chut" and "tsik"
LENGTH: 5.7–6 in (14–15 cm)
WINGSPAN: 9–10 in (23–25 cm)
AVERAGE WEIGHT: 0.6–1 oz (16–28 g)
MARKINGS: Olive-brown back, white undersides with dashed black streaks, orange-brown head stripe (usually brighter on males) bordered by black stripes, distinct white eye ring, light pink legs
ALIAS: Golden-crowned waterthrush, *Seiurus aurocapillus*
PREFERRED HABITAT: Deep interior of extensive, unbroken, mature deciduous and mixed forest uplands and slopes, with thick leaf litter and sparse ground cover
NESTING TERRITORY: 0.5–4.5 acres (0.2–1.8 ha)
FOOD: Caterpillars, beetles, grubs, ants, and other insects; snails; slugs; worms; spiders; also seeds and berries in fall and winter
NEST: Covered, dome shaped, about 5 in (13 cm) high and 6.5–9 in (16–23 cm) wide, made mostly of dead leaves, sometimes with pine needles, stems, grass, moss, and hair, with an opening slit in the side, on the ground, most often in the open, sometimes in a clump of plants or at the base of a shrub or sapling

Warblers migrate at night, when there's less turbulence and the air cools feverishly working muscles. In ideal conditions, on clear nights, advancing waves of up to two million migrating songbirds have been detected by radar. Most fly 500 to 2,000 feet (150 to 600 meters) high. They rest and catch insects to replenish their fat reserves for several days between flights.

Like many other warblers, male ovenbirds arrive in May on breeding territories to set up shop one to two weeks before the arrival of the opposite sex. Despite their booming calls, they're rarely actually seen. Though usually perching on a tree branch to proclaim their ground, ovenbirds are deep-forest pedestrians, pacing the ground in a head-bobbing, tail-wagging walk as they forage for creepy crawlies, their thrush-like olive attire blending with the leaf litter. If by chance they are spotted, however, they're not nearly so shy as thrush.

Even less often seen than the birds themselves are their dome-covered ground nests, resembling the old-fashioned Dutch ovens for which they're named. Constructed of the same leaves and pine needles that cover the forest floor, they look like little more than small, nondescript clumps of duff. Yet predators can and do often find the nests, especially in forests cut back and fragmented by roads and logging. Consequently, nestlings become accomplished walkers when only seven days old, before they can fly, and abandon their vulnerable nurseries. At that point, the family splits in two, perhaps broadening the chances of survival, with some of the young taken under the wing of their father, while the others go off separately with Mom.

AVERAGE CLUTCH: 4–5 olive-sized brown- and gray-specked white eggs

INCUBATION PERIOD: 11–14 days

FLEDGING AGE: 11–20 days

AVERAGE ANNUAL ADULT MORTALITY: 50%

LIFE SPAN: Up to 7 years in wild

PREDATORS: Broad-winged hawks, barred owls. Nests raided by blue jays, red squirrels, raccoons, skunks, weasels.

RANGE: Throughout northeastern United States to North Carolina, northern Georgia, and Arkansas; scattered across prairies to Rockies, north to Newfoundland, James Bay, and British Columbia

SPRING MIGRATION IN NORTH WOODS REGION: Early May to early June; peak, mid-May

FALL MIGRATION IN NORTH WOODS REGION: Mid-August to late September; peak, early to mid-September

WINTER WHEREABOUTS: Florida and southern Texas to northern Colombia, Venezuela, and Caribbean

NORMAL WARBLER BODY TEMPERATURE: 100°F (38°C)

WARBLER BODY TEMPERATURE WHILE MIGRATING: 115°F (46°C)

NUMBER OF DAYS A BLACKPOLL WARBLER TAKES TO FLY FROM MAINE TO SOUTH AMERICA: 4

AMOUNT OF BODY WEIGHT A BLACKPOLL WARBLER LOSES IN SOUTHWARD MIGRATION: 50%

AMOUNT OF TROPICAL RAIN FOREST DESTROYED EVERY DAY WORLDWIDE: 115 sq mi (300 km²)

NUMBER OF WARBLER SPECIES NESTING IN NORTH WOODS REGION: 28

NUMBER OF WARBLER SPECIES WORLDWIDE: 115

ALSO SEE: Yellow-Rumped Warbler, Red-Eyed Vireo, Hermit Thrush

RAVEN

Commanding Ancient Respect

From the time spear-bearing humans fanned out from Africa some 100,000 years ago, they have undoubtedly been intimates with the raven. The bold, black bird commonly forms close associations with northern big-game hunters, scavenging at wolf kills and following polar bears out onto Arctic pack ice to clean up seal carcasses. It has a wide vocabulary and often works in pairs, flushing out and ambushing prey. The raven's size, smarts, grace, and longevity, as well as its close association with death, must have always made a profound impression on people and sparked their imaginations. European cave paintings apparently investing birds with mystical significance date back as far as 32,000 years, and many authorities believe the magical avian depictions are ravens.

LENGTH: 22–27 in (55–68 cm)
WINGSPAN: 4–4.6 ft (1.2–1.4 m)
AVERAGE WEIGHT: 2–3.3 lb (0.9–1.5 kg)
BEAK LENGTH: Average 3 in (8 cm)
MARKINGS: Adults glossy black all over; juveniles duller, with some brown in wings and tail
Color origin: In Greek mythology, Apollo turned his snow-white raven messenger black in a fit of rage when it told him his girlfriend was unfaithful. The native peoples of the Pacific Northwest said higher spirits changed Raven to black because of his mischief. The Siberian Voguls said the raven was turned from white to black as punishment for eating corpses.
ALIAS: Northern raven, common raven, corbie, *Corvus corax*
NAME ORIGIN: Ancient German *khraben,* an imitation of the raven's harsh croak
NAME FOR A GROUP: An unkindness of ravens
CALLS: Wide repertoire, including loud, resonant, croaking "oook, oook, oook," deeper and less raspy than the "caw" of a crow; also a deep, bell-like "crong," a metallic "tok," and a buzzing burble like an electrical current. Males have deeper voices.
MIMICRY: Able to imitate many sounds, including human words

Northern cultures around the world had strong taboos against killing ravens, which figured prominently in their cosmologies. They play a role in most of the nearly universal Flood stories. Among Native Americans, the bird is sometimes named as the first of several animals that after the deluge, tried to gather mud to form a new world. In the Bible, the raven is sent by Noah to seek dry land. For the peoples of the Pacific Northwest and Alaska, the raven is not only the chief player in the Flood tale, but the bringer of the sun, moon, stars, and fresh water, as well as the creator of people. The Inuit said the raven, by flicking sparkling flakes of the mineral mica into the sky, created the Milky Way.

Early North Americans, Siberians, Chinese, Greeks, and Scandinavians thought ravens controlled or at least influenced the weather. Norse and Celtic gods and semidivine warriors often took the form of ravens or employed them as their messengers. Early Irish and Anglo-Saxon literature is also rife with references of ravens following armies to feast on the spoils of the battlefield. The Vikings embraced the gruesome association, hoisting the image of the black scavenger on their standards.

Christian lands pillaged by the hardy Northmen came to associate the raven with pagan religions, death, and ill omen. The raven was said to "shake contagion from her sable wing," and was blamed even for the pestilence that came in the aftermath of war. Ravens seen scavenging from dead livestock and wild game were held responsible for their death. European settlers brought their persecution of the great bird to North America. With the

PREFERRED HABITAT: Coniferous and mixed forests

HOME RANGE: 10–75 sq mi (27–195 km$_2$) for resident nesters. Nonbreeders can wander over more than 700 sq mi (1,800 km²).

FOOD: Carrion; birds' eggs and nestlings; crayfish; insects; mice, voles, and other small rodents; berries; seeds; wolf droppings when all else fails

NEST: Thick, bulky collection of sticks, twigs, clumps of grass and soil, and twigs, 1.7–5 ft (50–150 cm) wide, with a central depression lined with moss, lichens, bark shreds, and fur, 6–12 in (15–30 cm) wide; usually on a cliff ledge or on top of a tall pine or spruce

TELL-TALE NESTING SIGNS: Piles of fallen sticks and streaks of white droppings on or below cliffs or trees

AVERAGE CLUTCH: 3–5 plum-sized greenish eggs with dense brown-and-olive spotting or blotches

INCUBATION PERIOD: 18–21 days

FLEDGING AGE: 4–6 weeks

FIRST-YEAR MORTALITY: About 50%

AGE OF FIRST-TIME BREEDERS: 2–4 years

LIFE SPAN: Up to 13 years in wild; at least 29 years in captivity

PREDATORS: Great horned owls

RAVEN TAKEOFFS: Make 2 or 3 hops first, rather than lifting straight up like crows

RAVEN PLAY: Sometimes seen flying upside down and frolicking together in the sky, apparently playing tag and dropping sticks and other objects for each other to catch.

onslaught of guns, traps, poison, and forest-clearing lumberjacks, ravens retreated with the wolf, disappearing from New England in the 1800s, from Michigan's Lower Peninsula by 1900, and probably from the Adirondacks by 1930.

Early North Americans, Siberians, Chinese, Greeks, and Scandinavians thought ravens controlled or at least influenced the weather

---

Over the past fifty years, ravens have made a comeback, reestablishing breeding populations first in Maine, then in Vermont, in the 1960s and the Adirondacks and lower Michigan in the 1970s, and expanding south and west from northeastern Minnesota. While crows, which are much more adaptable and amenable to human presence, are still more numerous around settled areas, ravens are increasingly ruling the roost in the forests and mountains. The two birds are almost identical, but ravens are larger by about a third, have a stouter beak, and sport shaggy neck feathers not apparent on their smaller relatives. The best way to tell the two apart is to look for the raven's rounded, paddle-shaped tail in flight; the back of a crow's tail is straight cut. Ravens also tend to soar and flap their wings less than their smaller cousins and have a much deeper, hoarser voice.

ACCOLADES: Battle standard of Danish Vikings and William the Conqueror; most frequently depicted figure on west coast totem poles; official bird of the Yukon

ODIN'S RAVENS: Hugin and Mumin ("Thought" and "Memory") flew over the world every day and related all they saw and heard back to the ruler of the Norse gods, giving him universal knowledge.

"RAVEN'S KNOWLEDGE": Irish term meaning to see and know everything

RAVENSTONE: An Old English name for the site of executions

TOWER OF LONDON RAVENS: After the Great Fire of London in 1666, ravens were persecuted for scavenging, but King Charles II was warned to keep them at the Tower of London or disaster would strike the monarchy. Six ravens have been kept at the Tower castle ever since.

NOTABLE DEEDS: Ravens fed Elijah in the Jordanian desert, and a raven released from a wayward Viking ship flew west without returning, leading the way to the settlement of Iceland.

RANGE: Throughout north woods region, along Appalachians to Georgia, western United States to Rockies, north to Alaska and most of Canada to high Arctic

NUMBER OF U.S. CROW AND RAVEN SPECIES: 5

NUMBER OF CROW AND RAVEN SPECIES WORLDWIDE: 47

ALSO SEE: Coyote, Snowshoe Hare, Wolf

Ravens also don't migrate like crows; mates remain together on the same territory for life. They spruce up their relationships early each year, performing breathtaking courtship flights in the bitterly cold, clear skies of February. Soaring males call frequently and make sudden steep dives, often somersaulting just before pulling out of their descent. Couples also fly synchronized maneuvers, their wing tips virtually touching as they circle over their nest sites. Males usually fly slightly above their partners in the sky dance. Upon landing, they often nuzzle beaks together, and may preen and caress each other's breast and head feathers.

An ideal cliffside or treetop nesting spot may be used off and on by successive generations, some for up to 100 years. Old ravens' nests are also often used by hawks and owls. A couple usually spends two or three weeks building a new nest or renovating an old one, breaking off large, dead sticks from trees and piling them up. Both mates quiet down once egg laying begins, around mid- to late March, the female tending the nest while her mate brings home the bacon.

Things become noisy again when the nestlings hatch and start begging for food, though they fall silent at their parent's command when an outsider approaches the area. As they grow, the young cry out in a muffled crow-voiced "caw." For about the first eighteen days, fathers continue to be the main providers, while females brood their families. The males sometimes carry water in their throats for the nestlings to drink. After spending several days learning to fly, the young follow their parents over wide spaces for three or four months in search of food.

After they drift off from their parental abodes, young ravens often form widely wandering winter flocks with other adolescents. Studying such flocks in Maine for many years, preeminent ravenologist Bernd Heinrich discovered that they scavenge and hunt cooperatively, with scouts leading the others to new food sources whenever they're found. Since mating pairs don't take kindly to dinner guests in their territories, the flocks of younger ravens use force of numbers to belly up to carrion feasts. While a deer carcass might feed a territorial couple for weeks in winter, it can be stripped by a flock of several dozen ravens within a few days. While the going's good, each bird stashes portions of a big feed in hiding places beneath the snow and returns to them later.

RED-BREASTED NUTHATCH

Spike-Nosed Conifer Hopper

Nuthatches are munchkinlike birds with oversized beaks and feet, which they use to good effect. The remarkably strong grip of their long, curving claws enables them to scamper along in any direction, up, down, and around tree trunks and branches. By poking into bark fissures and crevices from an upside-down position, the stubby-tailed birds find bugs and grubs missed by brown creepers and downy woodpeckers working the same routes from the other direction. Nuthatches even follow woodpeckers to snap up the rattled insects left in their wake.

LENGTH: 4.5–4.7 in (11–12 cm)
WINGSPAN: 8–8.7 in (20–22 cm)
WEIGHT: 0.3–0.4 oz (8–13 g)
MARKINGS: Blue-gray back and wings; rusty red undersides; black eye stripe and crown; white cheeks, neck, and stripe above eyes
ALIAS: Red-bellied nuthatch, topsy-turvy bird, *Sitta canadensis*
CALLS: Oft-repeated, high, nasal beeps, written "ank, ank ank." Song, less often heard, is a rapid staccato like a high-pitched puttering of the lips.
PREFERRED HABITAT: Mixed and evergreen woods, often near beaver ponds and other forest edges
FOOD: Conifer seeds, nuts, berries, beetles, grubs, caterpillars, moths, wasps, crane flies, spiders, insect and spider eggs
NEST: Cavity 7–40 ft (2–12 m) high, usually in a dead or dying tree, often aspen or paper birch; sticky conifer resin around edges of opening
AVERAGE CLUTCH: 5–6 raspberry-sized reddish-brown-specked white eggs
INCUBATION PERIOD: 12–13 days
FLEDGING AGE: 18–21 days
RANGE: Throughout north woods region to New Jersey and Pennsylvania and along Appalachians to

Red-breasted nuthatches also spend a lot of time at flimsy branch tips, especially in winter, using their long, needlelike bills to pick seeds out of open evergreen cones. Because their vise-grip claws aren't adept at nimble tasks, they jam shelled seeds they collect from the ground into bark crevices so that they can extract the kernel. Similarly wedged nuts are "nut hacked" apart with their piercing beaks.

North Carolina; western United States to Rockies; north to southeastern Alaska, James Bay, and Labrador

WINTER WHEREABOUTS: Remain on breeding grounds or migrate as far south as northern Florida and Texas if food is scarce

*Wedged nuts are "nut hacked" apart
with their piercing beaks*

The beaks also come in handy for chiseling out nesting quarters in dead trees when an old woodpecker hole or natural cavity can't be found in April. Once a red-breasted nuthatch couple finishes the excavation, the duo collects wads of sap oozing from wounds in nearby spruce, pine, and fir trees. The sap is smeared thickly around the rim of the entrance. Some authorities speculate that the sticky goop may prevent or discourage predators, such as tree climbing snakes, from entering the nests. Others believe it is aimed primarily at keeping out pests and parasites, such as ants, mites, and ticks.

RED-EYED VIREO

The Loquacious Preacher Bird

Like a TV evangelist—"Do you believe? Do you repent?"—the red-eyed vireo, or preacher bird, seems to sermonize with an endless stream of rhetorical questions, its voice rising up and down in couplets all day long. Though difficult to see, male red-eyes make their presence known by belting out up to 3,000 songs an hour from the treetops, May until midsummer, even on hot days when most other birds are taking a siesta. They're even known to sing with their mouths full of insects.

While males call attention to themselves high in the canopy, female red-eyed vireos nest silently in the understory below. The nest usually hangs between the thin, forked outer branches of a sapling, which will not support raccoons or skunks and other predators. Dangers increase, though,

CALLS: Short, up-and-down whistled phrases of 2–5 notes, similar to robins' but slower, repeated sometimes 30–60 times a minute; also sharp, high single notes

MOST VIREO SONGS COUNTED IN 1 DAY: 22,197

LENGTH: 4.7–5.1 in (12–13 cm)

WINGSPAN: 6 in (15 cm)

WEIGHT: 0.6–0.7 oz (16–20 g)

MARKINGS: Greenish-brown back, gray cap, white streak over red eyes, white undersides

ALIAS: Preacher bird, greenlet, teacher, *Vireo olivaceus*

PREFERRED HABITAT: Deciduous and mixed forests with aspens, birch, maples, or beech and a continuous understory of saplings and shrubs

FOOD: Caterpillars, beetles, wasps, bees, ants, flies, spiders; berries if insects are scarce

NEST: Neat, deep, thin-walled, like a pencil cup, 2.4–3.5 in (6–9 cm) wide, of birch-bark strips, grass, wasp-nest paper, and cobwebs, camouflaged with lichens

AVERAGE CLUTCH: 3–4 olive-sized white eggs with dark brown marks; sometimes 2 broods a year

INCUBATION PERIOD: 12–14 days

FLEDGING AGE: 10–12 days

PREDATORS: Sharp-shinned hawks, raccoons, skunks, red squirrels, chipmunks

if forest fragmentation brings edge habitat closer. The sleek, sparrow-sized birds need at least an acre (0.4 hectare) of unbroken forest with an understory curtain of shrubs and saplings to nest successfully. In vulnerable forests, up to 75 percent of their nests fall victim to brown-headed cowbirds, which lay single eggs in the nests of other species, for them to raise. Most hosts do not recognize their own eggs or young, only the location of the nest. An impostor cowbird hatches first, grows faster, and aggressively elbows its foster siblings out of the way at feeding time, sometimes pushing them from the nest, often becoming the only survivor.

RANGE: Eastern United States to high plains, Oregon, north across boreal region of Canada

SPRING MIGRATION IN NORTH WOODS REGION: Early May to early June; peak, late May

FALL MIGRATION IN NORTH WOODS REGION: Late August to late September

---

Male red-eyes belt out up to 3,000 songs an hour from the treetops

---

Having raised their families—and many cowbirds—on the brief, intense abundance of caterpillars, beetles, and bugs in the north woods, vireos make their dash back to the Amazon jungle in August and September. Once there, they become vegetarians, dining on tropical fruits until the Northern Hemisphere tilts back toward the sun.

RED-WINGED BLACKBIRD

Flash of Scarlet Signals Spring

A dominant male red-winged blackbird in his prime is an iron-fisted patriarch commanding the best and biggest stretch of marsh, a sizable harem, and the fear and respect of his colony. He is a warrior troubadour who, many bird experts believe, has learned more songs than any of his rivals, warding them off with his virtuosity. While he sings, he flashes his bright scarlet epaulets, badges of age and experience that similarly convince others not to challenge him.

The flickering of red wing patches in flight, like technicolor strobe lights, is one

LENGTH: 7–10 in (17–25 cm)
WINGSPAN: 1–1.2 ft (30–36 cm)
AVERAGE WEIGHT: Males 2.4 oz (66 g); females 1.6 oz (45 g)
MARKINGS: Males black with scarlet-and-yellow wing epaulets; females streaked brown and beige, with yellowish orange tints around head; males in first breeding season brownish with slight red wing patches
ALIAS: Red-wing, marsh blackbird, *Agelaius phoeniceus*

of the earliest signs of spring. Male red-wings come first, arriving in flocks mixed with grackles and cowbirds, often when marshes are still frozen. They snap up weed seeds and tear into fluffy cattail seed heads for the tiny, overwintering caterpillars of the cattail worm moth nestled inside. Though red-wing males forage and roost together for a few weeks, they spend gradually more time each day staking out their turf in the marsh, singing boldly from prominent perches, chasing and fighting in a never-ending game of border encroachment. Less successful males are crowded out of prime marsh real estate and forced to establish territories in meadows or thickets.

Five wives is common for a well-situated male

Females, who arrive two to four weeks after the males, do not marry for love. They look for the richest, safest patch of marsh for raising a family, and mate with whatever lug happens to occupy it, usually in May. Males will breed with and defend as many females as are interested in settling in their domain. Each female maintains her own nesting zone within her mate's territory, driving away potential new concubines. Five wives is common for a well-situated male, though harems of up to fifteen have been noted.

Female red-wings are certainly not stand-by-your-man types. Although they may return to the same territory to mate every year, they show no qualms about

CALLS: Variety of loud clicks, clacks, high whistles, chirps, chatters, and staccato noises; song a gurgling "conk-a-ree," rolling at the end like a referee's whistle

PREFERRED HABITAT: Marshes, swamps, bogs, meadows, fields

AVERAGE TERRITORY: 0.06–1.1 acres (0.02–0.5 ha) in marshes, avg. 0.4 acre (0.16 ha); 0.3–7.5 acres (0.07–3 ha) in thickets and grassland, avg. 0.75 acre (0.3 ha)

FOOD: Caterpillars, dragonflies, damselflies, and other insects; invertebrates; seeds; small fruits

NEST: Small, deep, tightly woven basket of grasses and strips of cattail leaves built on cattails, reeds, small trees, or shrubs, usually less than 7 ft (2 m) above the water or ground

AVERAGE CLUTCH: 3–5 black-and-purple-speckled or -streaked light blue-green eggs, about the size of grapes

INCUBATION PERIOD: 10–12 days

FLEDGING AGE: 10–13 days

AGE OF FIRST-TIME BREEDERS: Males 2–3 years; females 1 year

NESTS PARASITIZED BY COWBIRDS: Up to 74%

AVERAGE ANNUAL ADULT MORTALITY: 40–60%

LIFE SPAN: Average 2–2.5 years; up to 14 years

PREDATORS: Sharp-shinned hawks, owls. Nests raided by raccoons, mink, weasels, crows, black rat snakes, water snakes, marsh wrens.

RANGE: All United States north to Alaska and across Canada to mid-boreal region

having flings with interloping scoundrels when the lord of the manor is away feeding. Studies suggest between one-quarter and a half of hatchlings are fathered through extramarital affairs, usually involving next-door neighbors.

Resembling big brown-streaked sparrows, female red-wings are effectively camouflaged in their nests. If predators are close by, the bright males try to distract or drive them away, exploding from cattails with a loud burst and splash of color. Blackbirds also commonly band together to mob owls, crows, hawks, foxes, and weasels.

Later in the summer, though they continue to roost in marshes, large flocks of red-wings forage for seeds and berries in dry upland areas, females and young flying separately from males. Flocks gradually gravitate to traditional migration staging areas, where many thousand may roost together between late August and September. Further south, some winter roosts swell to several million. Indeed, red-wings are believed to be the most numerous single species of land bird in North America, with an estimated fall population of 190 million.

SPRING MIGRATION IN NORTH WOODS REGION: Late March to early April

FALL MIGRATION IN NORTH WOODS REGION: Early September to mid-November

WINTER WHEREABOUTS: Most in southern United States to Florida and Texas, some to just south of north woods region

NUMBER OF BLACKBIRD FAMILY SPECIES NESTING IN NORTH WOODS REGION: 11

NUMBER OF BLACKBIRD FAMILY SPECIES WORLDWIDE: 94 (all in the Americas)

ALSO SEE: Cattail, Wetlands

RUFFED GROUSE

Drummer of the Forest

The abundance of ruffed grouse—which rises and falls in roughly ten-year cycles—made them vitally important to northern woodland peoples. One Ojibwa creation story tells of the grouse being the firstborn of the world's primal mother, Spirit Woman. The grouse stayed behind with her after all of her other bird children flew off. Similarly, the hare and the whitefish remained while the rest of her animal and fish offspring ran, swam, and waddled away. Like the grouse, the other two faithful children were important staple foods for northern hunters, and so became totem animals of large Ojibwa clans.

With only limited powers of flight, ruffed grouse are secretive chickens of the

FREQUENCY OF GROUSE DRUMMING: 40 Hz

BASS TUBA RANGE: About 50–250 Hz

RANGE OF HUMAN HEARING: About 33–16,700 Hz

NORMAL DENSITY IN PRIME HABITAT: 17–38 per sq mi (44–98/km²)

FALL DENSITY AT PEAK OF POPULATION CYCLE: 123–180 per sq mi (319–466/km²)

LENGTH: 16–19 in (40–48 cm)

AVERAGE WINGSPAN: 2 ft (60 cm)

AVERAGE WEIGHT: Males 1.3–1.4 lb (600–650 g); females 1.1–1.3 lb (500–600 g)

MARKINGS: Brown back and crested head, gray breast, black band at end of square-edged tail; black,

woods, commonly called partridges in many parts. They're intrinsically associated with aspens, on which they depend for much of their food and shelter. When flushed from their hiding places, they overwhelm observers, exploding out of nowhere so suddenly that they are out of view before the shock of their thunderous flapping wears off. Flushed grouse usually fly straight up with their tails fanned out and then arch swiftly, flying up to 100 yards (91 meters) to another well-concealed spot. In the winter, they might burst out from beneath powdery snow, where they take shelter during cold spells. Grouse can actually fly quite silently if they wish, but by stirring up a commotion, they throw potential predators off guard and warn others of their kind to flee.

In the spring, males actively broadcast their location in hopes of attracting a mate or two. Starting as early as late March, they climb onto carefully chosen fallen logs, usually in dense stands of young aspen where branch cover will obscure them from raptors. They then "drum" by flapping their wings, starting slowly and accelerating into a high-speed whirr for about ten seconds, like a motor being started. The low, deep thumping, almost felt more as a vibration in the listener's stomach, is inaudible to menacing owls. It is caused by the sound of air popping back into the vacuum created beneath the grouse's wings with each rapid, blurred beat he takes. Males repeat the drumming about once every five minutes and may signal back and forth to each other from up to half a mile (0.8 kilometers) away, marking off their breeding territories. Like songbirds, their sessions are especially persistent at dusk and dawn,

iridescent neck ruffs; bare skin over eyes usually orangish on males

ALIAS: Partridge, woods pheasant, birch partridge, pine hen, drumming grouse, drummer, tippet, long-tailed grouse, white flesher, wood grouse, *Bonasa umbellus*

BRAIN SIZE: 0.1 cu in (2 cm³)

HUMAN BRAIN SIZE: 79 cu in (1,300 cm³)

CALLS: Clucks, alarm whistles, hisses

PREFERRED HABITAT: Forests of aspens containing dense sapling stands mixed with thickets of alder and willow and areas of larger deciduous trees and evergreens for roosting in winter

HOME RANGE: 5–62 acres (2–25 ha) for individuals; about 50 acres (20 ha) for families

FOOD: Buds, catkins, and leaves of aspen most important, but hundreds of other species of seeds, nuts, berries, fruits, buds, leaves, mushrooms, and insects eaten; occasionally snakes and frogs; in winter relies heavily on buds of aspen, birch, hazel, and alder. Young eat 70% insects and worms in their first 2 weeks, 5% by late summer.

NEST: Ground depression lined with leaves and feathers

AVERAGE CLUTCH: 10–12 buff-colored walnut-sized eggs

INCUBATION PERIOD: 23–24 days

FLEDGING AGE: 10–12 days

NEST PREDATION RATE: 30–40%

CHICK MORTALITY IN THE FIRST 6 WEEKS: About 60%

LIFE SPAN: Few live more than 2 years, maximum about 8 years

though they sometimes jam through the night.

When a female shows up, her drummer boy goes into a song-and-dance routine as well, strutting in front of her with tail spread, comb erect, and wings hung low, and fanning his long neck feathers so they look like an Elizabethan ruff. All the while he chortles softly. The attraction, at least for the female, ends soon after mating. She steals off to lay her eggs and raise the young on her own, while the father resumes his drumming, soliciting all available females well into May. In September, when the angle of the sun is the same as in spring, some males may resume drumming briefly, just as songbirds sing a fleeting reprise.

Expectant mother grouse usually select nest sites at the base of large trees or under logs. A female takes two weeks or more to lay all of her eggs, waiting for the last to drop before she starts incubating so that they'll hatch simultaneously. Unlike most naked newborn songbirds, the wide-eyed, downy grouse hatchlings leave the nest and follow their mother as soon as they are dry, within a few hours of emerging from their shells, usually in late May or early June. They come into the world alert and instinctively knowing how to obey their mother's command calls to freeze, hide, come out, or run. If they're threatened, Mom resorts to the classic broken wing distraction display, leading a predator away and then flying up and circling back to the spot where the chicks remain hiding.

After the young fledge, families roost and often feed on aspen buds together in trees. Those that survive to September are gripped with a crazed wanderlust that sends them off to establish their own individual territories, serving to disperse the population and avoid inbreeding. In the weeks and months that follow, more than half of the inexperienced birds wander over a mile (1.6 kilometers), often seeming frantic and clumsy, sometimes traveling at night and flying into things. It's also a time when hundreds of thousands of them are dispatched by hunters across the north woods states.

PREDATORS: Great horned owls, barred owls, goshawks, foxes, bobcats, lynx, fishers. Eggs eaten by red squirrels, skunks, raccoons, mink, weasels, crows.

SCAT: Curved, gray-white droppings, 0.8–1.8 in (2–4 cm) long

SCAT PRODUCTION: Average of 4 droppings per hour

ACCOLADES: State bird of Pennsylvania

RANGE: Throughout north woods region to New Jersey, along Appalachians to northern Georgia, scattered through Midwest and northern prairies to Pacific, north to Alaska and forested region of Canada

NUMBER OF GROUSE SPECIES NESTING IN NORTH WOODS REGION: 3

ALSO SEE: Quaking Aspen, Eastern Hemlock, Snowshoe Hare

SONG SPARROW

Much Varied Virtuosity

Song sparrows, in Latin *Melospiza melodia*, are fully deserving of their name. Peals of exuberant song sparrow melodies, breaking late winter's still silence, are one of the first clear signs of the turning of the year. Males pour it out for hours on end, each bird drawing from a repertoire of eight to ten songs—sometimes as many as twenty—to create kaleidoscopic medleys. The females, for their part, sing short, soft tunes once they in turn arrive from the south. The most vocally versatile males command the greatest attention from the opposite sex and respect from rivals.

As the cacophony of red-winged blackbirds drops off in early summer, and warbler

Calls: Songs highly variable, but mostly in pattern of first note or phrase repeated 2 or 3 times, followed by complex string of buzzy trills, twitters, and whistles, often in rhythm of "Maids, maids, maids, put on your tea kettle-ettle-ettle," lasting 2–3 seconds

Length: 5–7 in (13–17 cm)

Wingspan: 4–9 in (10–23 cm)

Weight: Average 0.6–0.9 oz (17–25 g)

Markings: Streaky brown back and streaked white breast with telltale large dark spot in middle; tan eye stripe with reddish-brown band above

Alias: Ground Sparrow, bush sparrow, hedge sparrow, silver tongue, *Melospiza melodia*

Preferred habitat: Shrubby forest edges and clearings near lakes and rivers; small islands; thickets; marshes; swamps

Food: Grass and weed seeds, berries, beetles, grasshoppers, ants, flies, wasps

Nest: Cup of grass, bark strips, leaves and rootlets, on the ground in early spring, later in a shrub or tree

Average clutch: 3–5 light green or pale blue eggs covered in brown spots

Incubation period: 10–14 days

Fledging age: 17–20 days

choruses begin to thin, song sparrow refrains rise to the fore and continue through the hot days ahead. Song sparrows stay in top form because they hold on to nesting territories long enough to raise two broods of future songsters. Females usually spend four to ten days in April or early May building their first nests on the ground, hidden amid shrubs and the previous year's long, dry plant stems. Later, after the leaves open, they turn to the cover of bushes to locate a home for their second clutch.

Fathers help feed their offspring and take primary charge of them soon after they fledge, when mother birds are working on their second nests. Despite the equal amount of care given to the second brood, sparrows born in the first clutch have better chances for survival because they have more time to gain experience in their first summer.

After they fledge, young males spend the next couple of months learning the craft of their species, listening intently to the songs of surrounding adults. Adding their own improvisations, they begin singing ditties by autumn. By the time they begin their first breeding season the following spring, they've developed an expansive songbook that they'll follow for the rest of their lives.

PERCENTAGE OF EGGS LAID THAT PRODUCE SURVIVING FLEDGLINGS: 40
LIFE SPAN: Average of 2.5 years for adults; up to 11 years
PREDATORS: Sharp-shinned and Cooper's hawks; crows and blue jays raid nests
NESTS PARASITIZED BY COWBIRDS: About 23%
NUMBER OF SONG SPARROW SUBSPECIES ACROSS NORTH AMERCIA: 31
PERCENTAGE OF SONGBIRD SPECIES THAT SING 2 OR MORE SONGS: About 75
RANGE: Across northern United States to northern Georgia, Arkansas, and South Dakota; western states to Rockies, north to Alaska and southern half of Canada
SPRING MIGRATION IN NORTH WOODS REGION: Late March to early May; peak, early to mid-May
FALL MIGRATION IN NORTH WOODS REGION: Late August to early November; peak, late September to early October
WINTER WHEREABOUTS: Atlantic Coast, central New Hampshire and Vermont, Adirondacks, southern Michigan and Wisconsin, Iowa, south to Mexico
ALSO SEE: White-Throated Sparrow

Song sparrows return each spring to the same general locale where they hatched. Since they learn to sing in a particular milieu, generations of birds perpetuate distinctive musical styles in an area. Song sparrow enthusiasts estimate the birds have developed up to 900 local "dialects" across the continent.

SPOTTED SANDPIPER

Teeter-Tail of the Shoreline

Among spotted sandpipers, it's the female that loves 'em and leaves 'em. A spotted lass may breed with up to four males in a season, though two is more common. After an amorous liaison, she drops her eggs and moves on as soon as the next available fella comes along, leaving hubby number one to incubate and raise the motherless offspring.

Female sandpipers begin the role reversal by arriving first on the breeding grounds, establishing and defending territories from each other. Within minutes of the males' coming back, the larger, more aggressive females woo them with aerial displays, singing, strutting, and ruffling their neck feathers. Pairs stay together for about ten days, until all the eggs are laid, though a female usually helps out a little longer with her last clutch of the year. Multiple

LENGTH: 7–8 in (18–20 cm)
WINGSPAN: 15–16 in (37–40 cm)
WEIGHT: Males 1.2–1.4 oz (34–41 g); females 1.5–1.8 oz (43–50 g)
MARKINGS: Grayish-brown back, dark round spots on white breast and belly; females more heavily spotted than males
ALIAS: Gutter snipe, teeter-tail, sand lark, peep, spottie, peet-weet, *Actitis macularia*
CALL: Sharp, ringing whistle, commonly described as "peet"
PREFERRED HABITAT: Shores of lakes, ponds, rivers, marshes, mudflats
FOOD: Midge, fly and mayfly larvae, worms, beetles, grubs, grasshoppers, crickets, snails, fish fry

61

Aggressive females woo the males with aerial displays, singing, strutting, and ruffling their neck feathers

NEST: Grass- or moss-lined ground depression hidden amid long grass, rocks, or rotting logs on or near a shoreline
AVERAGE CLUTCH: 4 brown-spotted walnut-sized eggs
INCUBATION PERIOD: 19–22 days
FLEDGING AGE: 11–15 days
LIFESPAN: About 3 years, maximum 12 years in wild
PREDATORS: Mink, weasels, deer mice, gulls. Crows and grackles eat eggs or chicks.
RANGE: Northern United States to North Carolina, Indiana, Kansas, New Mexico, and California, north to Alaska and across Canada to tree line
FLYING SPEED: 18-30 MPH (30-50 km/h)
SPRING MIGRATION IN NORTH WOODS REGION: Late April to late May
FALL MIGRATION IN NORTH WOODS REGION: Late July to mid-October
WINTER WHEREABOUTS: Coastal South Carolina and Gulf of Mexico to Argentina

clutches may have evolved to offset the high predation of sandpiper eggs, laid on the ground in relatively open areas. Only about 20 to 40 percent of all eggs usually hatch successfully. If their clutch is lost, males may also mate again.

Sandpiper eggs are large and take longer to hatch than the eggs of many other species. But in June and early July, the young pop out of their shells fully feathered and are able to walk within four hours, and catch their own food when only a day or two old. Fathers continue to brood them for about ten days and tend them for at least a month. Meanwhile, footloose mothers head south ahead of everyone else, starting in July.

Sandpipers spend most of their time probing shorelines with their long beaks for insects, especially at dawn and dusk, their tails constantly bobbing or teetering up and down.

TREE SWALLOW

Swirling above the Waterfront

S pring, blessings, and fertility were long believed, from ancient Greece to China, to arrive on the wings of swallows. So high was their repute that killing a swallow or destroying its nest was considered ill luck, even a sin, in some cultures. Folk stories even told of benevolent swallows comforting Jesus at the Crucifixion, from which their name *svalow*, Old Scandinavian for "console," comes. Even in America, the return of cliff swallows every year on or about March 19 to San Juan Capistrano in southern California has spawned a legend, an annual festival, and a popular song.

Because swallows return so suddenly in early spring, swirling down from high in the air to skim the surface of the water for emerging insects, people once believed they hibernated in the mud beneath lakes

LENGTH: 5–7.3 in (13–16 cm)
WINGSPAN: 12–14 in (30–35cm)
WEIGHT: 0.6–0.8 oz (18–24 g)
MARKINGS: Like a uniform, with metallic, iridescent dark blue back and head, contrasting strongly with bright, clean white chin and undersides; very pointy wings; immatures and first-year females grayish-brown on top
ALIAS: White-bellied swallow, *Tachycineta bicolor*
CALLS: Thin, liquid twitter, single little notes, or a "weet, trit, weet" song ending in a liquid warble
PREFERRED HABITAT: Wetlands, beaver ponds, meadows, lakes, rivers
FOOD: 90% midges, blackflies, beetles, ants, stoneflies, aphids,

or the sea. Modern bird-banding projects have established that tree swallows come from winter homes spread around the Gulf of Mexico and the Caribbean. They migrate during the day, feeding on tiny flies transformed from larvae by early warm spells. Tree swallows arrive earlier than any other swallow species in a race for unoccupied nesting cavities in the north. They are the only swallows that have the ability to switch to berries when insects disappear during cold snaps.

Spending more time aloft than any other songbirds, swallows are in almost constant flight

---

Often returning to the same sites every year, tree swallows nest in early May, using tree cavities as close as fifty feet (fifteen meters) from each other. Unable with their tiny beaks to dig their own homes, they rely on old woodpecker holes or natural cavities. Dead, flooded trees in beaver ponds provide ideal sites, but the high demand by many species for such prime, sheltered housing limits the tree swallow population. Some even resort to nesting in floating hollow logs and stumps. A high percentage of tree swallows don't get to nest, creating a Wild West atmosphere of fighting among both females and males as birds try to wrest prime loft apartments from one another.

But swallows do have their fun side. They are often seen collecting feathers, mostly white ones, to line their nest cavi-

mayflies, gnats, and other flying insects; also moths, bees, other flying insects, bayberries, seeds

NEST: Usually in the cavity of a dead deciduous tree, especially birch, 5–20 ft (1.5–6 m) above the ground, lined with feathers, pine needles, and grass

AVERAGE CLUTCH: 4–6 white jelly bean–sized eggs

INCUBATION PERIOD: 13–16 days

AVERAGE NUMBER OF TIMES PER MINUTE HATCHING CHICKS PECK AT THEIR EGGSHELLS: 60

FLEDGING AGE: 18–22 days

EGGS THAT HATCH AND PRODUCE FLEDGED YOUNG: 83%

FIRST-YEAR MORTALITY: About 80%

ANNUAL ADULT MORTALITY: 40–60%

LIFE SPAN: Average 2.7 years; up to 11 years

PREDATORS: Sharp-shinned hawks, kestrels, owls, falcons. Nests raided by raccoons, weasels, crows, grackles, snakes, chipmunks, deer mice.

FLYING SPEED: Average 5–19 mph (8–30 km/h), faster in short bursts

RANGE: Northern United States to Virginia, Indiana, Missouri, South Dakota, Colorado, Utah, and California; north to Alaska and Canada almost to tree line

SPRING MIGRATION IN NORTH WOODS REGION: Early April to early May; peak, mid- to late April

FALL MIGRATION IN NORTH WOODS REGION: Mid-July to early October; peak, August and September

WINTER WHEREABOUTS: Mostly Florida and Gulf of Mexico, some south to Venezuela and sometimes

ties, playfully bobbing them in the air. They've even been observed swooping and plucking feathers off the backs of farm ducks. Though males arrive on the breeding grounds first and secure the nest sites, females do the renovations inside their quarters. Both take turns incubating.

After the young hatch, they are fed every two or three minutes. Spending more time aloft than any other songbirds, swallows are in almost constant flight, swooping gracefully to snap insects from the air. They glide in circles, then flap three or four times to gain altitude.

When nesting is finished and the young have fledged, around midsummer, swallows seem to acquire a festive spirit that brings them together in huge numbers. Flocks of thousands at Lake Champlain, Lake of the Woods, New England's coastal salt marshes, and wetlands across the north darken the sky in spectacular swirlings as they disperse in the morning to forage and return again at dusk. They migrate en masse in late August, forming even larger flocks when they land in the Florida Everglades. These can number into the millions.

north along the Atlantic Coast to Massachusetts

NUMBER OF SWALLOW SPECIES NESTING IN NORTH WOODS REGION: 6

NUMBER OF SWALLOW SPECIES WORLDWIDE: 75

ALSO SEE: Rain and Snow, Paper Birch, Yellow-Bellied Sapsucker

TURKEY VULTURE

The Graceful, Soaring Scavenger

Recent genetic investigations strongly support what dissenting taxonomists have long suspected: Despite their appearance, the vultures of the Americas are not even closely related to Old World vultures and other true raptors such as hawks and eagles. Apparently, they are rather a group of morphed storks that lost their long legs and necks and developed a decided taste for the macabre.

Still, turkey vultures are commonly mistaken for hawks, though they are actually much larger, second in size only to eagles in the north woods pantheon of soaring birds. They were not known to nest north of New Jersey and far southern Michigan before 1920, but have since ex-

AVERAGE GLIDE RATIO: 18 ft (5.5 m) forward to 1 ft (30 cm) of drop
LENGTH: 26–32 in (65–90 cm)
WINGSPAN: 5.8–6.6 ft (1.7–2 m)
WEIGHT: 4.4–5.3 lb (2–2.4 kg)
MARKINGS: Underside of wings black near front and gray at back, very dark brown body, red, featherless head
ALIAS: Turkey buzzard, red-headed buzzard, TV, *Cathartes aura*
PREFERRED HABITAT: Over open areas, large lakes, islands, swamps, ridges, cliffs
FOOD: Carrion, though may kill defenseless animals such as newborn rabbits

panded their range into the upper Midwest and northeast, nesting in Vermont for the first time in 1979 and continuing into Maine.

Turkey vultures are usually seen drifting or circling over fields, roads, cliffs, or lakes. They hold their six-foot- (1.8-meter) wide wings in a shallow V, slowly tilting from side to side on wind currents, almost never flapping. The two-toned underside of their wings is the chief distinguishing feature.

Vultures are highly skilled specialists, with an acute sense of smell not possessed by other birds

---

Because vultures evoke images of slow, parched death in the desert, there's a perception that they are the lowlifes of the bird world. These scavengers live on rotting carcasses, don't take time to make real nests, and even pee on their own legs to keep cool. When cornered, they vomit foul-smelling, half-decayed flesh and then hide their heads, ostrichlike, rather than fight. Turkey vultures don't sing, just hiss or growl on occasion. And their featherless, gnarled red heads (black on younger birds) do nothing for their standing in avian beauty contests.

But it's captivating to watch turkey vultures soar almost effortlessly overhead. Vultures are also notable as highly skilled specialists, with an acute sense of smell not possessed by other birds. They may forage

HOME RANGE: 50–180 sq mi (130–470 km²)

NEST: No nest made, but eggs laid in the hollow of a broken, dead treetop or a hole in a log or stump, often in a swamp or other remote site, or on a cliff or in a cave

AVERAGE CLUTCH: 2 brown-splotched nectarine-sized eggs

INCUBATION PERIOD: 38–41 days

FLEDGING AGE: 60–80 days

ANNUAL ADULT MORTALITY: 20–25%

LIFE SPAN: Up to 17 years in wild, 20 years in captivity

PREDATORS: Foxes, skunks, snakes. Other birds of prey may raid nests.

RANGE: Breeds in all of lower 48 states, but not in northern Maine and New Hampshire or parts of prairies and Pacific Northwest

SPRING MIGRATION IN NORTH WOODS REGION: Early April to late May

FALL MIGRATION IN NORTH WOODS REGION: August to early November; peak, early September to early October

WINTER WHEREABOUTS: Most in Florida to Louisiana, some north to Connecticut and Illinois or south to Paraguay

HIGHEST MIGRATION ALTITUDE: 21,000 ft (6,400 m)

AVERAGE DAILY MIGRATION DISTANCE: 17–43 mi (28–70 km)

NUMBER PASSING THROUGH PANAMA IN FALL: Up to 300,000, most from western United States

ESTIMATED WORLD POPULATION: Several million

AGE OF OLDEST NEW WORLD VULTURE FOSSILS: 60–70 million years

NUMBER OF U.S. VULTURE SPECIES: 3

all day over many miles before detecting the sweet scent of something dead. Then they home in with their keen eyes.

From their communal roosts and nest sites in remote woods and swamps, or on cliffs and small islands, turkey vultures set off when the morning mists have cleared and the sun has warmed the land enough

NUMBER OF VULTURE SPECIES WORLD-WIDE: 7 in Americas; 13 elsewhere, unrelated
ALSO SEE: Broad-Winged Hawk, Wind and Weather Systems

to create thermals—the columns of warm, rising air that vultures ride upward in circles. Their wings are too cumbersome to flap for very long. Though they usually forage alone, the sight of one vulture circling a find usually brings more. They'll eat anything from large mammals to fish and grasshoppers, as long as it isn't moving. Starting with the eyeballs, they'll strip the carcass to the bone. Vultures have been respected by people of many cultures as mythic figures connected with the mysteries of death. Tibetans and Zoroastrians still leave their dead at sacred sites to be eaten by the winged scavengers. The vulture's scientific name, *Cathartes*, of Greek origin, means "purifier." Ornithologists speculate that the vulture's bald head allows it to dig deep into a corpse without soiling its feathers.

As early spring warms, turkey vultures begin drifting back to the north from their winter haunts in the southeastern United States. Up to 3,000 in a single day have been seen over hawk watch sites, usually flying at 1,000 to 2,500 feet (300 to 750 meters) on high-pressure fronts. They often return to old nesting sites, where they pair off and devote spring and summer to raising a new family, with each parent taking turns incubating the eggs and feeding the young.

WHITE-THROATED SPARROW

Lingering Whistle Defines North

One of the most distinctive songs of the north is said to go, "Old Sam Peabody, Peabody, Peabody," or alternatively, "Oh, sweet poverty, poverty, poverty." While the tune, sung by the white-throated sparrow, is known to come in fifteen different versions, or song patterns, birds do not actually pronounce letters of the alphabet. Fanciful phrases attributed to them are merely human lyrics to their music, memory aids that fit the rhythms of their songs.

Whatever the interpretation, the song is one virtually everyone hears up north in late spring and early summer, hanging in the air, carrying over other sounds like a navy whistle calling order to the deck.

Like other songbirds, white-throated sparrows call to proclaim their turf and keep out intruders of the same species. They sing especially at sunrise and into evening, sometimes even pealing off a few

CALLS: Song a clear, lingering whistle, lasting 2–5 seconds, usually in 5 or 6 notes, changing in pitch, ending in subtly wavering triplets; single "tseet" call notes; loud clicks when frightened

NAME ORIGIN: Old English *spearwa*, meaning "flutterer"

LENGTH: 6–7 in (15–18 cm)

WINGSPAN: 9–10 in (23–25 cm)

WEIGHT: 0.8–1.1 oz (22–32 g)

MARKINGS: White throat, gray breast, white or tan head stripes, tiny yellow patch between eye and bill, reddish-brown back, gray undersides

ALIAS: Whistlebird, poor Sam Peabody, Peverly bird, Canadian song sparrow, Canada bird, nightingale, *Zonotrichia albicollis*

PREFERRED HABITAT: Shrubby edges and low, dense understory of partly open coniferous and mixed forests, usually with lots of spruce, fir, paper birch, and aspen; also thickets, bushy clearings, shrubby swamps, bogs, beaver ponds; up to tree line, at 4,000 ft (1,220 m), in Vermont mountains

BREEDING TERRITORY: 0.5–8 acres (0.2–3.2 ha)

FOOD: Grass and weed seeds; maple, beech, and oak buds; birch and hazel catkins; berries; caterpillars; dragonflies; beetles; grubs; flies; spiders; millipedes

bars in the dead of night. They usually whistle from a prominently exposed branch where they can easily be seen by their rivals. Each recognizes the others by their individual calls. Once they establish borders and neighbors get used to each other, squabbles diminish. The sparrows respond much more strongly if they detect a strange voice in the neighborhood. Less dominant males, usually one-year-olds, cannot establish their own territories and do not breed. Instead they become floaters, silently stealing through the bush, ready to take over a piece of real estate if something should happen to the proprietor. They often fill the vacancy within hours of the other bird's disappearance.

In contrast to the floaters, some female white-throats actually join in the mating chorus, normally an exclusively male rite among songbirds. It's a phenomenon of color-coded personalities. Singing females have white head stripes and are more aggressive than their tan-striped sisters. They join their mates in chasing away intruders from their territories until they begin nesting. White-striped males, however, don't appreciate any birds, even females, singing their tune and look upon them as competition. So they choose the more demure tan-striped females as partners, while the tan-striped males, being less aggressive and loquacious, find harmony with the feisty white-striped divas.

White-throats build their nests well hidden on or near the ground in mats of blueberries, bunchberries, or other shrubs in clearings or forest edges. While normally vegetarian, both parents switch to insects when their young hatch. Tan-striped mothers tend to be better providers for their young, but their husbands lend less of a helping hand than tan-striped males.

NEST: Cup of grass, twigs, roots, pine needles, and lichens, 3–5 in (8–13 cm) wide, usually on or near the ground and covered by a brush pile, a mat of dead leaves and ferns, or fallen branches

AVERAGE CLUTCH: 4 olive-sized light green, gray, or bluish eggs with numerous brown spots

INCUBATION PERIOD: 11–14 days

FLEDGING AGE: 12–14 days

NESTS LOST TO PREDATORS: 20–70%

LIFE SPAN: Up to 9 years

PREDATORS: Sharp-shinned hawks, kestrels, owls, merlins, foxes. Nests raided by red squirrels, chipmunks, garter snakes.

RANGE: Throughout north woods region to northeastern Pennsylvania, north across forested region of Canada to Rockies

SPRING MIGRATION IN NORTH WOODS REGION: Mid-April to late May; peak, late April to early May

FALL MIGRATION IN NORTH WOODS REGION: Mid-August to early November; peak, late September to early October

WINTER WHEREABOUTS: Most in southeastern states to Texas and Florida, some north to southeastern Wisconsin and coastal Maine

NUMBER OF SPARROW SPECIES NESTING IN NORTH WOODS REGION: 14

NUMBER OF NEW WORLD SPARROW AND RELATED OLD WORLD BUNTING SPECIES WORLDWIDE: 284

ALSO SEE: Yellow-Rumped Warbler

YELLOW-BELLIED SAPSUCKER

Making a Mark on the Forest

The red forehead patches sported by yellow-bellied sapsuckers and the males of most other types of woodpeckers in the north were a symbol of bravery to the Ojibwa, who hung them from their tobacco pipes. They said the patches were a gift from the trickster deity Nanaboujou, who had tried to copy the tree-knocking skill of his friend the giant woodpecker by placing two wooden pins in his nostrils and hammering away at a trunk. Instead, Nanaboujou knocked himself out and received a nasty wound. The giant woodpecker rescued him, stopped the bleeding, and in return was dabbed with the blood of Nanaboujou to wear as a symbol of honor.

Woodpeckers were similarly venerated in Europe and Asia, where they were closely associated with rain, thunder gods, and agriculture. The name for woodpeckers

LENGTH: 8–9 in (19 cm)

WINGSPAN: 9–10 in (22–25 cm)

WEIGHT: 1.5–2 oz (43–55 g)

MARKINGS: Black-and-white-lined back, faint yellowish belly, white wing patches, red forehead; throat red on male, white on females; immatures brownish

ALIAS: Yellow-belly, *Sphyrapieus varius*

NAME FOR A GROUP: A descent of woodpeckers

CALLS: Piercing, harsh, nasal whine; descending, slurred squeal; squeaks. Wings make a snipelike winnowing sound during courtship flights.

PREFERRED HABITAT: Dry, young, open deciduous or mixed forests with lots of paper birch, aspen, and clearings; hemlock, yellow birch, beech, basswood, maple, young white pine, and spruce also tapped for sap

BREEDING TERRITORY: 5–7.5 acres (2–3 ha)

FOOD: Wasps, flies, ants, beetles, moths, mayflies, caterpillars, sap, inner bark, berries

NUMBER OF BIRD SPECIES KNOWN TO FEED ON SAP OR INSECTS AT SAP-SUCKER HOLES: 35

NEST: Tree cavity with an opening about 1.5 in (4 cm) wide, usually 10–60 ft (3–18 m) up in an aspen; sometimes in a birch, beech, maple, or hemlock

in many languages was "rainbird." They received their reputation both because they produced thundering sounds when knocking and because they frequented oaks, the sacred tree of various cultures. The European green woodpecker, which, like the North American flicker, probes the ground with its beak for ants, was in Greek and other Indo-European mythologies the father of the inventor of the plow or hoe.

The much ballyhooed yellow-bellied sapsucker is both one of the most common and fascinating woodpeckers in the north woods. With their long, brushy tongues, sapsuckers lap up wasps, flies, moths, and other insects attracted to the sweet sap oozing from the rows of evenly spaced holes they drill into trees. Paper birch and aspen are favorites for the job. Early in the season, before those trees leaf out and yield a strong sap flow, yellow-bellies prefer hemlocks. Hummingbirds, yellow-rumped warblers, nuthatches, red squirrels, flying squirrels, and other creatures also frequent the sap wells. Sometimes, when the sap ferments, the whole party can get a little woozy. Bats, as well, come around at night to snatch sap-supping moths.

Sapsuckers also invest in their future housing needs, or at least that of future generations, when they drill holes in trees. A family of woodpeckers usually patronizes one or two favorite trunks for most of their meals, riddling them with sap wells. The holes eventually girdle the tree—cutting off the life-giving sap flow—or allow in wood-rotting fungi. It's estimated that the drilling of a pair of nesting sapsuckers leads to the eventual death of about one tree a year, making the birds important agents of forest change. In turn, the dead or dying trees provide the woodpeckers, and many other animals, with ideal nesting sites.

Aspens infected by false tinder fungus, a hoof-shaped gray polypore seen

AVERAGE CLUTCH: 4–6 shiny, white, olive-sized eggs

INCUBATION PERIOD: 12–13 days

FLEDGING AGE: 25–29 days

LIFE SPAN: Up to 6 years

PREDATORS: Sharp-shinned hawks, Cooper's hawks. Raccoons and red squirrels raid nests.

RANGE: Throughout north woods region, along Appalachians to West Virginia, west to North Dakota; western United States to Rockies and Black Hills; across forested region of Canada

SPRING MIGRATION IN NORTH WOODS REGION: Early April to early May; peak, mid-April

FALL MIGRATION IN NORTH WOODS REGION: Late August to late October; peak, late September

WINTER WHEREABOUTS: Most in Central America and West Indies, some as far north as Rhode Island, Kentucky, and Kansas

NUMBER OF CAVITY-NESTING NORTH WOODS BIRD SPECIES: More than 30

NUMBER OF TREE-DENNING NORTH WOODS MAMMAL SPECIES: At least 7

NUMBER OF WOODPECKER SPECIES NESTING IN NORTH WOODS REGION: 9

NUMBER OF WOODPECKER SPECIES WORLDWIDE: About 200

ALSO SEE: Fungi, Hummingbird, Red Oak, Red Squirrel, Quaking Aspen

on many trunks, are most commonly used by sapsuckers for their nest holes. The fungus rots the center of the trunk but leaves the outer sapwood alive, making for easy chiseling but strong walls. The availability of such trees is the biggest limiting factor on the sapsucker population. Yellow-bellies usually excavate new cavities every spring, though often in trees used before, resulting in what's been described as something resembling a multistoried New York tenement building. Indeed, flying squirrels often take up residence in old holes while sapsuckers are living on another floor. Many other species depend on old woodpecker holes for nesting or shelter as well.

Woodpeckers were similarly venerated in Europe and Asia, where they were closely associated with rain, thunder gods, and agriculture

---

Sapsuckers also seek out dead, dry trees that will reverberate well for courtship drumming. Their love code, much louder than their sap tapping, has an uneven cadence, with fast drumrolls often preceded by and ending in a few slow, tentative knocks. As with all woodpeckers, their strong head bones and neck muscles act as shock absorbers. Females also drum in territorial defense while their spouses dig out the nest site. Males also take the night shift incubating the eggs.

All woodpeckers can be identified by the way they perch, with their bodies parallel to a tree trunk, looking up. Their parrotlike claws, with two toes stretching backwards instead of one like other birds, and stiff tails propped against the tree hold them in place. The other common migratory woodpecker of the north woods, the flicker, utters a loud, ratcheting cry that sounds like a starter motor or a car engine trying unsuccessfully to turn over. The tiny, downy, and larger hairy woodpeckers stick around all year, mainly in deciduous forests, as does the crow-sized but elusive pileated woodpecker, which sports a huge beak and red plume that probably inspired Woody Woodpecker's hairstyle.

YELLOW-RUMPED WARBLER

Outgoing Bundle of Energy

There are more brightly colored summer wood warblers in the forest than any other group of birds. Legendary ornithologist Roger Tory Peterson called them the butterflies of the bird world. Unfortunately for people who delight in seeing them, many of these tiny, hyperactive insect-eaters are "skulkers" of the thick, tangled undergrowth. Or they frequent high, dense foliage, avoiding the gaze of all but the most dogged birders. Yellow-rumped warblers, generally the most common of all, break the mold, being exceedingly outgoing as they forage in small groups among the lower branches, affording the oft-heard, if somewhat embarrassing, cry, "I've got a great view of a yellow-rump!"

Yellow-rumps are also true northerners, the hardiest of warblers. They spend more time in the north woods, and winter farther north, than any of their brethren. Unlike most of the other warblers, they're

LENGTH: 5–6 in (12–15 cm)

WINGSPAN: 8–9 in (20–23 cm)

WEIGHT: 0.5 oz (12–14 g)

ADDITIONAL BULKING UP BEFORE MIGRATION: 0.15–0.2 oz (4–5 g)

MARKINGS: Yellow patches on top of head, in front of wings, and above base of tail. Males have black-streaked bluish-gray back, black mask and chest, and white throat and belly; females, gray-brown back, streaked breast, and white belly. Male colors fade to resemble female in fall.

ALIAS: Myrtle warbler, butter butt, *Dendroica coronata*

CALLS: Loud, sharp "chip"; song an undistinctive, flat, slow, gentle trill, usually over 1–3 seconds

PREFERRED HABITAT: Dry fir and spruce forest edges; also found in pine, cedar, hemlock, and mixed forests, and bogs

AVERAGE BREEDING TERRITORY: 1–2 acres (0.45–0.8 ha)

FOOD: Caterpillars; grubs; leaf beetles; ants; grasshoppers; mosquitoes; flies; spiders; insect eggs; bayberries; poison ivy; dogwood, mountain ash, and other berries; seeds; willow buds; sap

TIME TAKEN TO DIGEST AND PASS A SPRUCE BUDWORM: $2^{1}/_{2}$ hours

NEST: Deep cup, 3–6 in (7–15 cm) wide, of twigs and grass, lined with feathers, usually 5–20 ft (1.5–6 m) up in an evergreen

food generalists and can survive on berries, seeds, and even sap before the really good eating starts as insect numbers pick up. They're also known as myrtle warblers because of their winter subsistence on wax myrtle and bayberry, the fruits of which most other birds can only stomach small quantities of because of their high wax content. The berries, in fact, have been used to make candles since pioneer times.

Wintering most abundantly along the Atlantic and Gulf Coasts, yellow-rumps are stirred by the lengthening daylight soon after the spring solstice and begin showing up on northern nesting grounds about three weeks later, initiating a parade of migrant warblers that continues for two months. Most other species, though, come from roosts in the tropics and take four to five weeks to reach the northern United States.

Spring warbler migration peaks in mid- to late May, when insect populations are exploding in the north woods. It's often an all-you-can-eat bonanza, the reason they fly so far north to raise families. Populations of many warbler species go up dramatically with outbreaks of spruce budworm and other insects. Baby warblers, fed by their parents about every ten minutes, are stuffed with their own weight in insects each day. The high-protein diet turns hatchlings into fledglings in two weeks or less.

After a fairly quiet nesting period, with both parents attending, yellow-rumped warblers return to their noisy ways when the young fledge in July. They forage in small flocks, hunting flying insects from perches in the lower branches and up the trunks of trees. In the fall, they turn up at shorelines, open areas, and thickets. Switching to seeds and berries in cooler weather, most put off their return migration until late September or October.

AVERAGE CLUTCH: 4–5 gray-and-brown-speckled and -blotched white eggs, about the size of marbles

INCUBATION PERIOD: 11–13 days

FLEDGING AGE: 10–14 days

ANNUAL POPULATION MORTALITY: At least 44%

MAXIMUM LIFE SPAN: At least 7 years

PREDATORS: Sharp-shinned hawks, kestrels, raccoons, skunks, red squirrels, snakes

NESTS PARASITIZED BY COWBIRDS: About 30%

POPULATION DENSITY: Up to 250 pairs per sq mi (2.5 km²) in spruce-fir forests

RANGE: From northern Pennsylvania, Michigan, Wisconsin, and Minnesota to the tree line in Alaska and Canada; also in most states west of Rockies

SPRING MIGRATION IN NORTH WOODS REGION: Mid-April to late May; peak, early May

FALL MIGRATION IN NORTH WOODS: Mid-August to late October; peak, late September to early October

WINTER WHEREABOUTS: Coastal New England, western New York, and southeastern Wisconsin south to Panama and West Indies

AVERAGE DISTANCE COVERED BY A MIGRATING YELLOW-RUMP IN A NIGHT: 193 mi (312 km) in spring, 55 mi (88 km) in fall

ALSO SEE: Ovenbird, Red-Eyed Vireo, Yellow-Bellied Sapsucker, North Star and Little Dipper, Wind and Weather Systems

CREEPY CRAWLIES

There are more than one million animal species on Earth. By some estimates, 73 percent are insects. Other tiny invertebrates, such as spiders, mites, worms, snails, and springtails, make up most of the balance. Mammals account for just 0.04 percent of the total. Among the insects themselves, one-third are beetle species, of whom fireflies are the northland's flashiest representatives.

As anyone acquainted with the outdoors in spring and summer knows, the north woods has its share of creepy crawlies, with tens of thousands of known invertebrates. The region is legendary for its profusions of blackflies, mosquitoes, and other irrepressible flying insects. The same insects are also one of the main reasons the wilderness has so many beautiful insectivorous birds. There are plenty of striking dragonflies and spiders keeping bug numbers in check as well. Indeed, invertebrates are a vital link in the food chain, feeding fish, amphibians, many reptiles, bats, shrews, and bears.

The very process of decomposition, from which all new plant life springs, depends heavily on countless armies of springtails, beetles, mites, ants, worms, centipedes, and many others living above and beneath the ground. And without beautiful butterflies, moths, and, above all, bees to pollinate flowers, many species of plants and trees would perish. A world without insects would be virtually unrecognizable.

BEES, WASPS, AND HORNETS

Societies of Heavily Armed Females

It's true that only female bees, wasps, and hornets have stingers. They're actually modified ovipositors, or abdominal egg-laying tubes, used by most insects to deposit eggs with accuracy. A stinger moves up and down to saw into the skin with tiny barbs, while injecting venom through its hollow tube. While honeybee stingers are often so barbed that they break off in the skin, leading to the death of the bee, wasps and bumblebees can sting repeatedly. Hornets are reputed to be particularly painful, though yellow jackets are more aggressive and likely to administer multiple stings.

Having evolved their uniquely female instruments into awesome weapons, social bees and wasps not surprisingly form solidly matriarchal societies. The hardy bee usually seen in late April or early May is the husky, densely furred bumblebee queen (illustrated). Her insulation allows her to be active in temperatures too cool for other species, though she often avoids the midday heat. After hibernating alone beneath

MOST AGGRESSIVE STINGER IN NORTH WOODS: European yellow jacket

MOST PAINFUL STING: Spider wasps

MOST VENOMOUS STING: European hornet

CHEMICAL ALERT: Even if killed, social bees and wasps emit an alarm pheromone that, if it drifts to the nest, sends out their compatriots in attack mode.

HUMANS WITH SEVERE ALLERGIC REACTIONS TO INSECT BITES OR STINGS: 0.5–0.8% of population

AVERAGE ANNUAL BEE AND WASP STING FATALITIES IN UNITED STATES: Less than 50

HUMAN FATALITIES CAUSED BY VENOMOUS ANIMALS THAT ARE DUE TO BEES AND WASPS: About 50%

FAMOUS FATALITIES: Menes, first pharaoh of Egypt, died of a wasp sting c. 3200 B.C.

KILLER BEES: Accidental hybrid between an African honeybee subspecies brought to Brazil in 1956 and previously established European honeybees that has spread to Mexico and the United States, reaching Texas in 1990 and 4 other southwestern states since, blamed for a small number of American deaths

BUMBLEBEE WING BEATS PER SECOND: 150–200

BUMBLEBEE LENGTH: 0.5–0.9 in (1.3–2.3 cm)

the ground or within the cracks and crevices of logs or stumps all winter, bumblebee queens search out willow catkins and other early flowers for high-protein pollen needed to produce eggs. Having mated and obtained a year's supply of sperm the previous fall, the queen builds a small wax-chambered nest in the ground, often in abandoned mouse nests or under tree stumps, and lays eight to ten eggs. Some twenty to thirty days later, they have hatched, grown, pupated, and become working adults. These infertile female workers take over the job of collecting nectar and pollen, enlarging the nest, and raising successive generations of young. The queen concentrates on laying more eggs.

Toward the end of summer, when the colony has grown to 100 to 400 bumblebees, the queen lays a batch of unfertilized eggs that hatch into male drones. Still another set of eggs, given large chambers, extra food, and special care, become new queens. The sole job of the drones is to leave the nest, establish territories, and mate with young queens that come their way. They die soon afterward. The workers in the colony, along with the old queen, also perish with the killing frosts of fall. Only young, fertilized queens, after loading up on nectar from late-blooming goldenrods and asters, survive by crawling beneath the ground for the winter, with the future of a whole new colony resting with them.

The other major colonial nesting bee species in the north, though not nearly so common as bumbles, is the honeybee. Its colonies of up to 80,000 bees in tree cavities and crevices are like permanent cities, persisting through the winter, often lasting

BUMBLEBEE MARKINGS: Hairy yellow-and-black bodies, with smoky wings

DISTANCE OF A BUMBLEBEE FORAGING TRIP: Up to 6 mi (10 km)

AVERAGE AMOUNT OF HONEY IN A BUMBLEBEE NEST: About a teaspoon

LIFE SPAN OF A BUMBLEBEE WORKER (FROM HATCHING AS A LARVA): About 4 weeks

BEE FOOD: Nectar, pollen

LIFE SPAN OF HONEYBEE QUEEN: Usually 2–3 years; up to 5 years

LIFE SPAN OF A HONEYBEE WORKER: 6–8 weeks

HONEYBEE LENGTH: 0.4–0.6 in (1–1.6 cm)

HONEYBEE MARKINGS: Striped black or brown and yellow abdomen, mostly black head and thorax

FORAGING TRIPS REQUIRED TO MAKE 0.03 OZ (1 G) OF HONEY: About 60

NUMBER OF HONEYBEE LIFETIMES REQUIRED TO PRODUCE A TEASPOON OF HONEY: 12

MAXIMUM LIFETIME DISTANCE A HONEYBEE WORKER TRAVELS: 500 mi (800 km)

NUMBER OF CALORIES BURNED BY A FLYING BUMBLEBEE PER MINUTE: 0.5

AMOUNT OF HONEY NEEDED BY AN AVERAGE HONEYBEE COLONY TO GET THROUGH THE WINTER: 55 lb (25 kg)

HONEYBEE ACCOLADES: Official insect of Maine, Vermont, Wisconsin, and 13 other states

HONEYBEE COLONY POPULATION: 40,000–80,000 in summer, 5,000–20,000 in winter

AVERAGE YELLOW JACKET COLONY POPULATION: 10,000–15,000 by end of summer

YELLOW JACKET LENGTH: 0.5–0.7 in (1.2–1.8 cm)

YELLOW JACKET MARKINGS: Smooth bright-yellow-and-black bodies

for years or even decades. Honeybees transform nectar into large stores of honey for the cold months. Huddling together for warmth, wintering bees conserve their energy and live longer than quickly burned out summer workers.

Until sugar became widely available in the past few centuries, honey was Europe's main sweetener. Indo-European peoples learned the art of domestic beekeeping, or apiculture, more than 4,000 years ago, and brought the first honeybee colonies with them to North America in the early 1600s. Native peoples called honeybees the white man's flies. The bees spread quickly into the wild, since queens frequently lead swarms from crowded nests to start new colonies in late spring or early summer, leaving a pupal heir behind to assume the throne of the old colony. Since 1984, however, much of North America's wild honeybee population has been devastated by parasitic mites from Europe.

Some wasps are also colonial. Bald-faced hornets and yellow jackets, both members of the same wasp family, have life cycles very similar to that of bumblebees. They are the original paper producers, chewing wood fiber into sheets of saliva-soaked pulp that dries into the fine, gray paper walls of their nests. Starting out small, the nest expands in progressive layers as the colony grows through the summer. Paper wasps use the same material, but their umbrella-shaped nests consist of an unwalled, single-layer comb of paper cells suspended by a central stalk from a tree branch or shrub. Hornets also build in trees and bushes, where their irregularly shaped homes often have small branches running through them for support. Spherical

---

WASP FOOD: Insects, spiders, insect eggs, nectar, plant tissues and juices, honeydew

BALD-FACED HORNET LENGTH: 0.5–0.8 in (1.2–2 cm)

BALD-FACED HORNET MARKINGS: Black body with white markings on abdomen and head

ONLY TRUE HORNET SPECIES IN NORTH WOODS REGION: European hornet, 1.2 in (3 cm) long

PAPER WASP LENGTH: 0.6–0.8 in (1.5–2 cm)

PAPER WASP MARKINGS: Black, brown, or amber body with two large reddish spots on sides of abdomen, very thin waist, and long legs

LENGTH OF WASP AND YELLOW JACKET STINGERS: 0.015 in (4 cm)

MUD DAUBER LENGTH: 1.2–1.4 in (3–3.5 cm)

SWEAT BEES: Small metallic green bees, some species attracted to human sweat, may sting if touched but not as painful as major stingers

CARPENTER BEES: Resemble bumblebees but chew holes, 1/4–1/2 in (0.6–1.2 cm) around, in wood to lay eggs provisioned with pollen

PARASITOID ICHNEUMON WASP LENGTH: Up to 1.6 in (4 cm)

SMALLEST WASPS: Fairy flies, which parasitize insect eggs, as small as 0.01 in (0.2 mm)

BEE AND WASP PREDATORS: Spiders, bee flies, robber flies, flycatchers, skunks, mice, raccoons, bears

PORTION OF WORLD'S CROPS POLLINATED BY BEES: About 75%

PORTION OF WORLD'S CROPS POLLINATED BY WASPS: About 5%

RANGE OF BEES AND WASPS: All North America to the Arctic Circle

yellow jacket nests are found in excavated underground cavities or hanging by a single stalk from a tree branch. Yellow jackets often become pests to humans in late summer and early fall after their colonies begin to fall apart and the workers fan out looking for food at picnics, in garbage, or anywhere else they can find it.

Entomologists—bug experts—liken each selfless member of an insect colony to a single cell of an organism. The vast majority of bees and wasps, however, are solo fliers, hunting or foraging alone and very rarely stinging humans.

Most wasps are parasitoids, using their nonstinging ovipositors to inject their eggs into or on live insect victims. Spider wasps and sand wasps, on the other hand, dig holes in the ground for their eggs and stock

PORTION OF NORTH WOODS BEE SPECIES THAT ARE SOLITARY: More than 90%
NUMBER OF U.S. BUMBLEBEE SPECIES: About 50, with about 18 in north woods region
NUMBER OF NORTH AMERICAN YELLOW JACKET SPECIES: 18
NUMBER OF NORTH AMERICAN BEE SPECIES: About 3,500
NUMBER OF NORTH AMERICAN ICHNEUMON WASP SPECIES: More than 3,100
NUMBER OF BEE, WASP, ANT, AND SAWFLY SPECIES WORLDWIDE: At least 108,000
ALSO SEE: Moccasin Flower, Red Oak, Large-Flowered Trillium

them with flies, spiders, or caterpillars they have paralyzed with their stings. When the larvae hatch, their food is laid out in front of them, fresh, alive, and immobile. Mud dauber wasps work the same way, building numerous mud chambers, often stuck on the walls of human habitations, and leaving several spiders and one egg in each. Many of these species aren't readily recognizable as wasps, being small and black and white or all black. Spider wasps spend most of their time running along the ground rather than flying. At the same time, there are many species of flies and moths that look like bees or wasps, having evolved to imitate the bright colors that warn birds and other animals to stay away from stinging insects.

Over millions of years, bees and flowering plants have evolved in tandem, forming one of the most vital links in nature. Flowers produce nectar solely for the purpose of attracting bees and like-minded creatures. Bees lap up nectar with their tongues and pack it onto their hairy legs and bodies for transporting back to the nest. In the process, they also pick up and spread pollen as they buzz from blossom to blossom. Both the sweet fragrance and bright colors of flowers are designed to advertise their wares to pollinators. Plants have helped ensure their own survival by taking turns blooming—in succession, one species after another—through the year, allowing bees and others to stay fed and get around to them all.

BLACKFLIES

Scourge of the North

Just as the first fine days of May come along, the sun and warmth give rise to swarms of biting blackflies. Though they mass around the face, they are like commandos, landing silently behind ears or on necks, or burrowing under clothes. They are especially attracted to dark colors. Their bite is quite unlike the precise pinprick of a mosquito. Instead, they rip into the flesh with jagged, scissorlike jaws and slurp from a blood-filled bowl in the open wound. A set of long, barbed "stylets" also push into and hook under the severed skin, the reason the well-anchored little hunchbacks are so hard to brush off. The swollen, blood-encrusted ring of purple skin they leave behind is generally bigger and more itchy than the work of mosquitoes.

LENGTH: 0.0 5–0.2 in (1–5.5 mm)
MARKINGS: Most species black or dark brown, some dark gray, reddish-brown, or yellowish. *Simulium venustum* has white markings on legs.
ALIAS: Buffalo gnats, boxers, humpback gnats, turkey gnats, reed smut, family Simuliidea
BLACKFLY PUBLIC ENEMY NUMBER ONE: Simulium venustum, the "white-stockinged blackfly"
ESTIMATED LATE-SPRING DENSITIES: Up to billions per acre (0.4 ha)
AVERAGE NUMBER OF ADULTS EMERGING PER SQ YD (0.8 M²) ON PRIME STREAM HABITAT: 30,000
PREFERRED HABITAT: Areas with running water; some species in forests, others in open areas
DISPERSAL AFTER MATING: Up to 20 mi (36 km)
FOOD: Algae, plant particles, plankton, and bacteria in larval stage; blood, nectar, and honeydew when adults
ONE FULL BLOOD MEAL: 0.00006 oz (2 mg)
TIME IT TAKES FOR A FEMALE TO PRODUCE EGGS AFTER A FULL BLOOD MEAL: 4–7 days
EGGS PER BLOOD MEAL: 200–700. Female may produce 2 or 3 batches.
EGG-DEVELOPMENT PERIOD: 4–30 days, depending on temperature

Only female blackflies bite. It takes them up to three minutes of feeding to get enough blood to nourish their developing eggs. Fully tanked up, they are double their original size and must stagger away and lie low for one or two hours while they filter the blood's protein and drain its water content.

The north woods is prime blackfly country because it courses with the fast, clear waterways needed by their young. Females stick eggs to rocks, plants, and other debris in or beside rivers and streams. Groups of blackfly larvae are easy to see, forming dense greenish masses that look like moss on rocks. The larvae anchor themselves by secreting a silky goo onto surfaces and sinking tiny hooks at the end of their abdomens into it. As they sway in the current, they filter plankton—microscopic plants and animals—from the water with the bristles of two long brushes projecting from their mouths.

The species that attack in early May are blackflies that hatch in the fall and grow slowly as larvae beneath the ice through the winter, molting six to eight times. As rivers warm in spring, larvae spin cocoons and take several days to metamorphose into adults. Building to peaks in mid-May and June, depending on the weather, they die off quickly after five or six straight hot days, their tiny bodies drying out.

LARVAE: Greenish gray or beige, up to 0.6 in (1.5 cm) long

LIFE SPAN (FROM HATCHING AS A LARVA): Up to 1 year. Females live 3–6 weeks as adults, males much less.

NUMBER OF GENERATIONS PER YEAR: Most species have 1; a few have several.

PREDATORS: Dragonflies; damselflies; brook trout and other fish; bats; swallows, flycatchers, and other birds

FLYING SPEED: 1–2.5 mph (1.6–4 km/h)

LOWEST TEMPERATURE AT WHICH ADULTS ACTIVE: 50°F (10°C)

RANGE: Throughout North America

WINTER WHEREABOUTS: In streams, some as eggs, others as active larvae

PORTION OF WORLD'S CROPS POLLINATED BY FLY SPECIES: About 19%

NUMBER OF BIBLICAL PLAGUES OF EGYPT THAT WERE INSECT BASED: 6

FIRST APPEARANCE OF BLACKFLIES IN EVOLUTION: About 175 million years ago

NUMBER OF NORTH AMERICAN BLACKFLY SPECIES: 265, several dozen in north woods region

NUMBER OF BLACKFLY SPECIES WORLDWIDE: 1,660

ALSO SEE: Dragonflies, Blueberry, Mosquitoes, Yellow-Rumped Warbler

Most species of blackflies hatch from eggs in spring and do not become biting adults until June, July, or later. Their numbers are not as great as the early-spring hordes, and only a few species regularly bite humans. Most specialize in blood from birds, and many others don't drink blood at all, though their swarms can be bothersome. Luckily for nocturnal animals, most varieties restrict their feeding frenzies to daylight, though they become meaner and more numerous in the hours before sunset and on overcast, humid days. They become docile indoors, even inside tents or cars.

They are like commandos, landing silently

behind ears or on necks, or burrowing under clothes

Though universally reviled, blackflies play a vital role in the ecosystem. Their swarms draw tropical birds from as far away as South America to feast and raise their young on blackfly protein. Their larvae, as well, are an important food for brook trout and other stream fish. Blackflies themselves live primarily off plant nectar and are one of the most important pollinators of blueberries. Even purveyors of pain have a hand in creating sweetness and beauty.

DEERFLIES AND HORSEFLIES

Big, Persistent Biters

Deerflies and horseflies are the brutes of the biting-insect crowd, lacking the daintiness of mosquitoes or the stealth of blackflies. Instead, they zoom in and quickly seem to take a good-sized chunk of you. The sensation is akin to having a burning ember alight on your skin. A horde of horseflies streaming through an open vent on a hot July the Fourth in 1776 were notably loathed almost as much as the British by delegates finalizing the Declaration of Independence in Philadelphia.

Although more painful than the bites of blackflies or mosquitoes, those of the bigger flies do not swell or itch so much afterward, probably because the larger flies' quick work does not require a heavy injection of saliva, used by the smaller biters to keep blood from clotting while they suck. Their spongelike lower lips swiftly take up the blood that spills from incisions made by their mouth blades.

Like most other biting insects, only

SPECIES ILLUSTRATED: Deerfly *Chrysops callidus*

TOP HORSEFLY FLYING SPEED: 90 mph (145 km/h)

WIND SPEED AT WHICH THEY BECOME INACTIVE: 6 mph (10 km/h)

DEERFLY LENGTH: 0.3–0.6 in (8–15 mm)

HORSEFLY LENGTH: 0.4–1 in (10–25 mm)

AVERAGE HORSEFLY WEIGHT: 0.007 oz (0.2 g)

DEERFLY MARKINGS: Dark bodies of some species marked with black, brown, gray, orangish, or yellow stripes or spots; most have a large black dot or black patterns on each wing. Colorful eyes often have iridescent green, copper, or purple stripes or patterns.

HORSEFLY MARKINGS: Dark, usually less colorful than deerflies, with clear wings

HORSEFLY ALIAS: Gadflies, green-headed monsters, breeze flies, ear flies, tabanids, family Tabanidae

PREFERRED HABITAT: Shorelines, wetlands, clearings, and paths

FOOD: Larvae eat aquatic and soil insects, worms, snails, and other invertebrates; adults feed on nectar, pollen, plant juices, and honeydew.

EGGS PER FEMALE: Clumps of 100 to 1,000 long, flat, black, overlapping eggs

female deerflies and horseflies strike, using blood to produce eggs. As their name implies, deerflies, which are a little larger and fatter than houseflies, probably evolved to prey mainly on medium-sized animals such as deer. Most species attack both deer and humans high up on the body, circling around the head as they scout for a good place to land. They often follow a moving target with dogged tenacity and constant buzzing, less deterred by insect repellent than are mosquitoes and blackflies.

Horseflies, the fastest insects on the wing, are gargantuan moose feeders, usually hitting low on the legs. A moose can lose up to a cup of blood a day to the six-legged vampires. Humans are somewhat puny for horseflies' liking and are less often attacked by them than by the smaller deerflies.

Both horseflies and deerflies have very good long-distance vision. Horseflies are especially attracted to swimmers by the shimmer of wet skin in the sunlight. It may take many long dives underwater to get one off your trail. Along with deerflies, they are extremely partial to hot, sunny days and usually disappear quickly when the sun goes behind the clouds. Both keep out of sight in temperatures below 55°F (13°C).

Four to eight days after getting their blood meal, horseflies and deerflies lay their eggs in various wet habitats, often on stems or beneath leaves just above the surface. When they hatch, the larvae drop into the water or wet soil and become predators of aquatic insects and other invertebrates. They spend eight to nine months, through the winter, as larvae, capable of a painful bite if handled. In midspring, they begin crawling onto dry ground and spend about one to three weeks pupating into adults. The first take wing in late May or early June. Each species has its own emergence period through the summer. Males come out first, forming groups in clearings, on hills, or along paths and waiting for females to follow. Once mating is done, it's curtains for the males within a few days. Females live on for another couple of weeks, searching for blood for their eggs and tormenting their victims in the process.

> *EGG-DEVELOPMENT PERIOD:* 4–12 days
> *EGGS DESTROYED BY OTHER INSECTS:* About 50%
> *NUMBER OF LARVAL STAGES:* 5–11
> *LIFE SPAN (FROM HATCHING AS A LARVA):* 4 months to 3 years, but most species about a year. Adults live for 3–4 weeks.
> *PREDATORS:* Birds, dragonflies, wasps, robber flies
> *RANGE:* Throughout North America south of tree line
> *WINTER WHEREABOUTS:* Most as larvae in mud near or beneath streams, ponds, and wetlands
> *NUMBER OF NORTH AMERICAN DEERFLY AND HORSEFLY SPECIES:* About 350
> *NUMBER OF DEERFLY AND HORSEFLY SPECIES WORLDWIDE:* About 3,750
> *ALSO SEE:* Mosquitoes, Pegasus and Andromeda

DRAGONFLIES

A Mosquito's Worst Nightmare

Dragonflies are among the deadliest friends a human can have. They may look scary, but they don't harm people. Rather, they're like Blackhawk attack helicopters coming to the rescue, striking fear into the hearts of marauding mosquitoes and blackflies. Little wonder the Japanese considered them symbols of victory in war. A single bug-eating dragonfly in a clearing, or along a shoreline, can quickly clear swarms of biting insects away from a suffering human. One New England entrepreneur has even marketed dragonflies on tiny leashes, with one end clipped onto clothing, for summer walks in bug country.

From the moment they hatch in the water, dragonflies are fearsome predators. Dragonfly larvae, called nymphs, are stocky, crablike aquatic creatures that inhabit the muddy bottoms or weedy tangles of lake shallows, beaver ponds, rivers, and streams.

FLYING SPEED: Up to 35 mph (56 km/h)

COMMON WHITETAIL LENGTH: 1.7–1.9 in (4.2–4.8 cm)

GREEN DARNER LENGTH: 2.7–3.1 in (7–8 cm)

GREEN DARNER WINGSPAN: 4–4.4 in (10–11 cm)

LARGEST U.S. DRAGONFLY: Giant darner, 4–4.6 in (10–11.6 cm), in southwest

WINGSPANS OF ANCIENT DRAGONFLIES: Up to 2.5 ft (76 cm)

FIRST APPEARANCE OF DRAGONFLIES ON EARTH: At least 350 million years ago

ALIAS: Mosquito hawks, darning needles, horse stingers, snake charmers, snake doctors, order Odonata; larvae called nymphs, naiads, or bass bugs

BEST SENSE: Sight, with huge eyes containing some 30,000 separate lenses and estimated 80% of brain devoted to them, providing a 360° field of view

PREFERRED HABITAT: Various species specialize in beaver ponds and meadows, lakeshores, bogs, slow- or fast-flowing rivers and streams.

FOOD: Adults eat mosquitoes, blackflies, deerflies, horseflies, midges, butterflies; larvae eat other insect larvae, midges, butterflies, worms, snails, crayfish young, tadpoles, tiny fish.

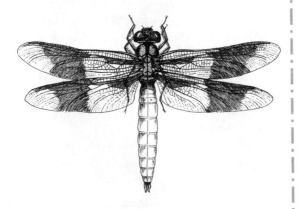

Like a living nightmare from the movie *Alien*, they have hooked, snap-action lower "lips" that spring forward in a fraction of a second to snatch prey. Usually after sunset in late spring and summer, fully grown nymphs crawl just above the surface on emergent plants and rocky shores and spend a couple of hours wiggling out of their juvenile skin, while keeping rectal gills at the tip of the abdomen in the water until their air-breathing equipment kicks in. The newly emerged dragonfly spends up to six more hours drying off and pumping fluid into the veins of its two pairs of wings. Finally, it lifts off on a maiden flight.

All dragonflies hold their wings horizontally when resting, unlike the somewhat similar damselflies, which hold their wings upward, folded together or half spread. Damselflies are also more slender and have a slower, more fluttery flight.

The first dragonfly to show up in spring is usually the green darner, one of the largest, fastest, and most common species in the northeast. Though most species overwinter as nymphs beneath the ice, some green darner populations migrate, flying south after cold fronts in early fall, often in squadrons of thousands. No one knows where they travel, though they are known as far south as Central America. Like monarch butterflies, only their descendants return, arriving as early as mid-April. Though the migrants mate, lay eggs, and generally die off by mid-June, nonmigratory green darners begin emerging soon after and fly through the summer. Then, after they dwindle away, the nymphs of the southbound population emerge to transform in September.

After spending two or three weeks after

AVERAGE NUMBER OF MOSQUITO LARVAE EATEN DURING NYMPH STAGE: 3,000

SUNBATHING: Dragonflies bask in the morning and shudder their wings to warm flight muscles enough to fly.

PEAK ACTIVITY PERIODS: Midday, warm, sunny weather

SHADY CHARACTERS: A few species, such as shadow darners and fawn darners, fly more in shade, on overcast days or at dusk.

EGG-DEVELOPMENT PERIOD: From a few days to 9 months, depending on species

NYMPHS: 0.08–2 in (2–50 mm) long; various shades of brown, green, or yellow, plain or heavily patterned

PERIOD SPENT AS A NYMPH: A few months to several years, depending on species

PERIOD SPENT AS AN ADULT: Up to 10 weeks

PREDATORS: Kingbirds, red-winged blackbirds, swallows, hawks, ducks, frogs, fish. Nymphs also eaten by giant water bugs and turtles.

PARASITES: Aquatic mites, tiny wasps

SPECIES THAT OFTEN LAND ON HUMANS: Black-shouldered spinyleg, chalk-fronted skimmer

PADDLE BUGS: Aquatic damselfly larvae, which propel forward by paddling a tail-end set of three long, flat external gills

RANGE: Throughout North America to the northern tree line

WINTER WHEREABOUTS: Most species overwinter as inactive nymphs at the bottoms of ponds, lakes, and streams. Some populations of

emergence feeding away from the water, male dragonflies return to establish and defend mating territories over prime egg-laying sites. The large darner species constantly patrol their realms for prey, mates, and interlopers, most cruising higher in the air than other families of dragonflies.

green darners migrate south; others lay overwintering eggs.

NUMBER OF U.S. DRAGONFLY AND DAMSELFLY SPECIES: 435

NUMBER OF DRAGONFLY AND DAMSELFLY SPECIES WORLDWIDE: More than 5,000

ALSO SEE: Mosquitoes, Monarch Butterfly

Skimmer family species, which are mostly partial to ponds, bogs, and slow waters, are among the most territorial and aggressive. One male's domain may cover an entire small pond, or many may occupy a larger water body. A common whitetail (illustrated)—an abundant skimmer throughout the north woods—usually commands 20 to 180 square yards (17 to 150 square meters) over a shallow stream pool or marsh. Scrambling from one of a number of oft-used perches, it engages in frequent but brief aerial dogfights, often accompanied by the loud sound of opposing wings thrashing together.

Dragonfly mating equipment is so varied and specialized, entomologists make no qualms about magnified examination of their private parts to make a positive ID on difficult species. Before mating, a male dragonfly doubles over to deposit sperm from the tip of his tail into a special storage space beneath the base of his abdomen. When a receptive female arrives in his territory, they form an acrobatic circle with their two bodies, the male holding her head by the tip of his tail while the female's tail swings forward to take the sperm from his cargo hold. The act takes only a number of seconds. A female can store the sperm for a long time and go on to mate with other dragons. Since the last one to mate with her usually has the biggest share of offspring, a male often jealously guards his partner, remaining attached to her or flying just above, driving off competitors until she lays her eggs. Ambitious males may try guarding two mates at once.

Varying egg-laying methods are largely responsible for the naming of major groups of dragonflies. Female skimmers "skim" low over the water for four or five minutes as they drop their eggs, two dozen or more at a time, each sinking to the bottom of the pond to hatch. Darners use the sharp tip of their abdomens to slice open stems just beneath the surface of the water and deposit their eggs inside. Spiketail dragonflies swiftly dunk into shallow water to inject one egg at a time into the bottom, while in weedy waters, baskettails drop just one big payload of eggs, which are strung together and become strewn over submerged vegetation.

FIREFLIES

Sex Flashers of the Wilderness

Compared to our own crude attempts at illumination, fireflies are far more efficient. Only 2 percent of their bioluminescent energy is lost as heat, compared with about 90 percent for most household light-bulbs. These high-tech beetles with the power of light confounded ancient philosophers, and even modern scientists have been unable to copy the wonder of "cold light" economically. We do know that the chemical luciferin and the enzyme luciferase react with oxygen in fireflies' abdomens to make them appear, as they did to the ancients, like sparks from a fire coming to life.

On clear, early summer nights, choruses of bellowing frogs and brilliant flashes of countless fireflies, seeming to multiply the stars, perform a mystical sound-and-light show over still lakes. An Ojibwa story traces firefly origins to a ferocious, celestial lacrosse game between young thunderbirds, the supernatural raptors responsible for rain, thunder, and lightning. The ball, made from the lightning of a great storm, was thrown far past the goal toward the Earth below. Its impact caused stars to fall from the sky, breaking into thousands of blinking pieces that became fireflies.

SPECIES ILLUSTRATED: Pyralis firefly (pg. 90), angulate firefly (pg. 89)

NUMBER OF FIREFLIES NEEDED TO EQUAL THE LIGHT OUTPUT OF A 60-WATT BULB: 25,000

LENGTH: 0.2–0.8 in (0.5–2 cm)

FULL-GROWN LARVAE: 0.4–0.6 in (1–1.5 cm)

MARKINGS: Most black or brown, with yellow, orange, or red trim, lines, or dabs

ALIAS: Lightning bugs, lampyrid beetles, glowworms, family Lampyridae

PREFERRED HABITAT: Moist ground beneath debris, bark, and decaying vegetation in meadows and wetlands; stream, pond, and lake margins; and moist open forests

FOOD: Larvae eat slugs, snails, worms, insect larvae, and mites; adults of some species eat nectar, pollen, and other species of fireflies.

EGG-DEVELOPMENT PERIOD: 3–4 weeks

PUPAL STAGE: About 2 weeks

LIFE SPAN: Up to 2 years

PREDATORS: Frogs, toads, spiders, birds, mice, bats

RANGE: Throughout North America south of the Arctic

WINTER WHEREABOUTS: Larvae hibernate in the ground.

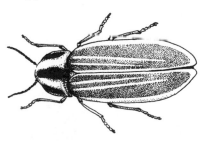

Though greenish or yellow firefly flashes seem most noticeable in June and early July, there are many species occupying various habitats, each flashing at a different time of the summer and of the night. Each variety has its own signal, a sexual Morse code ensuring the rendezvous of two bugs made for each other. This also makes it possible to flirt with fireflies by mimicking their blinking patterns with a flashlight, to which they respond. Females of some species are able to fake the flash of smaller species. Once seduced, the duped male fireflies are eaten.

Even as youngsters, fireflies are spindle-shaped, goo-sucking, killer glowworms. Already glowing in their eggs, they hatch beneath moist leaf litter and other debris in midsummer and spend most of their lives as carnivorous larvae, using poisonous jaws to paralyze, liquefy, and suck the insides from worms, snails, slugs, and other larvae. To top off their powers of alchemy, some fireflies contain steroids called bufo-dienolides that make birds and other predators puke. Birds learn quickly to pass up the meals that blink. At least one species of firefly that does not produce such steroids preys on other species that do, siphoning off the protective substance from them.

Larvae hibernate in soil chambers until late spring and emerge metamorphosed as adults, though some females remain wormlike with little or no wings. Their long, tanklike bodies are usually dark with yellow, red, or orange trim. Adults live only a few weeks and most do not eat at all. They have but one purpose left in the love-lit climax of their lives.

MAYFLIES

Fabled Fated Fliers Rise in Swarms

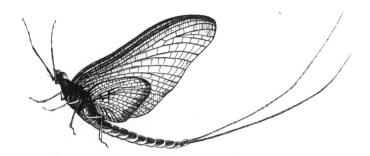

The sudden appearance of countless millions of bizarre, fairylike creatures filling the sky is a spectacular northern lakeside event. Seeming to materialize from nowhere, thick swarms of big-eyed, long-tailed mayflies flutter across open spaces and gravitate toward lights at evening, sometimes covering the sides of cottages, their triangular wings held upright together over their backs. Yet, within twenty-four hours they may be gone again, or lying lifeless in thick heaps along the shore and on the water.

Mayflies generally swarm in June and July. Smaller numbers, though, appear throughout spring and summer, making learned entomologists of the fly-fishing enthusiasts who have modeled their artificial lures on the vast variety of mayfly species for hundreds of years. Each species has a brief moment of glory. Most spend virtually all of their lives beneath the water as aquatic "nymphs" or "naiads," transforming to fly, mate, lay eggs, and die all within a day or two. Some do it all in ninety min-

MAXIMUM WATER-BOTTOM NYMPH DENSITIES: More than 8,000 per sq yd (0.8 m²)

LENGTH: 0.1–1.2 in (3–30 mm)

MARKINGS: Most species are various shades of brown or dusky yellow, some are black, olive, or reddish.

ALIAS: Shadflies, fishflies, dayflies, duns, spinners, lakeflies, drakes, trout flies, quills, cocktails, sailors, dotterels, mackerels, willow flies, cisco flies, river flies, cob flies, salmon flies, June bugs, order Ephemeroptera

NAME ORIGIN: In Greek mythology, the Ephemerides were beings that lived for only one day.

FEATHER FISHING FLIES IMITATING MAYFLIES: Blue wing olive, quill Gordon, March brown, royal coachman, dark Cahill, white-gloved howdy, Hendrickson

PREFERRED HABITAT: Varying species can be found in and around a wide range of waters,

utes. "Nature holds a couple of draughts from the cup of love to be fair payment for the pains of a lifetime," wrote Johann Goethe of the fabled fated fliers. Since the time of Aristotle, their evanescence has been taken as a metaphor for human life. Fittingly, the scientific name of their order, Ephemeroptera, means "living for a day with wings."

Mayflies are one of the most primitive of insects. With little time for wide dispersal, each species of the large, delicate insects tends to be geographically limited, which has made comparison of mayfly types an important aid in piecing together the history of continental drift.

Offspring of many varieties hatch in lakes, rivers, and streams within a few weeks of their parents' passing. The eggs of others may lie dormant for months. The nymphs have sets of gills along the sides of their distinctly segmented abdomens. They crawl along the bottom with sharply bent, pointy legs, hiding beneath rocks or amid weeds or burrowing into the mud, depending on the species, to avoid fish and other predators. Nymphs that survive may molt up to fifty times as they grow larger throughout the year.

The year's first mayflies are smaller species, emerging from snowmelt-swollen rivers, usually on sunny days in early May. Later in the summer, many continue appearing, especially around dusk or dawn. Mass emergences ensure that feasting trout, walleye, and other fish will not be able to eat all of them while they are most vulnerable.

from mud-bottomed lakes and weedy wetlands to fast, rocky streams.

MAXIMUM DEPTH NYMPHS FOUND AT: 200 ft (61 m)

FOOD: Nymphs mostly eat algae and bits of decaying vegetation.

EGGS PER FEMALE: 500–1,000

LIFE SPAN (FROM HATCHING AS A LARVA): 3–6 months for most species, others as short as 6 weeks or up to 2 years

PREDATORS: Trout, walleye, bass, suckers, frogs, salamanders, swallows, flycatchers and other birds, bats, crayfish, dragonflies, diving beetles, stone flies, water striders, and spiders. Snails and caddis fly larvae eat eggs.

RANGE: Throughout North America to the Arctic tundra

WINTER WHEREABOUTS: Water bottoms, as nymphs or eggs

AGE OF OLDEST MAYFLY FOSSILS: 300 million years

NUMBER OF U.S. MAYFLY SPECIES: 572

NUMBER OF MAYFLY SPECIES WORLDWIDE: 2,100

NUMBER OF RECENTLY EXTINCT NORTH AMERICAN MAYFLY SPECIES: At least 4

BIOINDICATORS: Mayfly numbers and diversity are important measures of environmental health for researchers because of the group's great range of habitat preferences and low tolerance for polluted water.

ALSO SEE: Brook Trout, Lakes

Congregating near shorelines and shallows just above deep water, transforming nymphs rise up as their old skin splits. Bursting from the top of their shells as they hit the surface, they appear as dull brown air cadets, called duns. In as little as ten seconds, as they drift along, their wings unfold, dry, and lift them up in clumsy maiden flights to the nearest landfall, usually waterside trees and shrubs. Before liftoff, they are basically helpless and ideal fish food. Those that make landfall spend up to another day molting again, the only insects known to do so after they've received their wings. Adults, also known as spinners, appear afterward in shiny, full flying colors and clear, intricately veined wings.

Since the time of Aristotle, their evanescence has been taken as a metaphor for human life

Adult mayflies do not eat. Instead, swarms of eligible bachelors fly synchronized courtship maneuvers over the water, repeatedly rising and floating back down. At the first opportunity, a male grabs a female that wanders into the swarm, mating with her in midair. The female lays her eggs in small batches on the water surface within an hour or so of mating, and then, spent, lays herself down on the waves, joining her lifeless mate. They leave behind only their unhatched offspring and inspiration for poets and philosophers. As Benjamin Franklin quoted a mayfly itself in a whimsical satire: "Alas! Art is long and life is short."

MONARCH BUTTERFLY

Amazing Migrant Bound for Mexico

Of all butterflies that flutter and glide, the monarch, for its beauty, familiarity, and extraordinary migrational feats, flies supreme in the imagination. Faced with the prospect of winter, most other butterflies and moths spin cocoons beneath bark or lay eggs before they die. Monarchs fill up on nectar, convert it into fat, and head south in late August and September. They employ the same migration strategy as hawks, spiraling upward on warm columns of rising air, called thermals, climbing up to 5,000 feet (1,500 meters), then gliding in the wind until they hook onto another thermal. At night, or on days when temperatures dip below 54°F (12°C), they rest, often roosting in trees en masse.

By November, up to hundreds of millions of monarchs from all over eastern North America converge on about a dozen volcanic mountains in central Mexico's

AVERAGE DISTANCE COVERED BY ONE GENERATION MIGRATING NORTH: 1,000 mi (1,700 km)

DISTANCE COVERED BY ONE GENERATION MIGRATING SOUTH: Up to 3,000 mi (4,800 km)

DURATION OF TRIP FROM NORTH WOODS REGION TO MEXICO: 6–8 weeks

AVERAGE DAILY MIGRATION DISTANCE: 44 mi (71 km)

CRUISING SPEED: 11 mph (18 km/h)

GLIDING SPEED: 7 mph (11 km/h)

WING BEATS PER SECOND: 5–12

MINIMUM TEMPERATURE NEEDED TO FLY: 55°F (13°C)

WINGSPAN: 3.7–4.1 in (9–10 cm)

WEIGHT: 0.01–0.03 oz (0.3–0.75 g)

MARKINGS: Black-veined, bright orange wings with white-spotted black borders; black bodies also marked with white. Males have a black spot on hind wings and thinner black veins than females.

ALIAS: Milkweed butterfly, King Billy, *Danaus plexippus*

PREFERRED HABITAT: Meadows, forest edges, marshes, shorelines

FOOD: Milkweed leaves for caterpillars; nectar for adults

MATING: Couples meet in afternoon and spend night together; both sexes may mate several times.

AVERAGE NUMBER OF EGGS PER FEMALE: 100–300 pinhead-sized green eggs attached singly beneath milkweed leaves

Sierra Madres. They gather in just a handful of colonies, each covering 2.5 to 7 acres (1 to 3 hectares), in stands of fir trees 10,000 feet (3,000 meters) above sea level. Yet none has ever made the trip before. Turning the sky and landscape orange, butterflies crowd onto tree limbs and go into intermittent semidormancy for several months, mountain temperatures around the freezing point allowing them to conserve energy. Mexicans living near wintering sites have traditionally said that monarchs are the souls of dead children, the butterflies' arrival coming around the time of All Souls' Day, on November 2, an important festival in Latin America known as the Day of the Dead.

The whereabouts of the monarch Mexican rendezvous was a mystery to the rest of the world until it was finally pinpointed in 1975 by American Kenneth Brugger, a participant in an international wing-tagging effort that was begun almost forty years before by the University of Toronto's Fred and Norah Urquhart. The discovery may have come just in time, with logging having reduced the wintering grounds to about 10 percent of what they once were. They are now designated as nature reserves by the Mexican government, but illegal cutting continues to encroach, with up to 75 percent of the population in the increasingly exposed colonies dying during severe storms in recent years.

While just one monarch generation flies all the way from its northern birthplace to Mexico and lives through winter, it takes a couple of generations to make it all the way back in spring. Overwintering monarchs may live far longer than previous generations because they remain chaste

EGG-DEVELOPMENT PERIOD: Usually about 4 days; up to 12

CATERPILLAR: Up to 2 in (5 cm) long; yellowish green after hatching, turning to bands of bright yellow, black, and white

TIME FROM HATCHING TO EMERGENCE AS AN ADULT: 3–4 weeks

ADULT SURVIVAL IN SPRING AND EARLY SUMMER: 2–6 weeks

SURVIVAL OF ADULTS EMERGING IN LATE SUMMER: 7–8 months

PREDATORS: Birds, mice, shrews, wasps, fire ants, spiders

LATE SUMMER NORTH AMERICAN POPULATION: 250–300 million

POPULATION CYCLE: Peaks about every 11 years

ACCOLADES: State insect of Vermont, Illinois, Texas, West Virginia, Idaho, and Alabama; official symbol of the North American Free Trade Agreement

RANGE: Throughout United States, except Rockies, and across most of southern Canada

LOOK-ALIKES: Viceroy butterfly smaller, with 2 white spots on front of forewings

MIGRATORY AND SEMIMIGRATORY BUTTERFLIES: Painted lady, red admiral, Compton tortoiseshell, mourning cloak, question mark, American lady, and at least 6 other species

LARGEST BUTTERFLY SPECIES: Queen Alexandra's birdwing, wingspan 11 in (28 cm)

NAME ORIGIN OF BUTTERFLY: From the butter-yellow color of European brimstone butterflies

NUMBER OF U.S. BUTTERFLY SPECIES: About 750

until longer days and temperatures above 70°F (21°C) stir them from their Mexican siesta. Then the delayed hormones kick in and they hold a mass love-in before setting off in March.

NUMBER OF BUTTERFLY SPECIES WORLD-WIDE: About 17,500
ALSO SEE: Broad-Winged Hawk, Moths

Having sexually matured, the Mexican migrants are at the end of their life cycle and burn out quickly as they race to be the first to lay eggs on milkweeds emerging from the soil in the northward march of spring. Their offspring hatch, grow, transform into adults, and continue the trip north.

Though monarch butterflies feed from and pollinate many different kinds of flowers, only the leaves of milkweed can nourish their young. Growing in meadows and fields, most species of milkweed produce toxins in their milky sap that protect them from most foraging animals and insects. Monarchs find milkweeds a safe haven on which to lay their eggs, and have evolved a tolerance for their poisonous tissues. In fact, milkweed toxins stored in the insect's body make both the caterpillars and adults unpalatable to most vertebrate predators. After heaving once from a monarch meal, birds steer clear of the butterfly's bright colors. The unpleasant reputation allows monarchs to flutter lazily about with relative impunity. The smaller viceroy butterfly, which looks so much like the monarch, also packs toxins, though not from milkweeds.

Starting off less than one-tenth of an inch (two millimeters) long, monarch caterpillars eat constantly for nine to fourteen days, go through five skin sheddings, and grow to 2,700 times their hatching weight. In human terms, it would be like an 8-pound (3.6-kilogram) infant putting on 11 tons. The caterpillar then transforms into a turquoise pupa and suspends itself from a silk pad stuck to a branch or leaf. The pupal covering gradually becomes transparent and, after about ten days, a butterfly emerges. It spends about an hour inflating its wings with fluid, then flies away. Two or three generations of monarchs hatch in northern areas after the first migrants return in late May or early June.

MOSQUITOES

Straw-Nosed Marauders

Most mosquitoes owe their survival to warm-hearted individuals—mammals and birds whose bodies course with warm blood. Aside from species that feed on amphibians and reptiles, female mosquitoes are straw-nosed marauders that produce their eggs from the protein of warm-blood sodas. Their antennae tracking systems lock onto the carbon dioxide exhaled by humans or animals and follow increasing concentrations to the source. As they get closer, body heat, odor, moisture, and sight also guide them. They're especially attracted by dark colors such as brown, gray, and navy blue. Mosquitoes also seem partial to some people's sweat more than others and are usually more attracted to women than men.

Upon landing, a mosquito drills into the flesh with several razor-thin stylets held within its long proboscis snout. As it sinks its sucking tube into a tiny blood vessel, it injects saliva containing anesthetic and an anticoagulant into the wound to keep the

DISTANCE HUMANS CAN BE DETECTED BY MOSQUITOES: Up to 100 ft (30 m)

WING BEATS PER SECOND: 300–600

FLYING SPEED: 3 mph (5 km/h) in calm air

LENGTH: 0.1–0.4 in (3–9 mm)

WEIGHT: 0.004 g

LARGEST U.S. SPECIES: *Psorophora ciliata,* about 1 in (2.5 cm) long, rare in north woods

MONSTER "MOSQUITOES": Crane flies, up to 2.2 in (5.5 cm) long, with very long legs, do not bite, but are attracted to lights.

WORST MOSQUITO COUNTRY: Exposed researchers in the Arctic report up to 9,000 bites per minute in summer.

COMMON NORTH WOODS VILLAINS: *Aedes communis* (illustrated) and *Aedes punctor* in late spring, *Aedes vexans* in summer

ALIAS: Scitters, flies, family Culicidae

NAME ORIGIN: Spanish *mosca,* meaning "little fly"

FOOD: Nectar, honeydew, plant juices, blood

AVERAGE BLOOD TAKEN: 1/1,000 of a tsp (2–3 milligrams)

MAXIMUM NUMBER OF LIFETIME FULL BLOOD MEALS FOR AEDES VEXANS: 8

AVERAGE NUMBER OF EGGS PER BLOOD MEAL: 60–300

LARVAE: Beige; 0.04–0.08 in (1–2 mm) long after hatching, grow to 0.3–0.6 in (7–15 mm)

blood coming. The body responds to foreign compounds from insect bites or stings by surrounding the wound with histamine, a chemical that marshals natural defenses such as white blood cells to sweep away and destroy toxins. Swelling, itching, and redness around the bite are all part of the allergic defense reaction. Reactions are worst with the first bites of spring. Outdoor types, though, often build up a resistance to the saliva of biting insects and are liberated from much scratching.

A mosquito needs a few minutes of uninterrupted siphoning to get a full tank. If brushed away before finishing, it tries biting again until it has the blood it needs. Females can double or even quadruple their weight in a single feeding, their abdomens ballooning red with blood. If the weather is warm, the acquired protein yields a batch of eggs a few days afterward. Both mosquitoes and blackflies may lay several clutches of eggs in their lifetimes, returning for blood each time. They need mate only once, storing the sperm internally for all future needs.

Most mosquito species go through just one generation in a year. Early-hatching varieties come alive en masse in pools of snowmelt in April and early May. Wormlike mosquito larvae are called wrigglers because they squirm rapidly from the surface to the bottom of the water to feed, then float vertically back up again to get air through a long tube at the end of their abdomens. They filter algae, particles of decaying vegetation, protozoa, and bacteria from the water with

NUMBER OF LARVAE PER ACRE (0.4 HA): Up to 30 million

LIFE SPAN (FROM HATCHING AS A LARVA): 1 month to 1 year, depending on species. Adults live 2 weeks to 3 months, depending on species; overwintering adults, 6–7 months.

PREDATORS: Flycatchers, swallows, warblers, and other birds; bats; dragonflies; wasps; spiders. Dytiscid beetles eat larvae.

MOON EFFECT: Studies show that mosquito numbers can increase up to fivefold on full-moon nights.

TEMPERATURE RESTRAINTS: Become sluggish below 60°F (16°C), inactive at 50°F (10°C)

ACCOLADES: Claimed as unofficial state "bird" by Minnesota and Alaska

RANGE: All of North America

WINTER WHEREABOUTS: Most species as eggs underwater or in ground depressions; some species as hibernating larvae in wetlands mud; others as adults in animal burrows or hollow logs

MOSQUITO EXPERTS: Culicidologists

AGE OF OLDEST MOSQUITO FOSSIL: 35 million years

NUMBER OF U.S. MOSQUITO SPECIES: About 170, more than 50 in north woods region

NUMBER OF MOSQUITO SPECIES WORLDWIDE: About 3,000

ALSO SEE: Blackflies, Dragonflies

long hairlike fans near their mouths. After shedding their skin four times over one to four weeks, depending on water temperature, they metamorphose into adults in floating curved brown pupal casings. The pupa, known as a tumbler, can't eat but can shoot to the bottom of the water if threatened. After a few days, the shell opens and becomes a floating launchpad for the winged adult.

An especially rainy April and warm May are ideal conditions for multitudes of mosquito larvae to hatch and survive into adulthood. As adults emerge, both males, which do not bite, and females feed primarily on nectar, as well as honeydew—sweet drops excreted by insects that suck plant juices. Once satiated on sweets, a day or so after emerging, female mosquitoes go looking for the boys, who hang out in thick, harmless swarms on spring and summer evenings. Each species tends to swarm over a particular kind of landmark, such as trees or watersides. Males use their brushy antennae to detect the distinct whine of female wing beats. Both sexes may mate several times. A few days later, females are out for blood.

As they get closer, body heat, odor, moisture, and sight also guide them. They're especially attracted by dark colors such as brown, gray, and navy blue

Starting about mid-May, mosquitoes usually build to a peak in June, when the most species are emerging, and then trail off all too slowly through the summer. Most adults live only a few weeks, and their eggs, laid in shallow puddles or depressions likely to flood again the following spring, cannot hatch until first being frozen by winter. A few species, however, go through several pestering generations throughout the summer. One breeds only in pitcher plants but does not suck blood. Some in the *Culex* genus hibernate as adults, using a blood meal in the fall to sustain them through the winter.

Some mosquito species found mainly south of the north woods region are known to spread diseases such as malaria, encephalitis, and dengue fever in warmer parts of the world. Malaria was contracted by several million people annually in the United States, mostly in the south, into the 1930s. The discovery of a vaccine for mosquito-borne yellow fever by American army doctors allowed the United States to complete the digging of the Panama Canal in 1914 where the epidemic-plagued French had failed before. Luckily, the AIDS virus is too fragile to survive in the harsh biochemical environment inside a mosquito.

Though each species of mosquito may have its own niche, most are stirred by rising and falling light levels, making them most annoying at dusk and dawn. During the heat of the day, they rest in the shade on plants and trees. Being slow fliers, they also take cover even in light wind. Camping in breezy locations, such as the east side of lakes, where prevailing winds have room to sweep in, is one of the best ways to avoid bugs.

Humans have probably been experimenting with ways of ridding themselves of biting pests since the dawn of time. Even wedge-capped capuchin monkeys—the famous organ-grinder monkeys—in Venezuela have been found to spread the caustic secretions of huge, cigar-sized millipedes over their fur to protect themselves from mosquitoes in the rainy season. Some Native Americans smeared themselves with animal grease and red ocher for protection, prompting early explorers to speak of seeing "red Indians." Homespun bug defenses such as eating garlic and vitamin B, or not washing, have been discredited. Concoctions containing the oil of citronella grass, a natural repellent, can keep mosquitoes away for fifteen or twenty minutes.

Ultimately, it was GIs fighting in the thick of mosquito-infested jungles in the South Pacific that brought the greatest relief to the north woods. During World War II, the army financed the development of the main ingredient of most repellents now in use, DEET, or diethyl-m-toluamide. The U.S. military is still the biggest funder of insect-repellent research in the world. No one is exactly sure how DEET works, though it may block sensors in the mosquito's antennae, mouth, and legs from detecting the lactic acid vapors given off by the skin, which stimulate mosquito feeding. Though DEET absorbed through the skin is shed in urine within twenty-four hours, without building up in body tissues, medical authorities recommend not using it on infants or toddlers and restricting older children to repellents with concentrations of less than 10 percent.

High-tech antibug gadgetry, on the other hand, has proven to be a big flop. Electric bug zappers do not dispatch many biting insects. Studies show that less than 1 percent of the insects they kill are mosquitoes and other biting flies. Instead they fry large numbers of insects that prey on biting pests and aquatic insects that are important food sources for birds and other beneficial insects. The American Society for Microbiology also notes that explosions of zapped bugs send body parts, bacteria, and viruses flying for at least 2 yards (1.8 meters) in all directions. Window screens, introduced in the 1880s, were a far greater advance.

MOTHS

Pollinators of the Night

When darkness descends on summer nights, the air around campfires, lanterns, and cabin lights becomes filled with swirling moths seemingly intent on self-destruction. Moths were once said to be the souls of the dead flying out of the night in search of the light. These days, the suicide fliers are thought to be drawn to the flames and light because they normally navigate a straight course by keeping constant the angle of moonlight or sunbeams falling on their eyes. Night lights created by humans disorient moths, causing them to flutter round and round the source without being able to get their bearings.

Moths take over from butterflies at night in pollinating a wide array of flowers as they suck up nectar with their long, coiled tongues. Nocturnally blooming flowers, such as evening primrose and jimsonweed, are usually white or light toned, making them easier to see in the darkness than the deeply colored flowers butterflies visit by day. Still, if some flowers are fragrant enough, they can attract pollinators around the clock.

Butterflies are actually only a small section of the much-larger moth-dominated order Lepidoptera. Unlike their relatives, butterflies have large knobs at the end of their antennae. Some moth species, such as wasp moths and hummingbird-like sphinx moths, are also active during the day and can even be as brightly patterned as butterflies. Most, however, have dull wings, which they keep outspread to blend with tree bark while resting. Butterflies, in contrast, usually rest with their wings folded together, except for when catching the sun's rays to increase their metabolic rates.

When they spread their wings to fly away, the large luna (illustrated), cecropia, and polyphemus moths, and some sphinx moths, flash a pair of large spots on them that look like eyes, which may startle an attacking predator. The otherwise concealed bold colors on the hind flappers of midsized underwing moths serve the same purpose. Underwing moths also have thin membranes stretched over tiny air cavities on their abdomens or thoraxes for picking up ultrasonic sound waves screeched by bats for their sonar tracking of flying prey. Tiger moths also have a special set of such "ears," which, in addition, make clicking sounds to warn bats of their extremely distasteful flavor. The youngsters of the Isabella tiger moth are the well-known fuzzy reddish-brown-and-black woolly bear caterpillars commonly seen along paths and roadsides in early autumn.

Though most often noticed when

DISTANCE A MALE CECROPIA MOTH CAN SMELL A FEMALE: Up to 7 mi (11 km)
OPTIMUM BREEZE FOR DISPERSAL AND TRACKING OF MOTH PHEROMONES: 2–2.5 mph (3–4 km/h)
WINGLESS MOTHS: Wormlike females of species such as bagworms, cankerworms, and white-marked tussock moths depend wholly on winged males following their scent.
TIME SPENT IN ADULT STAGE: Several days to several months
FOOD: Nectar, honeydew, overripe fruit, and carrion as adults; leaves, acorns, and other vegetation as caterpillars
CATERPILLAR WITH THE MOST VARIED TASTES: Fall webworm samples 636 different tree and plant species.
AVERAGE PERIOD BETWEEN FOREST TENT CATERPILLAR OUTBREAKS: 10 years
PREDATORS: Bats, birds, mice, predatory beetles, wasps, ants, spiders
MOTH RANGE: Throughout North America to the Arctic
WINTER WHEREABOUTS: Beneath bark, dead leaves, and other debris; wrapped in pine needles or inside galls. Most overwinter in eggs or cocoons, but some also as caterpillars or adults.
COMMON AUTUMN CATERPILLARS: Woolly bears and other tiger moth larvae, fall webworms
EARLY-SPRING AND LATE-FALL MOTHS: Pale-colored geometrids, which hibernate as adults
INCHWORMS: Very slender caterpillars of the geometrid moth family that loop their bodies into the air as they pull their back end up toward their front to move forward

adults, moths have the greatest impact on the ecosystem as caterpillars. Studies on caterpillars in northern forests have found that in total they outweigh all birds, moose, bears, and chipmunks put together.

Some species, including gypsy moths and the large, colorful cecropia and luna moths, do not even eat as adults, living only long enough to mate and lay eggs. Their offspring, though, are protein factories, eating up incredible quantities of leaves and concentrating nutrients into their plump, juicy bodies for birds and other animals. Even seed- and fruit-eating birds depend heavily on the high-protein caterpillar meals that allow their nestlings to reach adult size in a matter of weeks. Outbreaks of spruce bud-worm—a moth caterpillar—cause population explosions of many bird species, such as Cape May and bay-breasted warblers, as well as the defoliation of large tracts of evergreens, leading to more forest diversity.

OLDEST MOTH FOSSIL: 180 million years old

NUMBER OF SPECIES WHOSE CATERPIL-LARS EAT CLOTHES, FUR, AND FEATHERS: 2

MEXICAN JUMPING BEANS: Caused by movement of moth caterpillars eating into beans

NUMBER OF NORTH AMERICAN MOTH SPECIES: More than 11,670

NUMBER OF MOTH AND BUTTERFLY SPECIES WORLDWIDE: At least 165,000

ALSO SEE: Little Brown Bat, Monarch Butterfly, Red Oak, White and Red Spruce, Red-Winged Blackbird

To avoid becoming meals themselves, moth caterpillars employ a wide range of dining styles directed toward eating in anonymity. Some string out silk from spinnerets near the mouth to pull the edges of leaves up around them, or to tie bunches of coniferous needles together into snack shacks. Bagworm caterpillars live and munch within small hanging sacks of silk, twigs, and other bits of plant material. Tiny leaf miners create splotches or trails in leaves that start out small, where an egg hatches, and grow wider as the caterpillar winds through the leaf, ending at the point where it pupates and emerges as a moth. Other moth larvae hatch from eggs laid in plant tissues and cause some of the bulging galls common in goldenrod stems and oak trees. As the caterpillars eat away at a stem or acorn from the inside, the plant surrounds the area with hard, tumorlike gall tissue. The hidden munchers eat a hole out of the gall before transforming into adults.

Some moth larvae, such as fall webworms, eastern tent caterpillars, and chokecherry tentmakers live communally, spinning large silk nests for refuge. Forest tent caterpillars, which congregate on silken pads rather than in tents, can number up to 20,000 per tree during outbreaks, defoliating vast swaths of aspen, sugar maple, and red oak across the north. Most moth caterpillars also use silk safety lines if they fall or get blown off their perch, and to encase themselves in cocoons, in contrast to butterflies, which transform inside a skin covering as a chrysalis instead.

SPIDERS

Spinners of Insect Fate

Spiders are the very essence of "creepy" in the popular mind, the mere sight of one giving countless Miss Muffets the willies. Freud contended that spider phobias rise from a primal fear of a cannibal witch or ogre with long, pointy, bending fingers, subconsciously identified with the arachnid's legs. Despite the immense importance they have in controlling insect populations, spiders have long been associated with witches, and Halloween. Both Greek and Hindu goddesses were represented as spiders, spinners of fate, while flies were often regarded as the souls in transition from one life to the next. The image of a fly caught in a spider's web represented, to the ancients, the helplessness of humanity in the web of fate.

While only about half of all spiders spin webs, all of them have spinneret glands at the rear underside of their abdomens that produce silk. Jumping spiders, which stalk and leap upon their prey, remain anchored to a silk safety line in case they fall. Nocturnal wolf spiders run

Largest north woods species: Fishing spider (illustrated), with a leg span of up to 5 in (13 cm)

Estimated mass of insects eaten annually by spiders in the United States: More than combined weight of all Americans

Spiders per acre (0.4 ha) in northern forests: Up to 50,000; estimates of close to a million in southern fields

Name origin: Old English *spinthron*, meaning "spinner"

Alias: Arachnids

Arachnid name origin: In Greek mythology, the maiden Arachne was changed into a spider by Athena after defeating the goddess in a weaving contest.

Name for a group: A smother of spiders

Number of eyes: 8

Food: Insects and other spiders, mites, and daddy longlegs; tadpoles; tiny fish

Eggs per female: 2 to several thousand eggs, depending on species

Life span: Most species less than a year; a few up to several years

Predators: Birds, toads, frogs, salamanders, shrews, snakes, wasps, centipedes, other spiders. Eggs eaten by many insects.

Top wolf spider running speed: 10 in/sec (25 cm/sec)

Top fishing spider running speed on water: 30 in/sec (75 cm/sec)

down their prey but use silk to tie their shelters together. Silk is made of protein strands. The strands are coated in fungicides and bactericides to protect them from other hungry organisms. The antibiotic qualities of spiderwebs have made them in many cultures a common folk remedy for wounds. Layers of webs from large spiders have also been used for fishing nets by the natives of New Guinea.

Though a silk strand may be 1/100 the diameter of a human hair, it is twice as strong, for its size, as steel. Web strands are also incredibly elastic, stretching up to 30 percent before breaking. In the industrialized world, spider silk is used mostly for the crosshairs of optical equipment, but researchers are reproducing the genes of spiderwebs with the aim of creating building materials with the same diverse qualities.

Spiders can spin different types of silk from different glands for their varying needs. There are seven different kinds of silk in all, though no one species has all seven brands. The spider adjusts its spinneret valves to control the thickness, elasticity, and strength of the silk as it spins. Orb weaver spiders join strong strands, like girders, to a central point across a vertical space, then thread concentric rings through them with a special sticky silk that catches flying insects. A thick zigzag strand is woven through the webs of some species to make it visible to birds and mammals, which can see the big picture better than insects can. Spiders are always busy, usually building a new web every few days or less. Their work is best seen glistening with morning dew.

All spiders also have venom, which they inject into their victims through small, fanglike appendages. The paralyzing poison gives spiders the option of consuming their catch right away or wrapping it up and keeping it fresh and alive for later snacking. Spiders actually drink, rather than eat, sucking out their victims' bodily juices through a pump in their digestive system. They bite humans only in self-defense, though they can leave an irritating, swollen red mark. In parts of the north woods, only the very rare northern black widow spider presents any kind of a threat to humans. Its poi-

---

MAXIMUM TIME FISHING SPIDERS REMAIN SUBMERGED: At least 45 minutes

BIRDS THAT USE SPIDER SILK IN NESTS: Hummingbirds, vireos, flycatchers, tree-nesting warblers

HUMAN FATALITIES CAUSED BY VENOMOUS ANIMALS THAT ARE DUE TO SPIDERS: 10–15%

WINTER WHEREABOUTS: Most species hibernate or leave eggs in logs, beneath bark, or under dead leaves and grass.

FIRST APPEARANCE OF SPIDERS ON EARTH: Probably at least 180 million years ago

FAMOUS SPIDERS: Inky Beaky, Charlotte, Boris, Shelob, the Spiders from Mars

NUMBER OF U.S. SPIDER SPECIES: More than 3,850

NUMBER OF KNOWN SPIDER SPECIES WORLDWIDE: About 36,000

ALSO SEE: Fungi; Moose; Bees, Wasps, and Hornets

son usually causes fever, breathing trouble, and paralysis for one or two days, though it can be fatal to very small children or sick people. Black widows, however, are far more common to the south and found even in urban areas. As spiders go, the north woods is probably the safest part of the country.

Female black widows are also synonymous with the femme fatale because they're known to devour their mates after males have served their purpose. The practice actually occurs among many spiders. To avoid being eaten even before mating, the generally much smaller male may strum love notes on a strand of a potential mate's web, signal to her with his legs in a kind of sexual semaphore, or send a chemical message. If she appears receptive, he rushes in and fertilizes her. But most fleet-footed males then manage to hit the road before giving their hungry partners a chance to heartlessly devour them for a quick protein fix to nourish their eggs.

Most north woods spiders mate in early summer and then wrap their eggs in yellowish cocoons. Some, such as the *Dolomedes tenebrosus* fishing spider (illustrated), carry their egg sacks with them for a time. When they hatch, tiny spiderlings swarm to the highest point of the vegetation where they find themselves and spin a thin strand of silk, which catches in the breeze and lifts them up into the air, sometimes thousands of feet. This "ballooning" spreads them out over wide distances, keeping their populations from becoming too concentrated in one area. Ballooning spiders can sometimes cover bushes or shrubs with silk.

The ranks of eight-legged arachnids are swelled by many other species that, like true spiders, lack the antennae of insects. Daddy longlegs, or harvestmen, have only two simple eyes on a single "turret" and can neither spin silk nor inject venom. Instead, they mostly scavenge dead insects or forage for spider and insect eggs. If they themselves are captured, their detachable limbs continue to quiver after being severed, distracting the predator and giving the daddy longlegs a chance to escape. Unlike spiders and mites, they cannot regrow lost legs.

Ticks are also arachnids but live as parasites rather than hunters. The pinhead-sized nymph of the infamous deer tick, which normally feeds on the blood of mice as a youngster and on white-tailed deer when an adult, can spread Lyme disease among humans. Though there are some high-risk areas in west-central Wisconsin, the prevalence of the disease is generally much greater in the heavily populated Atlantic seaboard than it is in the north woods region. Similarly, the much larger wood tick, common on both wild animals and Rex at home, can spread Rocky Mountain spotted fever, but the incidence of the disease is negligible in northern forests compared with states to the south and southeast.

WATER STRIDERS

Staying Afloat on Tippytoes

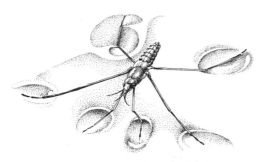

LENGTH: 0.1–0.5 in (2–15 mm)
MARKINGS: Various species may be black, dark gray, or yellow on top, with brown or gray markings, and white beneath; middle legs longer than body
WINGED STRIDERS: Some species, especially those in temporary ponds, have a winged stage and most often fly at night, sometimes attracted to lights.
ALIAS: Gerridae family
PREFERRED HABITAT: Calm water in streams, ponds, swamps, lake margins
FOOD: Springtails, mites, spiders, insects
EGG-DEVELOPMENT PERIOD: About 2 weeks
LIFE SPAN: About 6 months
PREDATORS: Fish

The water strider is a miracle bug, walking on water with seemingly the greatest of ease. It accomplishes the feat by spreading its weight out in a sprawled stance. Each leg is tipped with many tiny, stiff, waterproof hairs, which form a soft crust or film of closely packed molecules and prevent the insect from breaking the water's surface tension. If a solid object punctures the thin film, the strider falls through into the water.

Lying still, water striders are almost invisible. When they move, with their long, jointed legs acting like oars, their shadows glide across the shallow bottoms of their pools. They often congregate in large groups in calm channels, the water surface coming alive with their activity. They move quickly toward any small surface disturbance, looking for a meal that has dropped in—often another insect that has fallen into the water. Using their two short forelegs to grab their victims, water striders then pierce their prey with their needle-like mouthparts and suck out their life juices.

Hibernating beneath rocks and other debris on dry land near water, water striders appear as soon as the ice melts, and mate through spring and early summer. After signaling their intentions by creating special-frequency mating waves, couples may cling together in a love embrace for more than an hour. Females lay creamy-white, waterproof eggs on floating objects. Young water striders look like smaller versions of their parents.

FISH AND AQUATIC COMPANIONS

North country rivers and lakes have long been considered an angler's paradise, but rod and reel are not prerequisites for experiencing the inhabitants of the deep. Fish can be viewed jumping out of the water at low-flying insects at dusk, spawning near shore or along creek beds in spring or fall, or flitting amid the weeds of a small stream. Crayfish, though not really fish but crustaceans, are easy to find hiding beneath rocks by day and lurking in the shallows at night. Most fun of all are the north's numerous lake monsters, which offer anyone the opportunity of joining in the biggest fish stories of all.

BROOK TROUT

Wellspring of American Fishing

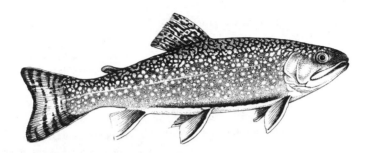

When colonists first arrived in New England in the 1600s, they found clear streams teeming with brook trout. The beautifully speckled fish quickly became a favorite supplementary food source. Adapting angling techniques from the old country to wild new habitats and the eccentricities of the brook trout gradually spawned the development of a distinctly American fly-fishing tradition. Anglers' singular passion for the brookie continues to this day, inspired in no small part by the untrammeled wilderness settings that their quarry needs to thrive. Eight states, including Vermont, New York, Michigan, and New Hampshire, embrace the fish as an official symbol.

Brook trout waters have recovered in many areas after long suffering from overfishing and habitat depredation caused by logging. But some of the most seemingly pristine trout country in the mountains of the east continues to be the hardest hit by acid rain. Above 2,000 feet (6,100 meters), brook trout no longer reproduce in any lakes surveyed in New England and more

AVERAGE ADULT LENGTH: 6–14 in (15–36 cm)
AVERAGE WEIGHT: 0.1–2 lb (45–900 g)
WORLD RECORD BROOK TROUT: 14.5 lb (6.6 kg), 31.5 in (80 cm) long, caught in Nipigon River, Ontario, 1916
WORLD RECORD LAKE TROUT (NETTED): 102 lbs (46.2 kg), 10.5 ft (3.2 m) long, caught in Lake Athabasca, Saskatchewan
MARKINGS: Dark olive-green back with lighter green swirls, sides splattered with white spots and red dots bordered by light blue; white belly; reddish fins
ALIAS: Speckled trout, squaretail (New England), brookie, native trout, eastern brook trout, coaster (Great Lakes), *Salvelinus fontinalis*
NAME FOR A GROUP: A hover of trout
PREFERRED HABITAT: Shallow, clear, cold headwater and spring-fed lakes, streams, and ponds with sand and gravel bottoms, lots of rocks, logs, and some vegetation;

than half of those sampled in the Adirondacks.

Neither brook trout nor their larger relative, the lake trout, are really trout at all. They're char. The early settlers named them for their resemblance to European brown trout, which have been introduced in many areas since the 1880s. The other part of the brook trout's name comes from its preference for cold, clear headwater streams. It can stand rushing water much better than most other large fish. It's also common in the headwater lakes of highland areas.

The best time to see brook trout is after the ice breaks up in spring, or when they're spawning in autumn. During those periods, they're near the shore, often jumping completely out of the water when flying insects are around. Brookies can't live in water temperatures warmer than 68°F (20°C), so they either keep to small, deeply shaded streams or, as the top layer on lakes and larger rivers warms up in June, head for deep, cooler water. They also need ample oxygen, which keeps them out of the lowest depths as summer wears on, concentrating them into a transition zone between the top and bottom layers of lakes, ten to forty feet (three to twelve meters) beneath the surface.

As the water cools again in late September, brook trout move into the shallows to feed. When the water temperature falls to 40 to 49°F (4.5 to 9.5°C), usually in October or November, they spawn in gravel or sandy beds, commonly three to seven feet (one to two meters) deep, returning to the same sites every year. The beds must have springwater percolating up through them, which keeps the buried eggs

often beneath overhanging trees and bushes in fall, winter, and spring; 10–40 ft (3–12 m) below the surface in summer

PREFERRED WATER TEMPERATURE: 54–59°F (12–15°C)

TIME WHEN MOST ACTIVE: Early morning and late evening

FOOD: Minnows, perch, sculpins, frogs, stone flies, mayflies, dragonfly nymphs, caddis fly and blackfly larvae, crayfish, snails, clams, worms

EGGS PER FEMALE: Average 200–1,000. Very large females produce up to 5,000.

EGG-DEVELOPMENT PERIOD: 2–5 months

AVERAGE EGG MORTALITY: 25–35%

AVERAGE SIZE AT END OF FIRST GROWING SEASON: 3 in (7.5 cm)

AGE OF FIRST-TIME BREEDERS: 8 months to 3 years

LIFE SPAN: Few live longer than 3–4 years; maximum more than 20 years.

PREDATORS: Mink, otters, osprey, pike, sea lampreys. Small trout also taken by kingfishers, herons, water snakes, snapping turtles, bass, walleye; eggs eaten by crayfish, whitefish, perch, and brown bullheads.

RANGE: Northeastern United States to eastern Minnesota, Iowa, southern Wisconsin, and Michigan; northeastern Ohio, along Appalachians to northern Georgia; eastern Canada to Hudson Bay; introduced in Alaska and Rocky Mountain and Pacific states

NUMBER OF SALMON FAMILY SPECIES NATIVE TO NORTH WOODS REGION: 15

clean and aerated and may protect them from acid-rain meltwater in the spring. Amid congregations of up to hundreds of trout, females spend up to two days plowing into the gravel and shaking about to create a nest, or redd, often with an eager male—which develops deep red lower sides during the spawning season—standing guard over her. She may fill three or four nests with eggs over several days of mating with various partners, spending up to an hour after each episode covering the clutch with gravel.

SALMON FAMILY SPECIES INTRODUCED IN NORTH WOODS REGION: Rainbow trout, brown trout, coho salmon, chinook salmon
NUMBER OF SALMON FAMILY SPECIES WORLDWIDE: 70
NUMBER OF NORTH AMERICAN FRESH-WATER FISH SPECIES: 754
ALSO SEE: Lakes, Minnows, Smallmouth Bass, Blackflies

The transparent orange or reddish eggs hatch from February to April, depending on how cold the water is, and the fry stay put beneath the gravel for about a month, living off large yolk sacks attached to their undersides. When they do move out, some keep to bigger water bodies, while others swim upstream to deep-forest creeks as shallow as six inches (fifteen centimeters) for the summer, where insect food is probably more plentiful.

Because trout are less active in the frigid water beneath the ice, those in larger water bodies do most of their growing in spring and fall, feeding in the rich, shallow waters. This is especially true of the brookie's much larger, greenish-gray cousin, the lake trout, which retreats down to about 70 feet (21 meters) or so in the coldest lower layer of lakes during the summer. Because of their deepwater needs, they are restricted to clear lakes that usually cover at least 50 acres (20 hectares). In the smaller lakes, they grow very slowly because they have only algae, plankton, and insect larvae to eat during the summer. In larger lakes, they can pick off fish such as perch and whitefish that enter into their summer zone. Adults average about 3 pounds (1.3 kilograms).

While near rocky shores and above boulder-strewn shoals in the fall, lake trout spawn at night—unlike day-spawning brookies—usually in 5 to 15 feet (1.5 to 4.5 meters) of water. The Ojibwa and other native groups took advantage of these rare, near-shore visits of the big lakers to net them. They also speared brook trout and whitefish as they were preoccupied with autumn spawning, and then smoked them for valuable winter stores.

CRAYFISH

Northland's Biggest Invertebrates

The shorelines of many lakes teem with crayfish. Their total biomass is commonly ten times as great as all fish present. Often only a few rocks need be removed near shore to reveal the miniature lobsterlike creatures hiding from the light of day. Crayfish are nocturnal crustaceans, preying and scavenging on smaller invertebrate animals. They are themselves the largest invertebrates in the north. Their exoskeletons are made out of chitin, a fingernail-like armor that covers all insects. But unlike insects, crayfish have

DENSITY PER SQ YD (0.8 M²) OF PRIME SHORELINE HABITAT: 4–40

LARGEST NORTH WOODS SPECIES: Robust crayfish, up to 7 in (18 cm) long

SMALLEST NORTH WOODS SPECIES: Northern clearwater crayfish, 2–4 in (5–10 cm) long

ALIAS: Crawfish, crawdads, family Astacidae

MARKINGS: Various species range from darkly mottled olive to gray-brown or rusty-orange.

PREFERRED HABITAT: Shallow water of lakes, streams, marshes, swamps

HOMES: Most common species beneath rocks or logs, marked by a semicircle of pushed-out gravel and mud

FOOD: Decomposing organic material, aquatic plants, algae, snails, insect larvae, fish eggs, and other recently molted crayfish

AVERAGE CLUTCH: 60–300, depending on species

LIFE SPAN: Most species 1–3 years, some up to 5 years

PREDATORS: Fish, turtles, frogs, snakes, gulls, herons, kingfishers, raccoons, mink, otters, mud puppies, dragonfly nymphs, giant water bugs

RANGE: Throughout United States and across Canada to James Bay and northern prairies

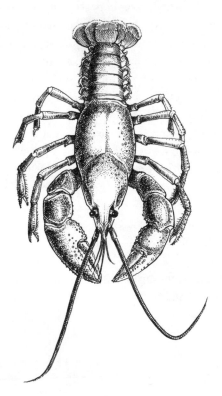

two sets of antennae, which they use to feel around and detect chemical scents in the water.

Crayfish are devoted mothers

to their clinging offspring

Despite their minimonster appearance, crayfish are devoted mothers to their clinging offspring. Most species mate from April to May or August to October. The following May, June, or July, females lie on their backs and bend their tails forward to stick eggs to their undersides. Even after they hatch, the young hang on beneath their mother's tail for two or three weeks. As they grow, young crayfish, like insects, shed their old exoskeletons six to ten times, tripling in size by their first winter. Their new, softer skin is inflated before it hardens to give them space to grow inside the new shell. In this soft stage, crayfish are delectable morsels for fish, birds, mammals, and Cajun-restaurant goers. To escape quickly, they flip their tails beneath them and catapult backward at high speed.

WINTER WHEREABOUTS: Deeper water, less active
NUMBER OF CRAYFISH SPECIES IN NORTH WOODS REGION: 10
NUMBER OF U.S. CRAYFISH SPECIES: 308
U.S. CRAYFISH SPECIES CONSIDERED AT RISK: 48%
NUMBER OF U.S. CRAYFISH SPECIES NOW PROBABLY EXTINCT: 2
NUMBER OF CRAYFISH SPECIES WORLD-WIDE: 469
ALSO SEE: Smallmouth Bass

LAKE MONSTERS

Relics from Past Ages?

In the north woods region, still waters indeed run deep, and abundantly, offering the best lake monster country this side of Loch Ness. There's certainly been no shortage of sightings. Generally, the lake leviathans are described as either long, winding, serpentlike creatures, or hump-backed, long-necked beasts resembling plesiosaurs, giant aquatic reptiles that lived in the dinosaur era more than 65 million years ago. Though fearsome-looking, they don't appear to be particularly nasty, at least in modern times. The odd, no doubt accidental capsizing of a small motorboat in calm water seems to be the worst they've managed.

Lake monster sightings are no recent phenomenon created by wayward Scots nostalgic for Nessie. Native peoples told of both good and bad beings inhabiting the waters they paddled. The Ojibwa feared the underwater manitou Mishipizheu, shown in pictographs as a great lynx with horns of power rising from its head, who whipped up storms with its tail and claimed many lives at rapids. But they could make offerings of tobacco for calm waters to the May-may-gway-siwuk, shy creatures resembling humans, but with strange faces and fishlike tails.

By the 1800s, there were many recorded lake monster incidents across the north, sometimes followed by farmers reporting missing cattle. In one of the most sensational accounts, a twenty-five-foot

LOCATIONS OF SIGHTINGS: Lakes Champlain, Ontario, Erie, Huron, Michigan; Lake Mendota, Wisc.; Lake Minnetonka, Minn.; Lake Samuel C. Moore, N.H.; Lake Pohenegamook, P.Q.; Lake Utopia, N.B.; Lake Simcoe, Ont.; Lake-of-the-Woods, N.Y.; Rock Lake, Wisc.; Leech Lake, Minn.; Niagara River, N.Y.; and Paint River, Mich.

LENGTH: Estimates range from 10–75 ft (3–23 m)

MARKINGS: Various monsters are dark gray, silver, green, mahogany, orange, brown, or black; head may be shaped like that of a horse or a dog, with fiery eyes and wide, gaping mouth; pointed, fishlike tail and dorsal fins, sometimes with 2 legs.

PREFERRED HABITAT: Deep, cold lakes, especially with rocky shores offering possible underwater cave lairs

FOOD: If related to plesiosaurs, whales, or other marine mammals, probably fish or plankton

FAMOUS LAKE MONSTERS AND SEA SERPENTS: Champ, Bozho, Ponik, Nessie, Ogopogo, Puff, Leviathan, Behemoth, Cetus, Hydra, Grendel, Cecil

LARGEST FRESHWATER FISH EVER CAUGHT IN NORTHEAST: 303 lb (140 kg), 8 ft (2.4 m) long (lake sturgeon in Lake Superior in 1922)

(7.6-meter) long serpent is said to have been caught in Lake Erie and coiled in a large crate at Sandusky Bay. The specimen, however, doesn't seem to have made its way into the hands of science.

Though the high-tech age has added lore of sonar fish finders detecting very large creatures, as with all great mysteries, there is no hard-and-fast evidence supporting the existence of lake monsters. But cryptozoologists—those who study reports of unknown animal species—are hot on the trail. Some believe the largest of these unknown critters, or "cryptids," could be rare, secretive descendants of plesiosaurs or zeuglodons, snakelike whales that flourished up to 20 million years ago. They cite the discovery of a living coelacanth, an ancient fish previously known only from fossils 70 to 320 million years old, off the coast of South Africa in 1938. Giant squid were similarly considered fishermen's tales before they began washing up onto the laps of biologists in the 1870s. Gorillas were dismissed as primitive fantasies until white men encountered and, inevitably, started shooting them in the mid–nineteenth century.

PLESIOSAURS: Were up to 43 ft (12 meters) long, with flippers and a long neck and tail

GIANT SQUIDS: Genus Architeuthis, up to 50 ft (15 m) long, the largest living invertebrates

LAKE CHAMPLAIN DIMENSIONS: 125 mi (206 km) long, 0.5–14 mi (9.8–22.5 km) wide, 400 ft (122 m) deep, 490 sq mi (1,270 km²) in area, (fourth-largest freshwater lake within United States)

ALSO SEE: Lakes; Pike; Otter; Pegasus and Andromeda; Eskers, Moraines, and Other Glacial Features

Other theories propose that various lake monsters may be remnant populations of well-known marine animals such as manatees, dolphins, or walruses, stranded after ancient seas receded. Seals have been found in Siberia's Lake Baikal and dolphins in China's Tung-t'ing Lake, both deep in the interior of Asia. Whale bones have been found near Lake Champlain, which was part of the postglacial Champlain Sea, an arm of the Atlantic that splashed the north and eastern slopes of the Adirondacks only 11,000 years ago.

Many residents around Lake Champlain certainly assert that the sea of the same name must have left something behind in their sizable drink. Since 1819, more than 300 monster sightings have been tallied on the lake. Quick to seize a custom-made publicity opportunity, fabled nineteenth-century promoter P. T. Barnum offered $50,000 to anyone who could bring him the body of the mysterious beast. To date, the most famous appearance of the monster, christened "Champ," was captured on a photo taken by a vacationing family, showing a long neck and head in the water, published in the *New York Times* on July 30, 1981. Other modern accounts describe Champ as plesiosaur-like, twenty to forty-five feet (six to fourteen meters) long, gray or rusty, with a horse-shaped head, two small horns, and a thick mane. At the south end of

the lake, Port Henry, New York, proclaims itself the home of Champ with hefty sales of T-shirts and souvenirs, and has passed a local ordinance for protection of the celebrity cryptid. The New York and Vermont legislatures have followed suit by backing efforts to declare Champ an endangered species.

Other plesiosaur or dragonike monsters, perhaps Champ's relatives, have been reported elsewhere in the east, including the Lake-of-the-Woods, north of Watertown, New York, and Lake Pohenegamook, in Quebec near the Maine border. Like Champ, Lake Pohenegamook's murky inhabitant has been adopted by the locals, who baptized it in 1974, gave it the name Ponik, and hold an annual Ponik festival. Further west, the snaky sort of lake monster seems to prevail. One of the most famous, Bozho, the Madison Monster, is said to be a greenish serpent with white spots and reckoned to be up to seventy feet (twenty-one meters) long. It has frequented the Wisconsin chain of Mendota, Monona, and Waubesa lakes for well over a century.

Lake monster sightings have been testified to by the reputable likes of sheriffs, priests, and coast guardsmen. Hard-bitten ichthyologists, or fish experts, however, have suggested that especially large sturgeon, known to live up to 150 years and reach 9 feet (2.7 meters) in length, could be behind all the hoopla. Sturgeon are themselves living relics from the dinosaur era. Rather than scales, they are covered with hard, armourlike plates, which rise to five long, sharp ridges along their backs and sides. These harmless, toothless bottom feeders are known to sometimes slowly raise their heads vertically above the surface or jump completely out of the water.

LEECHES

Stealthy Silent Suckers

L eeches figure prominently in the annals of camp and swimming infamy, even if more out of revulsion than for any real pain they inflict. The soft, slimy bloodsuckers can be abundant but are mainly nocturnal, hiding under submerged rocks, logs, and stumps by day, coming out only if they smell food.

Of the many common leeches in the north, only a few species are true blood-suckers that bite humans. Most are predators of insect larvae, snails, worms, and other bottom-dwelling invertebrates. Mercifully, the largest sucker, the giant horse leech, measuring up to fourteen inches (thirty-six centimeters), is toothless and indifferent to *Homo sapiens*. Those that do latch onto people, however, hold on tenaciously by a sucker mouth and a suction cup at the end of the tail. They inject an anticoagulant to keep their liquid lunch flowing and an anesthetic to keep their victims oblivious. Leeches can easily be removed, though, with salt, burns, or a good yank. Left to their own devices, they may continue slurping for anywhere from a

ALIAS: Bloodsuckers, class Hirudinea

NAME ORIGIN OF LEECH: Old English *laece,* meaning "physician"

NAME ORIGIN OF WORM: Proto-Indo-European *wrmi,* meaning "snake," possibly from the word *wer,* meaning "twist" or "turn"

NUMBER OF ORNATE LEECHES FOUND ON A SINGLE SNAPPING TURTLE: Up to 1,000

LENGTH OF AMERICAN MEDICINAL LEECH AND HORSE LEECH: 1–6 in (2.5–15 cm)

LARGEST NORTH WOODS SPECIES: Giant horse leech, up to 14 in (36 cm) long

LENGTH OF MOST LEECH SPECIES: 0.8–2.4 in (2–6 cm)

NUMBER OF LEECH BODY SEGMENTS: 34

NUMBER OF EYES: Most common bloodsuckers have 5 pairs; some species have none.

PREFERRED HABITAT: Shallow water with lots of rocks, stumps, and weeds

FOOD: Various species consume mammalian, waterfowl, turtle, frog, fish, snail, and clam blood or fluids; insect larvae; worms; tiny crustaceans; tadpoles; carrion; eggs of fish and amphibians; plankton.

BLOODSUCKER MOUTH: American medicinal and horse leeches have 3 serrated jaws, forking like a

minute to more than an hour, swelling from two to ten times their original weight.

The number one offender in most northern lakes is reputed to be the American medicinal leech, a finger-sized dark bloodsucker with a bright orange belly and rows of red and black spots on its back. It normally feeds on turtles, frogs, and fish. But if alerted by wave motions and the smell of dinner, it will rouse from daytime slumbers at the prospect of a juicy feast of human blood, which can keep its belly full for one to seven months. The similarly large American horse leech, which is dark gray with black spots, is another common adversary of swimmers, though it mostly preys on other invertebrates. The smaller, aptly named ornate leech, sporting fancy white markings on its dark green or gray back, also sometimes attaches itself to humans, often at liftovers at beaver dams. It usually contents itself with turtles and fish.

For more than 2,000 years, well into the mid-1800s, doctors commonly attached leeches to their patients as a remedy for just about anything. As barbaric as it sounds, "bleeding" may have had at least some beneficial effects. Many surgeons today apply leeches after operations for reattaching severed body parts and for skin grafts. The leeches drain off congested blood, giving capillaries time to grow back together without becoming deluged. Medical studies have also shown that a synthesized version of the leech anticoagulant hirudin is a more effective drug for heart patients than traditional blood thinners. Researchers are studying leech chemicals for possible treatments for arthritis, glaucoma, and cancer as well.

All leeches are hermaphrodites, having both male and female parts, with partners exchanging sperm when they meet. They leave their spongy egg-bearing cocoons at the water's edge over the winter. Horse leeches and some other species sometimes crawl onto land to migrate from one body of water to another, or to prey on terrestrial invertebrates at night.

clover; ornate leech and many others have a needlelike proboscis.

NUMBER OF FULL FEEDINGS NEEDED BY MOST BLOODSUCKERS TO REACH MATURITY: 3

LIFE SPAN: Up to 3 years

PREDATORS: Fish, waterfowl, garter snakes, salamanders

BIOINDICATORS: Leeches are used to measure water quality because they are highly sensitive to acidification and accumulate higher concentrations of contaminants than other aquatic invertebrates.

RANGE: Throughout North America to the Arctic

WINTER WHEREABOUTS: Buried in mud

NUMBER OF NORTH AMERICAN LEECH SPECIES: 63

NUMBER OF LEECH SPECIES WORLDWIDE: 650

ALSO SEE: Lakes; Humus and Soil; Eskers, Moraines, and Other Glacial Features

MINNOWS

Occupying Every Aquatic Habitat

A mong his many misadventures, the Ojibwa culture hero and comic deity Nanaboujou takes a Jonah-like role by being swallowed by a giant sturgeon. Nanaboujou rescues himself by killing the behemoth from the inside and then cutting it into small pieces, which float off to become the small fish of the world.

Minnows form the largest, and perhaps most important, single family of freshwater fish in the world

---

Most tiny fish, including darters in the perch family and the fry of many large species, are commonly called minnows. Some, in fact, are adult fish belonging to a group called darters—actually pint-sized perch that dart sharply about on the bottom of fast-flowing headwater streams.

AVERAGE ADULT LENGTH: 2–5 in (5–13 cm)
LENGTH OF LARGEST NATIVE MINNOW (FALLFISH): Up to 18 in (45 cm)
WORLD RECORD CARP: 58 lb (26 kg), caught in Lake Erie, 1957
ALIAS: Cyprinids, family Cyprinidae
NAME ORIGIN: Old English *myne*, meaning "small fish"
FOOD: Plankton, algae, aquatic insect larvae, fish fry
EGGS PER FEMALE: Up to 500
EGG-DEVELOPMENT PERIOD: 4–10 days
LIFE SPAN: Up to 8 years
PREDATORS: Trout, bass, pike, and many other large fish; kingfishers; mergansers; loons; wading birds
POPULAR BAIT MINNOWS: Fatheads, golden shiners, creek chub, stonerollers, common shiners
RANGE: Throughout North America to the Arctic
NUMBER OF NORTH AMERICAN MINNOW SPECIES: 221

119

Unlike darters, which have two fins on their backs, true minnows have just one, which is always soft, not spiny. Minnows have teeth in their throats instead of their jaws. They form the largest, and perhaps most important, single family of freshwater

fish in the world. Though most are 2 to 3 inches (5 to 8 centimeters) long, goldfish and carp—both Eurasian imports—are included in their ranks. Some carp in the Great Lakes can weigh in at 30 pounds (13.6 kilograms).

Ecologically, minnows also comprise one of the greatest links in the aquatic food chain, eating vast quantities of algae, plankton, plants, and insects and passing on their energy and nutrients to most of the other larger fish as well as fishing birds and mammals. More than two dozen species in the northeast and upper Midwest occupy every aquatic habitat, with each finding its own niche. Creek chub (illustrated) are probably the most common stream minnows. Northern redbelly dace, which average two inches (five centimeters) long, live in the tea-colored, acidic waters of boggy lakes and beaver ponds. Other minnows, such as fatheads—often the most abundant fish in small lakes, ponds, and slow brooks—are less tolerant of acid rain than other north country fish. Lake chub, which are twice as big, live in larger lakes but move into rocky streams to breed. Golden shiners are inhabitants of the clear, weedy waters of quiet lakeshores.

PERCH

Schools Seeking Warm Currents

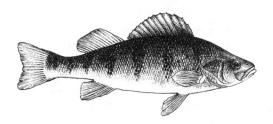

Perch find safety in numbers, but chance encounters with their schools provide sudden bonanzas for anglers, who may catch more of them than any other fish in the north, whether intentionally or not. From the time they hatch, perch fry form schools, often mixing with minnows, near the shore. They find no protection from their parents, who remain in adult groups and could very well be disposed to devour their own children. Transparent at first, the quarter-inch- (five-millimeter-) long hatchlings grow more slowly in colder water but live longer. In lakes with high population densities, adults may never exceed six inches (fifteen centimeters), while perch in the Great Lakes can be twice that size.

Perch move into shallows to feed at dusk and dawn, and rest at the bottom at night

AVERAGE NUMBER IN A SCHOOL: 50–200

AVERAGE ADULT LENGTH: 4–10 in (10–25 cm)

MAXIMUM LENGTH: 14 in (36 cm)

AVERAGE ADULT WEIGHT: 4–11 OZ (100–300 g)

MAXIMUM WEIGHT: 4 lb (1.8 kg)

MARKINGS: Green or yellow back and sides, usually with 7 dark vertical stripes; white or gray underside; 2 dark dorsal fins; orange lower fins; yellow or green eyes

ALIAS: Lake perch, American perch, panfish, *Perca flavescens*

PREFERRED HABITAT: Usually less than 30 ft (9.1 m) deep in lakes and rivers with clear, flowing water

FOOD: Zooplankton, aquatic insects, snails, leeches, crayfish, minnows, fish fry and eggs

LIFE SPAN: Often 7–9 years; up to 13 years

Like herds of bison or caribou, perch schools travel in definite migration patterns. After spawning, they move farther offshore as waters warm toward the center of lakes in summer. Preferring temperatures of between 68 and 75°F (20 and 24°C), perch generally stay in the warm upper layer. They move into shallows to feed at dusk and dawn, and rest at the bottom at night. In winter, the schools become more dispersed but continue to actively feed beneath the ice.

Male perch begin mating when they are three years old and females when they are four. They usually spawn at night and in early morning in weedy, shallow water near shore soon after ice-out, when the water is 45 to 54°F (7 to 12°C). Depending on her size, a female releases between 10,000 and 50,000 eggs in sticky strands up to 7 feet (3.1 meters) long. They hatch in about two to three weeks.

PREDATORS: Pike, walleye, trout, bass, loons, kingfishers, osprey
LAKE pH AT WHICH PERCH DISAPPEAR: 3.5
RANGE: Across northern half of United States with pockets southern to northern Florida, Alabama, Texas, Arizona, and California; across most of Canada to James Bay and northern prairie provinces
WINTER WHEREABOUTS: Remain active beneath ice
ALSO SEE: Walleye

PIKE

Stuff of Fishy Stories

Commanding fear and respect among its kind, the mighty pike is the big-game symbol of clear, weedy waters across the northern half of the continent. With treacherous teeth set in a huge pair of jaws, the long, stout, lunging beast takes the last bite in the proverbial chain of bigger fish eating littler fish. Ducklings, snakes, and young muskrats are also snapped up for good measure. Though the fearsome fish commonly weighs in at a few pounds, wily old prize codgers can reach 20 pounds (nine kilograms).

Monster-pike-and-angler duels are the stuff of the fishy stories stretching back into the reaches of time. Natives groups in Alaska told stories of remote demon lakes where giant pike could swallow a man whole, along with his canoe. Pike are also native to Asia and Europe, which were rife with stories of 100-pound (45-kilogram),

AVERAGE ADULT LENGTH: 18–30 in (45–75 cm)

AVERAGE ADULT WEIGHT: 2–5 lb (0.9–2.3 kg)

WORLD RECORD: 55 lb (25 kg), caught in Germany, 1986

WORLD RECORD MUSKIE: 69.8 lb (31.7 kg), caught in the Chippewa flowage, Wisconsin, 1949

MARKINGS: Green, olive, or almost brown on top, shading to lighter green on sides, lined with yellowish spots and flecked with gold; white or creamy belly; gold squiggly lines on cheeks; bright yellow eyes; green or yellow fins with dark splotches. Young have wavy white or yellow vertical bars.

ALIAS: Northern Pike, great northern pike, walleye pike, wolf, jackfish, American pike, yellow pike, northern shovelnose, hammerhandle, snake, slinker, *Esox lucieus,* and some 40 other local names

NAME ORIGIN: Originally *pikefish,* from Old English *pic,* meaning "pointed thing," also the origin of *peak* and *pick* (tool)

PREFERRED HABITAT: Weedy, warm, clear waters, from shallows to 15 ft (4.5 m) deep, in quiet bays, small lakes, and slow rivers

GREATEST DEPTH FOUND AT: More than 100 ft (30 m)

FOOD: 90% fish, including perch, suckers, catfish, shiners, bass,

alligator-like pike pulling mules and maidens into watery graves. Fishing guides of a few centuries ago claimed that pikes lived up to 200 years and were spontaneously formed from aquatic vegetation and ooze heated by the sun.

For much of the time, northern pike do seem to be one with their weedy surroundings. Largely sedentary creatures, they occupy hidden lairs within shallow beds of submerged plants, pickerelweed, or sedges, where they wait in ambush. When something comes within reach, they thrust out with lightning speed, just as the similarly built and sharp-toothed barracuda hunts in the sea. With a fish clamped in its jaws, a pike returns to its private quarters to swallow the meal headfirst. Fish approximately one-third of a northern's own length are preferred, though pike are found with more than two dozen perch in their stomachs.

Pike move a little deeper during the peak of summer heat and also for the winter, when they stay active but eat a little less. As soon as the ice starts melting from shorelines, they begin journeys to spawning grounds, usually about a mile (1.6 kilometers) upstream. Hundreds of pike may make a single run, which lasts about a week. Mating takes place during the day in 4 to 18 inches (10 to 45 centimeters) of water, often over spring-flooded banks of grass and shrubs or on marshy lake margins. Females may spend several days periodically releasing batches of five to sixty eggs as they vibrate alongside one or two milt-spewing partners, all thrashing their tails after each episode to scatter the roe.

Sticking to submerged branches and stalks of grass, eggs and immobile hatchlings are at the mercy of receding waters,

and pickerel; also frogs and crayfish; occasionally ducklings, snakes, mice, and young muskrats

EGGS PER FEMALE: Average 10,000–100,000 sticky clear amber eggs; maximum 595,000; each about 0.1 in (2.5 mm) wide. About half are infertile.

EGG-DEVELOPMENT PERIOD: Usually 12–14 days

PORTION OF EGGS YIELDING FRY THAT SURVIVE MORE THAN A FEW WEEKS: 0.2% in one study

HATCHLING LENGTH: 0.2–0.4 in (6–8 mm)

LENGTH BY END OF FIRST SUMMER: Most about 6–8 in (15–20 cm)

AGE OF FIRST-TIME BREEDERS: Males 2–3 years; females 2–4 years

LIFE SPAN: Often 6–9 years; up to 13 years in north woods region, 26 years in far north, 75 years in captivity. Females live longest.

PREDATORS: Osprey, eagles, and bears take small adults, usually while spawning. Herons, kingfishers, loons, mergansers, otters, mink, snapping turtles, perch, minnows, dragonfly nymphs, water tigers, and pike themselves eat young or eggs. Silver lamprey parasitize but rarely kill adults.

PIKE ACCOLADES: State fish of North Dakota

MUSKIE ACCOLADES: State fish of Wisconsin

THE MANNHEIM HOAX: The famous "Emperor's Pike," whose skeleton was long held at Mannheim Cathedral in Germany, was 19 feet (5.8 meters) long. When caught in 1497, it reportedly weighed 550 lb (247 kg) and bore a ring on its gills stating it was released by Emperor Frederick II, 267 years before. The

late cold spells, and caviar-loving predators. Surviving fry leave spawning areas several weeks after hatching, quickly switching from a diet of waterfleas and insect larvae to attacking baby fish hatched around the same time as they, such as white suckers. A pikelet 1 inch (2.5 centimeters) long will even fratricidally dine on one of its own just a fraction of an inch smaller.

Because pike fry hatch about two weeks earlier, they also tend to eat and outcompete muskellunge young. Grown-up muskies, however, average about half as long again and are at least twice as heavy as pike. The two fish occasionally interbreed, producing offspring called tiger muskies.

Sporting dark vertical bars along their sides, muskellunge are most abundant in Wisconsin among north woods states. They mostly lurk toward the edge of weeds or along rocky shoals. The water wolves are revered for presenting the greatest of freshwater fishing challenges. In waters where both fish are common, experienced rod handlers catch an average of three or four pike every two hours. The average muskie comes with a hundred hours of quasi-religious perseverance. There are stories of individual three-foot- (one-meter-) long muskies eluding anglers in a particular fishing hole for years, winning epic battles lasting up to seven hours.

The greatest fish of the northern lakes, however, is the lake sturgeon, which can reach up to 8 feet (2.4 meters) long and weigh 300 pounds (136 kilograms). Sturgeon are ancient fish, whose kind first appeared at least 80 million years ago. With a scaleless, armored body of pointy, dinosaur-like ridges, the gray or olive behemoths may be the source of most lake monster stories across North America. They are scavengers, feeding off water bottoms, 17 to 30 feet (5 to 9 meters) deep, with vacuumlike mouths and short barbels on their snouts, like catfish. Though caught commercially by the millions in the nineteenth century, they are a threatened species today, largely limited to the Great Lakes and some of its larger tributaries. Growing slowly, female sturgeon don't spawn until they are 14 to 26 years old, and can live more than 150 years.

skeleton was later discovered to contain the vertebra of half a dozen fish joined together.

PRIVY ETIQUETTE: Studies show fathead minnows have "alarm pheromones" that alert their fellows to danger, and that show up in the waste of pike that have eaten minnows. Evolution may have favored fastidious pike that dumped their loads off territory, thereby not giving their lairs away.

AGE OF OLDEST PIKE FAMILY FOSSIL: 62 million years

RANGE: New York to Montana, south along Appalachians to northern Georgia, Tennessee, Missouri, and Nebraska; north to Arctic Ocean in Alaska and across most of Canada; introduced in Vermont, New Hampshire, and many other states

NUMBER OF PIKE SPECIES NATIVE TO NORTH WOODS REGION: 4

NUMBER OF PIKE SPECIES WORLDWIDE: 5

ALSO SEE: Perch, Lake Monsters

SMALLMOUTH BASS

Maternal Males Watch Out for Fries

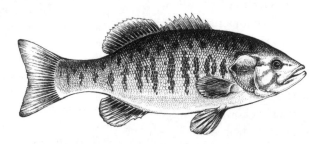

The sudden appearance of saucer-shaped impressions in near-shore sand and gravel shallows in late May and June can look like evidence of extraterrestrials lured by intergalactic rumors of good fishing. The circles, however, are entirely aquatic in origin, the love nests of male smallmouth bass with an impressively maternal bent.

Despite their reputation among anglers as feisty fighters, male smallmouths are truly sensitive, dedicated family fish. They spend up to two days sweeping away sand and debris with their tails to form their distinct pebble-bottomed nests, usually a few feet deep offshore. A male defends the site against all interlopers but steers fertile members of the opposite sex—whose background colors fade to sharply contrast with their dark markings—to the nest. After some fishy foreplay, with the he-bass rubbing and nipping, the passive female lays eggs in numerous four- to ten-second spurts over about two hours, interspersed with promenades around the nest. She then leaves him to care for them. Male and

ADULT LENGTH: Average 8–15 in (25–50 cm); rarely up to 20 in (50 cm)

AVERAGE ADULT WEIGHT: 0.5–3 lb (225–1,350 g)

WORLD RECORD: 11 lb 15 oz (5.4 kg), caught in Kentucky, 1955

MARKINGS: Usually green, sometimes brown or yellowish, with dark hash marks along sides and dark spots on back; white belly. Sunlight causes colors to temporarily lighten.

ALIAS: Bronzeback, northern smallmouth, hawg, black bass, green bass, *Micropterus dolomieui*

NAME FOR A GROUP: A shoal of bass

PREFERRED HABITAT: From steep shores to 20 ft (6 m) deep in clear, rocky lakes and slower stretches of rivers

FOOD: Crayfish, minnows, perch, darters, fish fry, small frogs, mayfly nymphs and other insect larvae, leeches, tadpoles, snails

WATER TEMPERATURE NEEDED FOR SPAWNING: Above 60°F (15°C)

female may both spawn with several other partners, usually at night, over a period of six to eighteen days.

Males fan the eggs, which stick to the gravel at the bottom of the nest, and guard them from caviar-gulping predators, even charging human swimmers. In rare instances, they have been known to bite. All the while, they eat only prey that comes within their nesting area. Black hatchlings, about the size of rice grains, are protected by their devoted dads for one to two weeks in the nest and another two to four weeks in open water, until the schools of tiny siblings begin to break up.

Despite their reputation among anglers as feisty fighters, male smallmouths are truly sensitive, dedicated family fish

---

Young bass must eat well in their first months if they are to survive the winter, during which they fast. If spring and summer are cool, delaying their hatching and development, most are goners. Heavy storms also destroy nests, and bass fry are more susceptible to acid rain than just about any other fish. Adverse weather often results in a bass-fishing drought three years later, when the lost generation would have reached the age when most smallmouths are caught.

Smallmouth bass spend hot summer days in shadows beneath rocky ledges and shoreline branches or in deeper water. They lie motionless most of the time

NEST: Circular, rock- and gravel-bottomed depression, 1–2.5 ft (30–76 cm) wide, usually sheltered by a large rock or log, 3–20 ft (1–6 m) deep near calm shores. Same sites often used for years.

CLUTCH: Up to 10,000 tiny yellowish eggs, often laid by several females

EGG-DEVELOPMENT PERIOD: 3–10 days

AVERAGE NUMBER OF HATCHLINGS: About 2,000

NEST FAILURE RATE: Often about 40%

AGE OF FIRST-TIME BREEDERS: Males 3–5 years; females 4–6 years

LIFE SPAN: Often 5–7 years; up to 20 years

PREDATORS: Pike, walleye, muskies. Osprey eat adults; young also taken by perch, catfish, rock bass, loons.

WATER TEMPERATURE AT WHICH BASS BECOME INACTIVE: 55°F (13°C)

NATURAL PH OF A CANADIAN SHIELD LAKE: 6.2–7

LAKE PH AT WHICH SMALLMOUTH BASS DISAPPEAR: 5.5

LAKE PH AT WHICH PIKE DISAPPEAR: 4.7

FISH THAT OFTEN LAY EGGS IN BASS NESTS: Common shiners, long-nosed gar

RANGE: Northeastern United States to high plains and midsouth. Introduced in parts of most other states.

WINTER WHEREABOUTS: Lying dormant in rubble and crevices at water bottom

OTHER NEST-TENDING FISH: Largemouth and rock bass, pumpkin-seeds and other sunfish, fathead minnows

NUMBER OF SUNFISH FAMILY SPECIES: 32 (restricted to North America)

ALSO SEE: Crayfish, Brook Trout

around rocks, logs, submerged tree roots, and other debris, waiting to ambush a swimming snack or two. Mealtime really arrives at dusk and dawn, when bass move into shallow rocky areas as crayfish, their favorite food, come out of their lairs to forage. After twilight fades, it's too dark for smallmouths to hunt.

Smallmouths lurk in clear, rocky waters across the north, but it was not always so. While they're native to the north-central U.S., their early popularity among fishing enthusiasts led to stocking in formerly bassless areas such as New England, northern Minnesota, and many other states. In 1874, the federal fish commission specially outfitted railroad cars to carry bass and other sport fish across the country. The introductions, however, often adversely affected the natural ecosystems of many northern lakes. Smallmouth bass outcompete native brook trout for food and easily pick off their young. Studies have found that two or three species of small fish also commonly disappear once bass come on the scene.

The nearly identical largemouth bass has also been introduced in many northern areas. Tending to be bigger than their smallmouth kin, largemouths are prized by anglers more for their heft than their fight, as well as for the challenge of finding them in the calm, weedy waters they inhabit. The rock bass, another relative, is more squat, bony, and homely, with blood-red eyes. Like smallmouth bass and all other members of the sunfish family, they feature males with a nest-building, fry-rearing inclination.

WALLEYE

Among the Most Savored of Game Fish

The walleye is one of the most beloved of all American sport fish, but nowhere so much as in the upper Midwest. It is venerated as the state fish of Minnesota and commemorated by the giant roadside walleye in the city of Garrison. The eagerly awaited opening of the walleye season in mid-May is by far the biggest fishing date of the year in the state. Thriving in thousands of northern lakes and rivers, the golden-hued whoppers are as tasty as perch but considerably larger, and put up a spirited fight before surrendering to fate as a fillet.

Walleyes are, in fact, really gargantuan perch, the biggest members of the family. But when the sun sets, loose schools of walleye go on roving picnics in search of their smaller relatives and other fish slumbering amid underwater debris and weeds. In cloudy-watered lakes, they also hunt during the day. They scan the darkness with large, light-sensitive eyes that shine orange-

AVERAGE ADULT LENGTH: 13–20 in (35–51 cm)
AVERAGE ADULT WEIGHT: 1–3 lb (0.45–1.4 kg); 6–9 lb (2.5–4 kg) in large, prime lakes
WORLD RECORD: 41 in (104 cm) long, 25 lb (11.3 kg), caught in Tennessee, 1960
MARKINGS: Variable, most often rough-scaled back and sides olive to dark brown flecked with yellow, with dark vertical bands on smaller fish; white underside, sometimes tinted yellow; lower tail fin tipped white, black spot on spiny dorsal fin; cloudy silver eyes
ALIAS: Yellow walleye, pickerel, wall-eyed pickerel, yellow pickerel, pike perch, yellow pike, walleye pike, *Stizostedion vitreum*
PEAK ACTIVITY PERIODS: Sunset to 11 P.M. and 3 A.M. to sunrise
PREFERRED HABITAT: Usually around 60 ft (15 m) deep in lakes and

red in the beam of a flashlight, like those of a deer or a cat. Up close, the eyes have the smoky look for which they're named. In traditional rural parlance, a blind animal is called wall-eyed because each of its cloudy eyes stares outward in a different direction—the opposite of cross-eyed.

Walleye are usually caught at dusk or dawn, on an overcast day, or in murky waters. Sunlight drives them to the shade near vegetation or beneath sunken logs and rocks, where they themselves may be vulnerable to predation by their chief nemesis and competitor, the pike.

Walleyes are, in fact, really gargantuan perch, the biggest members of the family

Throughout the winter, walleyes continue to prowl through near-blackness beneath the ice. Once the frozen mantle breaks apart on rivers in April, males cruise upstream to boulder-strewn riffles, rapids, waterfalls, and dams. In Wisconsin, they've been found to migrate up to 100 miles (62 kilometers). The opposite sex gradually joins them, and night spawning commences when water temperatures reach 44 to 48°F (7 to 9°C). Walleye-runs on tributaries of large lakes may last three weeks, peaking with hundreds of thrashing, spawning fish visible at a single stretch of frothy white water. Females, noticeably larger than their partners, usually release all of their eggs in frequent spurts over one night and leave, while males stick around to mate again.

large rivers with rock, sand, or gravel bottoms; often on shoals, venturing to both shallower and deeper waters to feed at night

HOME RANGE: Usually wander over 3–6 mi (5–10 km) in schools, but migrate much farther to spawn.

FOOD: Perch, minnows, darters, sunfish, suckers, ciscoes, whitefish, burbot, sunfish, bass, catfish, rock bass, sticklebacks, alewife, smelt, crayfish, frogs, mud puppies, snails, mayflies and other insects, rarely small rodents. Keen to eat each other when other fish wanting.

EGGS PER FEMALE: Average 25,000–100,000; up to 600,000

EGG-DEVELOPMENT PERIOD: 12–18 days

HATCHLING LENGTH: 1/50–1/25 in (6–9 mm)

FRY MORTALITY: Up to 99%

AGE OF FIRST-TIME BREEDERS: Males 2–4 years; females 3–6 years

LIFE SPAN: Usually about 7 years; up to 29 years

PREDATORS: Pike, muskies, osprey, otters. Young eaten by perch, older walleye, and other fish.

ACCOLADES: State fish of Minnesota and North Dakota, and "warmwater fish" of Vermont

RANGE: Western New Hampshire to North Dakota, south to Nebraska, Arkansas, western Georgia, and North Carolina; north in Canada to Hudson Bay and Mackenzie River delta. Introduced in parts of Maine and many other states.

NUMBER OF NORTH AMERICAN PERCH FAMILY SPECIES: About 150 (all but 3 darters)

RECENT EXTINCTIONS: Blue pickerel,

The sticky fertilized eggs settle downstream on rocky beds or sand, kept clear of vegetation by the fast current. Some eggs also develop on shallow lake shoals, where walleyes also spawn. In some years, cold weather, wind-whipped waves, or heavy currents can doom virtually a whole generation of walleye before or after they hatch. In good years, about 5 to 20 percent of the eggs produce fry.

once very common in Lake Erie, unsighted since the 1960s

NUMBER OF PERCH FAMILY SPECIES WORLDWIDE: 150–160

ALSO SEE: Pike, Perch

Hatchlings stay put to absorb their yolk sacks for ten to fifteen days before swimming toward the surface to dine on plankton. Perch take the opportunity to pick off as many of the potential menaces as possible while they're still small and vulnerable. By autumn, the survivors are about four inches (ten centimeters) long and are back near the bottom toward shore eating aquatic insect larvae and other invertebrates.

Keeping to more cloudy, shallow waters, the related sauger is a slightly smaller, more tubular fish. It greatly resembles the walleye, save mainly for dark brown splotching along its sides. Ascending spawning streams later in May, sauger sometimes crossbreed with the last walleye hangers-on at the rapids. They live mainly in large, slow rivers, silty bays, and weedy lakes, but are less adaptable than walleye, and therefore less common.

MAMMALS

Perhaps the most exciting wilderness experience of all is to encounter wild, free-roaming mammals. Partly it is because mammals are probably the most seldom-seen beasts, aside from ever-present and audible red squirrels and chipmunks. Not that other mammals are not around. There are often more mammals than birds in a forest, but most of them are tiny and hidden during the day. Among the north woods regions's denizens of the dark are eleven species of mice and voles, nine varieties of bats, nine weasel relatives, four bunnies, raccoons, porcupines, beavers, foxes, coyotes, wolves, and bobcats. Others, such as shrews and moles, seldom emerge above the ground or leaf litter.

Although mammals are elusive, their signatures are all around us: beaver lodges and dams, muskrat homes, bear-clawed trees, the rustling of mice scurrying in the night, paw and hoof prints in the mud and snow, and a galaxy of droppings, or scats. At the right time and place, a moose may be watched in the flesh, neck deep in a quiet bay, feasting on water lilies. In fact, parts of the north woods are some of the best places in the world to view moose, bears, and many other wild animals, or to hear the spine-tingling howls of a wolf pack at night.

BEAVER

Builder of Dams and Fortunes

While untold bounties of codfish first lured Europeans to return regularly to the northern shores of America, it was the beaver that beckoned them into the continent. With the European beaver becoming virtually extinct, visiting fishing vessels in the 1500s inadvertently tapped into a luxury market in beaver pelts, which natives on the shore were only too happy to trade for metal tools and implements. Both the beaver's abundance and the density of its soft inner fur, which it needed for warmth in frigid waters, made it more important to humans than any other furbearer. In the days before umbrellas, upper-class heads were kept fashionably dry with broad hats of beaver felt. Mercury, used to separate the fur from longer guard hairs and to break it down into felt, frequently caused mental deterioration among the ranks of ungloved hatmakers, giving rise to the expression "mad as a hatter."

The British, Dutch, and French char-

TIME IT TAKES A BEAVER TO CUT A TREE THAT IS 5 IN (12 CM) THICK: 3 minutes

THICKEST TREE EVER RECORDED CUT BY A BEAVER: 4 ft (1.2 m)

AVERAGE ANNUAL NUMBER OF TREES CUT BY AN ADULT: More than 200

AREA OF ASPEN FOREST NEEDED TO SUPPORT A COLONY ANNUALLY: 1–2 acres (0.4–0.8 ha)

AVERAGE AREA COVERED BY A BEAVER POND: 10 acres (4 ha)

DAM LENGTH: Average 100–200 ft (30–61 m); up to 5,000 ft (1,500 m) long and 10 ft (3 m) high

LONGEST MEASURED BEAVER CANAL: 750 ft (230 m), in Colorado

AVERAGE ADULT BODY LENGTH: 2–3 ft (60–90 cm)

TAIL LENGTH: 9–13 in (23–33 cm)

WEIGHT: 35–60 lb (16–27 kg)

HEAVIEST EVER FOUND: 110 lb (50 kg), in Wisconsin

MARKINGS: Glossy chestnut-brown body, scaly black tail

BEST SENSES: Smell and hearing

ALIAS: American beaver, *Castor canadensis*

CALLS: Mumble, hiss, or nasal blowing when angry; cry when frightened

PREFERRED HABITAT: Small, muddy lakes, ponds, meandering streams, and marshes flanked by aspen and birch stands and willow thickets

tered state monopolies to secure the northern forests' fur bounty in the early 1600s. Indeed, the Pilgrims of Plymouth were far more grateful at their Thanksgiving feasts for the beaver than the turkey, with the lucrative profits from fur-trading posts established in the Maine interior primarily responsible for keeping their colony afloat. Similarly, New York City was founded when beaver-pelt-seeking Dutchmen bought Manhattan Island from the natives as a base. The Dutch, though, centered their fur trading just south of the Mohawks' great hunting and trapping grounds in the Adirondacks, at Albany, where 60,000 beaver pelts a year were soon flooding in.

Even the opulence of modern New York's Waldorf-Astoria Hotel was ultimately founded upon the humble beaver and John Jacob Astor's American Fur Company, which established trading posts from the Great Lakes to the Pacific in the early 1800s. Astor invested his fur money in New York City real estate and became the richest man in the United States, with a fortune of more than $25 million when he died in 1848.

But the fur rush blazed a trail of ecological and social upheaval across the continent. Before the coming of white traders, woodland natives followed sustainable economies, fine-tuned through millennia, with each family's traditional hunting and trapping territory defined by a watershed. Families rotated their activities from one river branch to another within the basin, ensuring that beavers and other animals they hunted could rebuild their populations in each area.

The aboriginal system was disrupted by the steel-age goods and technology of Eu-

COLONY TERRITORY: 0.3–1.8 mi (0.6–2.2 km) along a stream or shoreline

HOME: Domed lodge of branches and mud, about 6.6 ft (2 m) high and 13.3–14.6 (4–8 m) wide, above waterline, hollowed out from an underwater entrance; built at the center of ponds or at side of deep lakes; occasionally in bank burrows

AVERAGE NUMBER OF BEAVERS PER LODGE: 5–9

FOOD: Water lilies, arrowhead, watercress, duckweed, yellow arum, cattails, grasses, sedges, leaves, berries, and ferns in summer; bark and twigs of aspen, willow, birch, poplar, mountain ash, and maples, and aquatic plant roots in winter

AVERAGE DAILY FOOD HELPING: 1–5.5 lb (0.5–2.5 kg) of bark and twigs in winter; about 12 oz (330 g) of green plants in summer

FORAGING DISTANCE FROM WATER: Usually less than 150 ft (45 m), rarely up to 300 ft (90 m) in wolf-inhabited areas, up to 650 ft (200 m) elsewhere

GESTATION PERIOD: $3\frac{1}{2}$ months

AVERAGE LITTER: 2–4

BIRTH WEIGHT: 0.5–1.5 lb (230–680 g)

AGE AT WHICH YOUNG BEAVERS LEAVE HOME: Usually 1 year; some at 2 years

AGE OF FIRST-TIME BREEDERS: 2–3 years

LIFE SPAN: Average 4–5 years, up to 20 years in wild, 23 years in captivity

PREDATORS: Wolves, rarely coyotes, foxes, mink, and otters

CAPACITY TO HOLD BREATH UNDERWATER: Up to 15 minutes

ropeans. Metal pots, axes, guns, and blankets offered huge time-saving advantages and luxuries, but hooked Native Americans into a European market economy, while they lost their own complex survival technologies. Traditional family trapping grounds were quickly exhausted to satisfy the new demands for fur. Both natives and traders pushed farther west. The Iroquois, seeking control of the trade routes, nearly wiped out, drove off, or absorbed the Mahican, Huron, Erie, Neutral, and many other nations in the Beaver Wars of the 1600s. A chain reaction of disruption spread across the continent until, by the late 1800s, there were few beavers, but much dependency.

Luckily, beavers were one of the first animals to benefit from the efforts of the early conservation movement. They were given legal protection and reintroduced or spread on their own into the largely beaverless north woods in the first decades of the twentieth century. Today's New York State beavers are largely the descendants of immigrants brought in from Michigan. Small refugee populations in Maine, Minnesota, and Wisconsin were also used to restock much of the country.

Both beavers and people are driven by the urge and ability to change and control their environment. A native tradition holds that the Creator took the power of speech away from beavers to keep them from becoming superior to humans. The Ojibwa said that beavers could change form into birds or other animals. They were highly respected and an important food source, especially their fleshy tails.

Beavers form essentially matriarchal societies. According to some experts, when one- to two-year-olds leave home for good, females choose

HEART RATE UNDERWATER: As low as 20% of normal rate

SWIMMING SPEED: Usually about 2.4 mph (4 km/h); up to 6 mph (10 km/h)

TRACKS: Front feet handlike, with 5 fingers, 2.5–4 in (6–10 cm) long; back feet webbed, 5–6.3 in (13–16 cm) long

SCATS: Usually in water, very rarely found, oval, dark brown, sawdust-like pellets, at least 0.8 in (2 cm) long. Nutrient-rich initial droppings are eaten again for full digestion

FAMOUS BEAVER HOT SPOTS: Albany (formerly Beaverwyck), Montreal (Hochelaga, Iroquoian for "where the beaver dams meet")

NUMBER OF BEAVER PELTS TRADED FOR A MUSKET IN 1700s: 10–12

NUMBER OF HATS MADE FROM ONE LARGE BEAVER PELT IN 1700s: About 18

ACCOLADES: Official mammal of New York, Oregon, and Canada

AGE OF OLDEST BEAVER FOSSILS: 35 million years

COMMON BEAVER POND INHABITANTS OR VISITORS: Muskrats, mink, moose, otters, great blue herons, black and wood ducks, mallards, hooded mergansers, woodpeckers, migrant geese, tree swallows, red-winged blackbirds, harriers, frogs, brook trout, minnows

RANGE: Throughout north woods region and at least parts of every other state, north to the tree line in Alaska and Canada

ESTIMATED NORTH AMERICAN BEAVER POPULATION: About 20 million

ALSO SEE: Quaking Aspen, Wolf

their mates for life and determine where they will live. If her partner dies, the female recruits a replacement and life goes on. If a matriarch dies, however, the colony usually breaks up. After mating in the water, beneath the ice, in January or February, mothers give birth sometime between late April and early June. Newborns are fully furred, and their eyes are open.

Beavers—the largest rodents in North America—can go to work wherever there is a stream and an ample supply of deciduous trees, especially aspen. If the water is shallow or intermittent, they build a dam, creating a reservoir deep enough to swim and dive in safety, one that will not freeze to the bottom in winter. The inundated area, often covering ten acres (four hectares) or more, is like a farm, growing the succulent water plants beavers eat in the summer. As well, it's a conduit for reaching and transporting felled hardwoods. Wherever the ground is soft, beavers may dig thin, shallow canals and tunnels into the woods and across peninsulas.

By controlling the water level, beavers ensure their lodge will not be flooded out or left high and dry by seasonal watershed fluctuations. A pair of beavers can build a dam in three or four days, with branches stuck diagonally into the mud so that the wall slopes downstream, braced against the force of the constrained water. Beavers scoop up mud with their paws to fill in the structure once all the branches are woven in place. They often build a series of dams along a stream, sometimes reaching up to 10 feet (3 meters) high.

Beavers in a well-established colony may not be busy at all during the relatively carefree days of spring and early summer. They are active mostly from dusk to dawn, occasionally warning each other to dive for safety with a loud tail slap on the water when danger approaches. From September until freeze-up, the colony works hard to build up a winter food supply of branches, extending their nocturnal toilings into the day. Beavers are often on land in this period, standing on their hind feet, propped up by their tails, cutting down trees. They cannot control where a tree falls, but heavy growth on the tree's sunny side usually topples it toward the water. A winter's larder of tasty trunks and branches, piled and submerged beside the lodge, may equal more than 1,000 cubic feet (30 cubic meters).

Flooded areas behind beaver dams become swampy, often creating rich habitat for a succession of plants and animals. After perhaps several generations, beavers may use up all the young broad-leaved trees they can safely reach and desert the area. Their dams slowly deteriorate and the ponds drain, leaving behind rich, silty soil that becomes a meadow. Eventually, the forest reclaims the spot. If fire later sweeps through, the aspen and birch that commonly sprout afterward are usually large enough within five to ten years to support another colony of beavers searching for a new homestead.

BLACK BEAR

Big Sleeper with Special Powers

Does a bear defecate in the woods? Well, not during hibernation. Neither does one urinate, eat, or drink, though females do give birth in late January or early February, nursing and tending their young between intermittent deep slumbers.

Bears are considered true hibernators, although their body temperature drops only seven to twelve degrees in winter, and they can wake easily. Denning bears have a unique chemistry that achieves wonders beyond the ability of other true hibernators. If most animals went without peeing for more than a few days, backed-up waste would result in fatal urea poisoning. Even hibernating woodchucks must relieve themselves once in a while. Bears, however, recycle urine from their bladders into new proteins. Water from the recycled urine and from fat reserves prevents dehydration. Unlike other animals denied food or room to move for long periods, a bear lives off its fat without losing muscle or bone mass. The fat fuel causes winter cholesterol levels to double, without resultant cardiovascular problems.

The system works so well that while most other species are going through their most difficult and dangerous season, 99 percent of all bears survive comfortably through winter. Scientists are working diligently to isolate the bear chemicals that could help humans suffering from kidney and bone diseases to recycle urea and calcium.

AVERAGE ADULT BODY LENGTH: Males 5–6 ft (1.5–1.8 m); females 4–5 ft (1.2–1.5 m)

HEIGHT AT SHOULDER: 2–3 ft (60–90 cm)

AVERAGE WEIGHT: Males 200–350 lb (91–159 kg); females 100–180 lb (45–82 kg)

BIGGEST EVER IN NORTH WOODS REGION: 876 lb (397 kg), in northeastern Minnesota, 1994

BIGGEST EVER FOUND: 880 lbs (399 kg), in North Carolina, 1998

MARKINGS: Completely black, except for tan or brown snout and sometimes a white patch on chest; rarely reddish, brown, or blond

PORTION OF BEARS THAT ARE BROWN: 6% in Minnesota, less than 0.01% in New York

ALIAS: American black bear, *Ursus americanus*

NAME ORIGIN: Proto-Indo-European *bheros*, meaning "brown," probably a euphemism for the bear's true name, which was too sacred to utter, a common occurrence among northern peoples around the world

NAME FOR A GROUP: A sloth of bears

CALLS: Grunts, loud blowing, teeth clacking

PREFERRED HABITAT: Mixed-age forests with thick understories, including large stands of trees

Mother bruins carry recycling to the point of ingesting their cubs' waste, recapturing the fluids lost through nursing. It also keeps the den clean. Although bears mate in June or July, embryos don't start developing until ten weeks before birth, when sows have stored enough nutrients needed to get them through winter. Newborns are a little bigger than chipmunks, very lightly furred, deaf, toothless, and blind. They are not, however, formless bits of mush sculpted by their mother's tongue, a folk belief responsible for the expression "licked into shape." Following only their sense of touch, they find their mother's nipples by moving toward the heat that can be felt from them.

Each year of a bear's life is like a big Viking feast. Although the black bear is the largest carnivore in the eastern United States, it concentrates on a changing smorgasbord of easily obtained food sources through the warm months. From 75 to more than 90 percent of its diet is vegetarian.

While most other species are going through their most difficult and dangerous season, 99 percent of all bears survive comfortably through winter

After sleeping off the previous year's banquet, bears emerge between mid-April and early May, groggy, 15 to 40 percent lighter, but not yet hungry. It takes about two weeks to clear the head and shake off the hibernative state before eating

less than 90 years old, berry-rich clearings, abundant oak or beech trees, wetlands, and rivers
AVERAGE CORE HOME RANGE: Males 8–25 sq mi (21–65 km²); females 2–10 sq mi (5–26 km²)
BEARS PER 10 SQ MI (26 KM²) OF SUITABLE HABITAT: 2–13
SAFETY TREES: While cubs are sleeping or their mothers are foraging, they are kept near big, branchy trees with deeply furrowed bark, especially white pines and hemlocks, that they can easily climb in case of danger, mainly from other bears.
FOOD: Berries, currants, acorns, nuts, cherries, grass, roots, leaves, buds, coniferous tree inner bark, ants, grubs, caterpillars, fish, frogs, eggs, birds, small mammals, fawns, moose calves, carrion
DAILY CALORIE INTAKE IN LATE SUMMER: Up to 20,000
AVERAGE NUMBER OF CALORIES BURNED DAILY DURING HIBERNATION: 4,000
RECOMMENDED DAILY HUMAN CALORIE INTAKE: 1,800–3,200
GESTATION PERIOD: 7 months, including 3–4 months delayed implantation
AVERAGE LITTER: 2–3
BIRTH WEIGHT: 7–14 oz (200–300 g)
FAT CONTENT OF BEAR MILK: 20–40%
FAT CONTENT OF HUMAN MILK: 4%
PERIOD CUBS STAY WITH MOTHERS: 16–17 months
AGE OF FIRST-TIME BREEDERS: Males 4–6 years; females 3–5 years
AVERAGE ANNUAL MORTALITY: Cubs about 20%; yearlings more than 35%; adults about 10%
ADULT LIFE SPAN: Average 3–5 years in hunted populations,

resumes. They start off light, with a green salad of grasses, sedges, horsetails, buds, and aspen and willow catkins, most in abundance before other vegetation sprouts in early spring. Roots, rotting logs filled with ants and grubs, and the occasional animal or spawning fish are important supplements. Late spring serves up fresh aspen leaves. Bears continue losing weight until they plunge into the main course with the ripening of the first berries in early July. Then they start steadily gaining a couple of pounds (one kilogram) or more a day. From August to October, eating goes into overdrive, as the bear spends up to twenty hours a day devouring high-fat-and-protein acorns, beechnuts and hazelnuts, and mountain ash berries, cherries, and other berries, sometimes venturing more than 60 miles (100 kilometers) from its home range to where the eating is good.

If nut and berry crops are plentiful, they may not bed down until November. As early as September, though, bears may begin preparing their winter sleeping

10–15 years in protected areas; up to 33 years

PREDATORS: Small cubs sometimes taken by adult male bears, wolves, eagles

HEARTBEATS PER MINUTE: About 40 when active, as low as 8 during hibernation

BREATHING RATE IN HIBERNATION: As low as once every 45 seconds

TOP RUNNING SPEED: About 35 mph (56 km/h)

BEST SENSES: Can smell carrion more than a mile away; hearing range wider than humans', probably twice as sensitive

EYESIGHT: Color vision about equal to humans'

TRACKS: Hind feet 6–7 in (15–18 cm) long, resembling wide human feet; front feet 4–6 in (10–15 cm) long

SCAT: Generally blunt and cylindrical, up to 2 in (5 cm) wide, varying in size, shape, and

chambers, spending up to ten days digging out a den, sometimes up to 5 feet (1.5 meters) deep. Before blissfully retiring, the stuffed bruins fast for about a week and then eat dry leaves, grass, pine needles, and hair that together form into a wad sealing their other end for the next six months or so.

Throughout its days of foraging, the black bear lumbers through forest and meadow with impunity, having few if any enemies to challenge it. Bears, though, are generally shy of humans and move away from their presence. Before the advent of the gun, the only way native hunters could readily kill a bear was to find one in its winter den, or to set a pit or falling-log trap for it. Hunters asked permission from the spirits that presided over bears to kill it (as they did with other animals) and offered apologies afterward. Bears were supremely respected as symbols of strength and courage, the primary Earth and healing spirits. Veneration of the bear, with remarkably similar lore, was also practiced by hunting cultures from eastern North America through Siberia to Scandinavia. The earliest evidence of religious thought on Earth is found in bear-cult cave shrines left by Neanderthals in central Europe at least 75,000 years ago.

In more recent times, bears have engendered widespread affection as cuddly, inanimate childhood companions and good-natured cartoon buffoons. In 1902, big-game-hunting president Theodore Roosevelt's refusal to shoot a bear that had been carefully leashed to a tree for his convenience captured the public's—and a toy manufacturer's—imagination and spawned the "teddy" bear. Later, a bear cub rescued

color with food eaten, distinctly containing loose masses of berries, seeds, nutshells, matted grass, ants, roots, and wood fibers

ACCOLADES: State animal of West Virginia, Louisiana, and New Mexico; on state seal of Missouri

FAMOUS BEARS: Yogi, Smokey, Winnie-the-Pooh, Fozzie, Gentle Ben, the Three Bears, Baloo, Paddington, Artio, Brer Bear

RANGE: Throughout most of north woods region and the Appalachians, Ozarks, Rockies, Pacific Coast, and Gulf of Mexico coast; Arizona, Utah, most of Canada, and Alaska

WINTER WHEREABOUTS: Den dug beneath roots of trees, logs, brush piles, rock ledges and crevices, in thick bush, lined with leaves, grass, moss, lichens, evergreen boughs, rotted wood

POPULATION ESTIMATES: Minnesota, 30,000; Maine, 23,000; Wisconsin, 13,000; Michigan, 12,000; New York, 5,000–6,000; New Hampshire, 4,200; Vermont, 3,000–3,500; North America, 450,000–750,000

BEARS TAKEN ANNUALLY BY HUNTERS: Maine, 4,000; Minnesota, 3,600; Wisconsin 3,000; Michigan, 2,000; New York, 600–1,000; Vermont, 500; New Hampshire, 400–500; North America, more than 40,000

AVERAGE NUMBER OF AMERICANS INJURED BY BEARS ANNUALLY: 30

AVERAGE NUMBER OF AMERICANS INJURED BY RODENTS ANNUALLY: 27,000

from a forest fire in New Mexico's Lincoln National Forest in 1944 became the inspiration for the famous fire-prevention poster icon Smokey the Bear.

Indeed, guns and habitat destruction have driven black bears from much of their original range, which once covered all of the United States except a small portion of the southwest and coastal Texas. Hunting is now strictly regulated, though most bears outside parks and other protected areas still die from bullets, usually before reaching the age of six. Many people also object to the practice of bear baiting, in which hunters perching in trees ambush their victims attracted to large quantities of rotting meat left below. While it's illegal to shoot mothers with cubs, it sometimes happens, raising concern because of the black bear's low reproductive rate. The species is also under threat from poachers seeking parts to export to Asia. Bear gallbladders, considered a panacea in traditional Asian medicine, have sold for as much as $20,000 in Taiwan and Korea.

NUMBER OF HUMANS KILLED BY BEARS IN NORTH AMERICA SINCE 1900: About 45
ODDS OF AMERICANS DYING OF OTHER CAUSES: Bee stings, 180 times more likely; traffic accidents, 160,000 times more likely
NUMBER OF U.S. BEAR SPECIES: 3
NUMBER OF BEAR SPECIES WORLDWIDE: 7
ALSO SEE: Big Dipper, Woodchuck, Blueberry, Beech

CHIPMUNK

Chip and Dale Are Frauds

Cute, cuddly, tame, adorable by popular acclaim, chipmunks are, in fact, highly secretive, independent, and aggressive animals. They usually don't enter the holes to their underground burrows while being watched. Though many will take food from campers' hands, chipmunks never become dependent on humans. They spend most of their days, from the time they emerge from hibernation in early spring, filling their cheeks to bulging with food and carrying it back to their burrows, often storing away a lifetime's supply in a single season. Lawrence Wishner, the dean of chipmunkology, who spent six years living among the tiny beasts, says they are driven by an "obsessive genetic fear of starvation."

The smorgasbord of nuts, seeds, berries, cones, mushrooms, and insects that forms most of their diet in the north woods supports up to thirty chipmunks per acre (0.4 hectare). One of the biggest factors preventing an explosion of chipmunks is their extreme dislike for one another. They live alone, and when they meet, there are almost always strong words, scraps, or

BODY TEMPERATURE: 95–108°F (35–42°C) when active, 41–45°F (5–7°C) in hibernation

BREATHS PER MINUTE: More than 60 when active, less than 20 in hibernation

NUMBER OF WILD CHERRY PITS ABLE TO HOLD IN CHEEKS: 48

AVERAGE ADULT BODY LENGTH: 5.5–6.5 in (14–16 cm)

TAIL LENGTH: 2.5–4.5 in (6.5–11.5 cm)

AVERAGE WEIGHT: 3.5–4 oz (75–105 g)

MARKINGS: Tawny-brown back and sides with 9 stripes; 2 stripes on face; white undersides and chin

ALIAS: Chipping squirrel, *Tamias striatus*

CALLS: "Chip," "chuck," trills, whistles or squeals, chatter

PREFERRED HABITAT: Mature, open upland hardwood forests and woodland edges with lots of logs, stumps, and rocks

HOME RANGE: ¼–1 acre (0.1–0.4 ha)

HOME: Burrow, about 3 ft, (1 m) underground, somewhat bigger than a large watermelon

FOOD: Acorns, beechnuts and hazel-

chases. Chip and Dale could never have been pals. If there are too many chipmunks in one area, the population becomes stressed, mating drops off, and miscarriages and maladies increase.

The constant discord explains much of the noisy chattering heard from chipmunks in the woods. They also pull together, however, whenever a fox, raccoon, or other mammal predator is spotted, by joining in on sharp, repeated choruses of warning "chips." For hawks and other large birds, the alarm call is a distinctly different, lower series of "chucks." When hordes of nervous, inexperienced five- to seven-week-old youngsters set off on their own looking for refuge in June, the pickings are prime for carnivores and the chips and chucks can reach fever pitch. The waifs that survive their troubled youth usually find sanctuary in old, empty burrows anywhere from 5 to more than 750 yards (5 to 700 meters) from their original homes within a few weeks of leaving.

When excavating new quarters, chipmunks finish them off by ingeniously digging a second entrance tunnel and pushing the dirt from it to seal the opening of their original three- to fifty-foot- (nine- to fifteen-meter-) long working shaft, hiding any obvious evidence of their occupation.

After a comfortable winter of intermittent sleep in leaf-lined chambers, male chipmunks resurface in late March or April in a lustful state. They call on female burrows, only to be thrashed and rejected until the fairer sex is ready. Then, love briefly conquers chipmunk belligerence and a couple will nuzzle, play, lunge, and squeak together for hours before and after mating. Beyond that, the relationship's over.

nuts, maple keys and other seeds, berries, cherries, mushrooms, buds, root bulbs, snails, slugs, insects, frogs, bird eggs
GESTATION PERIOD: 31 days
AVERAGE LITTER: 4–5
BIRTH WEIGHT: $\frac{1}{10}$ oz (3 g)
AGE UPON REACHING ADULT SIZE: 2–3 months
AGE OF FIRST-TIME BREEDERS: Males 1 year; females as young as 10 weeks
ANNUAL ADULT MORTALITY: 50% or more
LIFE SPAN: Average 1.3 years, with few living more than 3 years; up to 12 years
PREDATORS: Hawks, foxes, wolves, raccoons, weasels, snakes
TOP RUNNING SPEED: 7.5 mph (12 km/h)
TOP SWIMMING SPEED: 7 mph (11 km/h)
ACTIVITY PERIOD: Daytime
BEST SENSE: Hearing
WINTER FOOD STORES: Up to 7 quarts (6.7 l)
ENTER HIBERNATION: September–November
FAMOUS INDIVIDUALS: Chip and Dale; Simon, Alvin, and Theodore
RANGE: Northeastern United States to North Dakota, Kansas, Ozarks, Alabama, Georgia, and Virginia; north in eastern Canada to Labrador, James Bay, and Manitoba
WINTER WHEREABOUTS: In light hibernation beneath ground
NUMBER OF CHIPMUNK SPECIES IN NORTH WOODS REGION: 2
NUMBER OF U.S. CHIPMUNK SPECIES: 19, most in west
ALSO SEE: Broad-Winged Hawk, Mink, Red Pine, Red Squirrel, Humus and Soil

COYOTE

Newcomer to the North Woods

There's probably more than a grain of truth in the eastern coyote's alternative name "brush wolf." Coyotes were primarily native to the western plains until they spread east with the clearing of forests and settlement in the nineteenth century, finally reaching the Adirondacks and New England in the 1930s and becoming well established by the 1970s. Their spread coincided with the persecution and near extinction of the eastern red wolf. Though wolves normally drive off or even make lunch of their smaller cousins, it's believed that the vanguard of eastbound coyotes and remnant red wolf holdouts made a marriage of convenience when the presence of others of their own kind was wanting. Studies in northern Minnesota have found that when forest densities drop below the threshold of one wolf per fifteen

AVERAGE ADULT BODY LENGTH: 2.5–3 ft (76–91 cm)

TAIL LENGTH: 11–16 in (28–41 cm)

HEIGHT AT SHOULDER: 18–21 in (45–54 cm)

AVERAGE ADULT WEIGHT: 25–50 lb (11–22.7 kg)

MAXIMUM WEIGHT: More than 60 lb (27 kg)

MARKINGS: Grayish salt-and-pepper back and sides, often with a reddish hue; throat, chest, and undersides white or light gray

ALIAS: Brush wolf, prairie wolf, *Canis latrans*

PRONUNCIATION: Coyotl, meaning "barking dog" in the Aztec language, was pronounced by the Spanish, and later in the U.S. southwest, as "ky-o-tee," shortened in other areas to "ky-oat."

square miles (thirty-nine square kilometers), coyotes move in. The crossing is invariably between a male wolf and a female coyote.

Today, eastern coyotes are noticeably larger—about the size of collies or small, lean German shepherds—and darker than their western counterparts because of mixing with red wolves. As well, the few recognized surviving red wolves, in the southern United States, carry a significant infusion of coyote genes. Even among Minnesota's wolves, some 62 percent possess some coyote DNA. Recent genetic evidence reveals that even before the hybridization, the red wolf and coyote were actually kissing cousins, much more closely related to each other than to the larger northern gray wolf, whose ancestors migrated to Asia about 1 to 2 million years ago and developed separately before returning over a Bering Sea land bridge some 1.7 million years later. Meanwhile, the ancestral canids that remained in North America split off into coyotes and red wolves 150,000 to 300,000 years ago.

Supreme adaptability is the key to the coyote's expansion across the continent. Unlike wolves, which are big-game specialists that shrink from any sign of human settlement, coyotes evolved to maximize their opportunities in marginal hunting grounds not occupied by their more stout-snouted brethren. They became omnivorous, developed very flexible reproductive abilities, and learned to adjust their ways to meet almost any situation. Necessary for such powers of adaptability is a keen intelligence. The Aztecs and Navajo were so impressed with the cagey canine that they called it "God's dog." Coyote was the trick-

CALLS: High-pitched whines, yips, barks, howls, growls
PREFERRED HABITAT: Forest edges, meadows, swamps
HOME RANGE: Average 5–25 sq mi (13–65 km²), but spends most of time in territory of 2–3 sq mi (5–8 km²)
PORTION OF POPULATION WITHOUT TERRITORIES: 8–20%
FOOD: Mice, voles, hares, rabbits, groundhogs, squirrels, fawns, carrion, birds, eggs, frogs, insects, berries, cherries, grass. Adult deer most often taken in late winter.
GESTATION PERIOD: 60–63 days
AVERAGE LITTER: 4–8
AGE OF FIRST-TIME BREEDERS: Almost 2 years for most. Some females may breed at 10 months.
FIRST-YEAR MORTALITY: 40–80%
ANNUAL ADULT MORTALITY: 30–50%
LIFE SPAN: Few live more than 4 years in wild; up to 19 years in captivity.
PREDATORS: Wolves, bears
TOP RUNNING SPEED: More than 40 mph (64 km/h)
TRACKS: Oval, 2.5–3.5 in (6–8 cm) long
SCAT: Like dog droppings, but usually dark gray with hair and bone fragments and pointed at ends, averaging cigar thickness
ACCOLADES: Official state mammal of South Dakota
RANGE: All United States north to Alaska and across most of Canada
POPULATION ESTIMATES: New York, 20,000–30,000; Maine, 12,000; Vermont, 5,000
ALSO SEE: Wolf, Red Fox

ster deity for many western American native groups, responsible for placing people on Earth and providing for many of their needs and teachings.

Western ranchers were less enthused with the four-legged threat to their livestock. Giving voice to popular sentiment, Mark Twain once wrote that the coyote "is so spiritless and cowardly that even when his exposed teeth are pretending a threat, the rest of his face is apologizing for it." Yet, intense eradication efforts in the west utterly failed, with the U.S. Fish and Wildlife Service overseeing the killing of four million coyotes between 1930 and 1990 without reducing the population. When hunted and trapped intensively, coyotes become ever more wily and increase their birthrate by 30 to 100 percent, breeding younger and producing litters of up to nineteen pups.

Coyotes mate in the dead of winter, late January or February, so that when the pups arrive two months later, the melting snow will make for good mousing to nourish the litter. Emerging woodchucks also supply plenty of take-home meat. Fathers provide for both the young and their nursing partners, with whom they remain for life. They commonly move their pups between dens beneath rocky ledges, inside hollow logs, or in enlarged fox or woodchuck burrows in stream banks, brushy ravine slopes, or sandy ridges.

The Aztecs and Navajo were so impressed with the cagey canine that they called it "God's dog"

Though coyotes tend to hunt on their own, or sometimes in pairs, youngsters begin accompanying their parents in August or September. By that time, rising adolescent petulance may set some off on their own, usually dispersing from 25 to 100 miles (40 to 160 kilometers), sometimes more than 300 miles (480 kilometers). Others remain with the folks into winter, when they often scavenge or hunt deer as a family pack. One of the young may even stay behind to help raise the following spring's litter.

DEER MOUSE

Legions of the Night

When the sun goes down, the meek inherit the earth, emerging from every crack, crevice, and hole in the ground to skitter across their dark domains. Mice are usually the most numerous mammals in the forest and have among the most profound influences on the ecosystem. Forests usually teem with many hundreds per square mile, rivaling the total number of birds. Mice are far less conspicuous because they stick with the oldest of mammalian survival tactics, being tiny, nocturnal, and partly subterranean. It was only after a giant meteorite, comet, or some other shattering catastrophe struck the Earth sixty-six million years ago and ended the reign of the dinosaurs that furry sanimals began coming out into the light of day and putting on weight. Even today, rodents, which have sharp front gnawing teeth that grow throughout their lives, account for 40 percent of all mammal species worldwide.

POPULATION PER SQ MI (2.6 KM²): 600–19,000, generally tripling from winter to summer and fluctuating up to 10-fold between years of high and low tree seed crops

HEARTBEATS PER MINUTE: 320–860

HUMAN HEARTBEATS PER MINUTE: 60–200

TOP RUNNING SPEED: 8 mph (12.6 km/hr)

HIGH-JUMPING ABILITY: Up to 1 ft (30 cm)

NUMBER OF NAPS PER DAY: Up to 20

BODY LENGTH: 2.5–4 in (7–10 cm)

TAIL LENGTH: 2–4.5 in (5–11 cm)

WEIGHT: 0.4–1.2 oz (12–32 g)

MARKINGS: Gray to reddish-brown back and sides; white belly, feet, and chin

ALIAS: Woodland deer mouse, vesper mouse, singing mouse, *Peromyscus maniculatus*

CALLS: Shrill, buzzing trill lasting up to 10 seconds a burst; squeaks, chitters

PREFERRED HABITAT: Mature forests with rich soils, but found in woodlands of almost any type and age

HOME RANGE: About $\frac{1}{10}$–$\frac{1}{3}$ of an acre (0.04–0.13 ha)

HOME: Ground burrows, tree cavities, hollow logs, inside stumps and brush piles; usually 4–6 in (10–15 cm) in diameter, lined with

Mice have long had a dubious reputation in western civilization, defamed as the creation of witches or the devil, and as omens of all four horsemen of the Apocalypse. The very word *mouse* is evolved from a Sanskrit word meaning "thief."

But in native North American legends, the mouse is usually a good and trusted friend. Such respect may have been born out of an intrinsic understanding and reverence among hunting cultures of their food chain. A host of larger predators are directly dependent on the droves of mice that sprout from the earth. The abundance of prey, contrary to popular myth, has far more control over the numbers of predators than vice versa.

Forest mice populations rise and fall with the tree-seed cycles, which vary greatly from year to year to keep seedeaters in check. Mice, in turn, form one of the largest corps of seed distributors in the forest, unwittingly planting trees in forgotten caches and spreading minute herb pits and mushroom spores in their droppings. Those scats fertilize the soil, while mouse tunnels help air, water, and roots spread through the ground. Mice also limit outbreaks of tree-damaging insects by feasting on pine weevils, European sawflies, and others.

Deer mice are the most common squeakers in most of the north woods. Their rustling in the leaves and even singing, described in the writings of naturalist R. D. Lawrence as "an incredibly high, yet soft, crooning," can be heard throughout much of the night. More laidback than most of their relatives, deer mice rarely put up a fight against intruders into their territories unless population

shredded materials; usually several per mouse

FOOD: Mostly seeds, especially conifer and maple; also berries, nuts, buds, flowers, beetles, caterpillars, centipedes, grasshoppers, springtails, snails, spiders, moths, cocoons, and carrion of birds and small animals

FOOD CACHE SIZE: Up to 4.7 quarts (4.5 l)

GESTATION PERIOD: 22–23 days; 24–30 days if nursing a previous litter

AVERAGE LITTER: 3–6

LITTERS PER YEAR: Usually 2; up to 5

BIRTH WEIGHT: 1/20 oz (1.5 g)

INBRED INDIVIDUALS: Up to 10%

DISTANCE YOUNG DISPERSE FROM BIRTHPLACE: Up to 500 yd (457 m)

AGE UPON REACHING ADULT SIZE: About 6 weeks

AGE OF FIRST-TIME BREEDERS: Males 9 weeks; females about 7 weeks

NESTLING MORTALITY: About 50%

FIRST-YEAR MORTALITY: Up to 95%

LIFE SPAN: Probably up to 2–3 years in wild, 8 years in captivity

PREDATORS: Owls, snakes, weasels, foxes, coyotes, martens, raccoons, skunks, hawks, shrews, almost all other full or partial meat-eaters

AVERAGE NUMBER OF MICE EATEN BY A LONG-TAILED WEASEL IN ONE YEAR: 2,300

FAMOUS MICE: Mickey, Minnie, Mighty, Itchy, Jerry, Speedy Gonzalez, Topo Gigio, Algernon

GREATEST MOUSE ACHIEVEMENT IN SPACE: In 1960, 3 lab mice, Sally, Amy, and Moe, traveled 660 mi (1,100 km) above Cape Canaveral, higher than any other animal had gone, and returned alive.

densities get high. In winter, while occasionally scurrying beneath or above the snow, they mostly snuggle together for warmth in dens of up to twelve mice, living off stored seeds. They breed from April through August. The young are weaned and scattered, or drift away, about three or four weeks after birth, soon to mate and start their own families, allowing Mom to raise another brood as well.

Around campfires, deer mice can be quite tame, standing up on their hind feet, their large, beady black eyes searching hopefully for a discarded crumb or raisin. They'll also actively crawl into or industriously gnaw through food bags left on the ground. Unlike the "city mouse" image of the rather distantly related house mouse from Europe, the deer mouse is fastidious, carefully grooming and preening itself for up to twenty minutes at a time with its dexterous little paws.

A menagerie of other tiny creatures cross paths with deer mice throughout the wilderness. The almost identical white-footed mouse is more territorial than its amiable cousin and tends to drier forests than deer mice, where it spends much of its time in trees. The woodland jumping mouse, which, unlike other mice, hibernates six or seven months a year, frequents tangled debris along stream edges. Voles, which have shorter tails and ears than mice, making them look more beaver-like, skitter day and night through a variety of habitats. Red-backed voles abound in boggy or mossy spruce and fir forests, hemlock stands, and dense, log-strewn areas where there's plentiful regeneration after fires, blowdowns, or budworm epidemics. Around old beaver ponds and other open areas, the grass-eating meadow vole, or field mouse, at the peak of its two- to four-year population cycle, lives in densities up to ten times as high as its forest relatives. In captivity, meadow voles can produce up to seventeen litters a year, more than any other mammal on Earth.

PAST MEDICINAL USES: Ingested for a wide range of ailments, especially for children, from bad breath to bed-wetting

RANGE: Throughout United States except most areas east of Appalachians and around Gulf of Mexico; north to tree line in Alaska and Canada

WINTER WHEREABOUTS: Tunnels beneath snow and ground, living off caches of seeds and nuts; torpid for days at a time

HANTAVIRUS: Very rare disease, but potentially fatal to humans, spread by inhaling dust contaminated with infected deer mouse droppings or urine. Mouse-contaminated surfaces should be aired out and mopped, not swept, with disinfectant.

LARGEST MEMBER OF NATIVE MOUSE FAMILY IN NORTH WOODS REGION: Muskrat

NUMBER OF MOUSE, VOLE, AND LEMMING SPECIES NATIVE TO NORTH WOODS REGION: 11

INTRODUCED SPECIES: House mouse, Norway rat

Number of rodent species worldwide: About 1,600

ALSO SEE: Barred Owl, Red Pine, Humus and Soil, Falling Stars

FLYING SQUIRREL

Gliding through the Night Shift

Like inhabitants of a fairy realm, northern flying squirrels are unseen nocturnal creatures that sail through the air and visit hidden places where mushrooms flourish. Though the fur-caped aerialists are little known, they're as plentiful as the bigger red squirrels that chatter vociferously through the day. Night gliders sleep during the sunlit hours in tree holes or in spherical bark nests, and rise for the night shift soon after the bellicose reds and chipmunks call it a day.

Just as regular squirrels use well-worn routes that allow them to flash through the branches with hardly a thought, flying squirrels navigate along regular flight corridors, with takeoff spots marked by their urine and other body scents. Tossing themselves into the air, they spread their legs to unfold a continuous furred flap of skin reaching to each of their four feet, turning themselves into flying carpets. They can remain airborne for several seconds, usually landing near the ground on a tree trunk up to 160 feet (48 meters) away.

RATE OF GLIDING DESCENT: Averages 1 yd (91 cm) down for every 3 yd (273 cm) forward

POPULATION PER SQ MI (2.6 KM²) IN PRIME HABITAT: Up to 2,600

AVERAGE ADULT BODY LENGTH: 5.5–7.5 in (14–19 cm)

TAIL LENGTH: Almost as long as body, resembling a flattened bottlebrush; serves to stabilize glides and acts as an air brake when flipped upward

AVERAGE WEIGHT: 2.5–5 oz (70–140 g)

MARKINGS: Light grayish-tan to reddish-brown back; light-gray undersides. Large black eyes shine red in lights at night.

ALIAS: Glaucomys sabrinus

CALLS: Chucks, squeaks, sharp squeals, birdlike chirping, and calls beyond human hearing range

PREFERRED HABITAT: Mature coniferous and mixed forests

AVERAGE HOME RANGE: 7.5–30 acres (3–12 ha)

HOME: Old woodpecker holes or natural cavities lined with

Most glides, though, are closer to 20 yards (18 meters). Upon landing, they climb up and up until attaining a sufficient height to launch off again. The mouse-eyed sprites can also drop straight down by spinning in a tight spiral.

Like so much that rarely meets the eye in the wild, flying squirrels may play a vital role in the forest ecosystem that's only starting to be understood. The nocturnal nymphs are true mushroom fanatics, sniffing out and digging up even gumball-sized, subterranean fruiting fungi. Such mushrooms, called false truffles, may be largely spread in the droppings of their animal nibblers. A great variety of trees and plants in turn form close symbiotic relationships with these types of organisms, known as mycorrhizal fungi. Tree roots entwine with the fungal threads and provide them with sugars created through photosynthesis in return for nutrients and water collected from the ground by extensive fungal networks.

In winter, northern flying squirrels also eat lots of hanging tree lichens, a low-nutrition food on which few other mammals, save caribou, can get by. The aerial rodents also become quite social during winter, in contrast to the fierce individualism of daytime squirrels. On cold days, as many as nine flying squirrels will curl close together in tree cavities for warmth.

As the sun rises higher in the sky and mild days foreshadow spring in mid- to late March, the velvet-furred rodents develop a keen romantic interest in one another. New litters result in May. In summer, little Rockys leave the nest to learn to glide, remaining with their mothers until August or September.

shredded leaves, moss, lichens, grass, bark strips, fur, or feathers; in summer, also builds spherical nests of sticks, bark, moss, leaves, and lichens in forked branches, usually of an evergreen, and in witches'-broom tangles at top of black spruce, occasionally in a covered-over bird's nest. Each squirrel usually has several nests.
Food: Mushrooms, nuts, acorns, raspberries, and serviceberries in summer and fall; lichens, mushrooms, and conifer seeds in winter; maple sap and buds of aspen, alder, and willow in spring; also flowers, bird eggs and nestlings, mice, beetles, moths, mayflies, insect larvae, carrion; said to be the most carnivorous of squirrels
Gestation period: 37–42 days
Average litter: 2–4
Birth weight: 0.14–0.2 oz (4–6 g)
Weight of a nickel: 0.16 oz (4.5 g)
Age of first-time breeders: 9 months for females, later for males
Life span: Most less than 4 years; up to 14 years in captivity
Predators: Owls, hawks, ravens, martens, fishers, raccoons, weasels, foxes, wolves, coyotes
Range: Throughout north woods region to Red River Valley, along Appalachians to Tennessee; also in Pacific states, Utah, northern Rockies to Wyoming, and Black Hills; north to near tree line in Alaska and Canada
Number of flying squirrel species worldwide: 38
Also see: Fungi, Lichens, Red Squirrel, Black Spruce, Yellow-Bellied Sapsucker

LITTLE BROWN BAT

Good Fortune in the Night

The crusading efforts of Batman aside, bats remain enshrouded in myth and misconception, most of it bad. Little-seen specters of the night, the only mammals to really fly have been looked on since the Middle Ages of Western culture as unnatural, the associates of witches and vampires or the incarnation of the devil himself. In other cultures, bats represent fertility, because they have exceptionally long penises, spanning almost an inch (two centimeters) in the case of the little brown bat, nearly a quarter the span of its body.

In one Ojibwa tale, the bat was originally a squirrel that was burned, deformed, and blinded while heroically freeing the sun from the tangled branches of a tall tree. The sun rewarded its seriously singed rescuer with the power of flight and the ability to see in the dark. In the mystic East, the Chinese greeted bats as omens of good luck. The Wu Fu charm, traditionally

FREQUENCY OF BAT SONAR CALLS: 40–100 kHz

UPPER LIMIT OF HUMAN HEARING: 16.7 kHz

AVERAGE FREQUENCY OF HUMAN CONVERSATION: Less than 5 kHz

FLYING SPEED: 12–22 mph (20–35 km/h)

WING BEATS PER SECOND: 6–8

LENGTH: 3–4 in (8–10 cm)

WINGSPAN: 8.5–10.5 in (22–27 cm)

WEIGHT: $\frac{1}{4}$–$\frac{1}{2}$ oz (7–14 g)

BODY TEMPERATURE: 99–104°F (37–40°C) when active; up to 147°F (64°C) in nursery colonies; 36–47°F (2–8°C) in hibernation

HEARTBEATS PER MINUTE: More than 1,300 in flight, 100–200 when stationary, as low as 10–15 in hibernation

MARKINGS: Mostly medium brown, darker on shoulders, ears, face; lighter grayish-brown on undersides; dark brown wings and tail membrane almost hairless

ALIAS: Flittermouse, reremouse, *Myotis lucifugus*

NAME ORIGIN: Old Norse *bakke*, meaning "flutter"

PREFERRED HABITAT: Forage over lakes, streams, wetlands, ponds, meadows, and open forests

DAY ROOSTS: Usually in sunny spots near forest edges beneath loose bark, in tree cavities, caves, and brush piles, under rocks, and in crevices as narrow as 0.4 in (1 cm)

hung above the doors of Chinese homes, depicts five bats circling the tree of life, representing the five top human blessings—virtue, wealth, children, longevity, and a contented death.

Without doubt, bats do descend like a blessing on warm summer nights to devour the hordes of flying insects that torment larger mammals such as humans. The little brown bat, the most common species in the north woods, can catch and is believed to eat more than ten mosquitoes a minute on the wing, scooping them up in its wide tail membrane and flipping them into its mouth. In a single night, the little brown bat can eat enough insects to equal half its weight. For nursing females, it might be more than their entire weight. Extensive studies turn up fewer mosquito bites in areas with lots of bats.

While it is not true that bats are blind, hearing is certainly their most important sense for capturing large quantities of bugs. Using sonar, or echo location, little brown bats emit a steady stream of high-pitched squeaks that bounce off objects and insects within a range of six and a half feet (two meters). Their large ears and brain interpret the distance more accurately than human sonar devices. The sonar calls are too high for human hearing, though bats can make audible squeaks of fright if threatened.

Before engaging their sonar systems, bats depend on highly tuned internal temperature readings to tell them if it is worth going out to look for insects. Without temperatures high enough to guarantee plentiful insects, it is too dangerous for bats to gear up to full metabolism. Instead they go into semihibernation, even on cool nights

FOOD: Moths, mosquitoes, mayflies, midges, beetles, caddis flies, and other flying insects
NUMBER OF TIMES BATS CHEW PER SECOND: 7
AVERAGE TIME FOOD TAKES TO GO THROUGH A BAT'S SYSTEM: 20 minutes
GESTATION PERIOD: About 60 days after delayed implantation
AVERAGE LITTER: 1
FLEDGING AGE: 18–21 days
AGE OF FIRST-TIME BREEDERS: Males 2 years; females 1 year
LIFE SPAN: Average probably 10 years; up to 33 years
PREDATORS: Owls, hawks, martens, skunks, raccoons, snakes
RANGE: All United States except Florida, Texas, and southern California; north almost to tree line in Alaska and Canada
WINTER WHEREABOUTS: Large groups hibernate in caves and old mines.
NUMBER OF BATS HIBERNATING IN GATED ABANDONED MINES IN GREAT LAKES REGION: At least 300,000–400,000
WEIGHT LOSS DURING HIBERNATION: 20–40%
NIGHTTIME TEMPERATURE BRINGING BATS OUT OF HIBERNATION: 50°F (10°C)
AGE OF OLDEST BAT FOSSILS: 60 million years
OTHER ANIMALS THAT USE ECHO LOCATION: Shrews, dolphins, whales, cave-dwelling birds
MIGRATORY NORTHERN SPECIES: Red bat, hoary bat, silver-haired bat
NUMBER OF BAT SPECIES IN NORTH WOODS REGION: 9
NUMBER OF U.S. BAT SPECIES: 39
NUMBER OF BAT SPECIES WORLDWIDE: About 925

in the summer, with their body temperature and heart and respiratory rates dropping to put their systems on slow burn.

Although several northern bat species migrate to the southern states or Mexico for the winter, flying as high as 10,000 feet

(3,000 meters), little brown bats hibernate in colonies in cool, damp caves or abandoned mine shafts. One old mine in Michigan is home to 11,000 wintering bats. Another in New York State houses little browns 3,800 feet (1,160 meters) below the surface, the lowest depth mammals have been found at anywhere in the world. The bats travel up to 480 miles (800 kilometers) to return to traditional hibernacula—group hibernating sites—starting to swarm around them in mid-July or August. They mate in late summer, with both males and females having more than one partner and forming no pair bonds. By late September or October, they settle in for the winter, the males in tight clusters, the females hanging alone or in small groups.

Females come out of hibernation first, in mid-April or May, and fly to nursery colonies in brush piles, caves, or large tree cavities, where they give birth a couple of months later. Males and nonbreeding females, lacking the food needs of expectant mothers, slumber until warmer temperatures arrive in mid-May, then spread out to smaller summer roosting sites.

Contrary to myth, they do not become entangled in people's hair, and have a very low incidence of rabies. Little browns die soon after contracting the virus and their teeth are reportedly too small to even break human skin. An average of two Americans a year, however, die from a strain of rabies carried by silver-haired and pipistrelle bats, usually after handling the animals directly. Both species range into the southern reaches of the north woods.

Bats carry no other human diseases and very few parasites and, in fact, are quite clean, spending a half hour at a time grooming and cleaning their all-important ears with twists of their tiny thumbs. To admirers, they are charming, intelligent, even cute, like downy little mice with wings. Biologists believe bats may be closely related to primates. Like monkeys, apes, and humans, they have just two nipples for nursing their young.

Some bat species also form the biggest of all mammal colonies, save for perhaps humans. Caves in Texas hold colonies of up to 20 million Mexican free-tailed bats. Some of the caves were long mined for bat guano—decades-old accumulations of nitrogen-rich droppings—used for fertilizer and saltpeter, a prime ingredient of gunpowder. Texan bat guano supplied Confederate armies until the fall of Vicksburg on the Mississippi in 1863 effectively cut the South in half.

MINK

Among the Smallest of Carnivores

A mink's rich, luxurious coat, underlaid by an inner layer of supersoft, dense fur, is ideally suited for its semiaquatic lifestyle in sometimes frigid waters. Body oils spread during grooming keep it glossy and waterproof. Together with the fur's streamlined lay, its qualities have long attracted humans and made mink one of the most highly prized pelts to grace the backs of Park Avenue matrons. It takes about seventy to eighty mink to make a full-length coat. Fortunately for those in the wild, about 90 percent of the market today is supplied by commercially raised animals.

Mink are probably the most commonly seen species of the weasel family in the north woods, other than perhaps skunks, because they frequent shorelines and other open areas. For savage killers, they are deceptively cute, with little pointy faces, small round ears, and long, thin bodies on

BODY LENGTH: 12–20 in (33–52 cm)

TAIL LENGTH: 6–8 in (16–20 cm)

WEIGHT: Males 2–3.5 lb (0.9–1.6 kg); females 1.5–2.4 lb (0.7–1.1 kg)

MARKINGS: Light to dark brown or black, darkest on the back, with white chin patch, often a white chest spot

ALIAS: American mink, *Mustela vison*

CALLS: Snarls, squeaks, barks, hisses, purrs

PREFERRED HABITAT: Along forest streams, lakes, and marshes

AVERAGE BREEDING TERRITORY: 1.5–3.3 mi (2.5–5.5 km) of shoreline for males; for females 0.3–1.8 mi (0.5–3 km)

HOME: Maintains a number of dens in bank burrows about 4 in (10 cm)

155

short legs. Mink usually walk or run with their backs gracefully arched. Chancing upon a nonthreatening human, one may stop close by, stand up on its hind feet, and curiously check out the scene. Although they are mainly nocturnal, relentless hunting often keeps them going in daylight.

For savage killers,
they are deceptively cute

Weasels—mink included—are the smallest but among the fiercest and most agile of all carnivores. Mink often attack and eat animals larger than themselves, killing with a bite to the neck. Even muskrats—themselves ferocious—are attacked in their lodges and literally eaten out of house and home, the mink gaining both a meal and a new den. When the tables are turned, larger predators have great difficulty catching and outfighting a mink. Adding insult to injury, mink produce a stench from their anal musk glands more rank than that of any other member of the weasel family save the skunk. A mink cannot direct spray like a skunk, but it lets fly with its musky defense far more readily, at the slightest threat. *Mink* is, in fact, a Swedish word meaning "stinky animal."

Besides defense, musk glands are used by mink to communicate with one another and in seeking a mate between late February and early April. Indeed, the world of odors is everything to mink and other weasels. When hunting, even during a chase, mink use their noses more than their eyes, becoming so absorbed that they

wide, in log cavities, and under roots and rocks, sometimes in old groundhog holes or muskrat lodges

Food: Muskrats, crayfish, frogs, mice, voles, hares, squirrels, fish, waterfowl, small birds, eggs, garter snakes, salamanders, mussels, worms, snails, slugs, insects, grasses

Average daily food helping: About 4 oz (110 g)

Gestation period: 40–70 days, depending on delayed implantation

Average litter: 4–6, born late April to mid-May

Weaning age: About 6 weeks

Age of first-time breeders: Males 1½ years; females 1 year

Life span: Up to 8 years in wild, 14 years in captivity

Predators: Wolves, foxes, bears, bobcats, lynx, great-horned owls, snowy owls

Top running speed: 6–8 mph (10–12 km/h)

Swimming speed: 1.8–2.4 mph (3–4 km/h)

Dive duration: Usually 5–20 seconds; up to 2 minutes

Deepest dives: 16 ft (5 m)

Tracks: Round, 1–1.4 in (2.5–3.5 cm) wide, with 4 toes

Scat: Dark, 0.4 in (1 cm) long, in piles, with dense, fine fur, scales, and bone chips

Range: All United States except southwest; north to tree line in Alaska and Canada

Number of mink pelts collected annually in United States: Almost 3 million

World's smallest carnivore: Least weasel, 1–3 oz (28–85 g), boreal

have been known to run right over the feet of human spectators without seeming to notice them. Males hunt on long circuits that may take a week to complete, finding prey both at the bottom of deep, watery dives and on the forest floor. Dens along the route are often stocked with carcasses for the mink's next trip through, especially in winter. Up to a month's supply of food has been found in some mink storehouses.

species, rare in northeastern United States
NUMBER OF MUSTELID SPECIES IN NORTH WOODS REGION: 9
NUMBER OF MUSTELID SPECIES WORLD-WIDE: About 65
ALSO SEE: Skunk, Otter, Porcupine

Throughout the north woods, other weasel species that concentrate on different, though partly overlapping, habitats are tiny short-tailed weasels, which chase mice and voles right down into their tunnels along forest edges, wet meadows, and shrubby areas. About the size of skinny chipmunks and moving like greased lightning, they're usually too fast to be seen. In November, they turn in their brown summer duds to don royal ermine, the silky white coat for which they are named in winter, which traditionally trimmed the robes of kings and queens.

Less common are fishers and pine martens, once nearly wiped out by trapping and habitat loss. Reddish- to dark brown martens, about the size of sleek house cats, often climb trees as they prowl for red-backed voles, mice, grouse, and hares in mature evergreen and mixed forests. Frequenting denser forests and frozen swamps, where hares are even more common, the bigger, heavyset fisher hunts a wider variety of prey, including porcupines.

MOOSE

Reclaiming the Northland

In the moose-rich lands of Maine, northern Minnesota, Vermont, and New Hampshire, the great, silent, massive-muzzled monarch of the woods is celebrated as a cultural icon on innummerable signs and in place names, institution names, books, and fables. Indeed, as the moose reclaims more and more of the forest realm where it formerly roamed, it can't help but gain attention. In the 1980s, moose returned to the Adirondack Mountains, after disappearing from New York State 120 years before. And on Michigan's Upper Peninsula, they're growing in number after reintroduction from Canada nearly two decades ago, and spreading into Wisconsin, as are moose from Minnesota.

As, by far, the biggest animals in the northeast, moose are also often formidable pedestrians on wilderness stretches of highway. Even portly bears going into hibernation weigh much less than the lanky, stilted herbivores. Yet, for most of the year, the moose is like a towering, gentle farmhand. It is usually calm and benevolent even when awestruck canoeists drift close by as it feeds on succulent water lilies in the early morning or late afternoon. Some Eurasian moose were even once domesticated and ridden like horses by Siberians and Swedish cavalrymen.

In a story of the Penobscot people of Maine, the moose is one of the few large beasts not downsized by the deity Gluskabe before he set humans on Earth. The

AVERAGE ADULT BODY LENGTH: Males 7.9–10 ft (2.4–3 m); females 6.6–8.6 ft (2–2.6 m)

HEIGHT AT SHOULDER: 5–7 ft (1.5–2.1 m)

AVERAGE WEIGHT: Males 880–1,190 lb (400–540 kg); females 825–1,170 lb (375–530 kg)

BIGGEST EVER RECORDED: 1,800 lb (816 kg), 7.7 ft (2.3 m) tall at shoulder, in Alaska, 1897

AVERAGE DAILY FOOD HELPING: Up to 55–65 lb (25–29.5 kg) in summer and 33–45 lb (15–20.4 kg) in winter

MARKINGS: Dark brown body, in shades from almost black to rust; grayish-white lower legs and nostrils; calves reddish-brown

ANTLER SPREAD: Up to 5.6 ft (1.7 m)

ALIAS: Elk (European name), *Alces alces*

CALLS: Usually silent, but during rut, males make a hoarse, guttural, 2-syllable grunt or loud roar; females make a bleat or moo, up to 5 seconds long, audible for up to a couple of miles.

PREFERRED HABITAT: Forests with abundant patches of broadleaf trees up to 15 years old, diversely mixed with mature conifer stands, meadows, lakes, beaver ponds, and wetlands

HOME RANGE: 8–16 sq mi (20–40 km²) for males; 4–6 sq mi (10–15 km²) for females

FOOD: In summer, water lilies, pondweed, deciduous leaves,

big beast kept its size because of its humility and stated goodwill toward the newcomers. Moose were in turn highly valued by natives. A single animal could feed a family through much of the winter, in addition to yielding the favored leather for moccasins and wool from its mane for mittens and socks.

Look out, though, for a lovesick moose. During the fall rut, which peaks in late September and early October, males become aggressive and unpredictable, even crazed. Their mood starts to change in late August when, after their antlers have been growing for five months, they begin rubbing off the nourishing velvet lining on bushes and tree branches, coloring the huge racks orange-brown with dried blood. Males challenge each other to establish their status for the breeding ahead. Antlers are the measure of a moose, and the less impressive of two contesting bulls usually learns to back down before a fight develops, leaving only the psychological wounds of antler envy. Occasionally, they do drop the gloves, pushing head-to-head until one

ferns, horsetail, asters, jewelweed, grass, sedges; in winter, buds, twigs and bark of fir, beaked hazel, red and mountain maple, birch, mountain ash, aspen, poplar, willow, dogwood, Juneberry, and cherry

GESTATION PERIOD: 8 months

AVERAGE LITTER: Usually 1; 2 common in large tracts of abundant browse after fires or logging

BIRTH WEIGHT: 25–35 lb (12–17 kg)

AGE OF FIRST-TIME BREEDERS: Most males don't mate regularly until about 5 years old; most females start at 2½ years.

FIRST-YEAR MORTALITY: More than 50%

LIFE SPAN: Average 7–8 years; up to 18 years in wild, 20 years in captivity

PREDATORS: Wolves. Bears prey on calves.

TOP RUNNING SPEED: 35 mph (56 km/h)

AVERAGE SWIMMING SPEED: 6 mph (10 km/h)

AVERAGE TIME UNDERWATER: 30 seconds

159

loses ground and retreats. Most younger males, lacking the rack dimensions and strength of their elders, don't get to mate.

The biggest antlers also have the deepest, most impressive resonance for females listening to distant bulls thrashing them against branches. Females moan longingly for up to forty hours straight to attract bulls through the dense forest to their breeding arenas in meadows and boggy lake edges. Biologists in the role of female impersonators imitate the sound by squeezing their noses, cupping their hands, and calling. Great, long donkey ears and an acute sense of smell serve moose well in locating one another during the rut. Males also kick up the ground, pee, and then wallow in the depressions to perfume themselves. A courtship may last a week. With all the searching and challenging and waiting, bulls can drop up to 20 percent of their weight during the mating season.

Rutting moose seem to have trouble distinguishing their competitors from other things that are large and loud. In addition to chasing humans up trees, bulls have been known to demolish trucks in head-on collisions and even to challenge trains. On the other hand, males have also mistaken cattle for potential mates. In one celebrated Vermont love affair, a moose in 1986 wooed and occasionally nuzzled a brown-and-white Hereford named Jessica for seventy-six days. Like all moose, both his antlers and his interest finally dropped off in December and he slunk back into the woods.

Baby moose are similarly apt to follow humans or other species, mistaking them for their mothers. Females can be as dangerous as rutting bulls when guarding against such possibilities and generally

MAXIMUM TIME UNDERWATER: 50 seconds

DEEPEST DIVES: 20 ft (6 m)

TRACKS: Cloven hoofprints 6 in (15 cm) long, pointed in direction of travel

SCAT: Large piles of greenish-tinged, dark brown, pecan- to olive-sized, fibrous pellets in winter; less distinct, greenish-black or brown plops, like cow pies, in summer. Dried pellets can be burned as spruce-scented incense and have been varnished and sold as jewelery and Christmas tree decorations and, in Sweden, used to make fancy gray paper.

DAILY SCAT PRODUCTIVITY: Roughly 13 piles of more than 100 pellets

THE STUDY OF ANIMAL DROPPINGS: Microhistological analysis

ACCOLADES: Official state animal of Maine and Alaska

RANGE: Maine to Adirondacks and south to Connecticut, northern Minnesota, Michigan's Upper Peninsula, and eastern North Dakota, expanding into Wisconsin; across most of Canada to Alaska and northern Rocky Mountain states

RAMBLING YOUTH: After shooed away by mothers, some moose may continue to wander far; a yearling named Alice, tagged in the Adirondacks in 1998, turned up in Ontario's Algonquin Park, about 200 miles (320 km) away, three years later.

MYSTIC MOOSE: The Penobscot of Maine believed Mount Katahdin was inhabited by Pamola, a fierce spirit with the head of a moose, wings of an eagle, and body of a

seclude their offspring for as long as possible. Cows repair to islands, swamps, or waterside alder thickets safe from wolves in May or June to give birth. Newborn calves are about 3 feet (91 centimeters) long. Moose milk allows them to grow faster than any other mammal in North America, gaining more than 2 pounds (900 grams) a day in their first month and up to 7 pounds (3 kilograms) daily afterward.

During the summer, calves sometimes rest their heads or front legs over their mothers' necks when they tire of swimming. Moose escape swarms of blackflies, mosquitoes, and deerflies by taking to the water and feasting on water lilies and other salt-rich aquatic plants. In the winter, they repair to more heavy forest cover and switch to twigs and occasionally bark after the sap starts to run. The name moose is derived from the Algonkian word *moosee*, meaning "bark- or twig-eater."

With their long legs, moose are much better suited to deep snow than are white-tailed deer. Where winter conditions are mild enough to allow high densities of deer, moose often become scarce because of a parasite commonly called brain worm. The parasite evolved over millions of years to live off white-tailed deer without harming them. In moose, however, which are recent immigrants from Eurasia, arriving within the past 11,000 years, the brain worm causes disorientation, blindness, and eventually death. Snails feeding on deer dung spread the parasite when moose suck them up while browsing.

The burgeoning numbers of deer, and therefore brain worm, that came with the opening of northern forests by logging and settlement, together with heavy hunting pressure, sent moose populations into steep decline. Even in their Maine stronghold, the great ungulates were reduced to about 2,000 a hundred years ago. Moose hunting was finally banned in Maine and Minnesota for nearly fifty years during the middle of the twentieth century. As forests matured, though, deer herds had an increasingly difficult time and were devastated by severe winters from the 1950s to the 1970s, tipping the scales back toward moose in many areas.

man. A cartoonish version of the deity has been adopted as a popular mascot in northern Maine.

AVERAGE POPULATION INCREASE IN SPRING: 20–25%

POPULATION ESTIMATES: Maine, 29,000; New Hampshire, 10,000; Minnesota, 5,000; Vermont, 4,000; Michigan, less than 1,000; New York, 100

NUMBER OF MOOSE SHOT BY HUNTERS ANNUALLY IN NORTH WOODS STATES: About 2,600 in Maine; less than 1,000 in Minnesota; New Hampshire, and Vermont combined

AVERAGE NUMBER OF MOOSE HIT BY AUTOMOBILES ANNUALLY IN MAINE: About 700

ESTIMATED NORTH AMERICAN MOOSE POPULATION: 750,000

ALSO SEE: White-Tailed Deer, Wolf, Beaver, Porcupine, Deerflies, Spiders, Water Lily

OTTER

Playful Master Fish-Catcher

Quiet wilderness lakes and rivers are animated by the arrival in August of otter families from backwater natal retreats up small headwater streams and remote beaver ponds. Moving through the water in an undulating train of sleek dipping and rising bodies, appearing like one long, snaking lake monster, they often venture within clear reconnoitering distance of passing canoes. Looking beaverlike when just breaking the surface, their heads rise on long, weasely necks as they stop, snort, and turn to get a good look at their paddle-flapping companions on the water.

Otters are creatures of boundless enthusiasm and famed curiosity. They're said by some to be one of the few animals besides man known to engage in play even as adults. Dispassionate biologists caution that many otter antics, such as playing tag and diving for pebbles, serve as practice for hunting, and that instances of groups repeatedly using mud or snow slides are

AVERAGE ADULT BODY LENGTH: 21–32 in (53–82 cm)
TAIL LENGTH: 11–20 in (27–51 cm)
WEIGHT: 11–33 lb (5–15 kg)
MARKINGS: Dark brown to light chestnut back, lighter brown with some gray on sides; appears black when wet. Young born black.
ALIAS: Northern river otter, North American river otter, land otter, common otter, Canadian otter, fish otter, *Lontra canadensis*
CALLS: Coughing snorts, sniffs, grunts, chirps, growls, hisses, humming, and high whistles
PREFERRED HABITAT: Quiet wilderness lakes, rivers, creeks, and beaver ponds, interspersed with marshes and swamps, and in water with lots of submerged fallen trees and logjams
AVERAGE HOME RANGE: 15 mi (24 km) or more of shoreline in summer; 2 or 3 times as big in winter

fairly rare in the wild. Still, the aquatic animal's intelligence, hyperactivity, and keen interest in all things are universally acknowledged. The otter is sacred to many native groups throughout North America. It was one of the Ojibwa Midewiwin Society's most important spirit guides and protectors. Otter pelts, the most durable of all furs, were used for medicine bags, quivers, bow casings, hats, and robes.

The otter is sacred to many native groups throughout North America

For their part, otters have every reason to be upbeat creatures. They're largely impervious to the weather, have few if any natural enemies, and enjoy a food supply so plentiful and easily caught that they have lots of time to lounge and amuse themselves. Insulated by a layer of fat and by air bubbles trapped within their fur, otters glide stealthily underwater, taking fish unawares with lightning strikes. Though streamlined like seals, they're actually one of the largest members of the weasel family. Special flaps close tight within their ears and nostrils while submerged. Long, prominent, highly sensitive whiskers help otters probe darkened waters at night and beneath the ice of winter, picking up waves fanned by their prey. Their eyes, too, are so specialized for scanning the submerged nocturnal world that in the surface realm otters seem actually nearsighted.

Even in winter, otters have little trou-

HOME: Old bank burrows or lodges of muskrats and beavers, uprooted trees, eroded root tangles, hollow logs and stumps, rock crevices, dense thickets of willow and alder, old groundhog burrows; lined with grass, leaves, and sticks

FOOD: Mostly slower-moving fish 3–5 in (7–13 cm) long, including minnows, sunfish, catfish, suckers, perch, and sculpins; less often bass or trout; also crayfish, frogs, salamanders, mussels, water beetles, stonefly nymphs, worms, and snails; occasionally ducklings, muskrats, mice, water snakes, ground-nesting birds and their eggs, some grass, blueberries, algae, and aquatic vegetation

SUCCESS RATE OF FORAGING DIVES: Less than 20%

GESTATION PERIOD: 11–13 months, depending on delayed implantation

AVERAGE LITTER: 2–3

WEANING AGE: 4–5 months

DISPERSAL: Mothers leave young when 8–11 months old; siblings stay together until 12–13 months old.

AGE OF FIRST-TIME BREEDERS: Males 2–7 years; females 2–3 years

ANNUAL SURVIVAL IN TRAPPED POPULATIONS: 50–60% in first year; 55–70% for adults

LIFE SPAN: Up to 15 years in wild, 25 years in captivity

PREDATORS: May be taken on land by wolves, coyotes, and bobcats

PEAK ACTIVITY PERIODS: Predawn to midmorning, late afternoon to midnight

BEST SENSES: Touch, smell

MAXIMUM TIME UNDERWATER: 4 minutes

DEEPEST DIVES: 55 ft (17 m)

ble going about their business. They use the snow to their advantage, alternately running and sliding while journeying overland several kilometers from one body of water to another. To get into the water, they break through the ice at weak points around rocks, logs, and stumps, keeping several openings clear in a given area. Otters can also catch a breath at air pockets left beneath the ice by changing water levels. They also frequently slip through open spots at the spillways of beaver dams. With beavers creating ideal habitat for otters, peaceful coexistence between the two species is generally the rule.

In late April and May, male otters often join females, who have given birth a month or so before, at dens on or near small beaver ponds. Taking time out from maternal duties, mothers join their visitors to mate in the water for fifteen to twenty-five minutes at a time. After repeated performances, males usually depart, though some apparently return to lend a helping paw after the pups first leave the den and are taught to swim, when about two months old. Several weeks later, when the young are adept, families troop out to larger bodies of water where food is more plentiful. Here they may wander along many miles of shoreline, and become a common sight of late summer.

NORMAL SWIMMING SPEED: 3–7 mph (5–11 km/h)

RUNNING AND SLIDING SPEED OVER SNOW: Up to 18 mph (30 km/h)

DAILY ACTIVITY SPENT IN PLAY: About 6%

SCATS: Small, slimy lumps or splats, most often black, quickly washing away in rain to leave behind scattered fish scales, reddish bits of crayfish shells, and small bones

MINNESOTA POPULATION: About 12,000

OTTERS TRAPPED ANNUALLY IN MINNESOTA: About 2,000

OTTERS TRAPPED ANNUALLY IN NORTH AMERICA: About 50,000

RANGE: All north woods region to northern Connecticut; also in southern Atlantic and Gulf states, Pacific Northwest, Rockies, north to Alaska, and across most of Canada; being reintroduced into several Midwest and prairie states

NUMBER OF U.S. OTTER SPECIES: 2

NUMBER OF OTTER SPECIES WORLDWIDE: 13

PORCUPINE

Cute but Not Cuddly

Sometime within the past fifteen million years, porcupines, as well as raccoons, calmly waddled their way from South to North America after the two continents collided at the Isthmus of Panama. Armed with a dense coat of formidable quills, porcupines met with little resistance. Though they will attempt to escape up a tree when threatened, porcupines resort to their prickly defense if their slow-moving legs don't carry them away in time. The quills are modified hairs with hundreds of tiny overlapping barbs. Porcupines don't actually shoot their quills but cause them to stand on end, like bristling fur, when they are in danger. A swat from their tails can release hundreds on contact. Once embedded, the hollow quills swell, burn, and work their way into the flesh every time a victim's muscles contract, digging a millimeter deeper each hour. Eventually they emerge through the skin again, some distance from

NUMBER OF QUILLS: About 30,000
LENGTH OF QUILLS: Up to 5 in (13 cm)
AVERAGE ADULT BODY LENGTH: 1.6–2.8 ft (50–85 cm)
TAIL LENGTH: 6–8 in (15–20 cm)
AVERAGE HEIGHT AT SHOULDER: 12 in (30 cm); large males up to 18 in (46 cm)
WEIGHT: Average 7–20 lb (3.2–9 kg); large males up to 40 lb (18 kg)
MARKINGS: Black- or brown-tipped yellowish or gray-white quills, mixed with dark, dense underfur; black face
ALIAS: American porcupine, Canada porcupine, porky, quill pig, hedgehog (really another species), *Erithizon dorsatum*
NAME ORIGIN: Latin *porcus*, meaning "pig," and *spina*, "thorns"
CALLS: Snorts, nasal cooing, wails, barks, sniffs, teeth chattering
PREFERRED HABITAT: Coniferous and mixed forests and clearings. Hemlock stands with rock ledges favored in winter.
HOME RANGE: Males 75–375 acres (30–150 ha); females 30–200 acres (12–80 ha); average 17.5 acres (7 ha) in winter
HOME: Deep crevices beneath rock ledges and outcrops, caves, tree cavities, hollow logs, brush piles, ground burrows;

the entry point, though sometimes they spear right through the body.

A predator needs to learn only once to leave a porcupine alone. Bobcats, coyotes, and wolves, when extremely hungry and unable to catch anything else, may give it a try anyway. The fisher, however, is a skilled porcupine killer. It uses its speed and agility to snake around a porcupine's rear guard defense and viciously bite its face until it dies. Then, flipping the prickly corpse over, the fisher feasts on the soft, unprotected underbelly. After fishers were virtually wiped out by overtrapping, disappearing completely in Michigan and Wisconsin by the mid-1930s, unchecked tree-eating porcupine populations caused considerable damage to large stretches of forests. The big, skillful weasel was reintroduced in many regions in later decades, reestablishing a balance with far fewer spiny rodents. One Michigan study found ten porcupines per square mile (2.6 square kilometers) in forests without fishers, but only one porky per square mile in areas occupied by its arch nemesis.

A porcupine's quills were also of little help against native hunters. Because they are slow, can remain in the same tree for days at a time, and are about the only animal that can be killed simply with a large rock, porcupines were a godsend in times of scarce game. They were accordingly honored, and like the beaver's, their bones were kept away from dogs out of respect. Native peoples across the north woods region also wove elaborate dyed quillwork decorations into clothing, moccasins, belts, mats, necklaces, bracelets, and bags. Because the work was so time-consuming and highly valued, quill embroideries were

smell of porcupine pee, sometimes with large piles of scat, at entrance; used mainly in the winter

GESTATION PERIOD: 7 months

FOOD: Buds and catkins, especially sugar maple, basswood, aspen, willow, and alder in spring; leaves of aspen, basswood, beech, ash, and yellow birch, water lilies, raspberries, grass and other plants in summer; acorns, beechnuts, mushrooms and leaves in fall; buds, twigs, inner bark and needles of hemlock, pine, fir, and spruce in winter, along with some aspen, birch, beech, and sugar maple bark

AVERAGE LITTER: 1

BIRTH WEIGHT: About 1.1 lb (490 g)

WEANING AGE: 7–10 days

AGE OF FIRST-TIME BREEDERS: Males 2 years; females 18 months

LIFE SPAN: Often 7–8 years; up to 15 years in wild, 18 years in captivity

PREDATORS: Fishers, great horned owls, rarely bobcats, lynx, foxes, bears, wolves, coyotes

BEST SENSES: Smell, touch

TRACKS: Tail often leaves a trough up to 9 in (23 cm) wide in snow, often obscuring pigeon-toed, oval footprints 2.3–3.9 m (6–10 cm) long, with long claws.

SCAT: Black, gray, or yellowish, very fibrous, jelly-bean- or peanut-shell-sized pellets, sometimes curved, with distinct pine scent, usually clustered at base of a tree, often more clumped or strung together in summer

DAILY SCAT PRODUCTION: 75–200 pellets

DINING SIGNS: "Nip twigs" cut at 45° angle, with buds, nuts, or needles

used as a medium of exchange before the coming of Europeans.

Still, having so few effective predators, porcupines are relatively long-lived, allowing them to propagate sufficiently with just a single baby per mom a year. Of course, pincushion bodies seem a little impractical when it comes to sex. Porkies have it all figured out, though, when males go courting in female territories in October or November. Couples dance in circles when they meet, admiring each other's cute brush cuts, rubbing noses, and eliciting loud, high wails and low murmurings of lust. At the moment of truth, the female flips her tail up over her back so that the male can rest on its quill-less underside with his similarly unarmed belly. Later they return to their solitary lives, remaining active through the winter, eating buds and starch-rich inner tree bark, only the coldest nights keeping them den-bound.

Baby porcupines are born in May or early June, about ten inches (twenty-five centimeters) long, with open eyes and soft quills that harden as they dry. They can climb trees when only a day old. Their ready defense makes juvenile mortality extremely low. Four-month-old females leave home to establish their own territories. Males stay closer to Mom. Being slow, with a low-energy diet but with plenty to eat, porcupines usually don't travel too far. They spend most of their time in trees, as high as sixty-five feet (twenty meters) up, sleeping during the day and eating at night. Because they often feast on and sometimes kill the most common tree species in an area, they are an important agent of forest diversity.

Porcupines get salt from sodium-concentrated pockets of clay and other mineral licks, or by gnawing discarded antlers and bones or, more often than not, nocturnally chewing outhouse toilet seats. Sweat residues also make unattended ax handles and canoe paddles tasty entrées. Porkies even teethe on aluminum, though probably to wear down their rodent teeth, which always keep growing. Road-salt-enriched puddles of snowmelt in spring, and a misguided fearlessness, are largely responsible for their strong showing in roadkill stats.

removed, littered beneath feeding trees; bark gnawed in distinct patches on conifer trunks and in crosshatch patterns on deciduous trees
RANGE: Northern and western United States to Massachusetts, Kentucky, Illinois, Iowa, Kansas, and west Texas; also along Appalachians to Georgia and north to tree line in Alaska and Canada
ESTIMATED DAILY MAMMAL, BIRD, AND REPTILE ROADKILL TOLL IN UNITED STATES: More than 1 million
DATE PORCUPINES BRANCHED OFF FROM THE ANCESTORS OF GUINEA PIGS AND CHINCHILLAS: About 40 million years ago
NUMBER OF NORTH AMERICAN PORCUPINE SPECIES: 1
NUMBER OF PORCUPINE SPECIES WORLDWIDE: 23
ALSO SEE: Mink, Quaking Aspen, Eastern Hemlock, Water Lily, White-Tailed Deer

RACCOON

A Touch for Dexterity

The coonskin cap is an icon of the early American frontier, crowning the heads of heroes such as Daniel Boone and Davy Crockett. The ring-tailed hats, though, may not have been so common in the north woods, where raccoons were at the far limits of their range and were not as common as farther south. Today, the brazen, black-masked bandits in the north are probably more abundant scrounging around campgrounds and settled areas after dark than in the wilderness.

Raccoons are extremely bright. They reportedly beat dogs, cats, and foxes in animal IQ tests. And, like humans, raccoons have a very sensitive sense of touch. Their front paws, in fact, have many thousands more nerve endings than do human hands. With dexterous fingers, raccoons reach under crevices in shallow water, feeling their way to crayfish and frogs without actually seeing them or even seeming to

Body length: 1.3–2.5 ft (40–75 cm)
Tail length: 8–13 in (20–33 cm)
Height at shoulder: 9–10 in (23–26 cm)
Weight: 10–20 lb (4.5–9 kg)
Heaviest ever found: 62 lb (28 kg)
Markings: Two-tone gray- or brown-and-tan fur, with black mask over eyes, black-and-tan-striped tail
Alias: Coon, bandit, *Procyon lotor*
Calls: Chatter; low, fierce growl; a hoarse, staccato call when afraid. Cubs purr when content.
Preferred habitat: Near lakes, streams, and swamps in deciduous forests
Home range: 0.4–1.5 sq mi (1–4 km²)
Home: In holes about 20–40 ft (6–12 m) high in trees, often facing south; old groundhog, fox, or skunk burrows; or large abandoned birds' or squirrels' nests; and beneath large rocks
Food: Crayfish, frogs, clams, turtle and bird eggs, fish, birds, small rodents, snakes, snails, worms, insect larvae, berries, cherries, acorns, nuts, seeds, carrion
Gestation period: 63 days
Average litter: 3–7
Weaning age: 2–3 months
Age of first-time breeders: Males 22 months; females 10 months
Adult life span: Average 3–5 years; up to 12 years in wild, 16 years in captivity

pay attention. Cubs can climb even before they can see or hear. Driven by keen curiosity, raccoons explore the nocturnal world with their paws, constantly picking up objects and thoroughly feeling their food before eating. Biologists believe their sense of touch is actually enhanced by water. Raccoons are not really washing food when they wet it in a stream. Their scientific name, *lotor*, is Latin for "washer." The word *raccoon* itself is derived from the animal's Algonkian-language name, *aroughccon*, meaning "hand scratcher."

Like bears, raccoons are religiously omnivorous, and come autumn, they really pack on the pounds, gorging on acorns and whatever is plentiful to build up enough heft to nourish them in winter dens. A thick layer of fat may account for half their weight by the time the snow flies. Still, raccoons are not real hibernators and cannot survive long without eating. Hard winters can cause many to starve. On mild days, they come out to search for crayfish and torpid frogs beneath cracks in the ice. In February and early March, they also go looking for love. Males call on the opposite sex and, if invited into their quarters, mate with them repeatedly before moving on.

Female raccoons, like most mammals, are single mothers. Their cubs are usually born in April or early May. When they are a few months old, they join their mother on nighttime marauding expeditions. The cubs usually den up with Mom for their first winter and then leave home before she gives birth again.

In recent years, a strain of rabies to which raccoons are particularly susceptible has spread to the northeast from the south, arriving in New York State in 1990. The strain, however, is mainly confined to the eastern seaboard states, with no cases yet reported in Michigan, Wisconsin, or Minnesota. Raccoons should never be fed or closely approached.

PREDATORS: Cubs sometimes taken by coyotes, wolves, fishers, bobcats, foxes, great horned owls, and eagles.

TOP RUNNING SPEED: 15 mph (25 km/h)

TRACKS: Handlike, 2.5 in wide (6 cm) and 4.2 in (11 cm) long

SCAT: Usually blunt, sausage-shaped, shotgun-shell-sized, grayish, granular droppings; sometimes brown, black, reddish, yellow, or with blotches of white

ACCOLADES: Official state mammal of Tennessee

RANGE: All United States except for much of Rockies and southwest; also southeastern Canada to northern prairies

MINNESOTA RACCOON POPULATION: 800,000 to 1 million

RACCOONS SHOT AND TRAPPED ANNUALLY IN MINNESOTA: 175,000–250,000

RACCOONS SHOT AND TRAPPED ANNUALLY IN NORTH AMERICA: 2–4 million

CASES OF RABID RACCOONS ANNUALLY IN UNITED STATES: About 2,800 (38% of total cases)

AVERAGE ANNUAL NUMBER OF U.S. HUMAN RABIES FATALITIES: 1–2, most from bat rabies

RED FOX

Crafty Catlike Canine

From Aesop's fables to native North American legends, from Chaucer to Dante to Kafka, the fox is cited for its beguiling cunning and intelligence. Not all the press is good. Machiavelli said rulers must have the deceit of a fox. At the heart of such tales is an animal that employs a much broader range of strategies to fill its plate with a far greater variety of pickings than does its canine cousin, the wolf.

Foxes have a vegetarian bent and will go to great lengths to get what they want. But their staple is meadow voles, which they capture by first listening with sensitive ears for scurrying in the long grass or beneath as much as 4 to 5 inches (10 to 12.5 centimeters) of snow, and then making a precision pounce, like a cat, upon their unseen prey. The master mousers can reportedly hear a squeak up to 150 feet (45 meters) away. Similar feline-style stealth—including the silent footing of semiretractable claws—is used to get as close as possible to larger prey before making a fast,

AVERAGE ADULT BODY LENGTH: 2–2.3 ft (60–70 cm)

TAIL LENGTH: 1–1.5 ft (30–46 cm)

HEIGHT AT SHOULDER: 14–18 in (35–40 cm)

AVERAGE WEIGHT: 6.6–15.4 lb (3–7 kg)

MARKINGS: Orange- or yellow-red back and sides; white chin, chest, and tail tip; black legs. All-black "silver foxes" are less common color forms of same species.

ALIAS: Vulpes vulpes

NAME FOR A GROUP: A skulk or den of foxes

CALLS: A shrill, barking yelp, howls, whines

PREFERRED HABITAT: Forest edges, meadows, shorelines, open woods

HOME RANGE: 2–8 sq mi (5–20 km²)

HOME: Ground burrows up to 60 ft (24 m) long, often in dry, sandy south-facing hillsides; also in old groundhog burrows; with several entrances, 10 in (25 cm) wide; often stocked with food stores

FOOD: Voles, mice, hares, rabbits, woodchucks, chipmunks, squirrels, grouse, ducks, gulls, small birds, eggs, snakes, grasshoppers, beetles, crickets, berries, nuts, grass, carrion

AVERAGE DAILY FOOD HELPING: 0.7–1 lb (320–450 g)

GESTATION PERIOD: 51–53 days

AVERAGE LITTER: 4–6

WEANING AGE: 8–10 weeks

deadly dash. Foxes, in fact, are the only canid whose pupils turn into vertical cat-like slits during the day, protecting their light-sensitive eyes. A special reflective layer behind the retina causes a greenish eye shine in the dark.

Though normally silent, foxes let loose during the mating season, in late January or early February. Then competing males go nose-to-nose in screaming matches until one backs down. The celebrated bushy tails are also brandished with effect, with the owner of the biggest plume often winning out. Fights are rare, though contestants may jump up and push each other with their forepaws. The winner of a vixen's heart stays with her after the young are born in March or April and helps her raise them. Cubs remain in the den for about a month, nourished by a puppy chow of regurgitated meat. In the fall, the family breaks up.

Many young are killed crossing roads during dispersal. Winter also takes a heavy toll on foxes, especially where they're heavily trapped and hunted. In agricultural areas, up to 80 percent of annual fox mortality comes in the cold months. In the upper Midwest, many often survive the winter by extending their nocturnal hunting into daylight and feeding on the remains of animals killed by wolf packs.

Powers of great adaptability have given the red fox the most widespread carnivore on Earth, with the same species bounding across North America, Eurasia, and North Africa and introduced into Australia. Since colonial times, European foxes were also used for sport into parts of North America where native red foxes were not common, including much of New England. It's believed that interbreeding with the imports, together with the creation of more edge habitat with settlement, may have helped the native reds expand their range.

AGE OF FIRST-TIME BREEDERS: 10 months

ADULT LIFE SPAN: Rarely more than 4 years; up to 12 years in wild, 19 years in captivity

PREDATORS: Wolves, coyotes, bobcats, lynx, bears. Cubs killed by fishers and great horned owls.

BEST SENSES: Hearing, smell

TOP RUNNING SPEED: 30 mph (48 km/h)

MAXIMUM JUMPING DISTANCE: 15 ft (4.6 m)

TRACKS: Front feet 1.8 in (4.5 cm) wide and 3–3.4 in (5–6 cm) long, with 4 toes

SCAT: Like small dog droppings, about 2–3 in (5–8 cm) long, dark gray with hair and bone chips; waft a skunklike odor during winter mating season

FAMOUS FOXES: Reynard, Brer Fox, Seminole Sam, Russel

RANGE: Throughout most of North America to Alaska and high Arctic, but absent in large parts of southwest, eastern Oregon, and Washington

AVERAGE NUMBER OF AMERICANS BITTEN BY FOXES ANNUALLY: About 500

NUMBER OF FOXES SHOT OR TRAPPED IN MINNESOTA ANNUALLY: About 100,000

NUMBER OF FOX SPECIES IN NORTH WOODS REGION: 2

NUMBER OF FOX SPECIES WORLDWIDE: 13

ALSO SEE: Coyote, Woodchuck

RED SQUIRREL

Loud, Hot-Blooded Cone Hoarder

The red squirrel lives in the fast lane. It's a high-strung, cantankerous bundle of energy, racing at hyperspeed along branches and around tree trunks during the day. Its specialized vision makes instant trigonometric computations using vertical objects, mainly trees, to judge leaping distances between limbs. Sensing hairs guide the squirrel to twist and contort its body around obstacles as it navigates through the forest canopy. Potential competitors, such as jays, flying squirrels, even the larger gray squirrel, are chased off or soundly thrashed. Roosting owls are harangued until they fly off to find peace. Even trespassing humans may be incessantly berated with loud, angry chirping, the protester stamping its feet and jerking its tail violently with each syllable. The native

AVERAGE ADULT BODY LENGTH: 7–9 in (18–23 cm)

TAIL LENGTH: 4–6 in (10–15 cm)

WEIGHT: 5–9 oz (140–250 g)

MARKINGS: Reddish-brown back and tail, brighter in winter; white undersides and eye ring; flattened, bushy tail

ALIAS: American red squirrel, pine squirrel, chickaree, red robber, boomer, bummer, chatterbox, rusty squirrel, barking squirrel, *Tamiasciurus hudsonicus*

NAME ORIGIN: Greek *skiouros,* meaning "shadow tail." The Ojibwa name *adjidaumo* means "tail in the air."

CALLS: A loud, ratcheting "cherr," sharp squeaks, barks, squeals

PREFERRED HABITAT: Mature coniferous and mixed forests, bogs, cedar swamps

BREEDING TERRITORY: 0.25–5 acres (0.1–2 ha)

HOME: Nest, or "dray," made in tree cavities, often old pileated woodpecker holes; twig, leaf, and bark bundles in branches; or ground burrows, lined with shredded vegetation

FOOD: Mostly pine, spruce, and fir cones; also beechnuts; cherry pits; hazelnuts; acorns; maple keys; berries; mushrooms; cedar, birch, and aspen buds; bark; roots; sap; baby hares; bird eggs or nestlings

TOTAL WINTER FOOD STORES: Up to 10 bushels (350 l)

Abenaki people of Maine said the ferocious rodent was luckily shrunk to its present size by the guardian spirit Gluskabe to make the forest safe for the creation of humans.

Behind all the ill temper is the red squirrel's driving need to jealously guard from pilferers well-stocked food stores in its territory. Thousands of cones may be stashed in a tree cavity, in a hollow stump, or under a log or covered over at the base of a tree, where they stay moist, which keeps them from opening and losing their seeds. Ground caches are often covered with a midden of discarded cone scales, sometimes rising more than three feet (one meter) high below a feeding perch used by generations of squirrels. A red may polish off more than 100 spruce cones a day, each with an average of 80 seeds.

In late summer and fall, red squirrels tirelessly cut green cones from branches with their razor-sharp teeth and drop them to the ground for later collection. In an average year, they may collect up to two-thirds of the available cones of some conifer species. They also spread and dry mushrooms on sun-soaked bushes before storing them. These nonperishable supplies allow them to stay active throughout all but the coldest days of winter. Though

GESTATION PERIOD: 33–35 days

AVERAGE LITTER: 3–6

BIRTH WEIGHT: About ¼ oz (7 g)

WEANING AGE: 7–8 weeks

ANNUAL MORTALITY: 60–80% in first year, 20% in second year

LIFE SPAN: Few more than 3 years; up to 8 years in wild, more than 12 years in captivity

PREDATORS: Hawks, owls, martens, fishers, mink, weasels, foxes, coyotes, bobcats, lynx

POPULATION PER SQ MI (2.6 KM²) OF SPRUCE FOREST: 650–1,000

BEST SENSES: Sight, smell

TOP RUNNING SPEED: 15 mph (25 km/h)

MAXIMUM JUMPING DISTANCE: 8 ft (2.4 m)

RANGE: All northeastern United States to North Dakota, Iowa, Tennessee, and New Jersey; also in Rocky Mountains, Black Hills, Washington, Oregon, Utah, and Arizona; north to tree line in Alaska and Canada

NUMBER OF TREE SQUIRREL SPECIES IN NORTH WOODS REGION: 3

NUMBER OF U.S. TREE SQUIRREL SPECIES: 10

ALSO SEE: Blue Jay, Chipmunk, Snowshoe Hare, Mink, Red Pine

each type of evergreen tree produces a bumper crop of cones every two to seven years, a good stockpile can get a squirrel through a succeeding year of food scarcity. Two bad years in a row, however, can lower the red squirrel population by as much as 80 percent from peak levels.

The strong resins and tannins of raw nuts and seeds, even the poisons of many mushrooms, have no ill effects on squirrels. According to folk belief, squirrel meat may have psychedelic fallout. Woodlore traces the term *squirrelly* to trappers and others who went a little funny eating too many squirrels, suggesting active ingredients remain potent within their flesh.

Sometimes it seems as if the squirrels are a little crazy themselves, chasing each other round and round tree trunks in a dizzying whirl. While usually this is a part of their territorial squabbling, in late winter, and sometimes again in early summer, the chase involves males trying to outlast each other in pursuit of a receptive "cow" female. Each female is usually in heat for only one day in a season and ends the bond with her mate shortly after consummating it.

Its specialized vision makes instant trigonometric computations using vertical objects, mainly trees, to judge leaping distances between limbs

Around the time their own little ones arrive, usually in late April or May, red squirrels commonly lapse from strict vegetarianism to take advantage of the wide availability of birds' eggs, nestlings, and, especially, baby snowshoe hares up to two weeks old. The extra protein probably provides a valuable boost for mothers, who nurse their litters for seven to eight weeks. Young reds set off on their own later in the summer. Without the security of home and family, many don't make it very far in a world of hungry squirrel eaters. Those that manage to survive establish their own territories, where they learn every branch, perch, and hideout along their regular foraging routes and become very difficult for any predator to catch.

In hardwood forests, gray squirrels are a little less tense, possibly because they don't carry all their nuts in a few baskets, like the hot-blooded reds do. Instead, grays bury their food a nut or two at a time, relying on a wide dispersal to stay fed. In the north woods, many gray squirrels are actually black, a color that absorbs much more heat in winter.

SKUNK

The Sweet-Faced Stinker

I n the early 1600s, the colonists of New
England brought home fantastical stories
of a sweet-faced forest pussycat that struck
terror into the hearts of man and moose.
The local Abenaki people called the creature *seganku*, later simplified to skunk.
When French to the north caught wind of
the little stinker, they dubbed it *l'enfant du
diable*, "child of the devil."

A skunk has a double-barreled spray
that squirts from two little nozzlelike pro
jections on its anus. To fire, the skunk tight-
ens its sphincter, popping the nozzles out,
and lets fly an oily yellow-green fluid. About
a foot (thirty centimeters) out, the two
streams merge and turn into a fine misty

MAXIMUM SPRAYING RANGE: 20 ft
(6 m)
*AMOUNT OF SPRAY IN EACH FULLY
LOADED SCENT GLAND:* About 1 table-
spoon (15 ml)
AVERAGE ADULT BODY LENGTH: 1.1–1.7
ft (35–51 cm)
TAIL LENGTH: 7–12 in (17–30 cm)
AVERAGE WEIGHT: 4–10 lb (1.8–4.5 kg)
MARKINGS: Black body with two
wide white bands running down
back, joining at bushy tail and top
of head; also thin white vertical
line between eyes
ALIAS: Wood pussy, lined-backed
skunk, big skunk, Canada skunk,

spray. A skunk can shoot ten to thirteen feet (three to four meters) with accuracy. The stream is usually directed at an enemy's eyes, where it causes blinding pain for fifteen to twenty minutes unless washed out. The active ingredient, butylmercaptan, is a sulfide, bearing a stench that can carry over more than two square miles (six square kilometers). A skunk, however, stores only enough musk for four or five sprayings and takes several weeks to fully replenish an empty tank. The spray is a defense of last resort. If threatened, a skunk first lifts its tail, stamps its feet, arches its back, and growls. Finally, it forms a horseshoe—face and bum toward the assailant—flips up the tip of its tail, and squirts.

All members of the Mustelidae, or weasel, family have musk glands, used for marking territory and attracting mates. Skunk musk is so odious that it evolved as a perfect defense mechanism, allowing skunks to forgo the sleek, swift body design of their weasel brethren. Instead, with their malodorous reputation preceding them, they waddle casually about, seldom running from anything. The white stripes are an advertisement so that none can mistake them in their nocturnal wandering. In more recent times, the skunk's fearlessness, and its penchant for road-killed carrion, has made it one of the most common victims of the automobile.

Skunks are more common in open areas than deep forest and are probably more often seen around human habitations than in the bush. When temperatures drop to freezing, rather than slogging it out with lean winter hunting like other weasels, females and young skunks usually find hollow logs, or groundhog holes, or dig bur-

polecat (really a European animal), *Mephitis mephitis*

PREFERRED HABITAT: Forest edges, shorelines, thick brush, open areas

AVERAGE HOME RANGE: 0.4–2 sq mi (1–5.2 km²)

HOME: May have several dens in hollow logs, under rock piles, or in ground burrows about 60 cm (2 ft) deep

FOOD: In summer, mostly grasshoppers, crickets, bees, wasps, beetle grubs, caterpillars, and other insect larvae; also spiders, worms, snails, bird and turtle eggs, nestlings; more plant and other animal food in colder months, including mice, chipmunks, squirrels, frogs, salamanders, snakes, berries, grapes, nuts, roots, fungi, carrion

PORTION OF DIET MADE UP OF SPECIES CONSIDERED PESTS TO HUMANS: 70%

GESTATION PERIOD: 62–64 days

AVERAGE LITTER: 5–7

BIRTH WEIGHT: About 0.5 oz (14 g)

WEANING AGE: About 2 months

FIRST-YEAR MORTALITY: 50–70%

AGE OF FIRST-TIME BREEDERS: About 1 year

LIFE SPAN: Few longer than 3 years in wild, up to 12 years in captivity

PREDATORS: Great horned owls, rarely foxes, coyotes, wolves, bobcats

TOP RUNNING SPEED: 10 mph (16 km/h)

RANGE: All United States except small part of southwest; north across Canada to Hudson Bay

FAMOUS SKUNKS: Pepe Le Pew, Flower, Miss Mam'selle Hepzibah, Jimmy Skunk

FAMOUS SKUNK HOT SPOT: Chicago, meaning "Place of the Skunk"

rows, to nestle down inside. Adult males may brave the cold down to 14°F (−10°C). Skunks are not true hibernators because their body temperatures and heart and breathing rates are little altered.

A skunk stores enough musk for four or five sprayings and takes several weeks to fully replenish an empty tank

SKUNK SPRAY REMEDIES: Mixture of 1 qt (1 l) of 3% hydrogen peroxide, ¼ cup (50 ml) of baking soda, 1 tsp (5 ml) of dish soap; vinegar and detergent; tomato juice
CASES OF RABID SKUNKS ANNUALLY IN UNITED STATES: About 2,200 (30% of total cases)
NUMBER OF U.S. SKUNK SPECIES: 3
NUMBER OF SKUNK SPECIES WORLDWIDE: 13
ALSO SEE: Mink

Between late February and mid-March, skunks come out of their winter sleeps to mate. Young, called kits or skunklets, are born in May. Though their musk glands start working within about eight days, they must wait a couple more weeks for their eyes to open to take aim. After about two months, they follow their mother, single file, on nightly food-gathering journeys.

SNOWSHOE HARE

Humor, Mystery, and Procreation

Silent, inscrutable, yet somehow intrinsically funny, hares have always been subjects of fable and magic. A hare-headed supernatural teacher figures prominently in the lore of most northern Algonkian-speaking peoples. The Ojibwa called the spirit Nanaboujou. He is credited with remaking the world after a great flood, stocking it with game animals, and giving humans fire, the canoe, hunting weapons, and the sacred pipe for communicating with the spirits. In innumerable humorous and moral tales, and in both male and female manifestations, Nanaboujou, in the role of trickster, shows the pitfalls of improper social behavior through the trouble he makes for himself.

University of Michigan anthropologist Daniel Moerman theorizes that the hare's

BODY LENGTH: 15–20 in (38–50 cm)

EAR LENGTH: 2.4–2.8 in (6–7 cm)

WEIGHT: 3.3–5 lb (1.5–2.3 kg)

MARKINGS: Buffy, grayish-, or dark brown in summer, white in winter

ALIAS: Varying hare, showshoe rabbit, bush rabbit, *Lepus americanus*

NAME FOR A GROUP: A husk of hares

CALLS: Rarely, snorts, grunts, low chips; deep groan when fighting; loud bleat or scream when frightened

PREFERRED HABITAT: In summer, dense aspen, birch, and jack pine sapling forests, speckled alder and willow thickets; stands of low-limbed spruce and cedar in winter, often in frozen swamps and shrubby swales

HOME: Several lairs in depressions of leaves and litter under bushes or low-hanging evergreen boughs or in logs or old groundhog holes

FOOD: Herbs, grass, leaves, ferns, fungi, almost any green vegetation in summer; conifer needles, twigs, bark, buds, especially birch, aspen, alder, jack pine, and cedar, in winter

HARE BROWSE SIGNATURE: Twigs cut at sharp, 45° angle

NUMBER OF HARE OR RABBIT TASTE BUDS: 17,000

NUMBER OF HUMAN TASTE BUDS: 9,000

NUMBER OF TASTE BUDS ON AVERAGE BIRD: 200

GESTATION PERIOD: About 36 days

practice of eating its own droppings is at the root of its mystical status. After partial digestion and storage in its long appendix, a hare's food is excreted at night as soft, vitamin-rich, greenish pellets and is eaten again for full digestion. (Waste from food on its second time through is left as the familiar, berrylike rabbit "marbles.") Like the carrion eaten by ravens and coyotes—culture heroes in other regions—the hare's food is a transitional substance, somewhere between living matter and dust.

The abundance of snowshoe hares was of vital importance for native people, especially where bigger game was scarce in the winter. Leaving large tracks with their oversized "snowshoe" feet, specially adapted for staying aloft in deep snow, hares were readily trapped along their regularly traveled paths. But the disappearance of hares at the bottom end of their nine- to ten-year population cycle caused extreme privation for native hunters. Fear of cannibalism in times of famine helped give rise to stories of windigos, winter demons that ate humans who neglected their responsibilities or behaved badly.

In peak years in the far northern boreal forest, there can be up to 6,500 hares per square mile (2.5 kilometers). High densities quickly lead to stress, depletion of food and cover, and concentration of predators, bringing populations crashing down. Densities may drop to 3 or 4 hares per square mile. The cycles show up dramatically in hunting stats in Minnesota, where close to 300,000 hares may be shot one season and only 12,000 a few years later.

With their famed procreative exuberance—undoubtedly at the heart of the Easter Bunny's pre-Christian fertility-

AVERAGE LITTER: 2–4
BIRTH WEIGHT: 2.5–3 oz (70–80 g)
AGE OF FIRST-TIME BREEDERS: About 1 year
FIRST-YEAR MORTALITY: 60–97%
PREDATORS: Bobcats, coyotes, foxes, wolves, martens, mink, weasels, lynx, hawks, barred and great horned owls. Red squirrels eat a large portion of newborn hares.
TOP RUNNING SPEED: 30 mph (50 km/h)
MAXIMUM JUMPING DISTANCE: 13 ft (4 m)
MAXIMUM HIGH JUMP: 6.7 ft (2 m)
TRACKS: Hind feet, 4–6 in (10–15 cm) long, land ahead of much smaller, circular front feet; toes of hind feet spread 2–5 in (5–12.5 cm) wide.
SCAT: Vary with diet and season, often about the size of plump M&M's
FAMOUS BUNNIES: Bugs Bunny, Peter Cottontail, Thumper, Roger Rabbit, Harvey, Flopsy and Mopsy, Fiver, Bigwig, Brer Rabbit, the White Rabbit, Fletcher Rabbit, Raggylug
RANGE: Throughout north woods region and eastern seaboard to northern New Jersey, south along the Appalachians to Tennessee, west to North Dakota; also in Rockies, Washington, and Oregon and north to tree line in Alaska and Canada
NUMBER OF HARES AND RABBITS SHOT ANNUALLY IN UNITED STATES: Millions
NUMBER OF HARE AND RABBIT SPECIES NATIVE TO NORTH WOODS REGION: 4
NUMBER OF NATIVE U.S. HARE AND RABBIT SPECIES: 13
NUMBER OF HARE AND RABBIT SPECIES WORLDWIDE: About 50
ALSO SEE: White-Tailed Deer, Painted Turtle, Ruffed Grouse, Raven, Coyote, Red Squirrel, Quaking Aspen

symbol origins—hares can spring back from their cyclical lows. One promiscuous male, or buck, may mate with two dozen females. To do so, he may have to outrace and outfight a number of other bucks chasing the does, jumping up and administering boots to the head with his great furry hind feet in bouts of bunny jousting. Before she pairs off, a female may perform a mating dance, thumping her own feet on the ground. From the start of mating in March, does may have two to four litters a year.

Most hares are very short-lived. On top of high baby-bunny mortality, between half and nine-tenths of the adult population dies each year. Less than 2 percent see their fifth birthday. The hare's high reproductive rate provides a conveyor belt of little bunnies for a cafeteria full of predators. In extreme northern Minnesota and Maine, where the rarely seen lynx still prowls, hunting at night in dense thickets and swamps, the wildcat depends on snowshoe hares for 70 to 97 percent of its diet. For several years after hare populations crash, lynx mothers can't keep their kittens alive unless they move to better hunting grounds. In the rest of the north woods, bobcats are less dependent on snowshoes because they also eat a lot of cottontail rabbits and other prey.

Camouflage, stillness, and silence are a hare's first line of defense against predators. It stays put beneath ground cover, dropping its heart and breathing rates, and runs only when it's sure it's been spotted. Much of a hare's time is spent sleeping or grooming in one of several ground or litter depressions, called forms, beneath thick bushes, low evergreen boughs, or piles of snow. It comes out to forage in the evening and is most active around eleven P.M.

The snowshoe hare was once the north's main bunny, but with European settlement, new breeds of long-ears edged their way into the region. Eastern cottontails hopped farther north in Michigan, Wisconsin, and central Minnesota, as did the closely related New England cottontail in Vermont and New Hampshire. Unlike hares, which are born fully furred and able to run within hours, rabbits are slow starters, born helpless, naked, and blind in hidden nests. Cottontails have grayish- to reddish-brown backs and white undersides, and are about the same size as snowshoe hares, though not as hefty. European hares, introduced from Germany in 1893, are much larger, weighing seven to thirteen pounds (three to six kilograms) and sporting big donkey ears. Also called jackrabbits, they now inhabit the southern Adirondacks, Vermont, and New Hampshire but live mainly in agricultural areas. Unlike the snowshoe hare, the newcomers do not have the ability—vital to many more far-northern mammals—to put on a white winter coat.

WHITE-TAILED DEER

Speed, Grace, and Tension

White-tailed deer are all grace, beauty, tension, and bounce. They are wound like tightly coiled springs, their hooves kicking into the air after barely touching the ground. Watching deer leap over obstacles in the flash of an eye, covering up to twenty feet (six meters) in a single bound, their white tails waving good-bye, you might find it impossible to imagine any predator ever catching one.

A deer's life, however, is one of almost constant stress, with its survival dependent on its powers of flight. Its chronic nervousness would send blood-pressure levels skyrocketing in humans. White-tails, in a sense, eat on the run, not fully digesting their food during early-morning and evening grazings in clearings. Later, retreating to safe, sheltered spots in deep woods, they ruminate like cows, summoning the cud

TOP RUNNING SPEED: About 42 mph (70 km/h)

AVERAGE SWIMMING SPEED: About 4 mph (7 km/h)

MAXIMUM JUMPING DISTANCE: 29 ft (8.8 m)

MAXIMUM JUMPING HEIGHT: At least 7 ft (2.1 m)

ADULT BODY LENGTH: Males 6–7.2 ft (1.8–2.2 m); females 5.3–6.6 ft (1.6–2 m)

AVERAGE ADULT HEIGHT AT SHOULDER: 2.3–3.5 ft (0.7–1.1 m)

WEIGHT: Males 200–300 lb (90–135 kg); females 120–175 lb (55–80 kg)

MARKINGS: Reddish-brown back in summer; dull gray-brown in winter; white undersides; fawns with white-spotted backs

back up into their mouths to chew before swallowing it again for further processing in their four-chambered stomachs. All the while, their huge ears and sensitive nostrils scan far beyond the field of vision for every rustling or whiff of danger. When a threat is detected, a raised, waving tail of one deer is a flag to all the others, signaling them to flee. They're sneaky, and often circle around to get upwind of a predator. Normally only the young, sick, or injured are caught. As a last resort, a deer's sharp hooves can disembowel a predator.

In the north, the cold grip of winter is probably the greatest natural reaper of white-tailed deer. Some 15 to 20 percent of the herd commonly perishes in an average season. Alternatively, several years of mild winters can allow a deer population to double or triple.

When snow piles up 16 to 20 inches (40 to 50 centimeters) deep, foraging over wide areas becomes too exhausting for deer. Small family groups and lone males migrate, sometimes as much as 90 miles (140 kilometers), to traditional deer yards. The refuges are in lowland hemlock, spruce, and fir stands or cedar swamps, providing dense shelter from the wind and snow. Loose herds of fifty or so deer tramp down the snow and find some safety in numbers against predators. Food is limited, with deer relying on their fat reserves for up to a third of their energy needs through the season. When the best food is all eaten, deer turn to less nutritious, harder-to-digest species, such as balsam fir and spruce, to stay alive.

The often haggard and hungry deer that survive winter may increase their numbers by 30 to 40 percent when fawns

Alias: Long-tailed deer, bannertail, Virginia deer, American fallow deer, *Odocoileus virginianus*

Calls: Light squawks, snorts, grunts. Fawns bleat.

Preferred habitat: Mixed and deciduous forests with abundant clearings and scrub

Summer home range: 0.3–3 sq mi (0.8–8 km²)

Food: Grass, sedges, flowers, clover, wintergreen, seedling trees, fresh shoots, especially aspen, yellow birch, mountain maple, and chokecherry, in spring; aspen and other leaves, plants, berries, water lilies, mosses, and hair lichens in summer; acorns, beechnuts, grass, clover, large-leaved aster, evergreen herbs, mushrooms, and berries in fall; buds, twigs, conifer needles and bark, especially cedar, red maple, yellow birch, white pine, dogwood, aspen, hazel, and hemlock, in winter

Average daily food helping: 5.5–9 lb (2.5–4.1 kg)

Gestation period: 6½ months

Average litter: 1–2

Birth weight: 3.5–8 lb (1.6–3.6 kg)

Weaning age: About 6 weeks

Average fawn mortality in first 5 months: 20–40%

Age of first-time breeders: Does breed at six months in low-density populations, 2½ years in high densities.

Fat reserves in late fall: 10–25% of body weight

Adult life span: Usually 2–8 years; up to 13 years in wild, 20 years in captivity

Predators: Wolves, coyotes, bears; rarely bobcats, lynx, red foxes

are born in May and June. Up to 70 percent of newborns, though, may not survive their first few weeks after a severe winter. Does find hidden, secluded spots in deep forests or grassy thickets to have their babies. The fawns, with almost no odor and their white-spotted backs blending in with the sun-dappled surroundings, remain well concealed for several weeks, until they can run fast enough to keep up with the herd.

When a threat is detected, a raised, waving tail of one deer is a flag to all the others

---

While groups of a few does and their young travel together along regular deer trails throughout spring and summer, bucks lead more reclusive, solitary lives. Males start growing antlers in April—budding, horny manifestations of their rising testosterone levels. The largest, strongest deer in their prime, between four and six years old, grow the biggest antlers, signifying their status to both potential mates and rivals. Native shamans often wore antlers in recognition of the power they represented. The Iroquois crowned their chiefs with antlers, saying they were like antennae, making them supersensitive to their surroundings. Male deer shorn of their antlers, in fact, quickly lose their aggression and sexual drive.

Testosterone continues to build in bucks even after their antlers stop growing in September and they've rubbed off the

BEST SENSES: Smell, hearing

BROWSE SIGNS: Roughly chewed or broken twig ends. Lakeside cedars often have distinct winter browse lines, where deer standing on their hind legs reach up to 6 ft (1.8 m) above the snow.

TRACKS: Double, curved, wedge-shaped hoof marks, about 2.8 in (7 cm) long, pointed in direction of travel

SCAT: Peanut- to jelly-bean-sized, brown oval pellets, called "fewmets," in piles of 20–30, in winter, lasting up to a year. Less-often-seen soft clumps of irregular black pellets stuck together in summer dissolve more quickly.

DAILY SCAT PRODUCTIVITY: Average of 13 piles of 30–40 pellets each in winter

ACCOLADES: Official state mammal of Wisconsin, Michigan, New Hampshire, and 7 other states

RANGE: All United States except southwest, north across most of Canada to northern boreal forest

FIRST APPEARANCE OF DEER ON EARTH: 45 million years ago

DEER PER SQ MI (2.6 KM²): 0.6–5 in heavily forested areas, 15–40 in more open regions

POPULATION ESTIMATES: Michigan, 1.8 million; Wisconsin, 1.7 million; New York, 1 million; Minnesota, 1 million; Maine, 330,000; Vermont, 160,000; New Hampshire, 80,000

ESTIMATED U.S. WHITE-TAILED DEER POPULATION: 20–30 million

ANNUAL NUMBER OF DEER KILLED BY HUNTERS IN UNITED STATES: About 2 million

ANNUAL NUMBER OF ROAD-KILLED DEER IN UNITED STATES: About 700,000

once-soft velvety linings. As the November rut approaches, their necks swell to twice their normal size and they become gripped with a mixture of lust and rage, marking out territories and seeking mates, but eating little. After outpushing their rivals in head-to-head matches, victorious bucks may strike up mating liaisons, each lasting a day or two, with a number of does, coupling with them frequently and passionately during their brief time together.

(40,000 in Michigan, 30,000 in Wisconsin)

PORTION OF POPULATION SHOT BY POACHERS: 2–10%

NUMBER OF DEER SPECIES WORLDWIDE: About 40

ALSO SEE: Eastern Hemlock, Moose, Quaking Aspen, Wolf, Deerflies and Horseflies

Their antlers form a separation layer and break off in winter, providing a source of vital calcium and salt for mice, rabbits, porcupines, and other gnawing vegetarians.

Lying at the limit of the white-tailed deer range, most of the north woods originally bore few if any of the fleet-hoofed herbivores. To the south, early pioneer society denuded the wild of hundreds of thousands of deer annually for food and buckskins. By the beginning of the twentieth century, the continent's white-tail population stood at a low point of fewer than 500,000. Yet, at the same time, logging, fires, and settlement in the north gradually opened up vast new areas of prime browse for refugee deer from the south. Commercial hunters shot great numbers to supply venison to northern logging camps and a largely deerless south.

Deer numbers gradually multiplied with the enforcement of strict game laws. Today, there are more than twenty million white-tailed deer in the United States alone. The maturing of second-growth forests, though, have made things less hospitable for northern deer populations, which fell dramatically with a series of severe winters in the late 1960s and early '70s. The steady march of climatic warming since, however, has helped their recovery in many areas.

WOLF

Respected, Feared, and Slandered

Probably no other animal has a more complex psychological relationship with humans than the wolf. Despite an ancient, deep-rooted fear of the great canine among humans, "man's best friend" is a wolf, domesticated as a dog. All dogs descended from wolves at least 12,000 years ago, possibly much earlier, and the two can still interbreed. Like all domesticated animals, dogs have proportionally smaller brains than their ancestors. Originally, they were probably lone wolves who learned to follow human bands, living off their scraps. Gradually, the stragglers were accepted into a human social and behavioral structure not unlike their own, forming perhaps the strongest bond between species in history.

Actual documented attacks by wolves on people are extremely rare through the ages. There has never been an authenticated case of wild wolves killing humans in North America. Even rabies is very uncommon

AVERAGE ADULT BODY LENGTH:
3⅓–4⅓ ft (1–1.3 m)
TAIL LENGTH: 13–19 in (33–48 cm)
HEIGHT AT SHOULDER: 2–2¾ ft
(61–84 cm)
WEIGHT: Males 70–110 lb (32–50 kg); females 40–90 lb (18–41 kg)
GERMAN SHEPHERD SHOULDER HEIGHT: 2.3–2.6 ft (70–79 cm)
CRUSHING POWER OF A WOLF'S JAWS: About 1,400 lb/sq in (100 kg/cm²)
CRUSHING POWER OF A GERMAN SHEPHERD'S JAWS: About 700 lb/sq in (50 kg/cm²)
BIGGEST GRAY WOLF EVER FOUND: 196 lb (89 kg), in Alaska
NUMBER OF WOLVES IN A PACK: Average 5–6; up to 12
RUNNING SPEED: Can trot at 6 mph (10 km/h) for hours and sprint up to 42 mph (70 km/h)
AVERAGE DAILY DISTANCE TRAVELED: 9–18 mi (15–30 km)

among them. Natives told of picking up and playing with wolf pups from their dens, while the parents merely backed away.

Given the respect hunter-gatherer peoples in North America had for the wild wolf, which was regarded as wise and trustworthy, it is probable that modern animosity toward wolves evolved more with pasturalism. Reviled by shepherds, ranchers, and farmers for preying on their stock, big bad wolves became the nemeses of the Little Red Riding Hoods and Three Little Pigs of folklore. The most cursed of individuals assumed the form of the hated beast, becoming werewolves. At the end of the world, in Norse mythology, the ravenous Fenris Wolf would be let loose to wreak death and destruction.

From colonial times, it has been humans that have wrought bountied death and habitat destruction upon wolves across North America. By the late 1800s, the wild canines were eliminated from New England, New York, and most of the Midwest. Tens of thousands more were wiped out in the western states up to 1942 under a federal law sanctioning extermination on all federal lands. State bounties that continued into the mid-1950s and early '60s left only a few hundred wolves around the Boundary Waters Canoe Area Wilderness in northern Minnesota, as well as a refugee population on Isle Royale in Lake Superior and perhaps a tiny handful on Michigan's Upper Peninsula. Full protection under the federal Endangered Species Act was finally accorded in 1974. Populations have since grown manyfold and expanded into northern Wisconsin since 1975. The odd wolf still wanders into Maine from Canada, at least two in recent years being shot, illegally, by hunters.

DISTANCE WOLVES ABLE TO SMELL A MOOSE: Up to 1.5 mi (2.4 km)

UPPER LIMIT OF HEARING: 26 kHz (6 kHz above human limit)

MARKINGS: Back and sides usually salt-and-pepper gray or brown, sometimes black or creamy; reddish-brown face and legs; light gray to whitish undersides; amber or brown eyes

ALIAS: Midwestern wolves are variously claimed to be members of the eastern timber wolf or Great Plains wolf subspecies of the gray wolf, *Canis lupus,* or northern members of the separate southern red wolf species, *Canis rufus,* with the proposed designation of eastern or eastern Canadian wolf, *Canis lycaon*.

CALLS: Deep howls; growls; barks; whines

PREFERRED HABITAT: Extensive, unbroken forests; beaver meadows and open bog and marsh rendezvous sites for raising young in summer

PACK TERRITORY: 20–215 sq mi (52–557 km²)

WOLVES PER 100 SQ MI (260 KM²) IN NORTHERN MINNESOTA: 5–10

FOOD: Fawns, moose calves, beavers, hares, groundhogs, mice, voles, muskrats, squirrels, grouse, and insects in spring, summer, and fall; young, weak, or old deer and moose, hares, and carrion in winter and early spring

AVERAGE DAILY FOOD HELPING: 2.2–13 lb (1–6 kg)

TIME IT TAKES A PACK TO EAT A DEER: 18–32 hours

ABILITY TO GO WITHOUT FOOD: At least 17 days

One of the most persistent charges leveled against wolves is that they ravage populations of game species such as deer and moose. Countless modern studies have shown, however, that the availability of browse and the severity of winters have a far greater influence on prey populations than do wolves. In most cases, wolves usually take less than 2 to 7 percent of the deer in their winter yarding areas.

With longer legs, wider feet, and a leaner build than dogs of comparable size, wolves are made for long-endurance running in snow. If they can stay within 100 yards (91 meters) of a fleeing deer or moose, they stick with it for up to 25 miles (40 kilometers), running it down in deep snow, often on frozen lakes. They concentrate on deer in areas where they're common, and otherwise switch to moose and hunt over larger territories. A healthy adult moose standing its own ground can normally keep a pack at bay with its hooves. Most victims are young, old, or weakened animals. By eliminating those individuals, wolves help isolate disease, ease pressure on limited browse from nonbreeding older deer, and keep the weaker young from passing on their genes.

Wolves themselves carefully regulate their own numbers through their social structure to ensure overhunting doesn't put their food supply in jeopardy. Packs usually consist of a dominant mating pair, their offspring from several generations and sometimes aunts, uncles, or occasional lone wolves that are gradually accepted into the pack. Only the dominant female breeds, in late February or mid-March, and she may sometimes be the pack leader. When the cubs are born two months later, they may almost double

ATTACKS ON DEER OR MOOSE SUCCESSFULLY COMPLETED: 8–10%

AVERAGE ANNUAL NUMBER OF DEER TAKEN BY A PACK: 60–180

DEN FOR CUBS: In-ground burrow, 6–30 ft (1.6–9.1 m) long, sometimes an enlarged fox den, hollow log, or rock outcrop; near water

GESTATION PERIOD: 63 days

AVERAGE LITTER: 4–6

DISPERSAL RATE: About 25% of pups, 50% of yearlings, 25% of young adults, usually in late winter and early spring

FARTHEST RECORDED DISPERSAL: 551 miles (887 km), from near International Falls, Minnesota, to Saskatchewan, in 1980–81

AGE OF FIRST-TIME BREEDERS: Males 2–3 years; females 2 years

AVERAGE FIRST-YEAR MORTALITY: 50–60%

AVERAGE ANNUAL ADULT MORTALITY: 20%

LIFE SPAN: Average 4–8 years; up to 13 years in wild, 15 years in captivity

PREDATORS: Bears and large hawks may attack cubs.

TRACKS: Front feet 4–5 in (10–13 cm) long, back feet 3.2–3.8 in (8–9.5 cm) long, proportionally wider than a dog's feet

SCAT: Like dog droppings, but usually grayish, with fur, bone fragments, and pointed ends, usually 3–5 in (8–13 cm) long

DAILY SCAT PRODUCTIVITY: Usually about one dump a day, three when the eating's good

FAMOUS WOLVES: The Big Bad Wolf, Akala, Lobo, Fenis Wolf

RANGE: Most of Minnesota, northern Wisconsin, and Michigan's Upper Penninsula, north across most of

the size of the pack. All members help in raising them, but the cubs are at the bottom of the totem pole. They are the last to eat, and during hard winters all may perish. If some adults leave the pack or die, there's room for more cubs to survive and the pack's number remains relatively constant.

Packs also keep population densities low by maintaining very large territories for their long-distance hunts and by warning other wolves to stay away. In addition to marking their manor with urine and droppings, packs declare propriety over all the land within earshot of their howling, which on still nights can be heard up to three miles (five kilometers) away by others of their kind. Wolves also howl to locate each other when individuals are hunting separately, as they often do in the

Canada to Alaska: also parts of Wyoming, Montana, and Idaho
FIRST APPEARANCE OF CANINES: At least 25 million years ago
POPULATION ESTIMATES: About 2,500 in Minnesota, 250 in Wisconsin, more than 200 in Michigan's Upper Peninsula, 8,000–9,000 in Ontario
ANIMALS THAT DEPEND ON WOLF LEFTOVERS DURING THE WINTER: Foxes, martens, fishers, coyotes, ravens, eagles
NUMBER OF CANINE SPECIES NATIVE TO NORTH WOODS REGION: 4
NUMBER OF CANINE SPECIES WORLDWIDE: 37
ALSO SEE: Coyote, Moose, Raven, Red Fox, White-Tailed Deer

summer. Each wolf has its own distinct voice that can be recognized by others in the pack. Often, before or after a nightly foray, all join in a group howl in excited anticipation of a feast. Next to actually eating, it's probably when wolves are happiest, tails wagging, joyously bonding like humans in the warm glow, or drunken revelry, of a sing-along. The pack leader starts off with a deep, long howl, joined by the other adults at different pitches and the cubs with yips and whines. They are especially vocal in August and September, when cubs hone their singing abilities and howl at the drop of a hat.

While considerably more secure than they were a few decades ago, the wolves of the upper Midwest and south-central Canada have somewhat of an identity crisis. Smaller and generally more reddish than gray wolves to the north, they were long considered a separate species, *Canis lycaon*, the eastern wolf. But a reclassification based on physical structures in the 1940s demoted them to a mere subspecies of the gray wolf, designated the eastern timber wolf. Then in 1995, leading taxonomists decided that Midwestern wolves should really be considered members of the Great Plains wolf subspecies. Even more recent genetic research, however, strongly suggests that the packs of central Canada and possibly the upper Midwest are not gray wolves at all, but rather the northern version of the separate, nearly extinct red wolf species. Only 200 to 300 southern reds survive, more than half in captivity. A small population was reintroduced in North Carolina in 1987.

WOODCHUCK

Sleeping through Its Greatest Moment

Away from the bright lights and fanfare, almost all northern woodchucks are fast asleep on their one day of celebrity. Only at Gobbler's Knob in Punxsutawney, Pennsylvania, and a number of other woodchuck hot spots, do a select few bask in the limelight on Groundhog Day, coaxed in front of cameras by formally attired civic officials. A lot rides on Punxsutawney Phil and his colleagues. If Phil sees his shadow, it is supposed to mean six more weeks of winter—probably because February 2 is often a typically crisp, sunny midwinter day that produces a good shadow. If he fails to find a shadow, spring is said to be imminent. The tradition, brought to America by German and other settlers, is based on the old European folk belief that badgers and hedgehogs could predict the weather. February 2 has been observed as a church holiday, called Candlemas, since Christian times, though originally it was the pagan festival of Brigid, celebrating the first stirrings of spring. It was one of the many days farmers gathered

HEARTBEATS PER MINUTE: 80–100 when active, 4–15 in hibernation

BODY TEMPERATURE: 99°F (37°C) when active, 47°–37°F (8°–13°C) in hibernation

TIME BETWEEN BREATHS DURING HIBERNATION: As long as 6 minutes

AVERAGE WEIGHT LOSS DURING HIBERNATION: About 25–30% by adults, 50% by juveniles

AVERAGE ADULT BODY LENGTH: 16–20 in (40–50 cm)

TAIL LENGTH: 4–6 in (10–15 cm)

AVERAGE WEIGHT: 4–12 lbs (1.8–5.5 kg)

MARKINGS: Varying shades of coarse brown fur, darkest on feet, face, and tail

ALIAS: Woodchuck, groundhog, chuck, whistle pig, bulldozer, *Marmota monax*

NAME ORIGIN: Derived from Algonkian language name for the animal, called *wejack* by Ojibwa

CALLS: Loud, shrill warning whistle, like a sonic squeak; low churring when threatened; growls when fighting

PREFERRED HABITAT: Open woods, rocky hillsides, meadows, and forest edges with lots of grass or leafy ground cover and thick loam or sandy soil

HOME RANGE: Up to 330 ft (100 m) wide

to, among other things, guess the weather for the coming growing season.

In a sense, woodchucks do forecast the weather, since they know north woods winters rarely end even six weeks after Groundhog Day, as do the inhabitants of Vermont, who call themselves woodchucks for their ability to hunker down and wait out the season. The big rodents—giant members of the squirrel family—keep sleeping right on through. Woodchucks are true hibernators and remain curled tightly in a largely uninterrupted, deep sleep for six months. Their body temperature can drop to just above freezing, bringing their metabolism almost to a standstill, so they use just a trickle of their stored fat. When males emerge in late March or April, with snow still on the ground, they must have enough fat to live off for several weeks longer, until new vegetation sprouts. (They do eat some buds and bark at this time, but have not been observed actually tossing the leftover twigs away, leaving unanswered the age-old question of how much wood could a woodchuck actually chuck.)

Males awake with romance rather than breakfast on their minds. They immediately look for a mate, fighting off similarly minded rivals who get in their way. This period of early-spring woodchuck activity, coming at the leanest point in the year for wildlife and humans, often provided a much-needed meal for native people in past times. Though a courting male enters the winter den of a female wagging his tail like a puppy, more often than not, the randy marmot is chased right back out by the wakened, grouchy occupant.

When the gentleman caller finally finds an agreeable mate, he makes himself

HOME: Ground burrow, 13.2–16.5 ft (4–5 m) long, with a bed chamber 18 in (45 cm) wide and 12 in (30 cm) high, lined with grass and leaves

FOOD: Grass, leaves, herbs, flowers, clover, berries, seeds, bark, occasionally insects and snails, rarely bird eggs or nestlings; bark, buds, and twigs in early spring

AVERAGE DAILY FOOD HELPING: About 1.5 lb (700 g)

GESTATION PERIOD: 30 days

AVERAGE LITTER: 4–5

BIRTH WEIGHT: About 1 oz (30 g)

WEANING AGE: 5–6 weeks

AGE OF FIRST-TIME BREEDERS: 2 years for most

AVERAGE ANNUAL MORTALITY: About 75% for first-years, 30% for adults

ADULT LIFE SPAN: Up to 6 years in wild, 10 years in captivity

PREDATORS: Foxes, coyotes, wolves, bears, bobcats, lynx, hawks

TOP RUNNING SPEED: 10 mph (16 km/h)

HOBBIES: Eating; basking in sun on top of rocks, on warm ground, or in low branches; and meteorology

FAMOUS FORECASTERS: Punxsutawney Phil, Jimmy the Groundhog, General Beauregard Lee, Pee Wee, Penniechuck Chuck, Dunkirk Dave, Ruffles, Staten Island Chuck, Holland Huckleberry, Wiarton Willie

GROUNDHOG DAY SPECTATORS IN PUNXSUTAWNEY, PENNSYLVANIA: Up to 40,000

PUNXSUTAWNEY PHIL'S FORECASTING ACCURACY: 40–100%, depending on who's interpreting the weather

ANIMALS THAT USE OLD WOODCHUCK BURROWS: Foxes, skunks, raccoons, rabbits, hares, mink, porcupines, squirrels, mice, snakes

at home in her burrow for a month or so. It is the only time adult chucks shack up. When she is ready to give birth in May, the female terminates the honeymoon and kicks her loafing spouse out for good.

Young woodies begin viewing the surface world four to six weeks after they are born. Around the latter half of June, when they are too big for their natal burrow, their mother puts some young ones in old dens nearby or digs new burrows for them. She's not out of their life and continues to visit them. But the quarters are only temporary. About a month later, the young are gripped with wanderlust and drift away. They may go just a few hundred yards or much farther before either finding an abandoned burrow or digging their own.

RANGE: Northeastern United States to Virginia, Alabama, Ozarks, and eastern prairies; also northwestern Montana, Idaho, and northeastern Washington; north to Alaska and across southern half of Canada

CLOSEST NORTH WOODS RELATIVES: Squirrels, chipmunks

NUMBER OF U.S. MARMOT SPECIES: 5

NUMBER OF MARMOT SPECIES WORLD-WIDE: 14

ALSO SEE: Clouds, Red Fox

Woodchucks dig quickly, excavating up to 700 pounds (320 kilograms) of soil for a burrow. Their homes usually have two entrances, with additional escape holes that drop straight down into their tunnels. Burrows often start on hillsides or gullies, slope 3 to 6 feet (1 to 2 meters) below the surface, then rise up to the main grass-lined sleeping chamber, protecting it from flooding. There are additional toilet chambers, which are cleaned out regularly. Older woodchucks may have both a summer burrow in an open feeding area and a winter home in or at the edge of a forest.

Around early June, a woodchuck's metabolism begins to slow, allowing the stocky rodent to put on considerably more weight as it continues lunching through the day. Much of the weight is laid down as energy-rich brown fat, which yields twenty times as much heat as the white fat possessed by humans. Stuffed and sleepy by the time most of their remaining food withers with killing frosts in early autumn, the whistle pigs block off their hibernating chambers before turning in, allowing other animals to use the rest of the burrow through the winter. The young of the year, having to eat longer to catch up with larger, older woodchucks, go into hibernation a little later than their elders.

REPTILES AND AMPHIBIANS

For many, our earliest experiences with wildlife involve catching frogs at local ponds and creeks. Through our lives, the spring and summer night choruses of many and varied froggy voices speak of tranquillity and refuge from busy urban lives. From thumbnail-sized spring peepers to "banjo-plucking" green frogs, they clamor for attention in the business of propagating themselves each year.

By contrast, salamanders and newts scurry in the leaf litter, or glide through aquatic habitats, in a silence that masks their immense numbers. Rarely seen, they are the modern representatives of the first vertebrates to crawl onto dry land hundreds of millions of years ago.

Reptiles, too, are largely inaudible. Like amphibians, they are cold-blooded, and cannot produce their own body heat to keep from freezing when the temperature drops below 32°F (0°C). Consequently, the north woods, with its cold winters, hosts relatively few snakes and turtles, and no lizards in most areas. Of the region's nine kinds of turtle, only painted and snappers are really common. Among the sixteen native snake species, the ubiquitous garter snake is the one seen by most people nine out of ten times. Unlike the world's tropical realms, which seem to have the same attraction to all things lethal as they do to sun-seeking tourists, the north has just two poisonous snakes, both of which are rare and limited in distribution.

Many of the north's turtles, and particularly its snakes, are rare because of human hostility. Too often, fear and ignorance have won over the natural fascination and curiosity we have as children for these often colorful, limbless or shelled wonders.

Similarly, in a world under ecological stress, amphibians are among the first to suffer. Creatures of both water and land, literally breathing through their moist, permeable skin, they are especially susceptible to environmental adversities of all kinds. As night choruses fade in many areas, awareness of them as one of the Earth's vital signs has grown.

AMERICAN TOAD

Land-Loving Warty Wonder

Toad, that under cold stone
Days and nights hast thirty-one
Swelter'd venom sleeping got,
Boil thou first i' the charmed pot.

Shakespeare's witches in *Macbeth* were not the first to employ toad poison for dark deeds. England's King John, the villain of Robin Hood stories, was rumored to have been poisoned in 1216 via a cup of ale spiked with toad venom by a monk who had overheard the unpopular monarch's plans to raise the price of bread. The poison in question was a bitter white liquid that toads, when molested, exude from their "warts" and the parotid glands behind their heads. The secretion irritates the mucous membranes in the mouth, eyes, and nose of predators, but does not cause warts, as commonly believed. Toads can also puff up their bodies with air to nearly twice their normal size, handy for convincing snakes that they're too big to be swallowed.

AVERAGE ADULT LENGTH: Males 2–3 in (5–7.5 cm); females 2.5–4 in (6–10.5 cm)

MAXIMUM LENGTH: 8 in (20 cm)

MARKINGS: Mottled brown, tan, rust, or green on back and sides bearing numerous, bumpy "warts"; gray-white undersides; males' throats darker than females'

ALIAS: Eastern American toad, hop-toad, *Bufo americanus*

NAME FOR A GROUP: A knot of toads

CALLS: High, musical, cricketlike trills in 15–30 second bursts

PREFERRED HABITAT: Moist upland forests, meadows; shallow ponds and marshes in spring

FOOD: Beetles, ants, grasshoppers, spiders, flies, worms, insect larvae, slugs, millipedes, moths

ESTIMATED NUMBER OF INSECTS A TOAD EATS IN 3 MONTHS: 10,000

With their relatively thick, dry skin and terrestrial lifestyle, toads appear to be closer to reptiles than any other amphibian. Their hind legs are smaller than frogs' legs, limiting them to shorter hops or outright walking. Their coloring blends with fallen leaves and needles and can change slightly with their surroundings, becoming darker when they are in moist, brown earth. Moisture requirements keep toads mainly in soft dirt depressions or under debris during the day. They can dig quite quickly with their back feet.

After more than six months of winter dormancy below the frost line, toads reemerge around late April or May and retrace their steps over the following days or weeks back to almost the exact spot where they first emerged from the ponds of their youth. Upon arriving, males call out in slow trills that gradually speed up with their metabolism as the weather grows warmer. Though these breeding serenades commonly continue through June, toad socials can be very brief on any one pond, males eating little for the duration and their appreciably larger mates leaving as soon as they lay their eggs.

Hatching just days later, tiny black toad tadpoles soon school in dark, darting clouds. Sun-warmed waters in their shallow nursery pools allow them to develop faster than any other amphibians in the north, sprouting legs in six to nine weeks, just in time to escape the midsummer disappearance of many small ponds. Tiny enough to sit easily on a fingertip, the toadlets remain around the muddy, weedy water's edge for a time and then fan out on rainy nights, some traveling more than half a mile (0.8 kilometer). Most toads noticed by campers, hikers, and cottagers are the 1-inch (2.5-centimeter) long variety, still in their troubled youth stage, through which few survive. Those that do, continue to grow throughout their lives and may reach the size of bullfrogs.

EGGS PER FEMALE: Average 4,000–7,000, up to 12,000, released like double-strand, gooey strings of beads around submerged vegetation, rocks, or sticks

EGG-DEVELOPMENT PERIOD: 3–12 days

TADPOLES: Fat, black, with short wiggling tails

NEWLY TRANSFORMED TOADLET LENGTH: About 0.4 in (1 cm)

AGE OF FIRST-TIME BREEDERS: 2–4 years

LIFE SPAN: Few live past 3–4 years in wild; up to 36 years in captivity.

PREDATORS: Skunks, raccoons, hognose snakes, garter snakes, water snakes, broad-winged hawks, crows, owls

RANGE: Eastern United States to South Carolina, Louisiana, and edge of prairies, north to Labrador and southeastern Manitoba

WINTER WHEREABOUTS: Up to 4.3 ft (1.3 m) deep in sandy soil on land

ONLY OTHER NORTH WOODS TOAD SPECIES: Fowler's or Woodhouse's toad, on west side of Michigan's Lower Peninsula, southern New Hampshire, southeastern Vermont

NUMBER OF U.S. TOAD SPECIES: 18

NUMBER OF TOAD SPECIES WORLDWIDE: More than 300

ALSO SEE: Wood Frog, Spring Peeper

EASTERN NEWT

Amphibian with a Triple Life

Masters of change, newts take metamorphosis one step further than other amphibians. After usually spending two to five years completely on land, they change color, regrow tail fins, and return to breed and spend the rest of their active lives in ponds. Newts can also regenerate rough approximations of severed tails or legs. When threatened on land, they lift their tails high above their heads, ready to escape when a predator snatches the expendable appendage.

Normally, though, slow-moving newts—called "efts" during their terrestrial stage—are less harassed by predators than are other salamanders. They possess nasty glands on their backs containing the same poison, albeit at lower concentrations, that makes the famous Japanese fugu, or puffer fish, potentially fatal. After being swallowed by snakes and toads, efts have been known to survive for up to half an hour before being regurgitated and making their escape. Their bright orange-red color serves to

AVERAGE ADULT LENGTH: 2.5–5.5 in (6.5–14 cm)

EFT LENGTH: 1–4 in (2.5–10 cm)

HATCHLING LENGTH: 0.3–0.4 in (7–10 mm)

MARKINGS: Efts have black-spotted pale undersides and orange-red backs with black-bordered red spots, which are less distinct in Midwest; aquatic adults have yellow undersides and olive-green, yellow, or brown backs, spotted with black throughout; eastern adults also have large red spots on their backs, not present or much smaller on Midwest adults.

ALIAS: Red-spotted newt (eastern subspecies), central newt (midwestern subspecies), pond newt, red eft, *Notophthalmus viridenscens*

PREFERRED HABITAT: Beaver ponds, slow, clear stretches of streams, shallow bays, and swamps with abundant submerged vegetation or bottoms with thick leaf litter and few predatory fish; moist, mature forests with lots of logs and thick leaf litter in eft stage; found at up to 5,250 ft (1,600 m) in Adirondacks

FOOD: Larvae of mayflies, caddis flies, midges, and mosquitoes eaten in ponds, as well as water flies, frog eggs, tadpoles. Efts eat springtails, mites, fly larvae, beetles, grubs, spiders, caterpillars, snails, slugs, worms.

warn would-be assassins of the unpleasant taste in store for them if they bite, allowing efts to wander about in daylight, during rainy weather, far more often than most salamanders.

After spending the first two or three months of their lives in the water, feeding by night and hiding in bottom debris during the day, larval newts develop lungs and lose their feathery external gills and finned tail edges. Their moist brown skin turns red and becomes rough and dry as they crawl onto dry ground in August or September. These red efts are land-loving, carefree, prepubescent newts. They mostly live under logs or leaf litter during the day and roam about on moist nights, traveling up to 870 yards (800 meters) away from their natal ponds in their first year on land. Small groups of them sometimes gather to absorb radiant heat around the base of tree trunks in spring, or gravitate toward the moist beds of evaporated ponds in June. In August and September, they frequent large decaying mushrooms, where they can feast on fly larvae.

Newts can also regenerate rough approximations of severed tails or legs

---

When the time comes to grow up, efts migrate back toward the ponds of their origin. They often travel through the summer along streambeds and down slopes to get there, arriving in August or September. Some, perhaps still migrating in autumn, or in spring, colonize temporary pools along the way and mate with

---

EGGS: Females lay 200–375 per season over several weeks of multiple breedings, 6–10 per day deposited singly on submerged plants or bottom debris.

EGG-DEVELOPMENT PERIOD: 20–35 days

LARVAE MORTALITY: 97–99%

EFT-STAGE DURATION: Usually 2–5 years; up to 7 years

LIFE SPAN: Average 7–10 years; up to 15 years

PREDATORS: Insects and leeches eat eggs; dragonfly nymphs and diving beetles eat larvae; fish, herons, water snakes, and amphibian blood leeches prey on adults.

MINIMUM DOSE OF EFT TOXIN TO KILL A MOUSE: 0.16 micrograms

MINIMUM DOSE OF STRYCHNINE TO KILL A MOUSE: 10 micrograms

EFT POPULATION DENSITY IN IDEAL HABITAT: Up to 1 per 4 sq yd (3.3 m²)

DEEPEST DEPTH FOUND AT: 40 ft (13 m) in larger lakes

NEWT MYTH: It is untrue that the number of spots on a newt's back indicates its age.

RANGE: All eastern United States to northeastern Minnesota and eastern Texas, north to central Ontario and Maritime provinces.

WINTER WHEREABOUTS: Efts hibernate under logs, rocks, and other debris. Most adults active beneath ice; some hibernate in banks below frost line.

NUMBER OF U.S. NEWT SPECIES: 6

NUMBER OF NEWT SPECIES WORLDWIDE: 43

ALSO SEE: Beaver, Redback Salamander, Fungi

waysided newts there from other ponds, allowing crossbreeding between populations. As they become sexually mature, their skin turns soft and moist again; thin, finlike keels re-form on their tails; and they head back into the water. They also change color to olive. In the east, adults are called red-spotted newts because they retain the striking set of black-bordered vermilion spots trailing down their backs that are also sported by efts. Those west of southeastern Michigan comprise another subspecies, known as the central newt, that usually lacks the bold adult spots.

Though some breeding occurs in autumn, spring is the most popular season for newt nuptials. If a female is ready and willing, mating can occur quickly, with little ceremony. If she needs convincing, a male resorts to the all-important mating dance, for which he retains very rough skin on his inner hind legs, used to clasp her behind the neck and hold tightly for up to several hours. All the while, he ritually waves his tail over her to fan toward her nostrils a chemical aphrodisiac released from a gland at the base of his tail. Finally, he lets go, moves ahead of his mate, and drops a capsule of sperm that she picks up in her cloaca. Females can either fertilize their eggs immediately or store the sperm sac, along with those of several other males, for future fertilization.

Adults remain in the water for the rest of the summer. Some may hibernate during winter on land, below the frost line, but many remain active beneath the ice. If their pond ever dries up, newts turn brown again and either go searching for a new pool or wait several days in hopes that their old water hole fills up once more. This makes them particularly well adapted to survive changing conditions where beaver ponds are started or left to drain.

GARTER SNAKE

Forest's Most Successful Reptile

Garter snakes are common and familiar just about everywhere, primarily because they are more adaptable than most other snake species, which are in retreat across the country. Slithering farther north than any other reptile on the continent, garters are generalists, hunting anywhere and eating almost any prey they can get their expandable jaws around. Their horizontal black-and-yellow color pattern—resembling the old-fashioned garters used to hold up men's socks—blends well with the grass, leaves, and litter in many habitats, giving garter snakes the advantage of stealth when stalking, or when hiding from larger predators.

A foolproof reproductive system also allows garters to be quite fruitful. At group-hibernating spots, called "hibernacula," in April, sometimes with snow still on the ground, garters hold orgies, entwining in knots of many mating snakes for up to several hours. As each cold, bleary female

AVERAGE ADULT LENGTH: Males 12–19 in (30–50 cm); females 16–30 in (40–75 cm)
MAXIMUM LENGTH: 4 ft (124 cm)
MARKINGS: Usually 3 yellow stripes on a black, brown, or dark green background, sometimes with a reddish tint; undersides greenish-white, yellow, or bluish. New England's maritime garter subspecies has prominent black spots along stripes but a faint or absent center stripe; red-sided garter subspecies in western and central Minnesota has red bars or spots between yellow stripes.
ALIAS: Eastern garter snake, common garter snake, grass snake, *Thamnophis sirtalis*
NUMBER OF TIMES ADULTS SHED SKIN ANNUALLY: 2–4
PREFERRED HABITAT: Moist ground near water, but can be found almost anywhere
HOME RANGE: Up to 2 acres (0.8 ha)
HOME: Rests under rocks, logs
FOOD: Toads, salamanders, frogs, earthworms, insects, mice, voles, bird eggs and nestlings, fish, tadpoles
SALIVA: Recent studies suggest may contain toxins and enzymes that help immobilize amphibians and other small creatures; not venomous to humans, but may cause swelling or burning rash for some

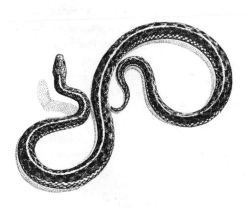

emerges from her winter sleep, she's joined by numerous waiting, writhing males, whose collective body temperature swiftly raises her own from about 39°F (4°C) to about 68°F (20°C), so she's no longer sluggish and vulnerable to predators. Some emerging males also derive the thermal benefits of this group hug by producing a female pheromone that dupes other fellows to their side until they've warmed up. As with all snakes, males have a choice of two penises, which pop up from the base of their tails. As well as producing many young at a time, females can store sperm from a single mating in their bodies to fertilize future eggs for up to five years. Thus a single female can slither far and wide to start a whole new population without needing to find a male.

Like many northern snake species, garters give birth to live young, usually around the end of August. Mothers may stay near their babies for several days afterward, and siblings often stick together for a few weeks, growing by frequently shedding their skin, including the clear scales that protect their unblinking eyes. Even as adults, snakes continue to grow, though much more slowly.

All snakes lack apparent noses or ears, are nearsighted, and probably do not have a sense of taste. Yet their senses are finely honed for survival. They smell by constantly darting their tongues out to pick up odors from particles in the air or whatever they touch. When they withdraw their tongues, the forked tips touch a set of twin sensory sacks at the roof of the mouth, called Jacobson's organs, which transmit the odors to the brain for identification. Snakes are also extremely sensitive to

DIGESTION: Large meals may take days, during which garters remain inactive, hiding beneath rocks or debris; a slow metabolism allows them to go weeks without food if necessary.

AVERAGE LITTER: 20–40

LENGTH AT BIRTH: About 5 in (12.5 cm)

FIRST-YEAR MORTALITY: 70–80%

AGE OF FIRST-TIME BREEDERS: 2 years

LIFE SPAN: Up to 20 years

PREDATORS: Broad-winged hawks, herons, ravens, crows, owls, mink, weasels, foxes, coyotes, raccoons, skunks, larger snakes

PEAK ACTIVITY PERIOD: During day, but takes cover during heat of summer and switches to night stalking

RANGE: All United States except southwest, north across Canada to James Bay and Great Slave Lake

WINTER WHEREABOUTS: Hibernates in large groups, often with other species, in rock piles, crevices, stumps, and decayed root passages 3 feet (91 cm) or more beneath the ground

LARGEST KNOWN GARTER COLONY: Estimated 75,000 snakes in several Manitoba limestone-crevice hibernacula, site of famous snake-pit scene in Indiana Jones movie *Raiders of the Lost Ark*

HIBERNATION CUE: Migrates to hibernaculum in September, but waits until ground surface forms frozen crust before retiring

AVERAGE WEIGHT LOSS DURING HIBERNATION: About 25%

FIRST APPEARANCE OF SNAKES: About 100 million years ago

VENOMOUS SNAKES OF NORTH WOODS REGION: Timber rattlesnake (southern New Hampshire, Vermont,

vibrations, which are relayed via the jaw-bone to the inner ear. They can judge from an animal's vibration whether it's small enough to be eaten.

Snakes themselves betray almost no body scent, and their heads appear tiny and harmless when poking through the grass. They strike like lightning, lunging up to half the length of their bodies, and usually eat prey headfirst and whole, the easiest way to both restrain and swallow still-struggling food. A snake's loosely hinged jaws can open almost 180 degrees. A garter has six rows of tiny, sharp, backward-curving teeth for drawing its mouth over prey rather than for chewing. To keep themselves from being eaten by mammals, garters when caught release a bad-tasting,

southeastern Adirondacks, west-central Wisconsin), massasauga rattlesnakes (Michigan's Lower Peninsula and west-central Wisconsin)

AVERAGE NUMBER OF AMERICANS BITTEN BY VENOMOUS SNAKES ANNUALLY: About 8,000

AVERAGE NUMBER OF U.S. SNAKE-BITE FATALITIES ANNUALLY: 15

PORTION OF VENOM FATALITIES CAUSED BY SNAKES: About 30%

NUMBER OF SNAKE SPECIES IN NORTH WOODS REGION: 16

NUMBER OF SNAKE SPECIES WORLDWIDE: More than 2,700

ALSO SEE: Draco

pale greenish-brown liquid from a gland at the base of their tails. The defense is not as effective against birds, which usually have a poor sense of taste.

Snakes have long engendered fear, reverence, and wonder the world over. The ancients viewed a snake's shedding of its skin as a symbol of rebirth. Hindu, Norse, and Egyptian cosmology all featured a great snake supporting or enfolding the world. The polar star, upon which the Earth's axis seems to spin, was said to be the eye of a serpent that fertilized the land. Similarly, China's snakelike dragons were powerful but beneficial beings that brought summer rains with their thunder. Zombie was a West African snake god and Quetzalcoatl, the great deity of the Aztecs and other Central American peoples, was a feathered snake.

Long ago, a now-vanished agricultural people that lived in large towns in the Ohio Valley left giant serpent-shaped earthen mounds. The enemies of the central figure of Ojibwa lore, Nanaboujou, were serpent people that lived beneath the water. But the Creator, Kitche Manitou, also gave snakes the job of protecting plants from overindulgent browsers.

GREEN FROG

Singing Shoreside Serenades

Frequently mistaken for bullfrogs, green frogs are actually far more common through most of the north woods than their more renowned relatives, who are absent from most of Minnesota, much of Wisconsin, and northern Maine and New Hampshire. Only a distinct ridge down each side of their backs readily sets greens apart from the bigger bulls. There's also no mistaking deep, drowning bullfrog choruses in June. Where both species are present, bullfrogs rule the waves on larger marshy bays, while their smaller look-alikes occupy the edges of slow, weedy rivers and ponds.

Once the ice disappears and late-April days consistently hover around 50°F (10°C), green frogs begin rousing from their muddy underwater winter beds. The ancient Greeks believed frogs were spontaneously formed from mud and could dissolve back into it, making them symbols of both fertility and resurrection. Their sudden appearance with life-giving rain

AVERAGE ADULT LENGTH: 2.4–3.6 in (6–9 cm)

MAXIMUM LENGTH: More than 4 in (11 cm)

MARKINGS: Green to olive-brown back, often with black spots or blotches; bright green above mouth; black hind leg bands; whitish undersides; distinct ridge down either side of back. Mature males have yellow throats and brown eardrum circles twice the size of the eyes.

ALIAS: *Rana clamitans*

SCIENTIFIC NAME MEANING: In Latin, *rana* is "frog" and *clamitans* means "loud calling."

CALLS: A deep, gulping "gunk," often described as sounding like the low twang of a banjo; 4 different variations, each sometimes repeated 2 or 3 times. Males also growl softly before or during fights.

HAYDN'S IMPRESSION OF A SINGING FROG: 2 violins, 1 viola, and 1 cello in Quartet No. 49 in D Major, Op. 5, No. 6 (no banjos)

PREFERRED HABITAT: Edges of slow, weedy rivers, ponds, marshes, swamps, and small, calm lakes or bays with lots of aquatic vegetation

HOME RANGE: 24–240 sq yd (20–200 m²)

MALE BREEDING TERRITORY: 3–20 ft (1–6 m) along water's edge

FOOD: Mostly beetles, flies, grasshoppers, ants, spiders, caterpillars,

also gave them status as rainmakers the world over. Stories of both the Iroquois and the Abenaki of Maine tell of a time when all the world's water was held inside a giant frog until their creation heroes, Ioskeha and Gluskabe, respectively, stabbed the bloated amphibian to release a deluge.

For the first part of spring, green frogs are fairly quiet, concentrating on eating and building up their strength. Then in June, when rising water temperatures warm their blood and passions, males inaugurate their long breeding season with deep, twanging choruses. Their verbal declarations continue well into summer, gradually trailing off in August.

At the start of the mating season, males spend two or three weeks carving out territories by the water's edge and establishing dominance hierarchies. The bigger the frog, the deeper its voice and the brighter yellow its chin. If not dissuaded by the sight and sound of one another, males will fight for territory, wrestling until one is dunked and sent packing. With all the time spent calling, patrolling, threatening, chasing, and fighting one another during the mating season, some males may lose up to a third of their weight. Subordinate frogs without their own territories are not harassed by property holders as long as they keep low in the water, like females, and call little attention to themselves.

After things are fairly settled, toward the end of June or early July, females, already bloated with eggs, inspect the breeding territories, looking for warm, shallow water and lots of aquatic veggy cover for their eggs. Once satisfied with a particular spot, a willing lass checks in

snails, and slugs; sometimes crayfish, little fish, and smaller frogs. Tadpoles eat algae, bacteria, and decaying vegetation.

EGGS PER FEMALE: 3,000–5,000 black-centered eggs, laid in a floating mat 6–12 in (15–30 cm) wide

EGG-DEVELOPMENT PERIOD: 3–7 days

TADPOLES: Green-brown with mottled tails and creamy, red-tinted bellies; fat-bodied

NEWLY TRANSFORMED FROGLET LENGTH: 1.2–1.6 in (3–4 cm)

AGE OF FIRST-TIME BREEDERS: Males 1–2 years, females 2–3 years

MAXIMUM LIFE SPAN: More than 5 years

PREDATORS: Snapping turtles, water snakes, raccoons, mink, foxes, herons, pike, and bass. Fish, dragonfly nymphs, giant water bugs, and leeches eat tadpoles.

FAMOUS FROGS: Kermit, Jeremy Fisher, Jeremiah, Dan'l Webster, Davey Croaket, Grandfather Frog

U.S. PROFESSIONAL-JUMPING-FROG SCHOOL: Croaker's College, Sacramento, California

RANGE: Throughout eastern United States to eastern Minnesota, Iowa, Missouri, eastern Texas, and northern Florida; north to Canada's southern boreal region

WINTER WHEREABOUTS: In mud between rocks and sunken logs at water's bottom

NUMBER OF FROG SPECIES NATIVE TO NORTH WOODS REGION: 9

NUMBER OF FROG SPECIES WORLDWIDE: 2,770–3,500

ALSO SEE: Leopard Frog, Lakes

with the local proprietor, who obligingly grasps all comers. As she releases her eggs, he gathers up thirty to fifty at a time with his hind legs, fertilizes them with his sperm, and then pushes them away. While they are thus engaged, for up to half an hour, a subordinate male may take over the breeding host's calling perch in hopes of hooking up with the next inquiring female.

Each egg is a tiny incubator, with a clear, porous membrane that swells like a balloon on contact with the water. In warm weather, they hatch in just a few days. The algae-eating tadpoles lead a fishy existence until transforming into frogs. Those hatching earlier in June may metamorphose in the same season, but most overwinter as tadpoles and transform the following summer. Almost immediately, they put their new legs to use, hopping onto land and, over the course of the summer, traveling up to 650 yards (600 meters) in search of new permanent bodies of water where they can settle. Along the way, they may sojourn in temporary ponds, puddles, creeks, and streams. It's one of the few times green frogs move far from the water's edge, but it allows them to colonize smaller pools that the almost totally aquatic bullfrog never reaches.

In their new homes, the young frogs feed close to the land during the day, then lie low to keep from being eaten by larger adults, who swim into the shallows to sing or hunt on the banks under the cover of night. While older frogs go into hibernation in early autumn, the young tend to follow them somewhat later, probably to build up enough fat reserves to get their little bodies through the long sleep.

Often on the same still rivers and bays, while green frogs feed on or near shore, the smaller mink frog moves in the opposite direction to forage in dense mats of water lily pads and other floating vegetation. It somewhat resembles a leopard frog, but with splotchy, less distinct markings on its olive-green back. The frog is named for the musky smell it produces if captured. Its hollow mating call, sounding like pieces of wood being struck together or the clatter of horses' hooves, can be heard on evenings from June to August. The nocturnal, bog- and creek-dwelling pickerel frog also sports a speckled leopard pattern, but with more squarish spots in straight rows on a light brown background. Found throughout the north woods east of Minnesota, pickerels are protected by skin secretions that are poisonous to other frogs and snakes.

LEOPARD FROG

Denizen of Pond and Meadow

Leopard frogs are probably the most-often-seen frogs because they are common both on land and in water. (In the latter, they lie stretched out, their eyes just breaking the surface.) They are, in fact, the most widespread frog species in North Amerca. With their attractive spotted markings, they blend well with the green grass and shadows of summer meadows or with algae beneath the water. Their main defense is sitting still, hopping only a short distance to a new hiding spot when chased. But they are still set upon by all manner of predators, from bullfrogs and cruel little boys to bass anglers and companies supplying high-school biology classes.

In late April or early May, rising water temperatures stir leopard frogs from their muddy winter beds deep beneath the water. They soon join the choir of spring peepers and other frogs already singing. Males, calling from under the water as well as above,

AVERAGE TIME BETWEEN SKIN SHEDDINGS FOR AMPHIBIANS: 1 month

FIRST APPEARANCE OF FROGS ON EARTH: 150–190 million years ago

AVERAGE ADULT LEOPARD FROG LENGTH: 2–4 in (5–10 cm)

MARKINGS: Black, irregular raisin-shaped spots on bright green or sometimes light brown or gray back; white undersides

ALIAS: Northern leopard frog, meadow frog, grass frog, *Rana pipiens*

CALLS: A deep staccato snore or chuckle about 1–3 seconds long (often described as the sound made by rubbing a balloon), usually followed by grunts; a piercing scream when attacked

PREFERRED HABITAT: Ponds, slow rivers, lakes, swamps, marshes, and moist meadows near water, with grasses 6–12 in (15–30 cm) high

FOOD: Grasshoppers, crickets, beetles, flies, spiders, snails, smaller frogs. Algae and decaying vegetation eaten by tadpoles.

EGGS PER FEMALE: 3,500–6,000 eggs, in spherical globs of jelly, about 6 in (15 cm) long and 2 in (5 cm) wide, often stuck to stems or twigs in shallow water

TADPOLES: Up to 5.5 in (9 cm) long, speckled olive backs, white bellies

make a snoring or chuckling noise to attract females.

Leopard frog eggs hatch ten to twenty days after being laid, yielding tadpoles that are like pieces of clay, constantly being remolded by metamorphoses to become something completely different. At first, tadpoles are tiny sluglike larvae, blind and with no mouths, hanging onto their egg jelly or to vegetation by sticky structures under their heads. They are nourished by absorbing their egg yolks. Gills filter oxygen from the water. Soon the pollywog's eyes clear, a mouth breaks open on its head, and it grows a tail, enabling it to swim and scrape up algae and decaying plant material to eat.

Over time, tiny hind legs begin to sprout and flaps of skin grow over the gills as lungs form. Front legs develop inside the covered gill chambers, breaking through the skin about a week before the amphibian uses them to crawl onto land. During the last stages of rapid change, the pollywog is like an awkward adolescent and cannot eat. Instead, it lives off the reabsorbed tissue of its shrinking tail, losing about 25 percent of its tadpole weight. Bones harden, true teeth form, eyes rise up from the head, a long tongue develops, and the intestine shortens to that of a meat-eater. Nine to thirteen weeks after hatching, the once fishlike creature has become a tiny froglet.

AGE OF FIRST-TIME BREEDERS: 2–4 years
TADPOLE MORTALITY IN FIRST 6 WEEKS: 95–99%
ANNUAL ADULT MORTALITY: Fluctuates greatly, averaging 60%
MAXIMUM LIFE SPAN: At least 4 years in wild, 9 years in captivity
PREDATORS: Dragonfly larvae, fish, aquatic insects. Leeches eat tadpoles; adults eaten by raccoons, mink, weasels, otters, garter snakes, water snakes, bullfrogs, great blue herons, kingfishers, bitterns, broad-winged hawks, turtles, bass, trout, pike, and many more species.
RANGE: Across northern United States to eastern Washington, south to northern Connecticut, Pennsylvania, Kentucky, Indiana, northern Illinois, Iowa, Nebraska, Colorado, New Mexico, Arizona, and northeastern California; north to Newfoundland and Great Slave Lake in Canada
ALSO SEE: Green Frog, Spring Peeper, Great Blue Heron

Leopards commonly travel a couple of hundred yards (180 meters), sometimes up to 2 miles (3.2 kilometers), between breeding ponds, grassy foraging areas, and deeper bodies of water to overwinter. Great numbers may migrate on rainy nights in spring and autumn, sometimes resulting in the death of hundreds or even thousands along a single stretch of road or highway. While still one of the most common of frogs, they have suffered steep declines in many parts of the country over the past forty years. Pesticides and herbicides were linked with population crashes after a dramatic drop in Wisconsin's leopard frog ranks in the 1970s. More recently, large numbers of deformities among leopard frogs in Minnesota and elsewhere have focused national attention on environmental threats to amphibians.

PAINTED TURTLE

Creature of Climate Control

In Iroquoian cosmology, the Earth rests on the back of a great turtle. The turtle had rescued the goddess Aataentsic after she fell from the sky into a vast ocean below. Mud scooped from the bottom of the sea by a muskrat or toad was placed over the turtle's back, forming the goddess's new realm, Turtle Island, the Earth. In a similar, Hindu story, the world was started on the back of Vishnu, transformed into a turtle after a great flood. Among some Algonkian-speaking peoples, who also had flood creation stories, the great turtle Makinak was the symbol of fertility.

Perhaps the best domed hero for the creation story would be the painted turtle, which spends much of its time, particularly in the morning, sunning itself above the water, usually on rocks and logs. Basking is more than just California dreaming for turtles, especially in the north. Temperature is everything to these cold-blooded creatures, whose body warmth rises and falls with that of their surroundings. Most reptiles need temperatures of at least 50°F (10°C) to function. But

AVERAGE ADULT SHELL LENGTH: 4–7 in (11–18 cm)

MAXIMUM SHELL LENGTH: 10 in (25 cm)

AVERAGE WEIGHT: Males 7–11 oz (200–310 g); females 11–16 oz (310–450 g)

MARKINGS: Olive, black, or brown shell, with sections divided by pale yellow lines, bright red dabs around the edges of shell, red-and-yellow streaks on dark gray skin of head and neck, red streaks on front legs; plastron (underside) usually all yellow on eastern subspecies in New England, yellow with a dark center blotch on midland subspecies in Adirondacks, Michigan's Lower Peninsula, and eastern Wisconsin, orange-red or red with elaborated black and yellow patterns on western subspecies in Minnesota, Wisconsin, and Michigan's Upper Peninsula

ALIAS: Mud turtle, pond turtle, *Chrysemys picta*

NAME FOR A GROUP: A bale of turtles

CALLS: Squeaks or sighs

PREFERRED HABITAT: Shallow, mud-bottomed bays, rivers, ponds, and marshes with plentiful lily pads, pickerelweed, or other aquatic plants and lots of logs or rocks for basking

FOOD: Lily pads, duckweed, and other aquatic plants; algae; snails; mayfly and caddis fly nymphs;

because they don't need to stoke an internal furnace with food to heat their bodies, the way warm-blooded mammals and birds do, their food requirements are much less. Painted turtles can't eat if their body temperature falls below 59°F (15°C). With a sun-powered metabolism, the more they bask, the faster they digest, and the more they can eat and store fat for the winter.

Temperature even determines gender, both for painted turtles and snappers. After mating, usually earlier in the spring, mother painted turtles crawl onto land on June afternoons in search of sandy stream banks or open hillsides, generally within 200 yards (183 meters) of water, in which to lay their eggs. They spend about forty-five minutes digging out 4-inch- (10-centimeter-) deep nests with their back feet, dropping their eggs, covering them up, and patting down the dirt with their plastrons before leaving them to incubate on their own. The location of the nest—whether it has a northern or southern exposure, or is partially shaded by plants—and the summer weather then dictates the sex of the developing embryos. Eggs that warm under fairly steady temperatures of 72 to 79°F (22 to 26°C) yield male turtles. At temperatures several degrees above or below that, Yertle becomes Myrtle.

Regardless of their gender, if there's already a chill in the ground when they burst from their eggshells in September, painted turtle hatchlings have to wait until spring to see the light of day. To survive the winter, they remain in their subterranean birth nests, living off their egg yolks. During cold snaps, they literally turn into turtcicles. Ice crystals form in their

beetles; tadpoles; crayfish; fish; fish eggs; salamanders; carrion. Young mostly eat aquatic insects.

AVERAGE CLUTCH: 5–10 capsule-shaped, wine-cork-sized white eggs. Some females may lay second clutch about 10 days later.

INCUBATION PERIOD: 60–100 days, depending on the temperature

NESTS LOST TO PREDATORS: Usually about 70%

HATCHLING SHELL LENGTH: About 1 in (2.5 cm)

ANNUAL ADULT SURVIVAL RATE: Up to 99%

AGE OF FIRST-TIME BREEDERS: Males 5–12 years; females 6–16 years

MAXIMUM LIFE SPAN: More than 40 years

PREDATORS: Eggs and hatchlings eaten by raccoons, skunks, foxes, mink, weasels, muskrats, crows, gulls, herons, bullfrogs, snakes, fish, and other turtles.

NUMBER OF ALGAE SPECIES THAT GROW ON SHELLS: 5

FAMOUS TURTLES: Yertle, Churchy La Femme, Brer Tarrypin, Makinak, Kumaa, Michelangelo, Donatello

RANGE: Northern United States, except northwestern third of Maine and far northern New Hampshire; south to Georgia and Louisiana; Oklahoma; Colorado; Idaho; and northern Oregon

WINTER WHEREABOUTS: Up to 3 ft (91 cm) deep in mud beneath water, or in bank burrows or muskrat lodges

NUMBER OF TURTLE SPECIES NATIVE TO NORTH WOODS REGION: 9

NUMBER OF TURTLE SPECIES WORLDWIDE: 257

ALSO SEE: Milky Way, Snapping Turtle, Wood Frog, Water Lily

blood, their hearts slow down to less than a beat per minute, and breathing stops altogether. Their temperature can drop to 18°F (−8°C), and up to 58 percent of their body fluids freeze without harming them. Within shrunken blood and tissue cells, a portion of unfrozen fluid remains. Though some frogs and insects have similar abilities, the painted turtle is the only reptile able to maintain this semi-freeze-dried state. A prolonged deep-freeze, however, occurring when there is not a deep enough overlying layer of snow to insulate the nest is fatal.

During cold snaps, they literally turn into turtcicles. Ice crystals form in their blood, their hearts slow down to less than a beat per minute, and breathing stops altogether

Once spring does arrive, hatchlings head straight for the water and stay there for the rest of their lives, save for brief sojourns by egg-laying females or occasionally by turtles relocating between feeding ponds and deeper water bodies for winter. Painted turtles eat, sleep, and hibernate underwater. Like all submerged turtles, they breathe by filtering water through special tissues in their mouths and in the cloaca, an all-purpose excretory and reproductive opening beneath the base of the tail. In the latter, the water is held in two small sacs, like aquatic lungs, that draw oxygen from the water into the blood in exchange for the body's carbon dioxide waste. Even if all the oxygen is used up during their muddy winter slumbers, however, the painted turtle can go without for up to 150 days, longer than any known vertebrate species.

Such abilities, together with their protective shells, also help give adult painted turtles perhaps the highest annual survival rate of any species ever studied, offsetting the very high predation rate on their nests and young. A recent study led by University of Michigan biologist Justin Congdon discovered that the more rare Blanding's turtle doesn't seem to ever grow old, and the same may be true of painted turtles. Unless struck by disease, predators, or accidents, the turtles don't physically decline and continue to lay eggs. Researchers are hoping to better understand aging in humans by learning the secrets of the turtle fountain of youth.

REDBACK SALAMANDER

Unseen in Multitudes

Salamanders are the oldest vertebrates on dry ground, closely resembling the first amphibians that evolved from fish and crawled out of the water almost 400 million years ago. Every summer, that moment in evolution is played out in the greatest historical reenactment on Earth, as amphibians emerge from their youthful aquatic stage to actually breathe air. With one foot in the water and the other on land, amphibians have lived through four planetary cataclysms, each causing the extinction of 50 to 95 percent of all species on Earth.

Even today, amphibians by far outnumber all land animals with backbones, comprising up to 75 percent of the vertebrate biomass in temperate forests. In the north woods, redback salamanders are the most numerous of all, totaling more than all the birds put together in one New Hampshire study. But they are seldom seen and never heard, being completely mute. They spend almost their entire lives in small hunting territories under fallen leaves, rocks, and

LIFE SPAN: Up to 30 years

AVERAGE LENGTH: 2.5–4 in (6–10 cm), including tail

MAXIMUM LENGTH: 5 in (12.7 cm)

MARKINGS: Reddish-brown back, dark gray sides, mottled with light gray near salt-and-pepper belly; "gray phase," with solid dark back, and sides, locally common in some eastern populations

ALIAS: Eastern Red-backed salamander, *Plethodon cinereus*

PREFERRED HABITAT: Mature deciduous, white pine, or hemlock forests with deep, moist soil strewn with logs and rocks

POPULATION DENSITY IN PRIME HABITAT: 1–4 salamanders every 5 sq yd (4.2 m²)

HOME RANGE: Usually stay within 2–3.5 sq ft (0.2–0.3 m²), but may travel more than 3 ft (91 cm) on wet nights

FOOD: Beetles, flies, ants, worms, spiders, mites, snails, slugs, sow bugs, centipedes

MATING SEASON: September–early October, on wet nights

AVERAGE CLUTCH: 6–10 eggs, hanging in bunches like grapes

INCUBATION PERIOD: 30–60 days

HATCHLING LENGTH: 0.8–1 in (2–2.5 cm)

AGE OF FIRST-TIME BREEDERS: About 2 years

PREDATORS: Snakes (especially ring-necked), owls, shrews, thrushes,

logs. Only in damp subsurfaces can they maintain the coating of moisture essential to their survival. So mysterious were salamanders to the ancients that the Greeks gave them their name, which means "fire animal," because they believed their moist skin allowed them to crawl through flames unscathed.

Without moist skin, salamanders would, in fact, be unable to breathe. Redbacks do not even have lungs. They use their skin and the roof of their mouths to filter oxygen from the air and to release carbon dioxide. Biologists speculate that they evolved in fast-flowing, cold streams. Without lungs, they were less buoyant and sank to the rocky bottom rather than being swept away with the current.

Evolution, however, has taken redback salamanders out of the water entirely. They go through their gilled aquatic stage inside the fluid of their egg cases, which the mother salamander hangs in a bunch from the ceiling of her nest cavity, usually in a rotting log, in June or early July. A mother stays with her eggs for up to two months. She wraps her body around the egg cluster, guarding it and keeping it moist but not mouldy with her skin secretions. The young look like miniature versions of adults when they hatch in August or September. They may stay in the nest with their mother for another one to three weeks before heading out on their own.

herons, and other birds; bigger salamanders

SENSE OF SMELL: Acute; grooves between mouth and nostrils detect scent of prey and other salamanders marking territories

CLOACA: All-purpose excretory opening at base of tail in most nonmammalian animals

RANGE: Throughout most of north woods region south to North Carolina, Ohio, and eastern Illinois and north to southeastern Canada

WINTER WHEREABOUTS: Underground, below frost line

AGE OF OLDEST AMPHIBIAN FOSSILS: 370 million years

LARGEST NORTH WOODS SALAMANDER: Mud puppy 10–20 in (25–50 cm)

NUMBER OF SALAMANDER SPECIES NATIVE TO NORTH WOODS REGION: 15

NUMBER OF SALAMANDER SPECIES WORLDWIDE: About 350

ALSO SEE: Eastern Newt, Humus and Soil, Falling Stars

Until setting up permanent residence on good hunting grounds, young salamanders are "floaters" and can have a tough time of it—especially so during dry summer weather, when larger, older salamanders occupy and fiercely defend territories in shrinking pockets of moisture within rotting logs and deep mineral soil. Up to thirty redbacks may stake out turf beneath or inside a large deadfall. Spring and early autumn, on the other hand, are times of plenty, when salamanders chance open-air adventures on moist nights or, much more rarely, rainy days. Such conditions serve up a bountiful buffet because the salamanders can cover more ground and imbibe in the vast selection of other little creatures beckoned to the wet surface.

REDBELLY SNAKE

The Little Serpent

Tiny denizens of darkness, pencil-thin redbelly snakes are seen not nearly as often as their numbers warrant. They spend the day hidden under rocks and logs, surfacing later to prey on other small crawling things that emerge under the cool cover of night. Smaller than any other snake in the north, redbellies themselves appear to be little more than long worms with backbones and brilliantly colored undersides. Variously described as timid and dainty when captured, they are apparently too small to bite, though they have been known to curl their upper lips in a nasty Elvis snarl. In contrast to its bright underside, the redbelly's rusty brown back blends with dead pine needles and other ground litter.

Redbelly snakes breed after emerging from hibernation in April, though some also mate in October, with females storing

AVERAGE LENGTH: 8–12 in (20–30 cm)
MAXIMUM LENGTH: 14 in (41 cm)
MARKINGS: Back and sides varying shades of brown, gray, or black, with dark or rust, sometimes indistinct, lines; bright pink or brick-red belly separated from sides by small dark spots; often with 3 yellow spots on neck, like a necklace; white chin and throat
ALIAS: Red-bellied snake, northern redbelly snake, *Storeria occipito-maculata*
PREFERRED HABITAT: Moist forests and woodland edges near bogs, marshes, lakes, and clearings
HOME: Under logs and rocks
FOOD: Slugs, earthworms, beetle grubs
AVERAGE LITTER: 7–8
AGE OF FIRST-TIME BREEDERS: 2 years

Described as timid and dainty when captured, redbelly snakes have been known to curl their upper lips in a nasty Elvis snarl

PREDATORS: Raccoons, milk snakes, crows, blue jays and other birds, turtles

ONLY DEFENSE: May release a mildly stinky musk if threatened

RANGE: Throughout eastern United States, except extreme northern Maine and southern Florida, to eastern Texas and eastern North Dakota; across southeast; Canada to Manitoba

sperm internally and fertilizing their eggs the following spring. Mothers give birth, rather than laying eggs, in late August or early September. Newborns, three or so inches (eight or nine centimeters) long, are dark with white neck rings. Like most snakes, they shed their skin for the first time about an hour or so after birth.

After spending much of the summer in meadows and clearings, redbelly snakes migrate in September and October, usually in rainy weather, back to forest hibernating spots. Dozens are occasionally seen migrating in the same direction. Slithering beneath stumps and into rock crevices, old animal burrows, and ant mounds, they sometimes share their hibernacula with the similar, though slightly larger, brown snake, which sports black spots down its dull brown back.

SNAPPING TURTLE

Relic of the Dinosaur Past

With its long, jagged-ridged dragon's tail, the snapping turtle is a living relic from the age of dinosaurs seventy million years ago. Effective, protective shells have given turtles little need to change through the ages. The snapper, though, is actually one of the few species of turtles that cannot fully retract its limbs into its dome when in danger. A small plastron, or underside shell, and very thick, meaty legs prevent the classic turtle defense. A razor-sharp beak and powerful jaws—capable of a painful, flesh-ripping bite—are instead the snapper's salvation.

Despite its fearsome reputation, the snapping turtle has pronounced vegetarian tastes. It is most carnivorous in the spring, before aquatic weeds are abundant, when it sniffs out water-bottom nooks and crannies for aquatic insects and crayfish and sucks up small, slow fish or frogs. Larger prey is dragged down to the depths to drown

Life span: Commonly more than 30 years, possibly up to 90 years

Oldest recorded age of a turtle (Marion's tortoise): 152 years

First appearance of turtles on Earth: 200–250 million years ago

Shell length: 8–14 in (20–35 cm)

Length from beak to tail tip: Up to 3.3 ft (1 m)

Average weight: 10–30 lb (4.5–13.6 kg)

World records: 65 lb (29 kg) "Minnesota Fats," caught in Popple River, Minnesota, in 1986, 4 ft (1.2 m) from head to tail tip, with a shell 19.5 in (44 cm) long, became a state fair celebrity before being tagged and returned to the wild. Largest snapper kept in captivity reached 86 lb (39 kg).

Markings: Black, brown, or olive shell, often covered with algae; dark gray or brown skin; underside plastron cross shaped and dull yellow or black

Alias: Common snapping turtle, snapper, *Chelydra serpentina*

Calls: Sometimes hisses when threatened

Preferred habitat: Muddy lake shallows, slow rivers, creeks, ponds, and marshes, with abundant submerged vegetation

Home range: About 7.5 acres (3 ha)

Food: Mostly algae, water shield, water lily roots, and other aquatic

before being ripped apart by the turtle's huge claws. But a snapping turtle almost always retreats swiftly when a larger animal comes near in the water. Only when trapped on land will it lunge quickly and accurately, up to eight inches (twenty centimeters), with its long neck outstretched. Once they bite, snappers hang on tenaciously. Some have had to have their jaw muscles cut before they let go.

Normally, snapping turtles don't chance being trapped on land. They spend most of their time underwater, often partly buried in mud during the day, sometimes poking their hooked snouts and eyes just above the surface while resting in shallows. They are active mainly at night.

From June to early July, however, females seek out dry, sandy, or gravelly sites for laying their eggs, usually within twenty yards (eighteen meters) of water. Working most often in the morning, they dig holes four to six inches (ten to fifteen centimeters) deep in shore embankments or hillsides with their hind feet, deposit their eggs, cover them up, and leave. The site must be in the open, where the sun can incubate the eggs. Under such exposed conditions, 50 to 90 percent of all nests are cleaned out by predators. Most of the tiny turtles that do hatch in September or early October have fairly soft shells and are soon eaten by birds and fish. To survive, they probably have to bury themselves in the mud quickly and go into hibernation before even having their first meal.

plants; insects; occasionally dead, ailing, or slow fish, crayfish, frogs, ducklings, baby muskrats, snakes, snails, leeches, carrion

MATING SEASON: Mainly after emerging from winter torpor, when water temperature reaches 61°F (16°C), in late April and May, but mating can occur throughout summer

AVERAGE CLUTCH: 20–70 rubbery round white eggs, like small Ping-Pong balls

INCUBATION PERIOD: 55–125 days, depending on temperature

HATCHLING SHELL LENGTH: 1–1.5 in (2.5–3.8 cm)

AGE OF FIRST-TIME BREEDERS: 16–18 years old

PREDATORS: Skunks, foxes, minks, muskrats, raccoons, and otters eat eggs; blue herons, crows, hawks, bullfrogs, snakes, and fish eat hatchlings. Adults killed by otters, and rarely by bears and coyotes.

BEST SENSE: Smell

RANGE: All eastern United States to Rockies, except northwestern third of Maine and far northern New Hampshire; also across southern Canada

WINTER WHEREABOUTS: Inactive beneath mud, vegetation, or logs at bottom of water, or dug into banks, often in groups

ALSO SEE: Painted Turtle, Leeches

While very few snappers make it to adulthood, those that do are longer-lived than any other animal in the north woods. Little wonder many cultures regarded turtles as symbols of longevity, tranquillity, and happiness. Their reproductive lives are far longer than those of humans. Females play the odds by producing a new clutch almost every spring until they are in their seventies.

SPRING PEEPER

The Loudest Animal on Earth

Ounce for ounce, or a fraction thereof, the spring peeper is probably the loudest animal on Earth. Only about the size of a nickel or quarter and rarely actually seen, peepers make themselves very conspicuous on late-April and May nights, when their high, musical calls join together in a resonating din. Choruses of untold numbers sound to some ears like distant sleigh bells. To sing, males squeeze air over their vocal cords and amplify the sound by inflating their throats into huge balloonlike bubbles, producing a springy note that can carry for at least a third of a mile (half a kilometer).

Spring peepers are one of the first frogs to sing in spring. Awakened in their beds beneath the leaf litter by the thawing of the earth, they rise en masse on the first rainy nights of the season, when temperatures hit about 48°F (9°C). In rare cases when conditions are ideal, the ground crawls with thousands of peepers, wood frogs, and blue- or yellow-spotted salamanders, drawn to their ancestral ponds like

SOUND LEVEL OF SPRING PEEPER CALL AT 4–8 IN (10–20 CM): 110–120 decibels

SOUND LEVEL OF JET ENGINE AT 70 YD (64 M): 120 decibels

SOUND LEVEL OF AVERAGE CONVERSATION: 60 decibels

SOUND LEVEL OF CONSPIRATORIAL, SUBDUED CONVERSATION: 40 decibels

AVERAGE ADULT LENGTH: 0.8–1.5 in (2–3.7 cm)

MARKINGS: Tan, greenish-brown, or gray back with dark X; black bands on legs; white throat and belly

ALIAS: Northern spring peeper, *Pseudacris crucifer*

CALLS: Shrill, piercing "peeeep" rising in pitch, lasting about a second, constantly repeated

PREFERRED HABITAT: Wetlands and small temporary ponds in spring; damp forests and bushy areas, even in uplands, in summer and fall

HOME RANGE: 4–18 ft (1.2–5.5 m) in diameter

BREEDING TERRITORY: 4–18 in (10–45 cm) wide

FOOD: Mosquitoes, gnats, ants, beetles, caterpillars, spiders, mites, sometimes worms and snails; algae when a tadpole

EGGS PER FEMALE: 200–1,000 eggs, laid singly or in small clusters

EGG-DEVELOPMENT PERIOD: 5–15 days

TADPOLES: Up to 1 in (2.5 cm) long, with gold-speckled green backs and white bellies

zombies, entranced by the urge to breed. Often migrating with patches of snow still on the ground, they slip under the ice at the edges of ponds.

Males immediately take up positions around the pool, several days before the opposite sex will be drawn by their ringing voices. Balladeers usually sit on floating twigs, tufts of grass, or low branches, allowing each shrill peep to resonate freely over the water. In Michigan, Wisconsin, and Minnesota, tiny chorus frogs sometimes join in, with a call that sounds like the teeth of a comb being flicked. During cold snaps, the frogs quiet down. But as the temperature warms, the singers pick up the tempo, with each member of a peeping choir calling out in counterpoint to the others around them, as often as once every second. Some researchers speculate that those with the fastest, deepest peeps attract the most females. If a male can draw an admirer plump with eggs, he jumps on her back and swims with her for hours, often all night, fertilizing hundreds of her eggs as she releases them onto submerged vegetation and debris.

AGE OF FIRST-TIME BREEDERS: 3–4 years

PREDATORS: Fish, other frogs, turtles, snakes, birds. Salamanders, dragonfly nymphs, diving beetles, giant water bugs, and fish eat tadpoles and eggs.

MAXIMUM JUMPING DISTANCE: More than 20 in (50 cm)

RANGE: All eastern United States to northern Florida, eastern Texas, Missouri, and northeastern Minnesota, north to midboreal eastern and central Canada

WINTER WHEREABOUTS: Hibernate beneath ground or leaf litter

FIRST APPEARANCE OF TREE FROGS IN EVOLUTION: 26 million years ago

NUMBER OF TREE FROG SPECIES NATIVE TO NORTH WOODS REGION: 5

NUMBER OF TREE FROG SPECIES WORLDWIDE: 630

ALSO SEE: Wood Frog

Peeper choruses fall silent by early June, though a few individualists sometimes call before retiring for the season in early autumn. While risking fatal late freezes, the spring peepers' early breeding gives tadpoles a chance to mature into tiny, bee-sized frogs by the end of July, as their small ponds are drying up in the summer heat. More than half of the ponds in a Michigan study usually evaporated before or during peeper transformation.

With remnants of their youthful tails still trailing behind their new legs, they spread out over wide areas and spend the rest of the year on land, hunting for insects at night, resting during the day under logs, rocks, and leaves. Clinging to vertical surfaces with sticky toe disks formed by bits of overlapping skin, like other members of the tree frog family, spring peepers climb up low bushes and stems. In addition to the amazing feat of projecting their voices great distances, the tiny frogs can leap more than seventeen times their own body length when moving from branch to branch.

WOOD FROG

The Deep-Freeze Forest Bandit

Hopping through dark forest interiors all the way to Alaska and the Arctic Circle, the wood frog ventures farther north than any amphibian on the continent. European explorers in search of the potentially lucrative Northwest Passage found instead only icebound seas and the improbable presence of the black-masked bandits on the barren wastes. Captain Francis Smith was dumbfounded upon making landfall near the Arctic Circle in May 1747 to find it thronging with vast multitudes of thunderously quacking wood frogs.

Even in the northern continental states, woodies are tough frogs, settling under a cover of dry forest litter in the autumn and waiting for the snow to fall. They can slumber on a bed of frosted leaves as cold as 21°F (−6°C) and withstand up to 65 percent of their internal fluids turning to ice crystals. To keep from completely freezing, they flood their bodies with glucose from stored carbohydrates in

Average adult length: 1.2–2.4 in (3–6 cm)

Maximum length: 3.3 in (8 cm)

Markings: Distinct yellow-lined black "mask" running behind each eye; brown, tan, gray, or reddish-brown back and sides; white undersides, sometimes darkly mottled; dark bars across legs; males darker brown during breeding season

Vocal sacs: Gleaming white when inflated at the sides of male's head

Alias: Robber frog, *Rana sylvatica*

Scientific name meaning: Sylvatica, from Latin *sylva*, meaning "wood"

Calls: Mating song sounds like high-pitched duck quacks; males also chirp when grabbed by other lusty fellows, to tell them they've made a mistake.

Preferred habitat: Damp portions of the forest floor; shrubby, temporary woodland ponds, swamps, and marshes in early spring; up to 3,800 ft (1,160 m) in altitude in New England

Home range: 3.5–440 sq yd (3–370 m²)

Food: Beetles, flies, mosquitoes, ants, caterpillars, spiders, snails, slugs. Tadpoles eat algae and bacteria.

Portion of males that get to mate each year: About 20%

Portion of males that mate twice in a season: About 1%

their livers. By thus elevating their blood sugar levels to some sixty times the summertime norm, they create a sweet natural antifreeze that prevents crystals forming within cells and causing damage.

As soon as the snow is mostly gone and the litter layer thawed in mid-April to early May, male wood frogs rise. As the world's most posthumously famous idler, Henry David Thoreau, wrote of the early-rising frog in the spring of 1859: "He is wholly of the earth, sensitive as its skin in which he lives and of which he is a part. His life relaxes with the thawing ground." The newly roused bachelors make straight for the leaf-filled meltwater pools, ponds, and wetlands from whence they hatched. There, floating largely unseen in the water, they begin quacking like phantom ducks as the thermometer rises toward 50°F (10°C). The larger females join them a few days later, each drawing half a dozen or more males around them in a cackling frenzy. He who holds on the tightest remains fastened onto the object of his desire anywhere from an hour to three days, when the pair finally spawn.

Parents have no time to lose to ensure their progeny develop legs before natal swimming holes dry up. The mating prom may be over in as little as a few days at a single pond. With gatherings starting earlier on open marshes than in dark, forest ravine pools, wood frog calls may be heard for two or three weeks before finally fading.

EGGS PER FEMALE: 400–2,500 black-centered eggs in a globular clump, 0.8–2 in (2–10 cm) wide, around a submerged stem or twig, turning green with algae after a week or so
EGG-DEVELOPMENT PERIOD: 10–30 days
TADPOLES: Hatch 0.3–0.4 in (7–10 mm) long, grow to 1.2–2 in (3–5 cm), with yellow-spotted olive backs and iridescent, pink-tinted bellies
PORTION OF EGGS THAT YIELD TADPOLES SURVIVING TO FROGDOM: About 4%
AGE OF FIRST-TIME BREEDERS: 2–3 years
MAXIMUM LIFE SPAN: At least 4 years
PREDATORS: Raccoons, mink, garter, ring-necked, and ribbon snakes; herons, bitterns, and other large birds. Turtles, red-spotted newts, yellow-spotted salamanders, diving beetles, leeches, and caddis fly larvae eat tadpoles.
RANGE: Northeastern United States to North Dakota, northern Illinois, Ozarks, Kentucky, northern Georgia and Virginia; north to the Arctic Circle in Alaska and Canada; western subspecies in Rockies
WINTER WHEREABOUTS: In the forest litter layer and under rocks, logs, and stumps
ALSO SEE: Spring Peeper, American Toad, Mosquitoes

In a choice spot, where a submerged branch lies well exposed to the sun, many wood frog mothers mass their gooey blobs of dark-centered eggs together. After a couple weeks, the tadpoles hatch and have aquatic childhoods as brief as forty days, developing faster than the larvae of any other North American frog. By early summer, the few that survive the cold, predators, and competition for food take to land as froglets.

PLANT KINGDOM

PLANTS

t is said that Native Americans had no word for "wilderness." The bush was their home, their provider, a vast pharmacopoeia and treasure trove of life-giving substances, with each plant having its place and purpose, its secrets and mysteries. Many native peoples saw plant spirits as benevolent healers aiding them against diseases sent by offended animal spirits when hunters did not show them proper veneration. Recognition of the curative powers of plants and appreciation of their beauty stretch far back into humanity's prehistory. Soil studies of 60,000-year-old Neanderthal grave sites have revealed that the dead were laid to rest on beds of spring flowers, all known in more recent times as traditional folk remedies.

Native or folk medicines, such as those mentioned in this book, are not recommended for those unschooled in their preparation. The same active ingredients that give plants their curative powers are also often poisonous in large concentrations.

In addition to the many hundreds of species of flowering plants, including trees and grasses, in the north woods, there are many other kinds of vegetation, such as spore-producing ferns and mosses. For convenience, this section includes fungi and lichens, which are not actually part of the plant kingdom at all, though they are popularly perceived as such. They predate the evolution of modern plants and reach back toward the origins of life.

BLUE BEAD LILY

Lush Leaves of Summer

HEIGHT: 6–16 in (15–40 cm)
ALIAS: Clintonia, yellow clintonia, corn lily, northern lily, dogberry, wild corn, *Clintonia borealis*
FLOWERS: Pale to greenish-yellow, loosely bell-shaped, 3–8 per plant at top of stem, each 0.8 in (2 cm) wide, with 3 petals and 3 petal-like sepals, 6 golden stamens, and a long green pistil
BERRIES: Navy blue, shiny, 0.4 in (8–10 mm) wide, each on a long stalk and containing 6–10 seeds
LEAVES: Up to 1 ft (30 cm) long, 1.6–3.6 in (4–9 cm) wide, thick, glossy, bright green above, downy on bottom, with bluntly pointed tip and parallel veins. Usually 3 arch from the base of the flowering stem, occasionally 2, 4, or 5.
ROOTS: A thin, knotted, branching rhizome near surface, producing colonies
PREFERRED HABITAT: Coniferous and mixed forests and alpine meadows
RANGE: Throughout north woods region to New Jersey, around Great Lakes and along Appalachians to Tennessee; north in eastern Canada to Hudson Bay and Manitoba

The blue bead lily, with its lush, tulip-like leaves, stands out in the heart of the summer forest like few other woodland plants. In patches receiving the most sunlight, sturdy green stems rise from between the glossy, rubbery leaves. Each stem bears several smooth, round berries, like navy-blue beads, giving the lily its name. The plant's other common name, yellow clintonia, is more applicable in late May and June, when its greenish-yellow flowers nod from the stem tops. Though the sharply pointed, flaring petals turn more purely yellow as they mature, they are far less striking than the single dark blue berry that each flower produces if pollinated.

Happily gobbled by chipmunks, the attractive berries are nonetheless bitter, and some authorities say mildly poisonous to humans. One tale, passed down from native groups, held that dogs poisoned their teeth with the berries before a hunt.

BLUEBERRY

Carb-Loading in the Bush

*It must be on charcoal they fatten their
  fruit.*
*I taste in them sometimes the flavor of
  soot.*
*And after all, really they're ebony
  skinned:*
*The blue's but a mist from the breath of
  the wind.*

—ROBERT FROST, *"Blueberries"*

Thick networks of buried root runners
ensure that blueberry patches survive
ground fires and rebound to flourish like
never before. Native Americans knew this
well and regularly burned choice areas to
encourage bountiful harvests. One native-
tended colony in Maine has been determined to be more than 900 years old.
Blueberries were an important food source
for woodland peoples. Dried or charred
berries, added to wild rice, meat, or bread,

HEIGHT: Usually 12–14 in (30–35
cm); up to 2 ft (60 cm)

ALIAS: Lowbush blueberry, low
sweet blueberry, late low blueberry, whortleberry, bilberry
(really European varieties of blueberry), deerberry, *Vaccinium
angustifolium*

FLOWERS: White, like tiny bells, up
to 0.2 in (6 mm) long, in clusters

LEAVES: 0.3–1.2 in (1–3 cm) long,
rounded, leathery, turning
reddish-purple in exposed areas,
bright crimson in fall

BERRIES: Green at first, turning
pink, reddish-purple, and finally
dark blue-purple when ripe in late
July and August

*AVERAGE NUMBER OF SEEDS PER
BERRY:* More than 100

FLAVOR CELLS: Most sweetness is in
the skin, making wild berries more
tasty than large, pulpy commercial varieties.

PREFERRED HABITAT: Dry, acidic soil
in rocky or sandy clearings; along
shorelines, islands, open hilltops,
and ridges; bog edges; jack pine
barrens; open spruce-fir forests;
and recently burned areas

COMMON DINERS: Bears, coyotes,
deer, foxes, raccoons, martens,
rabbits, chipmunks, mice, voles,
ruffed grouse, robins and other
thrushes, white-throated sparrows, blue jays, orioles, scarlet

225

provided vital nutrients during the long winter. Crushed blueberries were also used to make a blue-gray dye, later commonly used for the attire of New England whalers.

Blueberries are the most common and best loved of a galaxy of summer berries. Their ripening is perfectly timed, through millions of years of natural selection, for just after the late-spring/early-summer bug-population peak, when birds are searching for new sources of food. Even most fruit- and seed-eating birds nest when insect numbers are highest, because bug meals, with up to 70 percent protein, are needed for their hatchlings to reach adult size in the space of a couple of weeks. After the young have flown the coop, many birds are happy to switch back to fruits and berries, which are 3 to 13 percent protein.

Like most other summer berries, blueberries are high in carbohydrates, or sugars, and low in fats. Fruits and berries ripening later in the year are higher in the easily stored, longer-burning fats needed by birds in migration. Blueberries' conspicuous color advertises their presence to birds, while their sweet smell attracts many mammals, from mice to bears. Fluctuations in berry crops have a major effect on animal populations. By enticing wildlife with juicy flesh, blueberries and other fruit-producing plants have their seeds spread and fertilized by way of bird and mammal droppings.

tanagers, catbirds, chickadees, brown thrashers

NATIVE REMEDIES: Ojibwa used leaf tea as a blood purifier and inhaled the fumes of dried, heated flowers for mental illness. The leaves contain the chemical myrtillin, which acts like insulin to reduce blood sugar, as well as other minerals that serve as blood purifiers and are used to treat kidney problems. The same ingredient, though, can be toxic in high concentrations.

RANGE: Throughout north woods region south to New Jersey and along Appalachians to West Virginia

OTHER BERRY-BEARING HEATH PLANTS: Velvet-leaved blueberry, cranberry, bearberry, creeping snowberry, black huckleberry, wintergreen

NUMBER OF HEATH SPECIES WORLDWIDE: 1,300

ALSO SEE: Bees, Wasps, and Hornets; Black Bear; Blackflies; Moss

Most often, blueberry seeds take root and thrive in dry, rocky habitats, helping to hold down the thin layer of soil painstakingly built up by lichens, mosses, and grasses. Once established, lowbush blueberries spread out in dense, tangled colonies, sending forth underground stems that sprout new plants. As with other heath or open-area shrubs, the shed blueberry leaves are slightly toxic to tree seedlings in the surrounding litter, keeping them from growing up and shading out the shrubs.

In late May and June, blueberries produce tiny white flowers that hang downward and are pollinated by blackflies, small bees, and ants. Widely varying amounts of nectar in each flower increase cross-pollination by keeping insects flitting from one to another until they finally hit a jackpot.

BUNCHBERRY

Hair-Trigger Pollination

HEIGHT: 2–8 in (5–20 cm)
ALIAS: Pop flower, dwarf dog-wood, cracker berry, *Cornus canadensis*
FLOWERS: 4 large, white petals (actually "bracts," or modified leaves), with about a dozen tiny greenish-white true flowers in the center
BERRIES: Scarlet, in small clusters, 1 large seed in each berry, ripening in mid- to late summer; eaten by bears, voles, mice, grouse, thrushes, vireos, and sparrows. Seeds take 3 years to germinate.
LEAVES: 6 on flowering plants, 4 on sterile plants, all meeting at same level on stem; dark green, smooth-edged, with distinct parallel veins, turning deep red in autumn and staying on plant until spring
PREFERRED HABITAT: Moist, cool forests, often with rich, acidic soil
MAXIMUM LIFE SPAN: At least 36 years
RANGE: Throughout north woods region south along Appalachians to Virginia through Great Lakes states, northern prairies, and Pacific Northwest, scattered along Rockies to New Mexico; north across Canada to Alaska

Clumps or mats of shade-tolerant bunchberry spread their striking white flowers in June. The plant is actually a shrub, a member of the dogwood family. But since an erect woody stem wouldn't give it any more chance of getting extra light beneath the trees, it conserves the little energy it receives by growing its stem horizontally beneath the ground, often for many yards.

Bunchberry plants poking above the soil are actually branches attached to the buried stem. Because its root system can survive the winter, bunchberry can use its limited energy to grow slowly but steadily.

The cluster at the center of each flower is actually made up of many individual tiny flowers. They remain closed, their stamens tightly bound, until fully mature. Then, when an insect or animal, or falling debris, touches a spike sticking up from one of the closed petals, they pop open, springing their stamens forward and catapulting their pollen into the air.

227

CANADA MAYFLOWER

Multitudinous Tiny Forst Forb

anada mayflower is not often given its due, being passed off with names such as "false lily of the valley," implying secondary significance to a refined garden import. In fact, Canada mayflower was considered a true lily until a recent breaking up of that family by busybody botanists. But it remains one of the most common of all forest plants from Maine to Minnesota. The sheer ubiquity of its lacy white spires of blossoms, in multitudes throughout the region, could easily make it floral emblem of the north woods.

But Canada mayflowers are tiny and bloom early. The vast majority produce no

HEIGHT: 2–10 in (5–25 cm), usually under 6 in (15 cm)

ALIAS: Wild lily of the valley, false lily of the valley, Canada maianthemum, May lily, bead ruby, *Maianthemum canadense*

SCIENTIFIC NAME MEANING: From the Latin *Maius,* meaning "May"; the Romans named the month after Maia, the goddess of growth and spring. *Anthemun* means "flower."

ANGLO-SAXON NAME FOR MAY: Thrimil-cmonath, or "three-milk-month," referring to cows' ability to produce enough to be milked three time a day in midspring

FLOWERS: 10–40 minute white blossoms, 0.2 in (4–6 mm) wide, on an erect spike, 0.6–2.2 in (1.5–5.5 cm) long, above the leaves. Each flower has 4 jutting stamens.

POLLINATORS: Solitary bees, bee flies, syrphid flies

SUCCESS RATE OF FLOWERS PRODUCING BERRIES: 5–30%

BERRIES: About 0.2 in (4 mm) wide, initially hard, whitish, and translucent, turning green speckled with purple and finally red when ripe in autumn. Each contains 1–4 seeds.

LEAVES: 1–4 in (2–10 cm) long, 0.6–2 in (1.5–5 cm) wide, shiny, pointed, smooth-edged, with notched base that hugs around stem; 2 or rarely 3 on flowering plants, just 1 on sterile plants; turn brown and wither back from tips in autumn

flowers at all, just a single leaf that rises a couple of inches above the ground. They are so commonplace, they seem to go virtually unnoticed. Having been preformed in underground shoots during the previous growing season, tightly curled, pointed Mayflower leaves burst straight up through the rotting leaves of forest duff soon after the snow is gone. But unlike trout lilies in hardwood stands, which disappear from view in June, Mayflower plants persist until the frosts of autumn.

Most mayflower plants are clones, sprouting from networks of connected underground stems. Some colonies of loosely spaced, genetically identical plants can be up to 20 feet (6.1 meters) wide and sixty years old. Each single-leaved sterile plant is part of a team, sending energy to a select number of confreres growing in the best light and soil conditions. These lucky few are the breeders, sending up two or, less often, three leaves along a flowering stalk, which usually blooms in late May and June. Up close, the flowers look like little globes with white antennae and give off a strong, sweet perfume. Bending down to sample the fragrance comes with a reminder, however, of the old English superstition that smelling lilies can cause freckles.

STEM: Usually changes angle where it joins with leaves on flowering plants

ROOTS: Shallow, stringy, creeping white rhizomes, up to 4 ft (91 cm) long, with many fine, tan-colored rootlets ending in rounded swellings in fall

ANNUAL RHIZOME GROWTH RATE: 6–12 in (15–30 cm)

PREFERRED HABITAT: Wide range of mature upland forests

COMPANION PLANTS: Bunchberry, moccasin flower, violets, wintergreen, wood sorrel, twinflower, goldthread, red baneberry. Solomon's seal, starflower, blue bead lily

COMMON DINERS: Chipmunks, mice, hares, and grouse eat berries; slugs and leaf miner caterpillars nibble leaves.

RANGE: Throughout north woods region south along Appalachians to Georgia, west through Great Lakes states to Iowa, Nebraska, Wyoming, and Montana; across Canada into the northern territories

ALSO SEE: Trout Lily, Solomon's Seal, Chipmunk

About a month after starting to bloom, the flowers give way to hard little speckled green berries that ripen through the summer, becoming soft and red by fall. They're feasted upon by an assortment of birds and animals. The Ojibwa called the plant *gunkisaehminuk,* "chipmunk berry." The bittersweet berries are edible to humans, but have been known to cause frequent trips to the outhouse.

A closely related plant that can be mistaken for Canada mayflower at first glance is the three-leaved false Solomon's seal. With longer, more upwardly pointing leaves and a sparser spike of flowers, it most commonly grows amid the sphagnum of open or partially forested bogs and cedar swamps.

CATTAIL

Prolific Plants of the Marsh

HEIGHT: 3.3–10 ft (1–3 m)

ALIAS: Broad-leaved cattail, common cattail, swamp bulrush, cossack asparagus, reed mace, nailrod, *Typha latifolia*

FLOWERS: Cylindrical, velvety female seed head, 4–6 in (10–15 cm) long, lime green at first, turns dark brown after pollination; spiky male pollen head above, 4–8 in (10–20 cm) long, dark green at first, turns yellow

NUMBER OF SEEDS PER CATTAIL: 117,000–268,000

LEAVES: 0.4–1 in (1–2.5 cm) wide, very long and pointed, like swords

ROOT CONTENT: 30% starch, 8% crude protein

PREFERRED HABITAT: Wet soil or water up to 2.6 ft (80 cm) deep in marshes, swamps, wet meadows, open ponds, lakeshores, and shallow bays

COMMON CATTAIL-MARSH INHABITANTS: Muskrats, red-winged blackbirds, Canada geese, swamp sparrows, marsh wrens, bitterns, sora rails, pied-billed grebes, American coots

NATIVE USES: Iroquois, Ojibwa, and others dried and pounded autumn roots into a sweet flour for bread and puddings, or cooked them like potatoes; Abenaki drank juice from roots. Split dried leaves used for weaving baskets and mats; seed fluff stuffed into winter clothes and bedding.

Cattails rise up in the richest habitats in the wilderness. Like other marsh plants, they are extremely efficient at filtering nutrients and even impurities from the water. Cattail roots have a nutrient content similar to rice and corn, but have a much higher yield. A Syracuse University project in the 1950s estimated cattails could provide up to 30 tons (27 metric tons) of dry flour per acre (0.4 hectare), far more than wheat, rye, oats, or corn.

Fall cattail roots are especially nutritious, because as winter nears, the plants suck all their nutrients back into the roots. They continue to breathe air through dead, dry, hollow stalks sticking up through the ice and water. In spring, the nutrient stores are used to send up fresh green stalks, which rapidly overtake the previous year's pale, dead relics.

By June or July, spikes of male pollen heads form above the familiar dense, velvety female seed heads, which look like big hot dogs on roasting sticks. Wind blows yellow pollen to surrounding cattails. Seeds emerge in fall and winter on fluffy fibers that travel far on wind, water, or an animal's fur. Though tiny, they remain viable for up to five years. Once established, cattails spread like vines by sending out underground stems that establish circular colonies of clones around a parent plant. In ideal conditions, a single seed can produce a colony of almost 100 stalks within a year. Cattail-loving muskrats help keep things in check by eating the roots and stalks. If a marsh or pond dries up, cattail seeds, and those of many water plants, can remain dormant for a long time and sprout when water returns.

WAR EFFORT: During WWII, seed fluff used to stuff tank and airplane seats and life jackets.
RANGE: Throughout United States north to central Alaska and Newfoundland
NUMBER OF U.S. CATTAIL SPECIES: 3
NUMBER OF CATTAIL SPECIES WORLDWIDE: 10
ALSO SEE: Red-Winged Blackbird, Wetlands

DOLL'S EYES

Poison Berries with Striking Allure

> *HEIGHT:* 1–3 ft (30–90 cm)
> *ALIAS:* White baneberry, necklace weed, white beads, white cohosh, whiteberry, whiteheads, snake root, grapewort, herb Christopher, *Actaea alba, Actaea pachypoda, Actaea x ludovici*
> *FLOWERS:* A spike of small white flowers, composed mainly of stamens and stigmas, with petal-like sepals that fall off soon after opening in late May or June
> *BERRIES:* Large, oval, greenish at first, turning bright white, with a single black dot at tips, borne in a cluster on stout stalks that turn purple as berries ripen; several seeds tightly packed inside berries; very bitter and poisonous
> *LEAVES:* Composite, composed of 3 groups of 3–5 sharply pointed leaflets with large-toothed edges
> *ROOTS:* Thick rootstock
> *PREFERRED HABITAT:* Deciduous and mixed forests
> *RANGE:* All northeastern United States to eastern Minnesota and northeastern Kansas, south to eastern Oklahoma and Georgia; north to southeastern Canada

Scattered through hardwood forests of maple, beech, and yellow birch, bunches of doll's eyes stare boldly out from deep red stalks in August and September. The large, white, black-eyed berries command attention wherever they ripen. Yet, for all their allure, doll's eyes are reputed to be deadly poisonous. They're also known as white baneberries, from the Old English word *bona,* meaning "killer."

Authorities don't agree on just how poisonous doll's eyes are to humans. A single berry is said to be so bitter, it would discourage anyone to try another. Mice, ruffed grouse, and other animals seem to snap up the white fruits happily.

Some botanists classify red baneberry as a variety of the same species as doll's eyes, though it has bright red berries on much more slender stalks. It grows in small colonies, rather than singly, in mixed as well as deciduous forests.

FERNS

Descendants of Ancient Tropical Trees

One person's fiddlehead could be another's black gold—that is, if they lived hundreds of millions of years apart. Today's ferns are the diminutive remnants of the Carboniferous period 300 million years ago, when giant, tree-sized ferns and horsetails dominated the Earth's first steamy jungles. The buried, fossilized material of those jungles—preserved from rotting by the acidic conditions of vast bogs and swamps—forms today's coal deposits.

Ferns appeared long before plants developed flowers or seeds, reproducing instead by spores, like mushrooms. Ferns, however, are more advanced than algae, lichens, mosses, and fungi, which depend on the slow diffusion of water and nutrients through their tissues to grow. Vascular canals, like veins, transport a fern's supplies much more quickly, allowing it to grow both higher and faster.

TALLEST NORTH WOODS FERN: Ostrich fern, up to 6.7 ft (2 m)

SMALLEST NORTH WOODS FERN: Wall rue, usually about 3 in (6 cm)

SPORE CASINGS: Many species have "fruit dots" containing spores on the undersides of fronds; others have markedly different fertile fronds or spikes bearing dense clusters of spore casings. Spores released in dry weather, traveling on air currents.

NUMBER OF SPORES PRODUCED BY A SINGLE FROND: Millions

ALIAS: Fiddleheads, Filicales

NAME ORIGIN OF FERN: Proto-Indo-European *porno*, meaning "feather"

LIFE SPAN: Up to 100 years

FIRST APPEARANCE OF VASCULAR SPORE-PRODUCING PLANTS: 400 million years ago

NATIVE REMEDIES: Ojibwa boiled lady fern and sensitive fern into a tea for relieving pain and helping nursing mothers to produce milk; fresh, moistened lady fern was also slapped onto scrapes and bruises to ease pain. Natives used rattlesnake fern in a poultice for snake bites and brewed maidenhair fern tea for coughs and other respiratory ailments.

NAME FOR FERN ENTHUSIASTS: Pteridologists, or ferners

COMMON WETLAND SPECIES: Sensitive, ostrich, royal, lady, New York,

As the Earth's climate cooled, giant ferns perished in temperate zones, leaving behind only species that buried their woody trunks underground as horizontal stems, called rhizomes. The visible ferns that appear above the ground are the plant's leaves, called fronds. There are still some tree ferns in the tropics that reach heights of eighty feet (twenty-five meters) and are easily mistaken for palm trees.

Old European beliefs held that fern "seeds" were produced only on Midsumm-mer's Eve and had the power to make people invisible and to unlock doors. Ferns actually reproduce by dustlike spores, each of which is a single cell. It grows by dividing after it has landed in a suitable site. After several weeks, it produces a tiny, heart-shaped plant called a prothallium, usually less than a half an inch (1.2 centimeters) wide, lying flat and close to the ground.

marsh, cinnamon, oak, and crested shield ferns

SPECIES OF MAINLY HARDWOOD FORESTS: Maidenhair, bulblet, New York, Christmas, rattlesnake, and silvery glade ferns

RANGE: Throughout United States to high Arctic in Alaska and Canada

CLOSEST FERN RELATIVES: Horsetails, club mosses, spike mosses, quill-worts

NUMBER OF FERN SPECIES NATIVE TO NORTH WOODS REGION: About 75

NUMBER OF NORTH AMERICAN FERN SPECIES: About 325

NUMBER OF FERN SPECIES WORLDWIDE: About 12,000

ALSO SEE: Wetlands, Fungi

The prothallium is short-lived and, unlike its parent, reproduces sexually. As with primitive water plants, sperm travels through a film of rainwater or moisture from male to female organs on the plants' underside. The fertilized egg grows into a tiny fern, drawing nutrients from the prothallium until it sinks its own roots. The rhizome that develops sends up more fronds.

Ferns have evolved to inhabit a wide range of habitats, though most prefer shady, moist conditions. Graceful, circular clusters, or "crowns," of various wood fern species are very common throughout northern forests, from the diminutive, lacy bulblet ferns growing in rich, damp humus to the lofty, arching ostrich ferns (illustrated) in wet bottomlands. A few species, such as the thigh-high-canopy-forming bracken—the world's most widespread fern—settle both in forests and in dry, open expanses.

Many, including bracken, sensitive, bulblet, and lady ferns, are browned and withered by the first frosts of autumn. Some wood ferns, though, as well as rock-loving polypody, remain green through the winter. But most produce new curled fiddleheads in spring. Despite the fact that ostrich fern fiddle-heads hold the honor of being Wisconsin's official "state vegetable," and picking them is a rite of spring in New England, all ferns are probably somewhat toxic. Authorities warn against eating large amounts.

FUNGI

Tying the Forest Together

The mushrooms sprinkled throughout moist forest, especially after late-summer and autumn rains, and the fungal shelves climbing up trees offer only hints of the stunning pervasiveness of fungi. Aboveground structures such as mushrooms are only the external, spore-producing, fruiting bodies of extensive fungal organisms. Fungi spread networks of threadlike fibers, called mycelia, through every nook and cranny of the upper soil, forming a mesh on the undersides of decaying leaves, intertwining with roots, and entering rotting logs, live trees, mosses, dead animals, and droppings—literally tying the forest together. A thimbleful of soil can have more than a mile (1.6 kilometers) of microscopic fungal strands running through it.

BIGGEST MUSHROOM (FRUITING BODY): Giant puffball, up to 20 in (51 cm) wide and 48.5 lb (22 kg)

NUMBER OF SPORES OR MICROSCOPIC FUNGAL COLONIES IN 1 G (0.03 OZ) OF SOIL: 300,000–3 million

NUMBER OF SPORES IN A SINGLE MUSHROOM: Billions

AVERAGE SPORE DIAMETER: 0.0006 in (0.015 mm)

LENGTH OF TIME SPORES CAN REMAIN DORMANT: Up to 20 years

RATE OF GROWTH: Under ideal warm, moist conditions, a new fungus can sprout several kilometers of strands in a few days.

PEOPLE WHO STUDY MUSHROOMS: Mycologists

In a hardwood forest in Michigan, the network of a single golden-brown honey mushroom organism—an edible species with filaments that glow in the dark—is estimated to weigh more than 110 tons (100 metric tons) and be at least 1,500 years old. The world's biggest known fungus, another honey mushroom in Oregon, has a network of fibers covering more than three square miles (almost nine square kilometers), sporting mushrooms throughout, and is believed to be at least 2,400 years old.

Fungal networks are like veins and capillaries in the soil, keeping ecosystems alive. Fungi cannot produce chlorophyll, so must get their energy from plants. Latching onto dead vegetation to reclaim nutrients back into the life cycle, fungal strands secrete enzymes that dissolve the organic material into food molecules they can absorb. A succession of different fungus species is usually involved in the process of breaking down the sugars, cellulose, lignins, and hemicellulose that form leaves, wood, and other organic material, like the process of a pulp mill breaking down wood fiber.

About 90 percent of all dry vegetable material is consumed by decomposers rather than by herbivores, and 80 to 90 percent of the energy from decaying organic matter goes to fungi and bacteria. Without fungi and bacteria, all the carbon required for life would become locked up in a growing layer of dead material that would never break down. Life would peter out within a few decades.

Some fungal strands or spores spread into roots or wounds in the trunks of living trees as well, weakening them and speed-

PEOPLE WHO FEAR MUSHROOMS: Mycophobes

PEOPLE WHO ARE ADDICTED TO MUSHROOMS: Mycophagists

EDIBLE MUSHROOM NUTRIENTS: Folic acid, vitamins D and B7

COMMON POISONOUS MUSHROOMS: Death angel, fly agaric (illustrated), death cap. Most have gills on the undersides of their caps.

ORIGIN OF "TOADSTOOL": Folklore held that the whitish flakes on the caps of fly agaric were poisonous warts left by toads after sitting on the mushroom.

MUSHROOM SEX: Strands of two fungi grow and fuse together uniting nuclei of the opposite sex to create a reproductive spore-producing organism

FAIRY CIRCLES: Rings of dead grass, left in fields by mushrooms produced by a spreading central underground fungus. A 700-year-old fairy circle in France has a diameter of more than half a mile (1 km).

FAIRY STEPS: Long-lasting, woody bracket fungi on trees

ARTIST'S CONK: Large, common bracket fungus with smooth white underside that stains dark brown where scratched, long used for handicraft etchings

MYCORRHIZAL: From Latin *myco,* "fungus," and Greek *rhiza,* "root"

NORTH WOODS MUSHROOMS SYMBIOTIC WITH TREES AND PLANTS: About 15%

SPORE DISPERSAL: By wind, rain, insects, and mushroom-eating animals

MOST IMPORTANT ANIMAL DISPERSERS OF SPORES: Mites, both on their bodies and in their droppings

ing their demise. Logging can sometimes help nourish such fungi with the dead roots and stumps left behind, resulting in more formidable parasites for new trees or those left standing.

Many species of fungi engage in an interspecies chemical-trading network that is essential for more than 90 percent of all trees, shrubs, herbs, and grasses. By entwining their filaments around rootlets, these "mycorrhizal" fungi transfer water and nutrients, most notably nitrogen and phosphorus, to trees and plants. In return, trees and plants pass about 10 percent of their high-energy sugars, created through photosynthesis, on to the fungi. In effect, the fungi are middlemen that connect all living things beneath the ground, even transporting important materials from one plant to another and producing chemicals that protect trees from microbial diseases and parasitic fungi species.

Fungi also manufacture a stew of other chemicals for their own protection and competition. Some produce antibiotics to make it difficult for bacteria and other fungi to grow near them. In 1929 in Britain, Alexander Fleming isolated one of these substances from the penicillium mold and produced the first modern medical antibiotic, penicillin.

Defense chemicals are probably the active ingredients in most poisonous mushrooms, known as toadstools. Ancient people often learned ways of taking small doses of toxic mushrooms to achieve a state of ecstasy. The Roman writer Seneca called such mushrooms "voluptuous poison." Fly agaric (illustrated) was used ritually throughout much of Asia and Europe and is also common throughout North America. Soma, the sacred elixir of Indo-European peoples more than 4,000

PUNGENT-FUNGI SPORE SPREADERS: Flies are attracted to the rancid-meat smell of slimy stinkhorn fungi; northern flying squirrels sniff out and eat the underground fruiting bodies of some mycorrhizal fungi.

SPECIES THAT GLOW IN THE DARK: Jack-o'-lantern, luminescent panellus, honey mushroom (only its fiber network)

MEAT-EATING FUNGI: Some species, such as the large, edible oyster mushroom, a wood-rooting fungus, use looped strands to snare round-worms, or paralyze them with toxic drops, afterward secreting enzymes to digest them.

AMOUNT OF CARBON RETURNED TO THE AIR BY MICROORGANISMS ACCOUNTED FOR BY FUNGI: 13%

FIRST APPEARANCE OF FUNGI IN ANCIENT OCEANS: Probably about 2.5 billion years ago

OFFICIAL STATE MUSHROOM OF MINNESOTA: Morel

SITE OF ANNUAL NATIONAL MOREL HUNTING CHAMPIONSHIP: Boyne City, Michigan

NUMBER OF MYCORRHIZAL FUNGI SPECIES IN CONIFEROUS FORESTS: Up to 5,000

OTHER FORMS OF FUNGI: Yeasts, molds, mildew

NUMBER OF NAMED FUNGI SPECIES WORLDWIDE: More than 100,000

ESTIMATED NUMBER OF FUNGI SPECIES WORLDWIDE: 1.5 million

ALSO SEE: Lichens, Humus and Soil, Moccasin Flower, Indian Pipe, Flying Squirrel

years ago, is believed to have been made from a deadly mushroom that grew on the steppes of central Asia. It induced a battle rage among warriors that made them fearless and heedless of pain.

Fungal networks are like veins and capillaries in the soil, keeping ecosystems alive

Some mycologists and psychologists strongly suspect that the psychoactive, and sometimes deadly, ergot fungus may have touched off the infamous Salem witch trials of 1692, which resulted in nineteen people being hanged as witches. The victims of alleged spells, both people and cattle, experienced painful crawling-skin sensations, manic depression, hallucinations, headaches, and vomiting, all classic symptoms of ergot poisoning, caused by a fungus that infects rye, the main grain used in Salem and other farming communities at the time for bread. The damp conditions that lead to ergot outbreaks also correspond to the site and weather records from the time of the Salem witch hysteria.

INDIAN PIPE

Ghostly Plants without Chlorophyll

Deep in the darkest forest shade, where nary a green plant dares to venture, one may encounter a bowed, stunted ghoul. Appearing in small groups of what look like bizarre, emaciated fungi, Indian pipe is the custodian of the forest's inhospitable nether regions. Amazingly, it's actually a flower, though one that seems to have defected to the ranks of mushrooms. It survives by subversive means, getting the sunlight denied other forest-floor plants by stealing its energy from the roots of the light-hogging trees. Accordingly, it has no need for leaves and chlorophyll, the green cells that allow plants to capture sunlight and turn it into energy.

Indian pipe, however, is no welcome convert in a collegial world of mushrooms.

HEIGHT: 4–8 in (10–20 cm); rarely up to 1 ft (30 cm)

ALIAS: Ghost flower, ice plant, corpse plant, fairy-smoke, convulsionroot, fitroot, eyebright, Dutchman's pipe, convulsionweed, *Monotropa uniflora*

FLOWERS: White, waxy looking, bell-shaped, 0.6–0.8 in (1.5–2 cm) long, formed by 5 overlapping petals, with 10 yellow stamens surrounding round white pistil inside; scentless

SEEDS: Brown, dustlike, released from large, upright capsules at top of stem

STEM: White or pale pink, translucent, turning dark brown and woody in autumn

ROOTS: Small, dense ball of brittle brown rootlets covered by matted fungal fibers

PREFERRED HABITAT: Rich, acidic humus or mossy soil in deep forest shade, especially beneath pines and oaks, and in black spruce bogs

COMPANION PLANTS: Wintergreen, bunchberry

RANGE: Throughout eastern United States to Texas and Nebraska, and across north to Pacific Northwest; north far into boreal forest across Canada

ONLY OTHER MONOTROPA SPECIES: Pinesap, also in north woods

ALSO SEE: Fungi, Moccasin Flower

Rather than obtaining its nourishment directly, its dense rootlets cluster around and parasitize fungal fibers that themselves feed off tree roots.

The roots of closely related plants in the wintergreen family, such as shinleaf, pyrola, and prince's pine, maintain close, symbiotic bonds with certain kinds of fungi, sending them photosynthesized energy in sugar compounds in return for moisture and soil nutrients collected by the fungi. It may be that Indian pipe's ancestor somehow acquired the ability to tap into tree root fungi as well. Finding life easier as a parasite than a symbiont, it discarded its green attire, today bearing only tiny, gauzy visages along its stem of what were once real leaves. Seeming to enter a realm of shades between plant and mushroom, Indian pipe acquired its strange, not-quite-mortal aspect. As if its pallid, waxy appearance wasn't enough, the plant bruises black when handled. If picked, it bleeds a thick, gooey liquid. The whole business seriously creeped-out many nineteenth-century botanical writers, who denounced Indian pipe as "weird," "ghostly," and "degenerate."

Others saw dignity in the ghost flower. They found that once fertilized, it slowly, solemnly raises its head to stand straight up. The motion is noted in Indian pipe's scientific name *Monotropa*, which means "one turn." Once out of its "pipe" posture, the plant becomes hard, tough, and woody as it darkens to dusty brown. From late summer through to spring, it remains standing, though now lifeless, gradually releasing dustlike seeds from slits in the pipe-head capsule. But even as the plant lets its stem dry out, its roots form new flower buds, which push up as translucent, silvery sprouts early the following summer.

Native healers embraced the plant. They mixed its thick juice with water to use as an eye lotion and for colds and fevers. The dried root was also enlisted by nineteenth-century doctors to help cure fainting, epileptic fits, and nervous disorders.

Indian pipe's sister plant, pinesap, is more rare, growing mainly in pine and evergreen woods, where it, too, parasitizes tree root fungi. It is similar to Indian pipe, but is pale yellow, orangish, or sometimes tinted red, and has several nodding flowers at the top of a stem, rather than just one.

JACK-IN-THE-PULPIT

The Transsexual Preacher

In the forest cathedral, jack-in-the-pulpit is a silent preacher, ministering to the more brightly colored spring ephemerals. Wearing simple vestments of striped green, it may be easily overlooked at first. But the elegant, shade-loving flower holds secrets that, upon close inspection, prove to be as intriguing as its name.

The name springs from the plant's likeness to a figure, "Jack," standing in an antiquated church pulpit with a canopy (which was designed to project the preacher's voice). A modified leaf forms the hood-shaped canopy enclosing Jack, a thick column that pokes its head out from the top of the pulpit. The plant's name may actually mix the sacred and profane, since "Jack" was once a common nickname for the penis, while another name for the flower is

HEIGHT: Usually 12–16 in (30–40 cm); up to 3 ft (91 cm)

ALIAS: Woodland jack-in-the-pulpit, Indian turnip, marsh turnip, pepper turnip, wild turnip, bog onion, brown dragon, starchwort, dragon root, devil's ear, cuckoo plant, priest's-pintle, *Arisaema triphyllum*

FLOWERS: Green or purplish-brown hood, often striped, called a "spathe," about 1.5–3 in (4–8 cm) long, surrounding a thick, club-shaped "spadix," 1.2–2.4 in (3–6 cm) long, which bears many tiny yellow male or green female flowers near its base; blooms late April to June

BERRIES: Scarlet, waxy, corn kernel–shaped, about 0.4 in (1 cm) long, in a tight, dense, oval cluster of up to more than 2 dozen. Each berry has 1–3 seeds.

LEAVES: 3 dark green, pointed compound leaflets, 1 set on male plants and usually 2 on females, on separate stems from flower; with wavy edges, pale green undersides

ROOTS: Bulbous, starchy rhizome up to 2.4 in (6 cm) thick, with root filaments trailing from it. New rhizomes often form at ends of roots, sending up clones of the parent plant, forming colonies.

PREFERRED HABITAT: Rich, moist soil of forests; swamp and bog edges

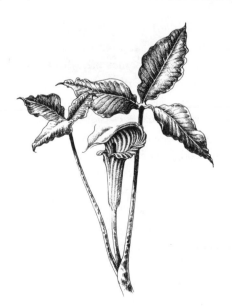

priest's-"pintle," an Old English word for the male member.

Jack-in-the-pulpit's flowers are very tiny, growing in clusters hidden down in the pulpit around the base of the column. Overhead, the drooping canopy keeps rain from pooling in the pulpit and drowning the dwarfish flowers.

The pulpit's stately lines may guide flying insects to its center. Thrips are common visitors, as are small fungus gnats, perhaps mesmerized by the preacher's perfumed homily into believing the plant is a mushroom on which they can lay their eggs. But once inside, the gnats are trapped by slippery, narrowing walls, forcing them down onto the floor of the pulpit. If they're lucky, it is a male plant and they can escape, covered with sticky pollen, by crawling out through a passage at the bottom of the pulpit. If they make the same mistake twice, though, and the next stop is a female plant, there is no way out, and they must remain there to pollinate the flowers. The sexual strategy leads some evolutionary entomologists to speculate that the plant may eventually evolve into a meat-eater, like pitcher plants or sundew.

Jack-in-the-pulpit begins life as a male, with pollen-bearing flowers. But as soon as it stores up enough nutrients and energy, often when about three years old, the preacher has a sex change. Jack becomes Jill, with all female flowers. While the jack and pulpit of a male plant wither with its flowers, the female spathe remains, protecting the fruits developing on the spadix until late summer. Then the hood falls away to reveal a cluster of bright green berries. Later turning scarlet, the berries flag hungry birds such as thrushes and wood ducks, who serve as flying seed dispensers. But if a jack-in-the-pulpit is damaged or conditions change somehow to diminish the nutrients needed to produce berries, the plant may opt to become a male again.

While its flowers, leaves, and stems wither and die with autumn's frosts, the plant survives winter by storing supplies in its rhizome, a small, bulbous underground stem just beneath the surface. This bulb also contains another of the jack-in-the-pulpit's secrets: minute, needle-shaped calcium oxalate crystals that if eaten, immediately burn and blister the mouth severely.

FIRST SIGN IN SPRING: A green or purplish pointed shoot pushes up from the ground, unfolding its leaves when 8–12 in (20–30 cm) high

CLOSE RELATIVES: Water arum, sweet flag, skunk cabbage, green dragon, arrow arum

MAXIMUM LIFE SPAN: At least 25 years

RANGE: Throughout eastern United States west to the high plains states and north into southern Ontario

WORLD'S LARGEST ARUM: Amorphophallus titanum, with a spathe and spadix up to 10 ft (3 m) long

NUMBER OF ARUM SPECIES WORLDWIDE: Probably more than 3,500, most in tropics

NUMBER OF ARISAEMA SPECIES WORLDWIDE: More than 100

ALSO SEE: Doll's Eyes, Pickerelweed

JEWELWEED

Custom-Made for Hummingbirds

Dangling like delicate orange earrings, sparkling in the dew, jewelweed flowers are the highlight of an exceptional plant. To start with, their color, orange, is one of the rarest in the wild, outside of autumn. The plant's succulent stems and its leaves also seep a watery, orange-tinted juice when crushed. Native Americans and others have long rubbed the liquid on the skin for quick relief from insect bites, poison ivy, nettle stings, athlete's foot, and general itching. Jewelweed juice has also been used to make yellow dye.

Unlike most forest plants, jewelweed lives only one year. Growing in dense patches on mucky ground, the plants' water-filled stems shoot up more than three feet (ninety-one centimeters) in the space of a few weeks. They begin to bloom around mid-July and continue until frosts in September create expanding ice crystals that destroy the tender stems from within. While they flourish, their flowers' uncommon color is perhaps key in flagging jewelweed's principal

HEIGHT: 1.7–5 ft (50–150 cm)
ALIAS: Spotted jewelweed, spotted touch-me-not, orange jewelweed, snapweed, silver leaf, *Impatiens capensis*
OJIBWA NAME: Muklkeebug, "frog petal"
FLOWERS: Intricate hanging, horn-shaped structures, 1–1.2 in (2.5–3 cm) long, orange, sometimes yellowish, speckled with rust-red. Top of flower cavity shows white pollen during male stage and pointed green pistil during female stage; cleistogamous buds are just 1/25 in (1–2 mm) long.
SEEDS: Pop out from green pods that are 0.6–0.8 in (1.5–2 cm) long
LEAVES: 1.2–3.6 in (3–9 cm) long, thin, light green, with pointed ends and large-toothed edges, appearing particularly silvery when glistening with dew; temporarily wilting in hot weather
STEM: Shiny light green, sometimes mauve, succulent, and translucent
ROOTS: Short, thin, pink, and claw-like
PREFERRED HABITAT: Along creeks, ravine bottoms, shorelines, beaver meadows, hardwood and cedar swamps, marshes, and low-lying soggy forest sites and clearings

partner in survival, the ruby-throated hummingbird. Storing nectar deep inside conical spurs, the flowers are ideal vessels for the hummingbirds' needlelike bills and long, probing tongues. With its nose in the flower, a tiny hummer picks up pollen on its forehead and then cross-fertilizes the next receptive plant it visits. Bees and wasps also seek out jewelweed nectar, though they usually cheat the flowers by biting holes through the back of the spur, bypassing the sexual organs.

But plants robbed of all their nectar, without receiving another's pollen, can still produce seeds. Jewelweed, like a number of other north woods species, has a backup system. Later in the summer, on its lower branches, it grows many very tiny flower buds that never open. Instead, they pollinate themselves internally. Called cleistogamous—"hidden marriage"—flowers, they have no nectar and require less energy for their production. The seeds they produce are genetic clones of a single parent, without the variation that makes cross-pollinated seeds more adaptable. But they ensure another generation will get a chance at life. It is an important contingency given that jewelweed is only an annual. Where conditions are drier or otherwise more difficult, the plants produce greater numbers of closed flowers. In Britain, where jewelweed became widespread after being imported from North America, there are no hummingbirds to cross-pollinate plants. Charles Darwin found only one in twenty in his country that produced regular flowers.

Regardless of how they are pollinated, fertilized jewelweed flowers develop small seedpods that feature the best known of all the plant's tricks. About a month after fertilization, a mere touch or even a strong wind will burst the ripened pods open, their seeds flying as far as seven feet (two meters). Seeds landing in water can be transported long distances to spread the plant. Mice and grouse eat any they find on the ground. The pods' hair-trigger propensity to explode is the source both for jewelweed's other common name, touch-me-not, and of the scientific designation for its genus, *Impatiens*.

COMPANION PLANTS: Ostrich fern, marsh marigold, blue marsh violet, gold thread, Jack-in-the-pulpit, raspberry, black currant, sweet flag, grasses

COMMON DINERS: Hummingbirds, bees, wasps, hawkmoths, hares, mice, ruffed grouse

RANGE: Throughout eastern United States west to Texas, Colorado, and North Dakota; also in Washington, Oregon, and Idaho and north across Canada to tree line

NUMBER OF U.S. IMPATIENS SPECIES: 11

NUMBER OF IMPATIENS SPECIES WORLDWIDE: About 400, mostly in tropical Asia and Africa

ALSO SEE: Hummingbird, Violets

LARGE-FLOWERED TRILLIUM

Six Years to First Flowering

Large-flowered trillium is one of the monarchs of the spring ephemerals. Like other early forest flowers, its reign is brief, taking over from the trout lilies and spring beauties in May, and lasting for two to four weeks, until deciduous tree leaves unfold and cut off the light overhead. Spring forest flowers take advantage of the time between the thawing of the soil and leaf-out, when the sheltered woods are actually warmer than open fields, to grow very rapidly. Naturalists say dead leaves may be heard rustling on still nights as the flowers push their way up from the ground—the sound of plants growing. Meadow flowers, on the other hand, with the benefit of the sun all the time, bloom throughout summer to early autumn.

Being sheltered by trees, forest flowers must depend on insects rather than the wind for pollination and seed dispersal.

HEIGHT: 12–18 in (30–45 cm)
ALIAS: White trillium, snow trillium, great white trillium, wake-robin, trinity lily, bathflower, white lily, *Trillium grandiflorum*
NAME ORIGIN: Latin *tres*, meaning "three," in reference to number of petals, leaves, and sepals on each plant
FLOWER: 3 white, pointed petals, 1–3 in (2.5–8 cm) long, fading to pink before they die; yellow organs at center; 3 narrow, sharply pointed green sepals beneath petals
SEEDS: 9–10 contained in a single, dark red, hexagonal capsule, or "berry," about 1 in (2.5 cm) long, appearing in mid- to late summer
LEAVES: Wide, pointed, smooth-edged leaves, 1.5–6 in (3.5–15 cm) long; 3 per plant, meeting together at stem below flower; wither by mid- to late summer
ROOTS: Thick, tuberlike rootstock. Roots reach at least 5 in (13 cm) below surface.
PREFERRED HABITAT: Rich soil in mature deciduous forests
COMPANION TREES: Sugar maple, beech
POLLINATORS: Bees, beetles, flies
SUMMER LIGHT LEVELS IN MATURE HARDWOOD FOREST: 1–5% of full sunlight
GREEN-STRIPED TRILLIUMS: Mutation caused by microorganisms spread by sucking insects

Spreading out tender, colorful petals to attract the six-legged pollinators, spring ephemerals are the essence of fleeting beauty. Trilliums are considered unspecialized flowers because, like the world's first flowers, which appeared at least 140 million years ago, their simple petals are on a horizontal plane, offering a broad landing pad for incoming insects. Herbivorous mammals tend to leave most flowers alone because many contain psychoactive chemicals that have a bitter taste.

Trillium seeds, and those of up to 40 percent of all herbaceous plants in deciduous forests, have nutritious green handles by which they are dragged by ants to their nest. Ants eat only the handles, leaving the seeds to sprout. Birds and small mammals probably eat trillium capsules and spread the seeds in their droppings as well.

RANGE: Western Maine to east-central Minnesota, scattered south to New Jersey and along Appalachians to Alabama and parts of Midwest to northeastern Iowa; north into southern Ontario and Quebec
OTHER FLOWERS WITH SEEDS SPREAD BY ANTS: Violets, trout lily, spring beauty, fringed polygala, Dutchman's breeches, wild ginger, bloodroot
NUMBER OF TRILLIUM SPECIES NATIVE TO NORTH WOODS REGION: 5
NUMBER OF U.S. TRILLIUM SPECIES: 42
NUMBER OF TRILLIUM SPECIES WORLDWIDE: About 48
ALSO SEE: Bees, Wasps, and Hornets; Blueberry; Sugar Maple; Jack-in-the-Pulpit

Reproduction requires great amounts of energy from plants. Trilliums, with the limited sunlight they receive in spring before the forest canopy unfurls, take about six years from the time the seeds sprout until they produce their first flowers, all the while storing energy captured by their leaves in their thick roots. If the leaves are picked, the plant usually dies. When it's ready, a trillium takes about one month to produce a flower. Because its sunlight window of opportunity is much shorter than that, the plant actually preforms the flower in a tightly packed bundle at the tip of its root the year before it blooms, allowing it to sprout and inflate as soon as the soil thaws enough to water its roots the following spring.

Many native peoples brewed tea from large-flowered trillium root for menstrual cramps or made it into a poultice to be placed on sore eyes. The Ojibwa innovated an early form of inoculation by spreading the juice of ground, boiled trillium roots on rheumatic joints and then puncturing the skin with thorns or bone needles.

Native Americans also ate red trillium roots as an herb to help stop bleeding after childbirth and for many other ailments. Red trillium, which also blooms in May from Maine to Michigan's Lower Peninsula, is more tolerant of acidic soil than white trillium and becomes more common in rocky northern woods, especially highland areas. It is dark purple-red with straight-edged, sharply triangular petals.

LICHENS

Two Organisms in One

Hard, brittle, and dormant when dry, with a little rainfall, lichens transform into a soft, spongy, glowing carpet, a delight to bare feet. A rocky open area can sport a riot of different lichen species, a veritable world unto itself. Deriving their sustenance from thin air, lichens are the hardiest of all "plants," though they are not really plants at all. They form the dominant ground cover in dense boreal forests, arctic tundra, and sometimes even rocky deserts. Some survive more than a year without water. Others thrive around hot springs at temperatures above 390°F (200°C), while in Antarctica, 400 species flourish. Crustose lichens form a wafer-thin living layer over bare rock on high Appalachian peaks and the Canadian Shield, continuing a process of colonization that began hundreds of millions of years ago when plant life first edged its way from the sea onto sterile, barren land.

Lichens gained a foothold on dry ground through a unique symbiosis of two organisms in one. All lichens are combinations of fungal threads entwined around cells of algae. Both life-forms make up their own kingdoms of species, separate from plants or animals. The fungi provide

OLDEST KNOWN LICHENS: Map lichen colonies up to 9,600 years old on Baffin Island in Canadian Arctic (also grows in north woods region)

AVERAGE ANNUAL RATE OF GROWTH OF MAP LICHENS: Less than 0.05 in (1 mm)

AVERAGE ANNUAL RATE OF GROWTH OF MOST NORTH WOODS LICHENS: 0.1–0.2 in (2–4 mm)

VARIETY OF COLORS: Green, gray, black, red, orange, brown, pink, white, yellow, lilac

NUMBER OF UNIQUE PIGMENTS, ANTIBIOTICS, DEFENSE TOXINS, AND OTHER BIOCHEMICAL COMPOUNDS KNOWN IN LICHENS: About 500

ESTIMATED PERCENTAGE OF LICHEN SPECIES WITH NATURAL ANTIBIOTICS: About 50%

DATE LICHENS WERE DISCOVERED TO BE A SYMBIOSIS OF FUNGI AND ALGAE: 1867, by Swiss botanist Simon Schwendener

NORTH WOODS LICHEN FEEDERS: Eaten primarily in winter by moose, deer, northern flying squirrels, red-backed voles, and spruce grouse; eaten in summer by snails, slugs, lichen moth and bagworm moth caterpillars, mites, springtails, barklice

NUMBER OF NORTH AMERICAN BIRD SPECIES KNOWN TO USE LICHENS FOR NESTING MATERIAL: 46

LICHEN LINE: Because many tree lichens cannot live if buried in

shelter, shade, and water-absorbant tissues for algae. The algae capture the sun's energy with their chlorophyll to make carbohydrates for both organisms from rainwater and carbon dioxide in the air. Although lichens have no roots, they stick to bare rock and produce acids that slowly break down stone, creating depressions to anchor themselves. Mineral grains of broken rock gradually mix with past generations of decayed lichens, a process that created the world's first organic soil on land. As mosses and larger plants evolved, they took root in these pockets, expanding the soil base to eventually clothe the Earth in an ever-thickening mantle that sustains all terrestrial life.

Crustose lichens are the pioneers, clinging flat on rock, bark, and soil and growing outward in crusty rings. About half of the northeast's lichen species are in the crustose group. They grow very slowly. Colonies of light green map lichens on some northern rocks date from the last retreat of the glaciers. Another type of crustose lichen grows along rocky waterlines, leaving even black tracings that mark the high-water point of lakes and streams.

Foliose lichens are also flat but are attached to rock, tree trunks, or humus by small filaments only at their center. Common species such as dog's tooth and waxpaper lichen often have curled edges and leaflike lobes. Rock tripe grows abundantly in circular black or dark brown clusters on granite and sandstone lakeshores and boulders. Crispy when dry, it becomes rubbery in the rain.

snow, the height of the snowpack in a forest is often distinctly marked, and observable in summer, by the point at which the lichens appear on trunks and branches.

LICHENOMETRY: The use of lichen colonies growing on rocks to date landslides, earthquakes, and the retreat of glaciers from a given area, with the oldest colonies present often originating from shortly after the event. Lichenologist Trevor Goward refers to lichens as the "minute hand on the geological clock of the north."

DOCTRINE OF SIGNATURES: Ancient belief that certain plants are shaped like parts of the body they can heal—thus wispy old-man's beard lichen was used to treat baldness, leafy lungwort lichen for respiratory problems, and dog's tooth lichen for rabies

DATE FIRST LAND PLANTS EMERGED: 400–500 million years ago

RANGE: Throughout North America, to the high Arctic

EARTH'S LAND SURFACE ON WHICH LICHENS ARE THE DOMINANT VEGETATION: 8%

PORTION OF WORLD'S KNOWN FUNGI SPECIES THAT FORM LICHENS: 20%

NUMBER OF NORTH AMERICAN LICHEN SPECIES: 3,600

NUMBER OF LICHEN SPECIES WORLDWIDE: 15,000–20,000

ALSO SEE: Fungi, Moss, Humus and Soil, Flying Squirrel

A third group, fruticose lichens, is made up of three-dimensional, often intricately shaped, species. False pixie cups (illustrated) look like tiny trumpets. British soldiers (also illustrated) are little light green sprouts topped with bold scarlet, like King George's redcoats in the Revolutionary War. Both are very common but less than an inch (2.5 centimeters) tall. They often grow in rocky clearings or light shade, together with silver-green reindeer and coral lichens, which are both used as miniature bushes in dioramas and model railroad sets. Pale yellow-green old man's beard hangs in wispy strands from trees, especially old spruce, fir, and jack pines. Old-growth forests in general have the greatest diversity of lichen species. A single spruce tree can host more than twenty different kinds of lichens, each occupying a different zone.

A lichen is named for the fungus rather than the alga in the pairing, because the fungal portion makes up about 95 percent of the lichen. More than one type of alga may also be present. Algae reproduce asexually, by cell division, within the lichen, while some fungi grow tube- or flask-shaped fruiting bodies that spread spores in the wind. The spores must land where the right kind of alga is already present in order for a new lichen to develop. But lichens reproduce mostly by fragmentation, with new colonies starting from broken-off pieces of old ones or from special powdery sheddings of fungal threads rolled with a few algae cells, like minute balls of lint.

Instead of dying when there is no water, lichens simply go dormant, often appearing dead. When it does rain, some species can hold up to thirty times their dry weight in water. But because they are designed to maximize water retention and do not lose any tissue during the cold months, lichens can't filter out air pollutants. Accumulated toxins in their tissues soon kill them, which is the reason they are rare near urban areas and are used by biologists as biomonitors. Rapid accumulation of radioactive fallout by Scandinavian lichens after the Chernobyl nuclear accident in 1986 led to the cull of thousands of reindeer, which feed primarily on lichens in winter.

Lichens' own natural, bitter acids make them unpalatable to humans. When food was scarce, however, native peoples sometimes resorted to eating rock tripe and other species in soups and stews, neutralizing the acids by boiling. Natives also found partially digested lichens from the stomachs of slain caribou much easier to eat. Many historians even believe that the manna that nourished the biblical Israelites may have been grayish-white lichens that are sometimes blown from rocky areas into the desert lowlands.

Lichens were also used in antiquity to produce soft-colored dyes and medicine. Natural acids in lichen dyes help protect wools against clothes moths. The word lichen is taken from the Greek term for "leprous," both because of its scaly appearance and because it was used to treat the disease. Lichens also provide fibers used in clothing, unique chemicals for cosmetics and for stabilizing perfumes, and the dye used in litmus paper.

MOCCASIN FLOWER

June's Preeminent Forest Orchid

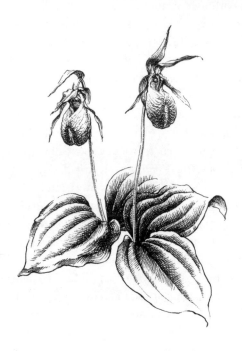

The standout beauties of June, moccasin flowers are the preeminent orchids of the northern forest. Though coming in many varieties, most orchids are like precious gems, transfixing, but all too rare to behold. Moccasin flower is the bountiful exception, generously displaying in small patches beneath pines, around the edges of bogs, and in other spots in mixed and evergreen woods. The Iroquois called the flowers the whippoorwill's shoes, whimsically similar to the flowers' other common name, pink lady's slippers. In New Hampshire, they're honored as the official state wildflower. Minnesota adopted the stunning, closely related showy lady's slipper as its floral emblem, but its pink-and-white

Alias: Pink lady's slipper, nerveroot, squirrel's shoes, stemless lady's slipper, old goose, two lips, Indian moccasin, *Cypripedium acaule*

Orchid name origin: From *orkhis,* Greek for "testicle," referring to the shape of roots of some species

Meaning of Cypripedium: Roughly, "Aphrodite's slippers," from the Greek Kypria, one of the goddess of love's titles, owing to her reputed birthplace in Cyprus, and *peridon,* a general reference to footwear

Height: 12–16 in (30–40 cm)

Flower: Pink, with 2 narrow, inconspicuous upper petals and 1 large, specialized lower petal curling inward to form a hollow sack, about 2 in (5 cm) long

Seeds: Up to millions produced by a single plant in a green capsule, about 1.5 in (4 cm) long, with three ribs, which split in autumn to release seeds to the wind

Leaves: 2 large, pointed leaves, 4–8 in (10–20 cm) long, attached near the base of the flower stem; shiny, dark green with parallel veins

Roots: Dense, numerous strands radiating beneath base of plant

Preferred habitat: Acidic soil in coniferous and mixed forests, especially beneath pines, and around bog edges; sometimes on oak ridges or in birch-aspen stands

flowers are restricted to wetlands throughout the north woods.

Like other orchids, the moccasin flower is highly specialized, near the summit of high-tech wildflower development. When it blooms, from late May through June, the flower's beautiful lower petal curves inward to form a large hollow chamber, like a slip-per. It's called an insect-ambush design. Bees are attracted to the flower's splash of pink and its slight scent. Pushing its way through the long slit where the two curled lips meet at the front of the flower, a bee is sadly surprised when it gets inside. There is little or no nectar to reward its efforts, and the front doors do not bend backward to let it out. There is light, however, coming from an opening at the top of the flower, which the bee follows to escape. Precisely placed stamens deposit their pollen on the bee's back on its way out through the nar-row passage.

Since the ungratified bee is not about to repeat the same mistake with nearby moccasin flowers, it leaves them alone. But the pollen remains stuck on a part of its back that it cannot clean with its legs. The insect's memory not being perfect, the bumblebee may be lured by a distant moc-casin flower's deceptive beauty at a later point, again crawling through and cross-pollinating it.

The whole process is still a long shot, dependent on limited encounters with forgetful bees. Studies show that only about 2 percent of moccasin flowers are successfully fertilized each year. They play the odds by being very long lived and by producing hundreds of thousands of seeds that spread like dust in the wind when their lucky number does come up. They often take a well-deserved break the following year by failing to bloom or even by remaining dormant beneath the ground. Moccasin flowers also propagate

COMPANION PLANTS: Bunchberry, wintergreen, blueberry, trailing arbutus, fringed polygala, violets, bearberry, leatherleaf, bog orchid
POLLINATORS: Bumblebees, leaf-cutting bees, mining bees
FOLK MEDICINES: Roots used as a sedative, to calm nerves, relieve headaches, and treat tremors, epilepsy, fever, and hysteria
LIFE SPAN: Mature plants average 24 years, younger plants average 5–6 years
RANGE: Throughout north woods region south to North Carolina and along Appalachians to Alabama; north across most of Canada to northern boreal forest
EDIBLE ORCHIDS: Seedpods of sev-eral closely related tropical species are the source of vanilla.
NUMBER OF ORCHID SPECIES NATIVE TO NORTH WOODS REGION: About 54
NUMBER OF NORTH AMERICAN ORCHID SPECIES: About 200, about half mainly in Florida
NUMBER OF ORCHID SPECIES WORLD-WIDE: About 19,000 named, proba-bly 25,000–30,000 in total
PERCENTAGE OF WORLD'S FLOWERING PLANTS THAT ARE ORCHIDS: 7–10%
ORCHID SPECIES AT RISK OR THREAT-ENED WITH EXTINCTION WORLDWIDE: 25–33%
ALSO SEE: Bees, Wasps, and Hor-nets; Fungi; Large-Flowered Trillium

themselves by spreading runners that send up more flowers, creating small colonies.

Orchid seeds are much smaller than those of all other flowering plants, lacking any significant store of protein to nourish them. Instead, upon germination, they swell into a minuscule root bulb and may then remain dormant for several years until the minute threads of a particular kind of symbiotic root fungus finds them. Growing right into the seed, the fungus provides it with the carbohydrates it needs to get started. Afterward, extensive fungal networks continue to collect nutrients and water for the orchid, while the plant transfers some of the sugars it produces through photosynthesis to the fungus. Growth is slow at first. It may take three or four years for a moccasin flower seed to send up its first leaf and a dozen years to produce a blossom.

Dependent on limited encounters with forgetful bees,

only about 2 percent of moccasin flowers are

successfully fertilized each year

All orchids are highly specialized for their own niche. Each forms a partnership with a different fungus species. A moccasin flower's needs are so specific that in less diverse environments, such as regularly sprayed forest plantations, few survive with the disappearance of bumblebees. Charles Darwin, recognizing in orchid diversity an ideal model for explaining how natural selection works, wrote an entire book on them as the sequel to his earth-shaking *Origin of Species*. The multitude of ways orchids are pollinated by insects, he concluded, "transcend in an incomparable manner the contrivances and adaptions which the most fertile imagination of man could invent." Or as Will Shakespeare before him wrote, "There are more things in heaven and Earth. . . ."

MOSS

Gathering in the Damp and Dark

Moss often grows thickest on the north side of trees because, in the Northern Hemisphere, the north side receives less sunlight and doesn't dry out as much as a southern exposure. Having no true roots, only filaments called "rhizoids" for anchors, moss thrives in moist conditions, getting all its nutrients from rain, snow, humidity, dust, or organic matter that collects on it. On the ground, species such as pincushion moss grow in rounded, fluffy clumps that minimize moisture loss.

The lack of roots allows moss to grow almost anywhere, without need of fertile soil. Some species grow only on moose droppings. Moss is often the second wave of vegetation established in rocky spots, latching onto pioneer lichens and taking

AVERAGE NUMBER OF SPORES IN THE SPORE CAPSULE OF COMMON HAIR CAP MOSS (ILLUSTRATED): 65 million

MOSS HEIGHT: 0.03 in–2.3 ft (0.5 mm–70 cm)

ALIAS: Bryophytes, class Musci

PEAT MOSS ABSORBENCY: Up to 27 times its dry weight in water

TIME IT TAKES A CLUB MOSS SPORE TO PRODUCE ANOTHER SPORE-PRODUCING PLANT: About 20 years

PIONEER USES OF HAIR CAP MOSS: For stuffing pillows and bedding and as dusters

CLOSEST MOSS RELATIVES: Liverworts

FIRE MOSS: Species that forms dense tufts with spore capsules borne on prominent long purple-red stalks, often dominates ground after severe forest fires

NUMBER OF YEARS FIRE MOSS SPORES CAN REMAIN DORMANT: 16

AGE OF OLDEST MOSS FOSSILS: 320 million years

NUMBER OF NORTH AMERICAN MOSS SPECIES: More than 1,300

NUMBER OF MOSS SPECIES WORLDWIDE: More than 15,000

NUMBER OF SPHAGNUM MOSS SPECIES WORLDWIDE: 350

NUMBER OF NORTH AMERICAN CLUB MOSS SPECIES: 27

NUMBER OF CLUB MOSS SPECIES WORLDWIDE: 350–400

ALSO SEE: Lichens, Humus and Soil, Wetlands

advantage of the moisture and nutrients they hold. Sometimes moss grows on bare granite rock. Over centuries, soft moss mats help build up a layer of organic soil as they decay, allowing more advanced plants to take root.

Though moss functions very much like lichen, it makes its own green chlorophyll and has no need of an algae-fungi partnership. In deciduous forests, species such as common hair cap moss, which grows in plush green mats, are like spring flowers, doing most of their growing after the snow melts and before tree leaves open and block off both rain and sunlight. Each hair cap moss plant, like most mosses, is either a male or female. Males have a tiny cup-shaped structure at their tips. They transfer their sperm to the female plant tips through a film of moisture coating the moss bed, or with the splash of a raindrop. A fertilized egg develops into a new plant with a spore capsule at the end of a long, fine stem rising above the green moss mat. The pressure inside sphagnum moss capsules is close to that of truck tires. When the capsules burst open, with an audible pop, spores are spread by the wind.

Aquatic moss grows with long, green, serrated leaves, like wet shag rugs, on top of rocks in fast-flowing streams, waterfalls, and headwaters. Water moss thrives on high levels of carbon dioxide, which in a fast-moving stream has not had a chance to escape into the air. Among the many minute life-forms inhabiting water-moss mats are one-celled diatomaceous plants, which contain glassy silica and sparkle in the light.

Sphagnum, or peat moss, on the other hand, colonizes and dominates the still, stagnant water of bogs, forming springy mats and hummocks several feet thick across the surface. Sphagnum grows in long strands with small leaves only one cell thick. The leaf's small green living cells are interspersed with much larger porous dead cells that balloon with water. Because of this super-absorbency, as well as its antiseptic qualities, dried sphagnum was widely used for diapers and wound dressings by Native Americans. The moss, in fact, was heavily used for dressings during the First World War and was introduced as a natural product for menstrual pads in the 1990s. As sphagnum mats grow and thicken, the large dead cells of long-covered layers continue to absorb and transfer water up to the top living layer, like a giant sponge.

A further kind of common "moss" is actually not a moss at all, but a distant relative of ferns. Club mosses, or running pines, are, like ferns, miniature descendants of large spore-bearing trees that flourished 300 million years ago. Some species, look like tiny evergreen trees, no more than a foot (25 cm) tall, attached to horizontal ground runners, often forming dense carpets. The fine yellow dust of the plants' club-shaped spore cones, released in autumn, was inhaled by natives to stop nosebleeds, creating, in effect, a nasal powder keg, since the highly flammable spores were also once used in fireworks, old-fashioned camera pan flashes, and theatrical explosions.

PICKERELWEED

Watery Beds of Purple Beauty

HEIGHT: 1–4 ft (30–120 cm), usually reaching 1–2 ft (30–60 cm) above water
ALIAS: *Pontederia condata*
FLOWERS: Small, bluish-purple, vase-shaped; many densely clustered on a vertical spike up to 4 in (10 cm) long
SEEDS: 1 per flower, covered by a ridged jacket about ¼ in (6 mm) long
LEAVES: Arrow-shaped, 2–10 in (5–25 cm) long, glossy, succulent, 1 per plant, on separate stalk attached at base of main stem underwater
STEM: Green, thick, erect, though often snaking, filled with air chambers
PREFERRED HABITAT: Up to 3.3 ft (1 m) deep in clear water of mud-bottomed streams and sheltered lakesides, around outlets or inlets
COMPANION PLANTS: Arrowhead, water lily, cattail
COMMON VISITORS: Pike, ducks, kingbirds, turtles, bullfrogs, muskrats, deer
RANGE: All eastern United States to eastern edge of prairies, north in eastern Canada to southern edge of boreal forest

Rising in dense purple swaths from quiet, shallow, muddy waters under full sun, pickerelweed is a joy for human and beast alike. The Ojibwa called the aquatic beauty *kinozhaeguhnsh,* "the pike's plant," because the great-fanged fish often lurks amid the plant's submerged tangled stems, waiting to ambush its prey. The English version became the plant's common name, pickerel being another name for pike, as well as walleye.

Though colonies of pickerelweed may cover hundreds of square yards, they are often populated by clones of the same plant, replicating itself by rapidly spreading rootstocks rather than by setting seed.

Each pickerelweed blossom remains open just for a single day, with the multiple-flowered spire gradually blooming from bottom to top between late July and early September. The finished flower heads droop down to let their seeds fall to the water.

SOLOMON'S SEAL

Mystically Decreed Herbal Healer

HEIGHT: 1.6–3.3 ft (50–100 cm)
ALIAS: Hairy Solomon's seal, true Solomon's seal, conquer-John, *Polygonatum pubescens*
OJIBWA NAME: Nauneebidaeodaekin, "those which grow together hanging"
FLOWERS: Greenish-white or white, bell-shaped, 0.4–0.6 in (1–1.5 cm) long, hanging in pairs, sometimes single, beneath arching stem
BERRIES: Bluish-black, containing several seeds, in late summer
LEAVES: 2–6 in (5–15 cm) long, 0.5–3 in (1.3–7.5 cm) wide, pointed at both ends, pale bottoms with conspicuous veins, stalkless, turning yellow in autumn
ROOTS: Deep, knotted white rhizome 0.4–0.8 in (1–2 cm) thick
PREFERRED HABITAT: Rich loam soil in upland hardwood forests, often mixed with white pine
RANGE: All north woods region south to Iowa and Ohio Valley, along Appalachians to Georgia and Delaware; also in eastern Canada to southern boreal forest

Mysterious circular scrawlings on the thick rootstocks of Solomon's seal are responsible for its name. Early Greek scholars likened them, on the Old World version of the plant, to Hebrew letters, and legend grew that they were a pharmacological seal of approval from the ring of history's first reputed botanist, King Solomon. The rhizomes of closely related plants have long been used for treating a wide sweep of maladies on both sides of the Atlantic. Many Native American groups applied it as a poultice for bruises, wounds, and black eyes. The Ojibwa brewed the roots into a tea to treat coughs and inhaled the steam from a preparation placed on hot stones.

In truth, the "Hebrew letters" are scars, marking where each year's stem has risen from the overwintering root. The graceful, arching stem rises from the ground in May, its pointed leaves unfolding to reveal tiny pairs of bell-like flowers dangling in a long row below them.

TRAILING ARBUTUS

Beloved Mayflower of Pilgrim Past

Legend has it that trailing arbutus, blooming just after the snow shrinks away, was the first flower the Pilgrims saw after their December landing and winter of death and privation at Plymouth. It's often called mayflower, like the Pilgrims' ship, and is venerated throughout New England. The old tradition of picking the strongly sweet-smelling blossoms and bringing them home as a spring greeting was outlawed in many states after they became scarce in more settled areas.

Trailing arbutus is really a short ground vine, its stem creeping along the surface, often covered by fallen leaves and pine needles.

In Ojibwa legend, the trailing arbutus is the gift of Hope, a beautiful pink-cheeked maiden, who came to Earth to grant a wish for an old man who wanted to be remembered for giving something lasting to his people. At his passing, she covered him with leaves and the white and pink blossoms that have since returned to inaugurate each spring.

HEIGHT: 0.8–2 in (2–5 cm)

ALIAS: Mayflower, ground laurel, Plymouth mayflower, winter pink, mountain pink, gravel plant, shad-flower, crocus, *Epigaea repens*

FLOWERS: 5 white or light pink, waxy-looking petals join to form a tube 0.4–0.8 in (1–2 cm) long; several bloom together in a tight bunch.

SEEDS: Minute, dark brown, numerous, held in rounded 5-chambered capsule; mature in late summer

LEAVES: Evergreen, 0.8–4 In (2–10 cm) long, 0.4–1.6 in (1–4 cm) wide, with rounded tips, smooth edges, shiny green and rough on top, hairy on bottom

STEM: Woody, covered by bristly, reddish-brown hairs, up to 1 ft (30 cm) long

PREFERRED HABITAT: Acidic sandy or mossy ground around coniferous and mixed forest edges and clearings

RANGE: All eastern United States to northern Florida, Mississippi, northeastern Illinois, and Minnesota; to northern boreal forest in eastern Canada to Manitoba

TROUT LILY

Early Spring's Green Mantle

I n early spring, about the first signs of growth on the hardwood forest floor are the pointed, tightly rolled purple leaves of trout lily, also called dogtooth violet, poking up en masse through the previous year's brown fallen leaves. With patches of snow still on the ground nearby, the scene resembles a rolling medieval battlefield with countless thousands of Lilliputian spears hoisted high. As they unfurl, the leaves—mottled like the skin of a brook trout—transform the ground into a transitory sea of green, speckled here and there with yellow clumps of flowers. The glory is short-lived. As soon as green spreads to the treetops, it drains from the ground, the

HEIGHT: 4–10 in (10–25 cm)

ALIAS: Dogtooth violet, yellow adder's tongue, fawn lily, yellow lily, yellow bells, yellow snowdrop, rattlesnake tooth, rattlesnake violet, yellow snake's tongue, lamb's tongue, snakeroot, *Erythronium americanum*

OJIBWA NAME: Numaegbugoneen, "sturgeon leaf"

FLOWERS: 1–1.4 in (3–3.5 cm) wide, nodding, with 3 backward-curving yellow petals with a purple strip on the back of each, and 3 petal-like deeper yellow sepals curving back even more; 6 orange or yellow sta-

leaves dying as they're cut off from the sun.

Many trout lily colonies are actually as old as the same arboreal giants that crowd them out every June. After its leaves crumble, a trout lily plant resumes its normal life deep underground, May's captured sunlight fueling it for the next ten months. Its bulb, or corm, is the plant's powerhouse and factory. After taking a summer siesta, it kicks into operation in late August. The next spring's leaves and flowers are formed in tightly packed buds on shoots that push toward the surface through autumn and winter. Trout lilies also spread runners up to ten inches (twenty-five centimeters) through the soil to create new bulbs. These cloned corms send up their own leaves in spring. The process repeats itself year after year, decade after decade, forming extensive subterranean networks that help hold the soil together. Some are up to 300 years old.

Many trout lily colonies are as old as the same arboreal giants that crowd them out every June

More than 99 percent of trout lily corms produce just one leaf. As the colony spreads randomly, eventually some bulbs grow in choice spots with enough light, moisture, nutrients, and shelter to support flowers. Still, it takes a seed or new corm in a good location at least five years to flower, producing bigger leaves each growing season and pushing deeper in the soil until the bulb is four to eight inches (ten to twenty centimeters) below the surface. Flowers often bloom

mens and a green pistil at center
SEEDS: Contained within oval green pod
LEAVES: Shiny, green, mottled with purple-brown or gray, 4–8 in (10–20 cm) long, 1–1.5 in (2–4 cm) wide, tapered at top and bottom, with smooth edges and parallel veins; cool to the touch; just 1 on non-flowering plants, 2 growing from the base of flowering stems
STEM: Light green, slightly leaning, extending 4–9 in (10–23 cm) straight below ground to bulb
ROOTS: Older corms brown and scaly; younger ones white, thin, and pointed, like a dog's canine tooth
PREFERRED HABITAT: Rich, moist soil in deciduous and sometimes mixed forests
COMPANION PLANTS: Spring beauty, red trillium, true and false Solomon's seal, wild sarsaparilla, jack-in-the-pulpit, starflower, violets
NUMBER OF TROUT LILIES PER SQ YD (0.8 M²) IN HARDWOOD FORESTS: 350 common; up to 900
PLANT BIOMASS CREATED BY TROUT LILIES EACH SPRING: Up to 175 lb/acre (165 kg/ha)
PAST MEDICINAL USES: Poultice from leaves used to treat skin disease, ulcers, and tumors; parts of plant also ingested to induce vomiting.
RANGE: Throughout north woods region and eastern United States to Georgia and Mississippi, west to Arkansas, Missouri, and Iowa, north into southeastern Canada
FIRST APPEARANCE OF LILY FAMILY: At least 35 million years ago

in small patches, usually about two weeks after first sprouting enclosed within two curled leaves. The blossoms nod toward the ground, protecting their nectar and pollen from rain. The backward-curving petals also close at night and during showers.

Only a small percentage of the flowers are fertilized, developing green pods holding a few seeds. Like trilliums and many other spring flowers, the seeds are spread by ants. Enticed by a nutritious, oily appendage attached to each seed, the insects carry the seeds back home for storage, later feasting on the attachments and chucking the rest in subterranean refuse chambers, which serve as protected seedbeds.

NUMBER OF ERYTHRONIUM *SPECIES NATIVE TO NORTH WOODS REGION:* 2
NUMBER OF U.S. ERYTHRONIUM *SPECIES:* 22
NUMBER OF OTHER ERYTHRONIUM *SPECIES ELSEWHERE IN WORLD:* 1, in Eurasia
NUMBER OF NORTH AMERICAN LILY SPECIES: About 140
NUMBER OF LILY SPECIES WORLDWIDE: About 485, or up to 5,000 if recent reclassifications of families discounted
ALSO SEE: Large-Flowered Trillium

Trout lily plays a vital role in the forest ecosystem that goes beyond its brief spring appearance. Because it dominates so thoroughly immediately after the snow melts, it draws up to almost half of all nutrients—such as nitrogen and potassium—accumulated from the breakdown of fallen leaves by bacteria working beneath winter's insulating snow. Without the trout lily's quick action, much of these nutrients would be washed away in spring runoff before the dormant roots of trees and other plants begin to stir. This enormous nutrient load, combined with abundant snowmelt and unobstructed sunlight, creates an incredible burst of trout lily leaves. When opening tree buds shade out the ground in late May, whatever nutrients not drawn into the trout lily corms are released by the plants' rapidly decaying leaves into the soil and absorbed by the rest of the forest vegetation.

VIOLETS

Sweet, Nutritious Flower of Love

Cherished by lovers, prophets, and generals, violets come not just in purple but in varying shades of white, blue, pink, and yellow as well. The color violet was actually named after one of the purple varieties. In the north, there are many species, adapted to a wide assortment of habitats, from hardwood and coniferous forests to wetland fringes and meadows, with the greatest profusion of bloomings coming in June.

In their highly varied colors and sizes, violets everywhere share a very similar design and layout. All feature a specialized lower, central petal that forms an organ- and nectar-bearing tube stretching toward the back of the flower. The front of the petal also serves as a landing platform for incoming flying insects, complete with runway markings in the form of brightly colored veins. Drawn by the flower's delicate scent, insects follow the veins straight

HEIGHT: 1–18 in (2.5–45 cm)
ALIAS: Family violeae
FLOWERS: 0.1–1.2 in (0.3–3 cm) wide, 5 petals, with nectar held in enclosure—called a spur—formed by the lowest petal
SEEDS: Sprung from dividing 3-chambered beige capsules, 0.2–1.1 in (4–12 mm) long; spread by ants, which eat attached fatty knobs but cannot break seed shell
LEAVES: Usually heart-shaped (notable exceptions being lanced-leaved and kidney-leaved violets), pointed at tips, and curled at base, with toothed edges; 0.4–4 in (1–10 cm) long, 0.4–5 in (1–12.5 cm) wide
ROOTS: Species with leaves and flowers on separate stalks have numerous thin roots and runners; species with leafy flower stalks have thick, branching woody roots.
DECIDUOUS FOREST SPECIES: Sweet white violet, Canada violet, downy yellow violet, woolly blue violet
CONIFEROUS FOREST SPECIES: Northern blue violet (illustrated), northern white violet, sweet white violet
WETLAND SPECIES: Marsh blue violet, sweet white violet, downy yellow violet, woolly blue violet, northern white violet

to the rich payload of nectar. Violets also display ultraviolet patterns, visible to bees and other pollinators but not to humans, which must make the veined petals even more striking in appearance.

Many of the same attributes that attract insects—alluring colors and structure and sweet scent—have also long endeared violets to humanity. The essential oils of Mediterranean violets are one of the oldest sources of perfumes. In Greek mythology, the flowers were created by Zeus as a sweet forage for the cow goddess Io, after whom they were named, rendered in Latin as *viola*. The blossoms and vitamin-rich leaves have also long been used by both Europeans and North American natives as ingredients for medicines, dyes, soups, salads, jams, syrups, candies, liqueurs, and dessert decorations.

But violets are probably more highly regarded for their symbolic value than for any practical benefit. Indeed, the woolly or common blue violet, which blooms in hardwood forests before leaf-out, is the official flower of four states: Wisconsin, Illinois, Rhode Island, and New Jersey.

Equated with modesty, chastity, love, and loyalty, violets have been worn by brides or thrown in their bouquets since the days of Helen of Troy. The garden pansy, developed from a small European violet, derives its name from the French *pensée*, meaning "thought" or "remembrance," after the custom of offering violets as a courting gift. Violets were also said to be the favorite flower of the prophet Muhammad and of Napoleon.

Most violet species actually reproduce mainly without their flowers, spreading thin underground runners that send up many clones instead. In addition, while cold weather or other mishaps often prevent insects from pollinating many violets, the plants still produce seeds with a second set of smaller flowers that never bloom. These "cleistogamous" buds are usually formed below or near the ground in summer and pollinate themselves without opening.

SHORELINE AND FOREST-EDGE SPECIES: lance-leaved violet, blue marsh violet, northern white violet, northern blue violet, dog violet, shore violet, Canada violet

WET MEADOW SPECIES: Northern white violet, marsh blue violet

MEADOW SPECIES: Dog violet, Canada violet, smooth yellow violet

COMMON DINERS: Bees, butterflies, mice, grouse, juncos, woodcocks, mourning doves, cutworms, fritillary butterfly caterpillars, slugs

NUMBER OF PARMA VIOLETS USED TO PRODUCE 1 LB (0.5 KG) OF ESSENTIAL OILS FOR PERFUME INDUSTRY: 2 million

RANGE: Throughout United States north to Alaska and northern Canada

NUMBER OF VIOLET SPECIES NATIVE TO NORTH WOODS: About 24 (much hybridization and debate on what to label species or subspecies)

NUMBER OF U.S. VIOLET SPECIES: About 100

NUMBER OF VIOLET SPECIES WORLDWIDE: About 500

ALSO SEE: Large-Flowered Trillium; Bees, Wasps, and Hornets

WATER LILY

Bloom of the Gods

The lotus flowers sacred to Buddhists, Hindus, ancient Egyptians, and Mayans are tropical relatives of the north woods water lily. Some water lilies are eaten in parts of Africa because of their hallucinogenic effects, which ethno-botanists speculate may have been at the root of the lotus's universal status as a sacred plant. The Buddha, Brahma, and Ra are often portrayed seated on lotus flowers. In these cultures, the lotus represents the primal womb of Mother Earth. Because it floats, radiant and serene, in stagnant ponds, the flower symbolizes the powers of light and beauty emerging from darkness. Similarly, the floating leaves, which remain dry on top, represent the inner self unsullied by the temptations of the senses.

Lily pads are designed to remain dry on top because, unlike land plants, their upper

ALIAS: Fragrant water lily, white water lily, water nymph, sweet-scented water lily, water cabbage, toad lily, lotus, *Nymphaea odorata*

OJIBWA NAME: Anung Pikobeesae, "star fallen in the water," from the story of a star maiden who became embodied as a water lily so that she could live on Earth close to people

FLOWERS: Up to 6 in (15 cm) wide, with many white petals around yellow center; strong fragrance similar to licorice; blooming late June to August

SEEDS: 600–700 per flower, mature in late summer or early fall

LEAVES: 2.5–12 in (7–30 cm) long, dark green, waxy on top, surface rather than their underside has air-breathing pores. If a lily pad is blown over, the waxy, waterproof top does not stick to the water as the slimy underside does. The red pigment of the leaf's bottom also increases its temperature slightly above that of the water. The extra heat helps the leaf get rid of the excess water through transpiration from pores on the upper surface, keeping the plant buoyant. Skipping-rope-like water lily stems have air tubes that keep them afloat as well. As soon as the ice is gone in spring, overwintering rootstocks send up new floating stems with leaf and flower buds ready to sprout, enabling the buds to reach the surface for light and air.

Root-eating Donacia beetle grubs siphon the water lily's air supply by tapping into the plant with special spines. Lily pads, meanwhile, are etched and pock-marked by tiny, dark nibbling waterlily leaf beetles and their grubby offspring, while midge larvae munch conspicuous snaking trails through the leaves. Among a plethora of other animals frequenting the plant are China-mark moth caterpillars, which eat through the pad from portable, airtight homes of woven leaf strips anchored beneath.

The resplendent flowers themselves provide sustenance to metallic adult Donacia beetles, bees, and flies. The flowers ensure cross-pollination by having their male, pollen-producing parts mature later than the female pistil. Laden with pollen picked up on older flowers, the insects stumble into the fluid-filled enclosure of stamens on the younger ones, washing off the pollen and fertilizing the plant. The flowers open early in the morning, but

purple-red on undersides, round or heart-shaped, with a V-shaped cut to the center; floating separately from flowers

ROOTS: Up to 3.3 ft (1 m) long and 2.5 in (6 cm) thick, lying horizontally

PREFERRED HABITAT: 6 in–15 ft (15 cm–5.5 m) deep in calm bays, ponds, and slow streams with deep organic silt bottoms

AVERAGE SODIUM CONTENT: 9,375 parts per million

AVERAGE SODIUM CONTENT OF LAND PLANTS: 9 parts per million

COMMON OCCUPANTS AND DINERS: Waterlily leaf beetles, Donacia beetles, China-mark moth caterpillars, fishing spiders, midge larvae, bees, caddis flies, aphids, pond snails, long-legged flies, dragonflies, leeches, frogs, painted turtles, wood ducks, muskrats, beavers, porcupines, deer, moose

NATIVE REMEDIES: Natives from Maine to Minnesota brewed root tea for coughs, sore throats, and tuberculosis and pounded roots into poultice for sores and swellings

MOST FAMOUS WATER LILY POND: Water garden of French impressionist Claude Monet, whose series of water lily paintings, in various light settings, are among his most celebrated

OTHER COMMON FLOATING PLANTS: Yellow bullhead lilies, water shield, bladderworts, floating arrowhead, pondweed, duckweed (the world's smallest flowering plant)

RANGE: All eastern United States to central Minnesota, Nebraska, and Texas, north into midboreal forest of eastern Canada; introduced in many western states

close by midafternoon, possibly conserving the pollen to ensure overlap between young and old flowers.

A flower blooms for three to five days, unless fertilized earlier, and then closes for good. At the same time, its stem begins to coil, gradually pulling the flower beneath the surface, where seeds develop for three to four weeks. Eventually, one to three dozen air-filled capsules containing many seeds break off from the shriveled stems in late summer and autumn and float away. As the slimy pod membrane dissolves, seeds sink to the bottom. They germinate in the spring and take about three years to produce a flower. New plants are also started by spreading rhizomes and by root fragments that break off and float away.

NUMBER OF NORTH AMERICAN WATER LILY SPECIES: 12

NUMBER OF WATER LILY FAMILY SPECIES WORLDWIDE: 60–90

ALSO SEE: Beaver, Moose, Porcupine

The flowers ensure cross-pollination by having their male,
pollen-producing parts mature later than the female pistil

Water lilies survive winter by withdrawing all their nutrients into thick rootstocks that are in turn a mainstay of beavers, moose, muskrats, and even fish-eating loons. The plant's high sodium levels also make it an important salt source for many vegetarian animals, such as porcupines. The rhizomes of yellow bullhead lilies, which tend to prefer slightly more shallow water, were collected from muskrat lodges or pulled up by native women in spring and late fall, when their nutrients were most concentrated. High in sugar and starch, they can be eaten like potatoes after soaking and boiling to get rid of bitter tannins. Seeds can also be eaten raw or ground into flour, while leaf and flower buds are eaten in salads.

WILD IRIS

Flower of Myth and Majesty

HEIGHT: 8–35 in (20–90 cm)
ALIAS: Blue flag, purple iris, *Iris versicolor*
FLOWERS: 2 or more per plant, each 2.4–3.2 in (6–8 cm) wide, with 3 violet true petals standing erect and 3 larger, down-curving sepals, which are violet with white-and-yellow bases veined with deep purple
SEEDS: Light brown, triangular, many held in green, 3-chambered, ridged pod 1.5–2 in (4–5 cm) long, maturing by late summer
LEAVES: Grasslike, 8–31 in (20–80 cm) long, 0.2–1.2 in (0.5–3 cm) wide
ROOTS: Soft, thick, spreading rhizomes with many fibrous rootlets
PREFERRED HABITAT: Moist ground and shallow water of shorelines, marshy sites, bog fringes, swamps, fens
RANGE: Throughout north woods region south to Virginia, Ohio, and Illinois, north in eastern Canada to Newfoundland and James Bay

Displaying one of the largest and most resplendent flowers in the wild, iris commands attention and captures the imagination wherever it blooms. Egyptian pharaohs topped their scepters with an iris design, its three petals representing wisdom, faith, and courage. In ancient Greece, Iris was the name of both the female messenger of the gods and her bridge to Earth, a rainbow. After taking a fancy to her, Zeus changed Iris into a flower to save her from the wrath of his wife, Hera. Other accounts hold that the flowers got their name because various iris species come in most colors of the rainbow. The colored part of the eye is called an iris for the same reason. In the twelfth century, Louis VII adopted as the symbol of French royalty the white iris, the fleur-de-Louis, later shortened to fleur-de-lis. Much later, Tennessee adopted purple iris as its state flower.

When wild iris blooms in early summer, bumblebees, butterflies, flies, and other insects actively seek out its ample pools of nectar, guided there by the prominent veins lining the flower's large purple sepals.

WILD SARSAPARILLA

The Original Backwoods Root Beer

The aromatic, nutritious root bark of wild sarsaparilla was the prime ingredient of homemade root beer beverages and medicinal pioneer teas, adopted from Native Americans. In Maine, the Penobscot used the root in cough medicine, while other groups included it in spring tonics and blood-purifying drinks. Perhaps not surprisingly, wild sarsaparilla is a member of the ginseng family. It is unrelated, however, to the true sarsaparilla of Central America, which yields a medicinal root extract that has been used to flavor soft drinks.

In many forests, large colonies of wild sarsaparilla form a second-story canopy with their outstretched leaves shading ground-cover plants below. Sarsaparilla's own tiny white flowers are also hidden beneath those leaves. Blooming in small spherical clusters in late May and June, they have no trouble attracting a wide assortment of pollinating flower flies and bees with their rich perfumed scent.

HEIGHT: 1–2 ft (30–60 cm)

ALIAS: American sarsaparilla, false sarsaparilla, *Aralia nudicaulis*

FLOWERS: Tiny, white, spiky, usually in 3 spherical clusters branching from a stem rising from the base of the plant, separate from leaf stem; sometimes 2 or up to 7 clusters

BERRIES: Purple-black, each usually containing 5 seeds, edible but disagreeable

LEAVES: Compound, with 3 groupings of 3–5 broadly pointed leaflets, each 2–5 in (5–12.5 cm) long, with finely serrated edges, purplish-brown at first, deep green in summer, yellow or bronze in September

ROOTS: Tough, woody horizontal rhizomes up to more than 2 ft (61 cm) long

PREFERRED HABITAT: Loam soil in mature deciduous and mixed forests; up to 3,000 ft (914 m) in mountains

RANGE: All northeastern United States, south along Appalachians to Georgia through Midwest, northern plains, and Rockies to Washington; north across Canada

WINTERGREEN

Little Leaf with Bubble Gum Flavor

The taste that flavors chewing gums, toothpaste, and cough drops is not hard to find in the north woods. Simply plucking a stiff, shiny little wintergreen leaf and giving it a quick chew yields instant *essence du bubble gum*. Wintergreen was used by native peoples throughout the north to flavor food, drink, and tobacco. Aromatic wintergreen tea, in fact, became something of a national drink after the Boston Tea Party in 1773 and the subsequent boycott of British-imported beverage leaves.

A chemical substance known as oil of wintergreen is also present in some other plants. Early manufacturers found it easiest to extract large quantities from the bark of "sweet" or cherry birch for food flavorings and perfume. Today, the flavor is widely synthesized. Because it soothes aches and irritations, the oil was also used in medi-

HEIGHT: 4–6 in (10–15 cm); rarely up to 8 in (20 cm)

ALIAS: Checkerberry, teaberry, mountain tea, spice berry, boxberry, deerberry, *Gaultheria procumbens*

FLOWERS: White, waxy-looking, barrel-shaped, 0.2–0.4 in (5–10 mm) long, blooming beneath leaves in summer

BERRIES: Scarlet, about 0.4 in (1 cm) wide, containing capsule with seeds inside

LEAVES: 0.4–2 in (1–5 cm) long, oval, pale on undersides; fragrant, shiny, flexible in first season, later turning dark green, stiff and leathery, and eventually reddish; 3–4 per stem

STEM: Short, bare, woody; actually one of many stalks, or branches, rising along length of buried, creeping rhizome

cine. It yields methyl salicylate, similar to the active ingredient in aspirin, also found in willow bark. One of its greatest uses, however, was as an ingredient to cover the taste of "miracle formulas"—comprised largely of alcohol—peddled by nineteenth-century snake-oil salesmen.

Still, wintergreen's mild powers as a stimulant and astringent seem to have been well known by Ojibwa paddlers, who said they chewed the plant's leaves during portages and other exhausting activities to increase their endurance. They also credited the plant's red berries with aiding digestion. Herbalists warn, however, that too much wintergreen oil can cause allergic reactions in some, especially children, who should be discouraged from eating the leaves and berries. The pitted berries are most palatable after they have spent a winter sweetening and mellowing on the vine, hanging beneath the plant's evergreen leaves deep in the snow. Perhaps that's why, though they're eaten by grouse, mouse, and bear alike, they're not snapped up as soon as they ripen in autumn.

COMPANION PLANTS: Goldthread, bluebead lilies, moccasin flowers, Canada mayflowers, bunchberry, wood sorrel, twinflowers, trailing arbutus

COMMON VISITORS: Mice, chipmunks, deer, bears, ruffed grouse, bumble-bees

MEDICINAL USES: Preventing tooth decay; soothing aching muscles; treating colds, stomachaches, toothaches, and rheumatism

PREFERRED HABITAT: Acidic, mossy, or sandy soil in mixed and coniferous forests and clearings

RANGE: Throughout north woods region, along Appalachians to Georgia and Alabama, west through Great Lakes states, and north into eastern Canada

NUMBER OF GAULTHERIA SPECIES NATIVE TO ONTARIO: 2

NUMBER OF GAULTHERIA SPECIES WORLDWIDE: About 200, most in the Andes of South America

ALSO SEE: Yellow Birch, Basswood

Wintergreen is sometimes called partridgeberry, which is more properly the name of a small, mat-forming forest ground vine, also a member of the heath family, which produces pairs of similar winter-persistent red berries. Both provide a ready food source for early migrant birds returning to their breeding territories in spring before insects become abundant.

Snowberry, wintergreen's closest relative in the north, also sounds the wintery theme, though its name actually alludes to the plant's white berries. Like wintergreen, it has tiny, waxy white bell flowers, but they're borne on vinelike, hairy branchlets forming mats over the ground in coniferous forests and sphagnum bogs. Its leaves are also very tiny, just a fraction of an inch long, lining the length of the branchlets.

WOOD SORREL

Far-Flung Shamrocks of Mossy Realms

Even when not in bloom, wood sorrel is very distinctive, its three glossy, smooth-edged leaflets forming three perfect hearts joined together at their pointed tips. The plant, which also grows in Europe and Asia, is often hailed as the original shamrock, a sacred symbol of the ancient Celtic druids used by Saint Patrick to explain the concept of the Holy Trinity to the pagan Irish. There are, however, several other leading shamrock candidates, including common clovers.

Growing happily in some of the deepest shade of northern evergreen forests, wood sorrel forecasts bad weather by folding together its dainty leaves (as it does at night) before rain or cold weather. Like

HEIGHT: 2–4 in (5–10 cm); rarely up to 6 in (15 cm)
ALIAS: Common wood sorrel, mountain woods sorrel, upright wood sorrel, white wood sorrel, true wood sorrel, shamrock, *Oxalis montana, Oxalis acetosella*
NAME ORIGIN OF SHAMROCK: Irish *seamrog,* meaning "little clover"
FLOWERS: 0.6–0.8 in (1.5–2 cm) wide, 5 small white, sometimes light pink, petals with thin dark pink stripes and a tiny yellow dot at the base of each petal; 1 per plant, on a separate stem from leaves
SEEDS: Have white ridges; shot out from small, round pod
LEAVES: Like tiny, distinct, smooth-edged, glossy clovers, 0.4–1.2 in (1–3 cm) wide
PREFERRED HABITAT: Acidic, thin, mossy, or sandy soil in mature coniferous and mixed forests and in bogs
RANGE: All north woods region to New Jersey and Ohio and along Appalachians to Georgia; north to midboreal forest of eastern Canada

many plants growing under coniferous trees, it is itself an evergreen, bolstered by sugary antifreeze compounds that allow its leaves to persist, dormant but alive, beneath the snow. Also, as with many woodland herbs, wood sorrel stays close to the ground, where carbon dioxide levels are 25 percent higher than in open areas.

TREES AND SHRUBS

Looking out from a hilltop over the seemingly endless expanse of forest across much of the north, one may find it hard to imagine how loggers could ever have cleared such vast tracts of green. Yet virtually the entire region has been visited by the ax and saw. A hundred or more years ago, many states had less than half the forest cover they now enjoy. Most of today's red and white pines—signature trees of the north woods—have grown up in the years since, though they are shadows of the towering old-growth bounty that once dominated much of the forest.

Luckily, the northeast and upper Midwest are blessed not only with the great pines, but also with many trees characteristic of two quite different forest zones to the north and south. On hills and lower mountain slopes, sugar maples and other hardwoods transform the countryside with rich hues of red, orange, and yellow in autumn. At the same time, the boreal zone's wealth of beautiful white-barked paper birch, aspen, and Christmas-tree forests of fragrant fir and spruce overlap throughout the region.

Together these trees clothe the land and give it its character. They are the greatest expressions and storehouses of the life force in the wilderness. The lion's share of the sunlight is captured by tree leaves and needles and used to power phenomenal growth. Every day, each mature tree sucks up thousands of gallons of water from the ground through its roots, releasing much of it in turn through pores in its leaves, moistening the forest air. Life is indeed at its richest inside a deep, dark forest.

BALSAM FIR

The Fragrance of the Forest

Balsam is derived from an ancient Hebrew word for aromatic tree resins used for balms—soothing ointments or salves. In the north woods, it is the rich, sweet essence of the region. The balsam fir's thick, sticky resin literally bubbles up beneath its bark, oozing from old knots and wounds and caking its buds and cones, making them difficult for squirrels and crossbills to eat. When fungus attacks, a fir increases sap production, laying it on thick where invading fungal strands seek to penetrate the tree's soft wood. Natives and lumberjacks took their cues from the trees and squeezed fir "gum" from the blisters to use as an effective antiseptic seal for cuts and wounds. The clear resin has also long been used for Canada balsam, a glue for mounting specimens on microscope slides and securing lenses in microscopes themselves and other optical equipment.

The gooey sap common to all northern conifers is, in fact, the key to their survival

AVERAGE MATURE HEIGHT: 40–60 ft (12–18 m)

AVERAGE MATURE TRUNK WIDTH: 1–1.5 ft (30–46 cm)

TALLEST IN UNITED STATES: 116 ft (35 m), in Porcupine Mountains Wilderness State Park, Michigan

LIFE SPAN: Average 60–70 years; up to about 200 years

ALIAS: Balm of Gilead, blister fir, white fir, Canada balsam, eastern fir, church steeple, silver pine, *Abies balsamea*

BARK: Gray and smooth, with horizontal specks and raised blisters filled with resin when young. Brownish scales form on older trees.

NEEDLES: 0.8–1.2 in (2–3 cm) long, blunt, dark green on top, 2 white lines on underside; curving upward in flat, horizontal rows on lower branches; remain on branch 3–4 years through winters too harsh for the watery sap of most deciduous trees. It acts as a sugar-rich natural antifreeze in the roots and branches, allowing the tree to hang on to its dormant waxy needles through the winter. As soon as temperatures rise above freezing, the needles can start photosynthesizing, allowing them to be productive through the entire short growing season.

Balsam fir, along with white spruce and Scotch pine, continues to be the most popular choice for Christmas trees and wreaths everywhere today

In pagan times, Germans celebrated the winter-solstice Yule festival by bringing evergreen boughs—holding the promise of spring and providing shelter for visiting elves—into their homes. Hundreds of years later, they brought the *Tannenbaum* tradition with them to America. Balsam fir, along with white spruce and Scotch pine, continues to be the most popular choice for Christmas trees and wreaths everywhere today. The fragrant needles also fill souvenir pillows of the north woods sold in New England gift shops.

In a forest of Christmas trees, firs can be distinguished from spruce at a distance by the way they taper more narrowly to a perfect point. Up close, fir can be seen to have flat needles, unlike four-sided spruce needles, which are easily rolled between the thumb and forefinger.

SEX: Usually reaches puberty after 20 years. Purple-red male flower conelets, $\frac{1}{4}$ in (6 mm) long, are clustered at base of needles along twigs; much larger, dark female cones stand erect higher up on tree; wind-pollinated in late May and June.

CONES: 2–4 in (5–10 cm) long, dark purplish, erect, near top of tree; mature in several months, by autumn, then disintegrate on the branch, leaving behind pointy spindles; big crops every 2–4 years

SEEDS: Tiny, attached to wing 0.4–0.6 in (1–1.5 cm) long, about 135 per cone, 60,000 lb (130,000/kg), most falling late August to October

WOOD: White, soft, knotty, weak, fairly brittle, with straight, coarse grain, 24 lb/cu ft (385 kg/m³)

HEAT EQUIVALENT TO 100 GALLONS OF OIL: 1.9 cords

PREFERRED HABITAT: Moist lowlands of silt loam soil, or in dry, sandy uplands, often on north-facing slopes; dominant tree from 3,200 ft (975 m) to tree line in mountains

COMPANION TREES AND SHRUBS: Spruce, jack pine, aspen, paper birch, red maple, white pine, hemlock, cedar, chokecherry, beaked hazel, mountain maple, Juneberry

ASSOCIATED PLANTS: Canada mayflower, large-leaved aster, bunchberry, wintergreen, blue bead lily, goldthread, bracken ferns

COMMON NESTERS: Yellow-rumped warblers, evening grosbeaks

FREQUENT VISITORS: Red squirrels, mice, voles, bears, moose. Ruffed and spruce grouse eat seeds, buds, inner bark, or needles, though not

Because balsam is more tolerant of moist soil and shade than white and red spruce, it forms pure stands much more often, its seedlings dominating the forest floor even where spruce tower above. Fir, however, is shorter-lived and more prone to many stresses. With a lower cellulose content, its wood is not as dense as that of spruce, allowing rot to set in when some trees are as young as forty years old. Weakened firs, anchored by shallow roots, are easily toppled by the wind.

Fir forests can also be especially volatile tinderboxes. Spruce budworms love balsam fir above all other trees, creating huge tracts of soft, dry, dead and dying wood during outbreaks. The thick layer of needle litter on the ground also makes coniferous forests more prone to fires than deciduous trees. When humidity levels drop below 30 percent—as they often do in May and June in boreal forests—the fire hazard becomes extreme. Trees dry out, trying to keep their needles moist, and lose billions of gallons of water to the air through transpiration. Such conditions lead to the most severe forest fires, spreading at up to 150 feet (46 meters) a minute.

a preferred food for most. Used for winter shelter by deer, hares, martens, and fishers.

COMMON NIBBLERS AND AILMENTS: Spruce budworms, ambrosia beetles, longhorn beetles, balsam woolly adelgids, hemlock looper caterpillars, wood wasps, red heart fungus, rust fungi

AVERAGE NUMBER OF FIR SAPLINGS IN A HEALTHY FIR-SPRUCE FOREST: 1,600 per acre (0.4 ha)

AVERAGE NUMBER OF SPRUCE SAPLINGS IN A HEALTHY FIR-SPRUCE FOREST: 200 per acre (0.4 ha)

AREA COVERED BY CHRISTMAS TREE FARMS IN UNITED STATES: About 1 million acres (400,000 ha)

RANGE: Throughout north woods region to northern Iowa and Connecticut and scattered along Appalachians to Virginia; to northern boreal forest across Canada to Alberta

NUMBER OF U.S. FIR SPECIES: 9

NUMBER OF FIR SPECIES WORLDWIDE: About 40

ALSO SEE: White and Red Spruce, White Cedar, Humus and Soil

On the subalpine slopes of the Appalachians and Adirondacks, where it's often too cold for budworms and too moist for fires to be regular occurrences, balsam fir forests experience a different form of mass die-off. Older trees that are most exposed to damaging winds and rime—ice forming when cloud moisture freezes over them—eventually succumb and topple, thereby exposing other firs behind them to the same stresses. The process commonly moves in distinct waves across the slope, with young spruce saplings springing up in the wake of their elders' demise until the next death wave reaches them sixty or seventy years later.

BASSWOOD

Rope, Honey, and Porcupine Fodder

Though never a dominant tree in the mixed and hardwood forest, basswood has been highly important to both beast and *Homo sapiens*. To the Ojibwa, Ottawa, and Iroquois, it was the tree that binds. Basswood's inner bark holds some of the longest, strongest, toughest natural fibers on the continent. It was used for rope, thread, twine, thongs, nets, and woven bags. In spring, natives easily stripped bark from the trees and either soaked it for several weeks—the softer material rotting away to leave only the strongest fibers—or boiled and pounded it until stringy and malleable. They then twisted the strands together to make flexible white rope and string esteemed by its native makers for being softer on the hands and less likely to kink and tangle than the white traders' hemp. Birch bark containers, clothes,

AVERAGE MATURE HEIGHT: 60–80 ft (18–24 m)

MAXIMUM HEIGHT: 132 ft (40 m)

AVERAGE MATURE TRUNK WIDTH: 2–2.5 ft (60–75 cm)

LIFE SPAN: Large, mature trees commonly 200 years old

ALIAS: Linden, lime, American basswood, whitewood, bass, *Tilia americana*

NAME ORIGIN: From "bast," the fibrous inner bark, or phloem, of trees used to make rope

BARK: Dark gray, with long, thin, flat ridges

LEAVES: 5–8 in (13–20 cm) long, 3–6 in (7.5–15 cm) wide, slightly lopsided, with a pointed tip and large-toothed edges; long stems; turn crispy brown from edges toward center in fall

SEX: Clusters of 10–20 small fragrant yellow flowers joined by a single stalk to the midpoint of a narrow leaflike blade 3–5 in (7.5–12.5 cm) long. Each flower has 5 petals and both male and female parts.

SEEDS: Bunches of several hard, pea-sized green nutlets covered by soft rust-brown hairs and holding 1–2 seeds; hang on trees into winter; take 2 years to germinate

WOOD: Creamy-white to light brown, smooth, soft, fine-grained, even-textured, weak, 29 lb/cu ft (465 kg/m³)

lodge poles, reed mats, even wounds, were all held together by the wonder fiber.

The settlers also took to basswood in a big way, though not so much for its rope. They worked the wood, taking the lead of the Iroquois, who carved False Face masks right on the trunks of live trees, then cut them off and hollowed them out. Softest and lightest of all the hardwoods, with a fine, smooth, straight grain that is easily worked, basswood has long been highly valued by carvers. It was lathed to make bowls and platters, and carved into wooden spoons and toys. Today, it is still crafted into duck decoys, wood sculptures, and models.

In the forest, basswood never forms pure stands. In the dark understory, shade-tolerant basswood saplings have the virtue of patience. With huge, lopsided leaves, often bigger than a fully spread hand, they grow slowly. When a spot opens up in the canopy, they shoot up and join the big trees. When an old basswood dies, rather than give up a hard-won place in the sun, its still-living base sprouts new shoots, creating a clump of trunks where there had been just one.

Even when basswood leaves are only high above on mature trees, porcupines make the effort to reach them. In many areas, basswoods are one of the most important foods of the moving pincushions. The mild-tasting leaves are about 13 percent protein.

Roots: Deep, widespread, well anchored

Preferred habitat: Deciduous forests with deep, rich soils, often on hillsides; less often in mixed forests

Associated trees: Sugar maple, yellow birch, beech, black cherry, ironwood

Frequent visitors: Porcupines, deer, chipmunks, squirrels. Mice and ruffed grouse eat seeds, leaves, or buds.

Common nibblers: Basswood leaf roller and forest tent caterpillars

Average leaf decomposition time: 2.5 years

False Face masks: Fierce images of the spirits that protected against disease and crop blights worn during Iroquois False Face ceremonies before the start of each growing season; were carved from living basswood trees so that the mask would hold life

Range: Throughout eastern United States to eastern prairies and north into southeastern Canada

Number of U.S. Tilia species: 1

Number of Tilia species worldwide: About 20

Also see: Porcupine; Bees, Wasps, and Hornets

The strong, sweet scent of basswood flowers, sometimes noticeable for more than half a mile (0.8 kilometer), also attracts droves of bees that cross-pollinate the widely scattered trees. While basswood blooms in late June and July, its nectar is the focus for local hives, where it is made into a high-quality, strong-tasting white honey. Perhaps the flowers and honey are what prompted the ancient Greeks to associate the closely related European linden tree with sweetness, modesty, gentleness, and conjugal love. The trees were said to be the husbands of the dryads, the wood nymphs.

BEECH

Signpost of the Ages

Or shall I rather the sad verse repeat
Which on the beech's bark I lately writ?

—Virgil, c. first century B.C.

A stand of beech trees can have an almost surreal, storybook presence, the silvery smooth, curvaceous trunks like the gnarled limbs of sentient giants. The thin, seamless bark of beech trees is more like living skin than the bark of most other trees. On oaks, maples, and conifers, dead bark cells gradually build up, crack open, and form deep ridges or plates. Dead beech-bark cells are soon shed like powder from the tree's surface.

Like skin, beech bark scars permanently, forming wound cork that rises up

AVERAGE MATURE HEIGHT: 60–80 ft (18–24 m)
MAXIMUM HEIGHT: 160 ft (49 m)
AVERAGE MATURE TRUNK WIDTH: 2–3.3 ft (60–100 cm)
LIFE SPAN: Commonly 200–300 years, maximum more than 400 years
ALIAS: American beech, white beech, gray beech, red beech, beechnut tree, *Fagus grandifolia*
BARK: Smooth, light bluish-gray, thin
LEAVES: 2–5 in (5–13 cm) long, shiny green, oval, pointed at end, serrated, with straight, prominent veins, papery texture
SEX: Clusters of greenish-yellow male flowers like round tassels, each 0.8 in (2 cm) wide, hanging on long stalks; tiny reddish females on short stalks near branch tips; open with leaves; wind-pollinated
NUTS: Three-sided nuts, 0.5 in (13 mm) long, usually 2 contained in round, bristled reddish-brown husk; 22% protein, 42% fat; fall for several weeks after first heavy frosts; big crops every 2–8 years
BUDS: Spearlike, 0.2–0.8 in (1–2 cm) long, slender, very pointy
WOOD: Pale to reddish-brown heartwood, thin whitish sapwood, hard, strong, stiff, 42 lb/cu ft (670 kg/m³), close-grained, long- and hot-burning
ROOTS: Dense, widespread mat of

like a bump along the scar. These qualities made beech a favorite signpost for lovers' initials and other graffiti long before a soon-to-be famous woodsman scrawled "D. Boon cilled A BAR On Tree in the Year 1760" on a Tennessee beech that lived until 1916. In fact, the word *book* is believed to be derived from the old Germanic word for beech, *boko*, because ancient runic inscriptions were carved on beechwood tablets.

According to one story, the tree actually triggered the greatest revolution of the written word ever, after Johannes Gutenberg, one day in the fifteenth century, idly carved some letters in beech bark, then wrapped the still-damp letter shavings up in paper and carried them home. When he later discovered that they left impressions on the paper, a lightbulb went on and the printing press was born.

Their thin skin does not allow beech trees to survive the most severe winters or to withstand fires. While common in the east, the tree doesn't venture above low mountain slopes, and it peters out on Michigan's Upper Peninsula and in eastern Wisconsin. Wounds also allow wood-rotting fungi into the tree, a common cause of demise for many beeches. In New England and the Adirondacks, the trunks of a large portion of the trees are pockmarked by beech bark disease. The epidemic is initiated by the European beech scale insect, an illegal immigrant that snuck into Nova Scotia in 1890. Trees tapped by the sucking villains become infected by bark canker fungi, giving them their blighted appearance, often eventually killing them.

In good conditions, beech can be very long lived. It is forty to sixty years old before it even starts producing nuts, which are fed upon by hordes of

fine rootlets, usually shallow, but can reach 5 ft (1.5 m) down in deep soils. Tree sends out suckering shoots.

PREFERRED HABITAT: Upland hardwood forests with rich, sandy loam soil, up to 3,200 ft (980 m) in mountains

COMPANION TREES AND SHRUBS: Sugar maple, yellow birch, hemlock, basswood, white pine, red maple, red spruce, black cherry, beaked hazel

ASSOCIATED PLANTS: Large-flowered trillium, trout lily, spring beauty, Canada mayflower

COMMON NESTERS: Red-eyed vireos

COMMON AILMENTS: Thin bark susceptible to frost cracks, small ground fires, and sucking insects such as beech scale and aphids; infected by more than 70 species of fungi, more than any other hardwood tree. Roots siphoned by beechdrops, sticklike parasitic plants that grow near the trunk.

RANGE: Eastern United States to the eastern two-thirds of Michigan's Upper Peninsula and Lake Michigan hinterlands of Wisconsin, south to eastern Texas and northern Florida, north into southeastern Canada

NUMBER OF NORTH AMERICAN BEECH SPECIES: 1

NUMBER OF BEECH SPECIES WORLDWIDE: 10

ALSO SEE: Sugar Maple, Black Bear, Blue Jay

deer, squirrels, foxes, raccoons, porcupines, mice, ducks, blue jays, and grouse. Black bears cause beech wounds by clawing their way up the trunks to get at big nut crops. More damaging still, bears often leave "bear nests" in the crotches of trees, where they sit and pull in branches while gorging— breaking limbs and twigs as they munch.

The word book *is believed to be derived from the old Germanic word for beech,* boko

---

The nutritious nuts are edible to humans as well, as noted by the tree's scientific name *Fagus*, from the Greek word for "eat." The original Indo-European word for "beech," *bhagos*, may have meant the same thing.

Beechnuts, like maple seeds, sprout fairly big, strong seedlings, whose roots can penetrate the forest's thick litter layer. Like maples, they are content in the shade, growing very slowly until a mature tree falls and brings the sun's light down on them. Eventually, they come to dominate the canopy. In more open areas, older beech trees often propagate themselves by spreading out sucker roots, resulting in clumps of beeches around a mature tree.

In contrast to sugar maples, beech tend to turn a dull yellow or bronze in the autumn. On lower branches and saplings, these leaves often don't fall, because their stem bases do not fully form the corky abscission layer that on most trees separates autumn leaves from the twig. Instead, they remain on the branch, becoming bleached by the winter sun, until they are pushed off by new leaves in the spring. Early settlers often stuffed such dry, dead beech leaves into their mattresses because they were springier than straw.

BLACK ASH

Fabled Trees in Many Cultures

Ash trees occupied an important place in early mystical beliefs on both sides of the Atlantic. A common story among Algonkian-speaking peoples tells of the first humans emerging from a hole made in an ash by an arrow shot by the supernatural culture hero Gluskabe. Similarly, the Romans, Greeks, Vikings, and others all had legends of the first people coming from an ash or other tree. The Norse world tree, Yggdrasil, which held heaven and Earth, was a European ash, similar to the black ash.

Though a member of the southern olive family, the slender, straight-trunked black ash is common in swampy areas in

The wood's elasticity also made it an important source of snowshoe frames

AVERAGE MATURE HEIGHT: 40–60 ft (12–18 m)
MAXIMUM HEIGHT: 100 ft (30 m)
AVERAGE MATURE TRUNK WIDTH: 8–24 in (20–60 cm)
ALIAS: Swamp ash, basket ash, hoop ash, brown ash, *Fraxinus nigra*
BARK: Soft, gray, corky with flaky ridges
LEAVES: Composites of 7–11 opposite, narrowly pointed, dark green leaflets, each 4–5 in (10–13 cm) long, with fine teeth on edges; pale yellow turning rust early in autumn
SEX: Clusters of tiny, shaggy, greenish-yellow, petal-less male flowers in May; smaller ragged females usually on separate trees

the north, often in pure stands. It moves into the edges of swamps as they begin to dry up, though it may be surrounded by shallow water in spring and early summer. In its wet habitat, it usually grows slowly, not leafing out until June and starting to change color after the first frosts of late summer. Black ash is easy to pick out because it is the only tree in the north woods with oval leaflets spreading out in pairs opposite to each other.

Black ash wood has a unique quality—when cut into short, peeled logs, soaked, and thoroughly beaten—of separating at the divisions between its annual growth rings. The Abenaki people of northern New England, the Iroquois, the Ojibwa, and many other groups cut the resulting thin circular sheets into strips for weaving baskets. Pioneers used them for barrel hoops and woven chair seats. The wood's elasticity also made it an important source of snowshoe frames, a vital tool of survival in northern woodlands. The tree's upland cousin, white ash, has stronger wood and was even more favored for snowshoes wherever it grew, primarily east of Minnesota. It's also famous as the main source of baseball bats, as well as many other sporting goods.

SEEDS: 1–1.5 in (2.5–4 cm) long, green, flat, with paddle-shaped wings, ripening in dense, hanging clusters in September; eaten by pine grosbeaks, purple finches, wood ducks, squirrels, mice
WOOD: Dark grayish-brown heartwood, whitish sapwood, coarse grain, stiff, medium strength, 35 lb/cu ft (560 kg/m³)
ROOTS: Very shallow
PREFERRED HABITAT: Rich, moist organic or loam soil in swamp forests, floodplains, watersides, and other low, moist sites
COMPANION TREES: Red maple, speckled alder, yellow birch, white cedar, black spruce, tamarack, balsam poplar, willow
RANGE: All north woods region to edge of prairies, south to Iowa, Indiana, and northern Virginia; north to midboreal region of eastern Canada

BLACK SPRUCE

The Hardy Bog Dweller

Dark, spindly stands of black spruce, with little moss-draped branches hanging down like shriveled, drooping arms of ghouls, give some people the heebie-jeebies as they drive into expanses of northern boreal forests. Yet to others, the trees evoke a somber, sublime solitude.

A specialist in adversity, black spruce takes root in remote environs where few other trees, or humans, venture. It perseveres on vast swaths of rocky, thin-soiled hillsides in northern Minnesota, at the highest treed limits of the Appalachians,

AVERAGE MATURE HEIGHT: 10–30 ft (3–9 m) in wetlands, 30–60 ft (9–18 m) on dry sites

AVERAGE MATURE TRUNK WIDTH: 6–10 in (15–25 cm)

TALLEST IN UNITED STATES: 78 ft (23.8 m), in Taylor County, Wisconsin

LIFE SPAN: Average 180–220 years; up to 250 years

ALIAS: Bog spruce, swamp spruce, shortleaf black spruce, *Picea mariana*

BARK: Dark gray-brown, thin, very flaky

NEEDLES: $\frac{1}{4}$–$\frac{1}{2}$ in (6–12 mm) long, dark green, shed after 10 or more years

SEX: Small crimson male flower conelets and deep red female conelets in dense clusters in crown, appearing in May and early June; puberty 15–30 years old

CONES: 0.8–1.3 in (2–3 cm) long, oval, brown to purplish, with thin, dense scales that open gradually to release very tiny winged seeds over several years

ROOTS: Very shallow, extensive, intricate; trees prone to being blown down

PREFERRED HABITAT: Bogs, swamps, watersides, or dry, thin-soiled uplands

COMPANION TREES: Tamarack, white spruce, jack pine, paper birch,

and, more than anywhere else, in the thick, wet moss fringing stagnant northern wetlands. Bogs maintain a microclimate that is cooler than the surrounding forests. Black spruce, one of the first cold-resistant trees to follow the retreat of the glaciers back into the northern states, remained clustered around bogs long after temperate tree species took over more fertile, hospitable ground.

Black spruce can make-do-with-less better than all the trees that crowd it out in good soils. Its stringy roots—which were split and used by native peoples to sew the seams of birch-bark canoes and containers—spread and intertwine through a bog's spongy moss mat or the thin soil of a rocky slope. Though black spruce's persistent, tiny, wind-borne seeds commonly sprout on open ground immediately after a fire, once established it can get by on a minimum of nutrients in acidic wetland and rocky settings, growing slowly, managing to sprout only tiny branches. Some, growing closest to the center of an open bog, at a mountain tree line, or in the shadow of their own kind, can be a century old and only ten feet tall. If a soggy moss mat builds up around the tree or the bog's water table rises, a black spruce's lowest branches can grow into the moss and sprout up as new trees.

quaking aspen, fir, red maple, speckled alder

ASSOCIATED PLANTS: Feather moss, sphagnum moss, lichens, Labrador tea, leatherleaf, bog laurel, bog orchid

COMMON NESTERS: Spruce grouse, kinglets, olive-sided flycatchers, gray jays, blackburnian warblers, northern parula warblers, red squirrels

FREQUENT VISITORS: Chipmunks, red-backed voles, mice, nuthatches, pine grosbeaks, pine siskins, white-winged crossbills and boreal chickadees eat seeds; moose, porcupines, and hares browse bark or needles.

RANGE: Throughout north woods region to southeastern Minnesota, southeastern Michigan, Pennsylvania, and northern New Jersey; north to Alaska and across Canada to tree line

AGE OF OLDEST SPRUCE FOSSILS: 55–65 million years

NUMBER OF SPRUCE SPECIES NATIVE TO NORTH WOODS REGION: 3

NUMBER OF U.S. SPRUCE SPECIES: 7

NUMBER OF SPRUCE SPECIES WORLDWIDE: 30–40

For early lumberjacks, the dwarfen trees were useful only as a source of home brew and chewing gum, from its branches and resinous sap, respectively. Today, however, they are cut extensively, mostly for pulp and paper.

CHOKECHERRY

Harsh Fruits Mellowing with Age

Since time immemorial, cherries have drawn hungry crowds seeking their sweet, juicy flesh. Cherry-eating creatures propagate the trees by swallowing the pits and spreading them in their droppings. Some, though, such as evening grosbeaks and chipmunks, cheat the trees by biting into the pits to eat the seeds inside. Bears tear branches off to get at the small, red fruits, sometimes harming or killing most of the trees in a thicket during big crop years in August and September.

Chokecherries are not as dangerous as their name suggests, though they can taste harsh and astringent, causing the mouth to pucker and dry. The riper they become, especially when tempered by a frost, the sweeter and more palatable they are. But eating large numbers with their pits, or eating those of any other cherries, can cause vomiting and even death. The pits, inner

AVERAGE MATURE HEIGHT: 6.6–13.2 ft (2–4 m)

MAXIMUM HEIGHT: 33 ft (10 m) in rich, moist soil

AVERAGE MATURE TRUNK WIDTH: 2–6 in (5–15 cm), usually with multiple bent, leaning trunks

MAXIMUM TRUNK WIDTH: 22 in (56 cm)

ALIAS: Prunus virginiana

LEAVES: Dark green, 0.8–4.8 in (2–12 cm) long, 0.4–2.4 in (1–6 cm) wide, egg-shaped, broader than other cherry species, with finely serrated edges; turn dull yellow in fall

BARK: Smooth or finely scaled, dark gray; almost black on older trees

SEX: White blossoms, 0.4 in (8–10 mm) wide, clustered tightly around an erect central stalk, 2–6 in (5–15 cm) long at branch tips, with male and female parts found together in each tiny, 5-petaled flower; blooming in late May and early June, a week or more after leaves open; cross-pollinated by mosquitoes and other flying insects

CHERRIES: Bright red to purple-black, pea-sized, with large stones

BUDS: Brown, 0.2–0.4 in (6–12 mm) long, sharply pointed

WOOD: Light brown, hard, dense but weak and porous

bark, and leaves of all cherry species are laced with prussic acid, or hydrogen cyanide, from which cyanide can be produced. A couple pounds (one kilo) of cherry leaves is said to contain enough poison to kill thirty humans.

When cooked and dried, however, pit-bearing chokecherries are safe. The Ojibwa mashed and dried them to mix into their cakes. Farther west, they were one of the main wild berries added to flavor and sweeten pemmican. Cherries were also dried or powdered for winter, when they were added to soup.

Pin cherry, with smooth, shiny reddish-brown bark laced with hash marks, tends to grow in clumps and patches, as does chokecherry. But it's more limited to drier, open, rocky areas, most often where there's been fires or logging, hence its other common name, fire cherry. Pin cherry's blossoms and shiny, red, long-stemmed fruits appear a little earlier than the chokecherry's. Fast growing and spreading by root suckers, it quickly colonizes open spaces in the early years after a disturbance. Pin cherry is a nurse tree for spruce and other slower-growing, shade-tolerant evergreen seedlings inching their way up beneath it, providing them with shelter and building up a fertile layer of humus with its fallen, decomposing leaves.

Black cherry, on the other hand, differs considerably from its shrubby relatives, becoming a tall, flaky-barked tree deep in the forest. It still needs open sunlight to get started, though, often getting its chance in the space opened up by an old, wind-fallen tree in maple and beech forests. Less tolerant of extreme cold than the smaller cherries, black cherry doesn't reach the most northern parts of Maine and Minnesota and the eastern end of Michigan's Upper Peninsula.

ROOTS: Deep, extensive, spreading by rhizomes
PREFERRED HABITAT: Mixed with deciduous trees and shrubs along streams, forest and wetland fringes, open woods, rocky ridges, and clearings, up to 2,000 ft (853 m) in Appalachians. Small numbers persist even in mature forests.
COMPANION TREES AND SHRUBS: Elderberry, raspberry, pin cherry, dogwood
FREQUENT VISITORS: Bears, foxes, moose, deer, chipmunks, red squirrels, raccoons, hares, skunks, mice, ruffed grouse, crows, evening grosbeaks, robins and other thrushes, blue jays, grackles, cedar waxwings, white-throated sparrows, northern orioles, scarlet tanagers, rose-breasted grosbeaks, woodpeckers, flycatchers, bluebirds, cardinals, catbirds, brown thrashers
RANGE: Throughout northeastern and western United States to Texas, northern Arkansas, Kentucky, and Delaware, and along Appalachians to North Carolina; north to Alaska panhandle and Newfoundland
NUMBER OF U.S. CHERRY AND PLUM SPECIES: About 30
NUMBER OF CHERRY AND PLUM SPECIES WORLDWIDE: Almost 200
ALSO SEE: Yellow Birch, Mosquitoes, Black Bear

EASTERN HEMLOCK

Creating Clear, Sheltered Havens

Eastern hemlock is not the poisonous herb Socrates was obliged to imbibe by the leading citizens of Athens in 399 B.C. The Old World toxic shrub lent its name to our broad, graceful evergreen because European settlers fancied that the scent of its burning needles was similar to that of poison hemlock. But they learned from the natives that the lacy twigs and needles, far from being toxic, could be brewed into a nutritious tea.

Hemlocks have it made in the shade. They thrive in mature mixed forests along cool, rocky lakeshores, ridge tops, and north-facing hillsides, usually on thinner, moister soil than is preferred by sugar

AVERAGE MATURE HEIGHT: 60–80 ft (18–24 m)

AVERAGE MATURE TRUNK WIDTH: 2–3 ft (60–90 cm)

TALLEST IN UNITED STATES: 166 ft (50.6 m), in Great Smoky Mountains National Park, North Carolina

LIFE SPAN: Commonly 300–400 years; up to 988 years

ALIAS: Eastern hemlock, Canada hemlock, common hemlock, hemlock gum tree, hemlock spruce, white hemlock, weeping spruce, *Tsuga canadensis*

BARK: Scaly, orange-brown on young trees, becoming deeply furrowed with purplish gray-brown ridges with age

NEEDLES: Flat, 0.4–0.8 in (1–2 cm) long, dark, shiny green on top, two white lines on underside; last about 3 years on branch

SEX: Tiny yellow male flower cones at base of needles; larger, pale green female flower cones at twig tips; appearing in May; puberty at 15–30 years

CONES: 0.5–0.8 in (1.3–2 cm) long, pale green ripening to reddish-brown, dropping seeds October through winter; big crops generally every 1–3 years

WOOD: Light yellow-brown with reddish tinge, rough, harder than most softwoods, 29 lb/cu ft

maples. Where lower branches on other evergreens die and drop off as the shade above grows too great, densely needled hemlock limbs stretch out and flourish. Little sunlight penetrates through to nourish undergrowth on the forest floor, making hemlock groves ideal clear, sheltered campsites. A thick mat of constantly falling needles provides a soft bed while making the ground too acidic for most plants, save the occasional yellow birch or white cedar taking root in a dead log or stump.

Deer and porcupines make themselves comfy in spacious hemlock stands in the winter, when the fine, intricately branched twigs of the trees' flexible upsweeping boughs keep out deep snow. Congregating white-tails create wintering yards below, nibbling voraciously on delectable hemlock and yellow-birch buds, twigs, and seedlings.

The great, ancient hemlock groves that once flourished across much of the north, however, have never really recovered from the coming of the steel ax and saw. From colonial times, loggers sought out eastern hemlocks along with the big pines, but for different reasons. Hemlock bark is very rich in tannins, natural chemicals that help protect trees from insects and animals, and long used by tanners to turn hides into leather. Bark was stripped from the felled trees from May to August, when it was looser and easier to peel, and carted off to tanneries, while the debarked logs were usually left lying in the forest because their wood was too knotty and brittle to be bothered with in the days of plentiful pine and spruce. Some peeled hemlock, though, peppered river drives

(465 kg/m³), very sparky when burned

HEAT EQUIVALENT TO 100 GALLONS OF OIL: 1.65 cords

ROOTS: Usually shallow, widespread, very fibrous, sometimes stilted; deeper in better-drained soils

PREFERRED HABITAT: Cool, moist, rocky, acidic ground in mature mixed forests, often near shorelines, on north-facing slopes, on rocky shelves with deep-seeping water, and in humid ravines; up to 2,400 ft (730 m) in mountains

COMPANION TREES AND SHRUBS: Yellow birch, white cedar, white pine, white spruce, red spruce, sugar maple, hobblebush, mountain maple, striped maple

ASSOCIATED PLANTS: Canada mayflower, goldthread, wood sorrel, starflower, oak fern, northern beech fern, club moss

COMMON NESTERS: Blackburnian warblers, black-throated green warblers, golden-crowned kinglets, veeries, juncos, pine siskins, saw-whet owls, sharp-shinned and red-shouldered hawks

BEAR HAVENS: Mothers and cubs often stay close to the safety of the hemlock's easily climbed branches in spring and sometimes hibernate at the hollow base of very large trees, which can be more than 4 ft (1.2 m) wide.

FREQUENT VISITORS: Red squirrels, red-backed voles, mice, ruffed grouse, red-breasted nuthatches. Chickadees and white-winged crossbills eat seeds; deer, porcupines, moose, and hares eat buds, twigs, or bark; yellow-bellied sapsuckers drink sap late April to mid-May.

because they slipped easily through the bark-bearing spruce and pine, opening up passages to counteract potential logjams.

More than 100 tanneries surrounded the Adirondacks in the 1840s. After felling about two-thirds of the mountains' hemlocks, many operations went west with the rest of the country, beckoned by the great cattle drives that began on the range in Texas and other prairie lands. From slaughterhouses to the south, hides were shipped upriver to the numerous tanneries of northern Wisconsin's hemlock country. The introduction of synthetic chemicals for tanning in the 1920s provided a reprieve for the remaining hemlocks of the north woods, though some are still cut for rough construction timbers and pulp.

Once gone, hemlocks are not readily replaced. In Wisconsin, less than 1 percent of what was once 18,000 square miles of hemlock-dominated old-growth remains. The state's remnant stands, as well as those in regions such as northern Michigan's Porcupine Mountains, are usually too small to keep bloated wintering deer populations from gobbling up almost all of the hemlock seedlings and sapling twigs.

Even in the best conditions, sun-shy young hemlocks root in deep shade, usually on rotting logs and stumps and mossy mounds, and then grow very slowly. A 200-year-old hemlock can look like a sapling but suddenly shoot up ten inches (twenty-five centimeters) in one growing season when an opening appears in the canopy above. Given their chance, the deep green centuries-old trees eventually come to dwarf their neighbors in mature forests.

COMMON NIBBLERS AND AILMENTS: Caterpillars of hemlock looper, porcelain gray, hemlock angle, bicolored, gypsy, and gray spruce looper moths; spruce budworms; hemlock borers; strawberry pine weevils; black vine weevils; wood-boring beetles; hemlock scale insects; heart rot; root rot; and needle rust fungi

ACCOLADES: State tree of Pennsylvania

RANGE: Maine to east-central Minnesota, southwestern Wisconsin, Kentucky, and Maryland, and along Appalachians to Alabama; north into southeastern Canada

NUMBER OF U.S. HEMLOCK SPECIES: 5

NUMBER OF HEMLOCK SPECIES WORLDWIDE: 10

ALSO SEE: Yellow Birch, White Pine, White-Tailed Deer, Porcupine, Black Bear

JACK PINE

Fire Frees Seeds to Sprout

Average mature height: 40–65 ft (12–20 m)

Average mature trunk width: 8–12 in (20–30 cm)

Tallest in United States: 97 ft (29.6 m), in Highland, Wisconsin

Average height of 20-year-old jack pines: 18–32 ft (5.5–10 m)

Average natural interval between fires in jack pine forests: Less than 50 years

Life span without fire: Commonly 60–200 years; up to 240 years

Alias: Scrub pine, gray pine, Banksian pine, pine princess, princy, *Pinus banksiana*

Name origin of pine: From proto-Indo-European *pit*, meaning "resin"

Bark: Reddish-brown to gray when young, turning with age to dark brown or gray, in large furrowed flakes

Needles: 0.8–2 in (2–5 cm) long, thick, stiff, rough, pointy, curved, in bunches of 2, stay on branch 2–3 years

Sex: Tiny, dark purplish female flowers near branch tips; light brown males in clusters at base of shoots in May; puberty at 5–10 years

Cones: 1–3 in (2.5–7.5 cm) long, curved, in pairs, green at first, turning gray with age, sometimes fused into branch

Number of stored seeds per acre (0.4 ha) of jack pine forest: Up to 2 million

Jack pine is the runt of the litter next to the majestic taller pines. Though usually straight when growing in large stands of its own kind, out in the open it is often twisted, knotty, and scruffy-looking, with its small tufts of needles on downward-bending branches. Early settlers thought the trees poisoned the ground and futilely tried to clear them, only to find more sprouting up.

The truth is that jack pine is one of the few trees that will grow on very poor ground. It takes root in dry, sandy, rocky sites, dominating large swaths of northern Michigan's pine barrens. Having evolved with the frequent-fire ecology of the northern boreal forest, it specializes in growing in burned-over areas, particularly if damage to the soil has been too severe for competing pioneer species such as aspen. Unable to live in the shade of other trees, pure, even-aged stands of jack pines mark the spot of such disturbance.

Jack pine is one of the few trees that will grow on very poor ground

---

Having little chance of success without their specific site requirements, jack pines do not even bother to release their seeds at regular intervals like other trees. Instead, most cones remain on the tree for up to twenty-five years, tightly closed, sealed in resin, until fire or very hot temperatures in direct sunlight open them. Fire also releases minerals from burned vegetation into the soil to nourish the new seedlings, which grow up from the ashes more quickly than other conifers, except tamarack. If no new fires come along in their life span, jack pines are eventually replaced in many sites by shade-tolerant species, such as fir, white spruce, and red maple, growing beneath them.

WOOD: Pale brown heartwood, whitish sapwood, rough, 31 lb/cu ft (495 kg/m³), resinous aroma
HEAT EQUIVALENT TO 100 GALLONS OF OIL: 1.4 cords
ROOTS: Widespread, often with deep taproot
PREFERRED HABITAT: Usually on dry, sterile, acidic, sandy, or rocky sites, commonly on outwash plains and open shorelines, usually less than 2,000 ft (610 m) in elevation
COMPANION TREES: Red pine, aspen, paper birch, red oak, black spruce, red maple, white pine, fir, white spruce
RANGE: Central Maine, scattered in New Hampshire, northeastern Vermont, northern and eastern Adirondacks, northern Michigan, Lake Michigan shore to northwestern Indiana and Illinois, most of Wisconsin, northeastern Minnesota, and boreal forest region across most of Canada to Rockies; planted in Alaska and some eastern and central states
NUMBER OF PINE SPECIES NATIVE TO NORTH WOODS REGION: 4
NUMBER OF U.S. PINE SPECIES: 43
NUMBER OF PINE SPECIES WORLDWIDE: 80–90
ALSO SEE: Red Pine, Quaking Aspen

PAPER BIRCH

Water Resistant, Born to Burn

Birch bark has a special quality that makes it famous: It resists water and decomposition. A natural wax base makes the bark impermeable, allowing it to last for years on the moist forest floor and still burn long after the wood it surrounds turns to mush. Fossilized birch has been found in Siberia with bark still in its original state, while birch-bark manuscripts in central Asia are up to 2,000 years old. This characteristic was of inestimable importance to northern woodland peoples, who were dependent on the bark for their wigwams, canoes, containers, and moose-calling

TIME IT TAKES A PAPER BIRCH LOG TO ROT: 1–2 years

TIME IT TAKES A PINE OR SPRUCE LOG TO ROT: 5–10 years

AVERAGE MATURE HEIGHT: 40–70 ft (12–21 m)

AVERAGE MATURE TRUNK WIDTH: 10–12 in (25–30 cm)

TALLEST IN UNITED STATES: 107 ft (25 m), in Cheboygan County, Minnesota

LIFE SPAN: Usually 80–140 years; up to 225 years

ALIAS: White birch, canoe birch, silver birch, *Betula papyrifera*

BARK: Reddish-brown for about ten years until peeling back to reveal mature, papery white bark with prominent black hash marks, called lenticels, which allow air through the bark. Stripping bark off trees leaves black scars and can kill them.

LEAVES: Light green, about 2–4 in (5–10 cm) long, spade-shaped, serrated, amber or yellow in fall

SEX: Hanging greenish-tan, tassel-like male catkins, 3–4 in (7–10 cm) long, at twig tips; upright green female flowers, 1.2–1.6 in (3–4 cm) long, farther back on branch; open before leaves in May for unhindered wind pollination; puberty at about 15 years

SEEDS: Winged, ⅙ in (4 mm) long, 3.3 million to a kilogram, released from brown, hanging cones 1.6–2 in

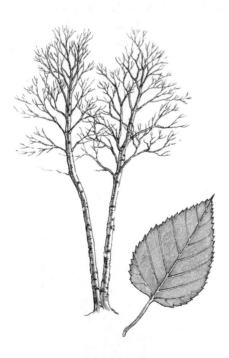

cones, as a quick fire starter even when wet, and to wrap their dead for burial.

Birch bark was an ideal material for the perfect design that is the canoe. It took two people about two weeks to make one, with men usually supervising and women doing most of the work. Bark was most easily stripped in early summer, whole tree lengths being used. Seams were stitched together with pliable black spruce, cedar, or tamarack roots and sealed with spruce gum. Ribs were made from strong, flexible spruce or cedar boughs. The canoes were swift, light to portage, and easy to fix, their materials abundant everywhere. European explorers and fur traders quickly adopted birch-bark canoes as the best means of traveling in the waterway-laced northern interior. Birch was also used to make boats in the boreal forests of Russia, but the true canoe—one of the first native words Columbus learned—is a New World perfection.

Perhaps because of its beauty, birch was considered a magical tree in northern Europe. Brooms were made out of its twigs to sweep away evil, and the Maypole of pagan spring rites was a birch. Various Ojibwa stories tell of birch bark acquiring its black marks from the magician-deity Nanaboujou's thrashing the tree for allowing some meat it was supposed to be guarding to be stolen by birds, or from a collision with pursuing thunderbirds whom the deity craftily dodged.

Though its thin, flammable bark makes paper birch an unlikely fire survivor, flames are actually its salvation. Having evolved around the cycle of renewal brought by frequent lightning strikes in tinder-dry, resin-soaked boreal forests, birch was born to

(4–5 cm) long, September to November, some falling through the winter; big crops every 2 years

Buds: Greenish-brown, gummy, 0.2 in (5–7 mm) long

Wood: Thick, creamy-white sapwood, pale brown heartwood, strong, hard, smooth, close-grained, 40 lb/cu ft (640 kg/m^3), very warm burning

Roots: Generally shallow, less than 2 ft (61 cm) deep

Preferred habitat: Cool, moist silt loam or sandy bottomlands to upper slopes and ridges of disturbed sites, forest openings, or lakeshores

Companion trees and shrubs: Quaking aspen, red maple, white spruce, red spruce, balsam fir, white pine, red oak, jack pine, black spruce, pin cherry, chokecherry, beaked hazel, willow, red osier dogwood

Associated plants: Bunchberry, wintergreen, blue bead lily, starflower, wild sarsaparilla, blueberry, raspberry, bracken fern

Frequent visitors: Common redpolls, pine siskins, chickadees, yellow-bellied sapsuckers, downy and hairy woodpeckers, nuthatches, black-and-white warblers, ruffed grouse, hares, porcupines, beavers, deer, moose

Common nibblers: Bronze birch borer beetle larvae, birch leaf miners, forest tent caterpillars, birch skeletonizers, gypsy moth caterpillars, sawflies, birch casebearers, ambrosia beetles

Accolades: Official tree of New Hampshire and Saskatchewan

Range: All north woods region to Connecticut, along Appalachians to

burn. The tree cannot grow in shade, but by flaming faster than almost any other natural material, birch bark fosters the heat conditions for regeneration. Newly burned-over areas provide sunlight and expose mineral soil for birch to take root and prosper, often in pure stands. Winged, confetti-sized birch seeds, released from August into winter, can travel great distances to find such sites, especially when blown across the surface of the snow. Birch also resprouts from the base of stumps, producing clumps of two to six trunks, nurtured by surviving root systems that give

North Carolina, scattered across lower Midwest and northern prairie states to Washington; north to tree line in Alaska and Canada

NUMBER OF BIRCH SPECIES NATIVE TO NORTH WOODS REGION: 11

NUMBER OF U.S. BIRCH SPECIES: 23

NUMBER OF BIRCH SPECIES WORLD-WIDE: About 60

ALSO SEE: Yellow Birch, Black Spruce, Quaking Aspen, Beaver, Black-Capped Chickadee

them a leg up on the seeds of the competition. Like other pioneer species, paper birch in general grows more rapidly than the progeny of most other trees, reaching up to ten feet (three meters) in its first five years.

Because birch trees grow quickly, however, their trunks are composed mostly of porous sapwood and contain considerable moisture and sugars, relished by wood-rotting fungi (the reason it's hard to find a fallen birch log worth burning). The wood is also low in the rot-resistant chemicals common in conifers. When little more than sixty years old, paper birch tends to become susceptible to heart-rot, wood-boring insects, and the woodpeckers that seek them, causing the tree to gradually die from the top down. Such trees provide ideal sites for cavity-nesting birds and animals. The upper branches are often already in advanced decay before the trunk finally topples.

QUAKING ASPEN

Stirred in the Slightest Breeze

Murmuring and shimmering in the slightest breeze, the quaking aspen has a name that fits. The quaking is due to long, flat leaf stems that are more easily swayed by the wind than if they were round. According to certain European legends, aspens shake because the wood of Christ's cross was made from one. North American natives called the tree "noisy leaf" or "noisy tree," while in several European languages it is referred to, at least by the men, as "woman's tongue."

Along with paper birch—which it resembles, though aspen bark is not papery and peeling or as white—aspen was long considered a scrawny "weed tree" because it

AVERAGE MATURE HEIGHT: 40–80 ft (12–24 m)

AVERAGE MATURE TRUNK WIDTH: 7–12 in (18–30 cm)

TALLEST IN UNITED STATES: 144 ft (34.7 m), in Kootenai National Forest, Montana

LIFE SPAN: Commonly 60–120 years; up to 200 years

ALIAS: Trembling aspen, quiverleaf, popple, golden aspen, smalltooth aspen, mountain aspen, trembling poplar, *Populus tremuloides*

BARK: Smooth, glossy, pale green when young, becoming silver gray or whitish, lightest on south side, with rough black patches and horizontal marks; dark gray and furrowed with age

LEAVES: Squat and rounded, with small pointed tips, 1.5–3 in (4–7.5 cm) long, finely toothed edges, green above, silvery pale below

SEX: Hanging yellowish-green flowering strands, called catkins, 1.5–3 in (4–8 cm) long, usually either all male or all female on a tree, opening before leaves in mid-April to May for efficient wind pollination; puberty as early as 2–3 years for clones, 15–20 years for trees starting from seed

SEEDS: Tiny, light brown, attached to fluff, 3 million to a pound (450 g); released after female catkin

springs up so quickly and numerously after fires or clear-cutting. The coming of logging and the slash fires that followed increased the presence of the white-barked trees manyfold across the north woods. Today, Minnesota in particular is dominated by aspen forests. The wood-products industry, in recent decades, has learned how to turn the abundance into gold, with aspen providing great quantities of chipboard, plywood, and much of the pulpwood used for paper, especially magazine stock. The fast-growing trees are profitable to cut when only forty years old and quickly replace themselves, ensuring continued predominance in many areas.

In the absence of major disturbances, the short-lived, sun-loving trees begin to give way in sixty years or so to shade-tolerant spruce, fir, and other species that are nurtured in aspen's nutrient-rich leaf litter. Meanwhile, tiny, light aspen seeds, borne on tufts of fluff in June, travel for miles in the wind and swiftly find any new forest openings.

Most aspens, though, are clones produced by numerous suckers sent up from the surviving roots of trees that have been burned, overbrowsed, or cut down. If a fire or logging occurs in April, the sprouts can emerge in the same season. Several acres may be covered by clones of a few trees, creating extremely dense stands of 10,000 to 50,000 new shoots per acre (0.4 hectare). Those numbers drop quickly, and within a few decades, there are a few hundred survivors per acre. But, if a forest is ravaged frequently enough, aspen root networks can survive indefinitely. One group of clones in Minnesota is estimated to be

reaches about 4 in (10 cm) long; big crops every 4–5 years

Buds: Dark brown, conical, $\frac{1}{4}$–$\frac{1}{3}$ in (6–8 mm) long

Wood: Grayish-white, close-grained, soft, brittle, weak, 28 lb/cu ft (450 kg/m³), but much heavier when green because it holds a lot of water

Heat equivalent to 100 gallons of oil: 1.5 cords

Roots: Mostly shallow, very widespread, producing numerous suckers; thin sinker roots reach down 10 ft (3 m)

Preferred habitat: Moist, well-drained sandy, loam, or gravel soils, from bottomlands to upper slopes, where previous forest cleared by fire or other disturbances, and at edges of beaver ponds, streams, and wetlands

Companion trees and shrubs: Paper birch, fir, spruce, jack pine, red maple, white cedar, bigtooth aspen, balsam poplar, chokecherry, speckled alder, beaked hazel, red osier dogwood, mountain maple

Associated plants: Large-leaved aster, raspberry, bunchberry, Canada mayflower, blue bead lily, wild sarsaparilla, starflower, goldenrod, fragrant bedstraw, bracken fern

Common nesters: Woodpeckers, broad-winged hawks, ruffed grouse, yellow-rumped warblers, ovenbirds, robins, hermit thrushes, warbling vireos, juncos

Common nibblers: Forest tent caterpillars and caterpillars of gypsy moths, big poplar sphinx moths, tiger swallowtails, and viceroy;

about 8,000 years old. In Utah, a stand of more than 47,000 genetically identical quaking aspens is estimated to be 1 million years old and to weigh 13.2 million pounds (6 million kilograms), making it, by some definitions, the world's largest and oldest organism.

North American natives called the tree "noisy leaf" or "noisy tree," while in several European languages it is referred to, at least by the men, as "woman's tongue"

The sun-fed vitality that can make an aspen clone sprout from two to six and a half feet (two meters) in its first year packs an abundant store of energy for other life-forms. In winter, ruffed grouse and evening grosbeaks depend heavily on aspen buds. Moose, deer, and porcupines feast on the tree's freshly sprouted twigs and catkins in spring. The catkins contain about 20 percent crude protein, more than cereal crops. The fresh new leaves are usually the main course for bears in late May and June, while aspen bark is the beaver's favorite winter food. Hares and mice also prize the bark, which is a living layer that photosynthesizes like leaves.

Young trees and fresh spring shoots, which have not yet built up natural chemical phenol defenses against browsers and insects, are preferred as food. Older leaves can double their phenolic concentration within three days of an insect attack on nearby branches. Such chemicals may have been responsible for the extremely bitter taste of the medicine pioneers and lumberjacks brewed from boiling the inner bark of aspen in water.

Among the nutrients packed into aspen leaves, and most plants, are

some 300 other known leaf-eating caterpillars, beetles, and other insects

FUNGAL FEEDERS: False tinder conk commonly infects 40–70% of mature aspens; also other bracket fungi, Hypoxylon canker, root rot and leaf rust fungi.

RANGE: All north woods region to New Jersey, West Virginia, and northern Missouri, scattered across northern prairies, Rockies, and western states; north almost to tree line in Alaska and much of Canada

PHOTOSYNTHESIS: The production of sugars, starches, and other materials from water, minerals, carbon dioxide, and sunlight in green plant cells

FIRST APPEARANCE OF POPLARS: About 100 million years ago

NUMBER OF POPLAR SPECIES NATIVE TO NORTH WOODS REGION: 4

NUMBER OF U.S. POPLAR SPECIES: 7

NUMBER OF POPLAR SPECIES WORLD-WIDE: 35

ALSO SEE: Black Bear, Beaver, Red Pine, Ruffed Grouse, Yellow-Bellied Sapsucker

beta-carotenes, molecules that trap and transfer the sun's energy for photo-synthesis in chlorophyll-containing tissues. They are a vital link for all animal life. When leaves are eaten, each beta-carotene molecule breaks into two vitamin A molecules. Beta-carotenes give carrots, oranges, squash, and egg yolks their color. A related molecule, xanthophyll, which protects chlorophyll from burning up in the sun's rays, gives quaking aspen its pale yellow color in autumn. Bigtooth aspen, usually growing on drier sites with its larger leaves and a fuller crown, turns a more brilliant gold about a week earlier. The yellow pigments are uncovered after trees withdraw nutrients from leaves (to be stored in branches during winter), stopping the production of chlorophyll, which normally colors leaves by reflecting green light while absorbing the other colors of the spectrum in the sun's rays.

RED MAPLE

Flowering Early for a Head Start

Red maple is named for its bright purple-red shoots, buds, flowers, seeds, and unfolding leaves in spring. Early settlers made red ink and dye by boiling its bark. In fall, however, its leaves are not simply red. Unlike most other trees, red maples most often feature either all male or all female flowers on one tree. Come autumn, the female trees change various shades of yellow or orange, while males, which are much more numerous, range from orange-red to scarlet.

While red maple is not as shade-tolerant as sugar maple, it is not nearly as fussy about where it takes up residence. In hardwood forests, it wins out mainly in areas that are wetter for longer periods of the year, or on dry, sandy sites. In places where the woods become more boreal in

AVERAGE MATURE HEIGHT: 50–90 ft (15–27 m)

AVERAGE MATURE TRUNK WIDTH: 1.5–2.5 ft (46–76 cm)

TALLEST IN UNITED STATES: 141 ft (43 m), in Great Smoky Mountains National Park, Tennessee

LIFE SPAN: Commonly 100–150 years

ALIAS: Swamp maple, scarlet maple, soft maple, water maple, curled maple, *Acer rubrum*

BARK: Smooth, silvery gray on young trees, darker and ridged when older

LEAVES: 3–5 in (7–13 cm) long, toothed edges, V-shaped notches between lobes, pale undersides

SEX: Clusters of tiny bright red flowers, females on long stems, males in short bunches with yellow anthers; mainly wind-pollinated, but honeybees also collect pollen; open long before leaves

SEEDS: 0.5–1 in (1.3–2.5 cm) long with wings, in pairs; traveling up to 525 ft (160 m) in moderate winds

WOOD: Light brown, moderately strong, hard, 38 lb/cu ft (610 kg/m³)

PREFERRED HABITAT: Wet sites around swamps, sandy loam bottomlands, bogs, and beaver ponds or dry, rocky, sandy soils

character, such as northern Minnesota and many Appalachian slopes, red maples often persevere while their sugary cousins dwindle, springing up on disturbed sites that previously held conifers or on the forest fringe. Red maple seeds are smaller and lighter than those of sugar maple, so can travel farther to find such sites. They also get a head start because red maples flower earlier than most other trees, often with snow still on the ground, and release seeds in late June.

Mountain maple, a hardy understory shrub or small tree, usually under 20 feet (6.1 meters) tall, is also a common maple in forests dominated by evergreens, aspens, and birch. Its leaves resemble those of red maple, but are more crinkly, with distinctly indented veins, and are more rounded at the base. Another small species, striped maple, reaches as far west as Michigan's Upper Peninsula. It stands out in hardwood and mixed forest understories with huge three-pointed leaves and distinctive vertical white stripes on the green bark of its thin stems. Silver maple, with deeply notched leaves, grows in swamps and on floodplains, but rarely anywhere else.

COMPANION TREES: Black ash, red oak, white pine, black spruce, white spruce, red spruce, balsam fir, tamarack, white cedar, yellow birch

ASSOCIATED PLANTS: Jewelweed, goldthread, jack-in-the-pulpit, poison ivy, sensitive fern, cinnamon fern, and sphagnum moss

COMMON NESTERS: Great blue herons, yellow-bellied sapsuckers, robins, goldfinches, red-tailed hawks, hairy and downy woodpeckers

FREQUENT VISITORS: White-tailed deer, beavers, porcupines, and rose-breasted grosbeaks browse twigs and buds; chipmunks, squirrels, and mice eat seeds.

ACCOLADES: State tree of Rhode Island

RANGE: All eastern United States to edge of prairies and north to Newfoundland and central Ontario

NUMBER OF MAPLE SPECIES NATIVE TO NORTH WOODS REGION: 9

NUMBER OF U.S. MAPLE SPECIES: 15

NUMBER OF MAPLE SPECIES WORLDWIDE: About 150

ALSO SEE: Sugar Maple

RED OAK

Beware of an oak,
It draws the stroke

The tall, wide crown of oak trees makes them particularly susceptible to being struck by lightning. Even in predominantly beech forests, oak is estimated to be hit by lightning ten to twenty times as often as beech. When hit, oak often bursts into flame. The ancient Europeans saw in this spectacular phenomenon a direct connection with the gods, and the thunder tree was venerated above all others.

The most ancient Greek traditions depicted Zeus, the thunder god, as an oak or at least living in one. Oaks were sacred to Thor and Jehovah, both thunder-and-lightning deities. Oak was similarly the supreme god of the Gauls, and the name of the Finnish thunder god was Ukko, meaning

AVERAGE MATURE HEIGHT: 60–80 ft (18–24 m)
AVERAGE MATURE TRUNK WIDTH: 1–3 ft (30–90 cm)
TALLEST IN UNITED STATES: 139 ft (42 m), in Great Smoky Mountains National Park, Tennessee
LIFE SPAN: 200–300 years
ALIAS: Northern red oak, eastern red oak, mountain red oak, gray oak, champion oak, *Quercus rubra*
BARK: Smooth and gray when young; form broad, flat ridges separated by fissures on older trees
LEAVES: 5–9 in (13–23 cm) long, 3–6 in (7–15 cm) wide, with 7–11

"oak." Sacred oak groves were the scenes of oracles by Greek priestesses, ceremonies by the druids, and Roman women beseeching oak nymphs for safe births. Roman poets wrote that acorns were the first food to sustain newborn humans. Even the oak tree's parasite, mistletoe, was deified and is still hung at Christmas. Unable to shake pagan reverence for sites of sacred oaks, where sacrifices were made to older deities, the Christian Church eventually took the sites by blessing them and erecting crucifixes and images of Mary.

The stately red oak, with its wide-sweeping, often horizontal branches, is still commonly admired and planted as an ornamental tree along American boulevards and parks. Unfortunately, the strong, level limbs also made it an ideal hanging tree for Revolutionary hero Nathan Hale, when he reportedly told the British that he regretted only having one life to give for his country.

In the north woods, red oak groves are most often found on dry, rocky ridge tops and south-facing slopes, where deep roots and tough, waxy leaves give the trees an advantage in finding and retaining scarce groundwater. Elsewhere, red oak is eventually crowded and shaded out in mature hardwood stands by faster-growing, more shade-tolerant maples and beech. Oak also cannot withstand prolonged periods of extreme cold and becomes increasingly scarce toward the Canadian border and on mountain slopes. Even where it is rare, red oak is very noticeable from a distance in the spring because its high levels of tannin—a bitter-tasting, acidic defense chemical against animal browsing—makes newly unfolding leaves bright red. Later,

pointed lobes between V-shaped notches; unfold later than maple and beech in spring

SEX: Dangling, greenish-yellow male catkins 4–5 in (10–13 cm) long; tiny green female flowers with 2–4 petals at the junction of twigs near the edge of canopy; open with or after leaves

ACORNS: 0.8–1.2 in (2–3 cm) long, woody, reddish-brown, with brown cap of scales; very bitter tasting, contain 8% protein, 37% fat; 2 summers to ripen; 100–4,000 per tree, with big crops usually every 2–5 years; puberty at about 25 years

BUDS: About 0.2 in (6 mm) long, pointy, shiny reddish-brown

WOOD: Reddish-brown to pink heartwood, whitish sapwood, coarse-grained, very strong, hard, 43 lb/cu ft (690 kg/m³), very warm burning

HEAT EQUIVALENT TO 100 GALLONS OF OIL: 1 cord

ROOTS: Deep, widespread, often with taproot

PREFERRED HABITAT: Most common on rocky ridge tops and dry, sandy uplands, though grows better in richer soils; up to 1,400–1,500 ft (427–457 m) in Adirondacks and New Hampshire

COMPANION TREES AND SHRUBS: White pine, red pine, jack pine, aspen, red maple, beaked hazel, bush honeysuckle

ASSOCIATED PLANTS: Blueberry, snowberry, poison ivy

FREQUENT VISITORS: Blue jays, scarlet tanagers, ruffed grouse, wood ducks, crows, nuthatches, and many mammals eat acorns;

chlorophyll production kicks in to turn them green. When the green fades in October, the tannin pigment reemerges to color hilltop oaks rusty-brown. The leaves remain long after maples and other trees drop theirs. Tannin is also the compound, released by slowly rotting vegetation, that turns swamp water brown.

As autumn draws near, red oak stands become the center of attraction for a great variety of wildlife. Deer, raccoons, foxes, chipmunks, ruffed grouse, wood ducks, flickers, and nuthatches come from far and wide to munch on acorns, one of the most nutritious woodland foods. Bears fatten up for hibernation by climbing up oaks and pulling limbs toward them to get at the acorns, often leaving conspicuous "bear nests" of broken branches behind. Squirrels, blue jays, and white-footed mice help spread the seeds by storing acorns in various locations. Those they fail to retrieve have a high germination rate. Populations of diners in some areas may rise and fall from year to year with acorn crop cycles. Millions of migrating passenger pigeons, which once blackened the skies over the north woods, were dependent on acorn and beechnut crops. Their extinction is believed to have greatly limited the oak's ability to spread.

The great white oak, with its round-lobed leaves, reaches only the southern portions of the north woods in New England, the edges of the Adirondacks, Michigan's Lower Peninsula, and scattered areas of northern Wisconsin. Yielding the best-quality wood of any oak, prized in shipbuilding, vast stands of white oak to the south ranked next to white pine in importance to loggers in past centuries. Because white oak wood is so dense and heavy, early river drives had to lash timbers of pine to it to keep it from sinking. Today, both red and white oak are used for floors, furniture, and trimmings.

moose, deer, and hares browse leaves.

COMMON NIBBLERS AND AILMENTS: Gypsy moth and forest tent caterpillars, oak leaf shredders, acorn weevils, wood-boring beetles, oak leaf rollers, filbert worm moth, sap beetles, gall-causing wasps, flies, beetles, aphids, oak wilt and shoestring root rot fungi

ACCOLADES: Official tree of New Jersey and Prince Edward Island

RANGE: All north woods region, except central Adirondacks; west to eastern edge of prairies, south to Oklahoma, Louisiana, and Georgia, north to Gulf of St. Lawrence and central Ontario

NUMBER OF OAK SPECIES NATIVE TO NORTH WOODS REGION: 9

NUMBER OF NORTH AMERICAN OAK SPECIES: 40–45

NUMBER OF OAK SPECIES WORLDWIDE: More than 200

ALSO SEE: Blue Jay, Red Squirrel, Black Bear, Thunder and Lightning

RED PINE

Drawing Strength from Adversity

Though red pine is often called Norway pine, it is a true-blue native American tree. A tough, resilient, almost invincible giant of the forest, it springs from underdog seeds that stand little chance of success in competition on fertile ground. Red pine grows poorly in shade but thrives along exposed, rocky lakeshores, steep slopes, and severely burned-over areas, places where the soil is too sandy, dry, and poor or where winter winds are too severe for many other species to prosper. With its strong roots set in these harsh niches, red pine can endure for hundreds of years, withstanding disasters that claim most trees.

More saturated with thick, protective resin than the other pines, red pine is resistant to most harmful insects and fungi, and can live through cold snaps of more than −58°F (−50°C). Large trees often survive

AVERAGE MATURE HEIGHT: 60–80 ft (18–25 m)

AVERAGE MATURE TRUNK WIDTH: 1–3 ft (30–91 cm)

TALLEST IN UNITED STATES: 135 ft (41 m), in Highland, Wisconsin

HEIGHT AT 50 YEARS OLD: 45–75 ft (14–23 m)

LIFE SPAN: 300 years common; up to 400 years

ALIAS: Norway pine, hard pine, Canadian red pine, bull pine, *Pinus resinosa*

NAME ORIGIN AS NORWAY PINE: Either due to early association with the town of Norway, in Maine, or to resemblance to European species now known as Austrian pine

BARK: Flaky, reddish- or pinkish-brown, furrowing into long, plate-like, flat ridges on older trees

NEEDLES: 4–6.5 in (10–16 cm) long, dark green, coarse, thick, stiff, 2 to a stalk, sharp points and finely toothed edges; lasting 4–5 years

SEX: Bunches of purplish male flower conelets, 0.4–0.8 in (1–2 cm) long, appearing at base of shoots in late May or early June; purple or scarlet female flower conelets, 0.1–0.2 in (2–4 mm), higher up on tree, partly hidden by tufts of needles at branch tips; puberty at 15–60 years

CONES: 1.5–2.7 in (4–7 cm) long, squat, dark at first, fading to tan-brown; opening in their second

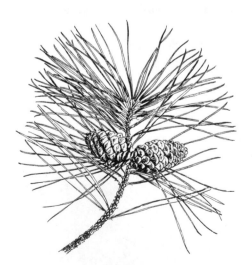

forest fires because their thick bark scorches but doesn't readily burn and there are usually no branches for the flames to climb on the lower half to three-quarters of the trunk. Red pines also often grow well-spaced apart from each other and have relatively narrow crowns, while their buds are protected within thick bunches of long, slow-burning needles, helping to protect the trees in all but the most intense forest fires.

Though most old-growth red pine was cut long ago, the qualities that make the tree so resistant made it the most favored species for tree plantations in many northern areas. Minnesota, in particular, has sought to replace the ancient pines removed from most of the state with extensive plantings of red pine, which it has adopted as its official tree. Large monoculture plantations, however, are far from the ideal of nature, with few understory plants and shrubs and little wildlife diversity. Dense rows of planted trees are also more vulnerable to fire than sparser natural red pine stands.

Whether in natural settings or plantations, red pine cones are not immune from the attentions of squirrels and birds such as crossbills. To ensure some seeds survive, the species follows the strategy of most conifers and many other trees. In most years, only a small number of pinecones are produced, with few escaping the hungry jaws of seedeaters. But every three to seven years, red pines over a large area produce up to a

September, dropping most seeds October to November, some falling through to next summer; up to 725 per tree in good crop years
SEEDS: Winged, about 0.5 in (1.3 cm) long, average 30–45 per cone; land up to 500 ft (150 m) from parent trees
WOOD: Light to reddish-brown heartwood, yellowish-white sapwood, straight-grained, harder than white pine, 28 lb/cu ft (450 kg/m²), very resinous
HEAT EQUIVALENT TO 100 GALLONS OF OIL: 1.5 cords
ROOTS: Widespread, moderately deep, very strong
PREFERRED HABITAT: Usually sandy, dry, acidic soils, outwash plains, rocky, wind-swept lakeshores (most often on east sides), islands, ridges, steep, exposed slopes; up to 2,700 ft (820 m) in Adirondacks
COMPANION TREES: White pine, jack pine, hemlock, aspen, red oak, cedar, balsam fir, sugar maple
FREQUENT VISITORS: Red squirrels and red crossbills eat seeds; porcupines, moose, deer, and hares eat seedlings, twigs, bark, or needles.
RANGE: Throughout north woods region to northern Illinois, southern Michigan, West Virginia, and New Jersey; north to Cape Breton and western Ontario

fivefold increase in cones, nurtured by particularly warm temperatures and plentiful rainfall in June and July almost two years before, when the buds that yield them begin forming. With up to 35,000 cones per acre (0.4 hectare) suddenly available, birds and squirrels cannot possibly eat or store all the seeds, allowing some to germinate the following year. Any population rise in seedeaters that results from the bounty is reversed when only a few cones are forthcoming the following year.

SPECKLED ALDER

Little Tree with Special Powers

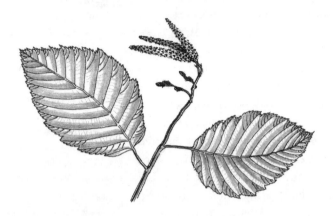

Being small shrubby trees, alders weren't given a second glance by the first lumberjacks chopping their way through the north's forests. The Finnish loggers, however, seemed to have some intuition about these trees' special powers. When they introduced the swede saw—which cut trees twice as fast as the old one-person crosscut saw—into north woods lumber camps in the 1920s, they used alder wood for their homemade saw frames, saying it had a spirit that kept lumberjacks from cutting themselves.

Before the saw-happy Finns came along, native peoples boiled alder bark to make a poultice for wounds and to treat rheumatism. Like willow and quaking aspen, the bark contains salicin, the active ingredient in aspirin. The inner bark, combined with the roots, bark, and berries of various other plants and trees, was also used to make red and yellowish-brown dyes for porcupine quillwork from Maine to Minnesota.

AVERAGE MATURE HEIGHT: 6–20 ft (1.8–6 m)

MAXIMUM HEIGHT: 66 ft (20 m)

AVERAGE MATURE TRUNK WIDTH: 1–2 in (2.5–5 cm)

ALIAS: Tag alder, black alder, gray alder, hoary alder, *Alnus incana rugosa*

BARK: Reddish-brown, thin; smooth surface densely speckled with small, horizontal, pale marks

LEAVES: 2–4 in (5–10 cm) long, oval, pointed, dull green, with serrated edges and straight, distinct veins that feel like ribs on the underside; wrinkled above; fall while still green in autumn

SEX: Bunches of 3–5 dangling, cylindrical male catkins, 0.8 in (2 cm) long, appear in late summer and expand to 2–4 in (5–10 cm) in April and early May, before leaves unfold, along with clusters of 2 or 3 oval female flowers, 0.6–1.2 in (1.5–3 cm) long.

Perhaps more than anyone else, beavers know the value of alder. The tree, thriving in fast-growing, dense curtains along shorelines, is their most common dam-building material. The water-tolerant trunks and branches are particularly durable in beaver constructions. They're also well designed for deprivations caused by the bucktoothed builders, with multiple stems sprouting from the spiky stumps left behind. Alders send up clones from underground shoots, as well, and reroot at branches that bend to the ground.

Like willow and quaking aspen, the bark contains salicin, the active ingredient in aspirin

In fact, speckled alder's unique qualities make it vitally important as a nourisher of all life in the forest—plant and animal, terrestrial and aquatic. Because its abundant cone clusters begin forming in late summer and don't release nutlets until autumn of the following year, alder feeds high-energy seeds, flowers, and buds throughout the year to grouse, wood warblers, and a large variety of other birds and animals. Thick, extensive lakefront or swampside alder tangles also provide shelter for both birds and mammals. Its dense, colonial rooting networks, which reach into streams and lakes to get oxygen from running water, help stabilize banks, while crooked, overhanging stems and branches provide shade and cover for fish and other creatures.

Unlike other trees, alder can also fix nitrogen from the air passages in the

SEEDS: 0.4–0.6 in (1–1.5 cm) long. Oval, woody cones open in fall to release winged seeds; cone may remain on tree for several more years.

BUDS: Dark red-brown, on a distinct stalk

WOOD: Light, soft, pale brown, not very strong

ROOTS: Shallow, with clusters of coral-like nodules

PREFERRED HABITAT: Shorelines, shrub swamp thickets of river and creek floodplains, wet meadows

COMPANION TREES: White cedar, red maple, fir, red spruce, black ash, black spruce, tamarack, balsam poplar, willow, red oisier dogwood, elder, chokecherry

ASSOCIATED PLANTS: Sedges, grasses, cattails, wild iris, jewelweed, sweet flag, winterberry, cinnamon fern

COMMON NESTERS: Hummingbirds, goldfinches, red-winded blackbirds, hermit thrushes, alder flycatchers, woodcocks, catbirds, golden-winged warblers

FREQUENT VISITORS: Chickadees, goldfinches, redpolls, and pine siskins eat seeds; ruffed grouse eat buds and catkins; muskrats, hares, deer, and moose sometimes browse leaves and twigs. Breeding tree frogs and spring peepers sing from branches. Also beavers, snipes, swamp sparrows.

COMMON NIBBLERS: Caterpillars of luna, large looper, rusty tussock, and cutworm moths; soldier, flathead borer, and alder leaf beetles

RANGE: Throughout north woods region south to New Jersey, West Virginia, south rim of Great Lakes,

ground. Though it constitutes about 80 percent of the atmosphere, nitrogen is one nutrient most plants cannot absorb in its gaseous form. But it is needed to make proteins and enzymes in all life-forms. Alder, along with legumes such as clover and beans, has clusters of knobby chambers, called nodules, on its rootlets, containing bacteria that take the compound from the air and transform it into ammonia, a form plants can absorb. This ability promotes extremely rapid growth in alders.

eastern Iowa and South Dakota; across Canada to tree line

NUMBER OF ALDER SPECIES NATIVE TO NORTH WOODS REGION: 3
NUMBER OF U.S. ALDER SPECIES: 8
NUMBER OF ALDER SPECIES WORLDWIDE: About 30
ALSO SEE: Beaver, Porcupine, Fungi

Alder leaves contain three or four times as much nitrogen as the leaves and needles of most trees. When they are shed, they provide about 140 pounds of the chemical per acre (160 kilograms per hectare). In the water, they feed aquatic insect larvae, injecting precious nitrogen into the entire aquatic food chain. On the ground, nitrogen compounds from fallen alder leaves are absorbed by other trees and plants. The high nitrogen content also causes the leaves to decay more quickly than most others, in about a year. Although it cannot grow in shade, alder has soil-enriching powers that make it an important pioneer species in burned- or cut-over areas. If logging companies, spraying to destroy "weed trees," kill too many alders, they may impoverish the soil and decrease the long-term chances of success for commercially grown trees.

SUGAR MAPLE

Northern Sweetness and Color

Blazing autumn colors and sweet maple syrup are two of the best-loved treats of the north woods. New England's forests, in particular, are world famous for both. Sugar maples are the trees responsible, dominating upland forests across much of the region, though giving way to evergreens in the colder northern reaches and higher mountain altitudes. Little wonder Vermont, New York, and New Hampshire all recognize the species as their state tree.

The secret to the sugar maple's dominance is its tough, early-sprouting seedlings and their extreme shade tolerance. They often cover the forest floor, up to 60,000 per acre (0.4 hectare). Though most die within a few years in the limited light, some may last fifteen to thirty years. If a space opens in the canopy, the lucky sap directly below wins the lottery and shoots upward. Once

TOTAL SPRING SAP COLLECTED PER TREE: 1–8 pints

AVERAGE NUMBER OF PINTS OF SAP TO MAKE ONE PINT OF MAPLE SYRUP: 35–40

AVERAGE SUGAR CONTENT OF SUGAR MAPLE SAP: 2–3%

AVERAGE SUGAR CONTENT OF RED AND SILVER MAPLE AND YELLOW AND PAPER BIRCH: 1%

AVERAGE SUGAR CONTENT OF MAPLE SYRUP: 66%

FLOW RATE OF SPRING SAP WITHIN SUGAR MAPLE: 1–4 ft (30–120 cm) per hour

AVERAGE U.S. MAPLE SYRUP PRODUCTION: 1.8 million gallons

AVERAGE MATURE HEIGHT: 60–90 ft (18–27 m)

AVERAGE MATURE TRUNK WIDTH: 2–3 ft (60–90 cm)

MINIMUM WIDTH FOR SAP TAPPING: 10 in (25 cm), usually when 25–30 years old

TALLEST IN UNITED STATES: 151 ft (46 m), in Great Smoky Mountains National Park

AVERAGE LIFE SPAN: 200–300 years

MAXIMUM LIFE SPAN: 400 years

ALIAS: Hard maple, rock maple, sweet maple, black maple, sugar tree, curly maple, *Acer saccharum*

LATIN NAME ORIGIN: *Acer,* from the word for "sharp," because Roman spears were made of maple shafts

BARK: Dark gray, long, flat ridges curling out on one side

there, it hogs all the sunshine. A maple branch, with its large, abundant leaves, captures or reflects 90 percent of the sunlight hitting it. Beneath the eight to twelve leaf layers of the canopy of a mature maple, few plants other than its own offspring can grow in the summer.

The amount of sunlight sugar maples receive is critical for both autumn colors and maple-syrup production in spring. Warm, sunny fall days spur the production of sugars in leaves. But cool nights below 45°F (7°C) cause a waterproof abcission layer to form at the end of leaf stems, trapping the sugars in the leaves. With the stem sealed, chlorophyll production stops and the leaf's green pigment fades. Red anthocyanin pigments are then formed, owing to the accumulation of sugars—the same pigments that color cherries, grapes, beets, radishes, and many other vegetables and flowers. Sugar maple leaves can also turn yellow and orange. But the sunnier the autumn, the brighter the colors, with the best oranges and scarlets appearing on the most exposed or southern side of trees. Acidic soils make for the deepest reds.

Sugar maples are among the first trees to change color in September, having withdrawn much of the nutrients from their leaves back into their branches. Eventually, as anthocyanins that remain break down, red and orange leaves join those in shadier parts of the tree in fading to yellow. Jack Frost is not responsible for painting leaves. He shrivels and oxidizes them, turning them brown.

In Ojibwa legend, a stand of bright autumn maples near a waterfall hid Nokomis, grandmother of the fabled magician Nanaboujou, from a band of evil

LEAVES: 3–7 in (7.5–13 cm) wide, U-shaped space between lobes, smooth edges; growing in opposite pairs on branch
SEX: Clusters of tiny greenish-yellow flowers hanging like tassels from long stems at branch tips, sprouting with leaves in May
SEEDS: 1.5 in (4 cm) long, green, winged, joined in pairs; shed in autumn
NUMBER OF SEEDS PRODUCED IN A 1-ACRE (0.4-HA) SUGAR MAPLE STAND: 200,000–5 million, big crops every 2–5 years
AVERAGE NUMBER OF MAPLES IN A 15-YEAR-OLD 2.5-ACRE (1-HA) STAND: 50,000
AVERAGE NUMBER OF MATURE SUGAR MAPLES IN A 2.5-ACRE (1-HA) STAND: 38
BUDS: Reddish-brown, pointed
WOOD: Light yellow-brown, close-grained and often wavy, hard, heavy, strong and durable, 46 lb/cu ft (735 kg/m³)
ROOTS: Deep, widespread
PREFERRED HABITAT: Rich, deep, moist, well-drained sandy loam soil on glacial-till hills
COMPANION TREES: Beech, yellow birch, white pine, hemlock, basswood, red maple, black cherry, red oak, beaked hazel, Juneberry,
ASSOCIATED PLANTS: Trout lily, white trillium, violets, Canada mayflower
COMMON NESTERS: Red-eyed vireos
COMMON SAP-SIPPERS: Yellow-bellied sapsuckers, red squirrels, flying squirrels, chickadees, mourning cloak butterflies, noctuid moths
FREQUENT BROWSERS: Evening grosbeaks, ruffed grouse, purple finches, porcupines, deer, moose

windigo spirits chasing her. Through the mist of the waterfall, the windigos were convinced they were staring at a blazing fire in which Nokomis must have died. Nanaboujou rewarded the sugar maples by giving them sweet, strong-flowing sap.

Native peoples across the northern woodlands collected sugar maple sap by placing a flat stick, hollowed alder stem, or reed in a gash in the bark and collecting the drips in birch-bark containers or hollow logs. The first run of sap, during the time of greatest privation at the end of winter, was greeted with ceremonies of thanksgiving. A family group commonly spent the better part of a month tapping hundreds of trees and collecting up to several thousand gallons of sap in a hereditary sugar bush within their traditional hunting grounds. The sap was boiled, then strained or dried in the sun on birch bark. Much of the maple sugar produced was stored for use into the following winter. Until about the 1840s, this was the main source of sugar for pioneers as well.

COMMON NIBBLERS AND AILMENTS: Forest tent caterpillars, sugar maple borers, Bruce spanworms, maple trumpet skeletonizers, honey fungus, yellow cap fungus, stereum fungus, spongy rot fungus, mossy top fungus

SECRETS OF MAPLE RESILIENCE: Glassy crystals in leaf tissues and hard veins wear down caterpillars' teeth. Tannins in leaves taste raunchy to mammals.

RANGE: Throughout north woods region north to Gulf of St. Lawrence and central Ontario, west to edge of prairies, south to Missouri, Tennessee, and Georgia

ALSO SEE: Red Maple, Beech, Big Dipper, Deer Mouse, Lakes

March days up to 41°F (5°C) and nights below freezing increase pressure within the tree, which stores sugars during winter in the deadwood tissues of the trunk. Sap flows only if there is a taphole or natural wound in the tree, providing an outlet for the pressurized, melted sugar-water solution. The end comes when sap-swollen buds start producing amino acids, which get into the tree's circulation, giving any resulting syrup a bitter taste.

The wider and deeper the crown of a sugar maple, the more light it captures and the more abundant and sweeter its sap. Over the past few decades, the crowns of many sugar maples in the northeast have withered under the combined assault of acid rain, invading gypsy moths from Europe, lower snowfalls, and higher temperatures. Because soil nutrients dissolve into acidic water solutions more readily than usual, they are washed away in acid rain runoff more quickly than they can be replenished by decaying vegetation. At the same time, acid precipitation frees up ten to thirty times as much aluminium into soil solution as is normal. Aluminium is toxic to trees. To avoid absorbing it, roots diminish their uptake, further starving themselves of nutrients in the process. Once undernourished, trees fall easy prey to heart-rot or root rot fungi and other natural afflictions.

TAMARACK

The Deciduous Conifer

The lacy, dangling limbs of tamaracks are unique among north woods coniferous trees in that they shed their soft needles every fall. Tamarack needles are soft because they do not need the waxy coating and strong cells that allow other conifer needles to survive winter. Before dropping, the needles turn bright yellow in September or October, enlivening the dark environs of the bogs and swamps where they're found.

Tamaracks can afford to shed their needles because they usually grow close to running water and draw new nutrients

AVERAGE MATURE HEIGHT: 35–70 ft (11–21 m)

AVERAGE MATURE TRUNK WIDTH: 1–2 ft (30–60 cm)

TALLEST IN UNITED STATES: 96 ft (29.3 m), in Seymour, Maine

LIFE SPAN: Average 150–200 years; up to 330 years

ALIAS: Eastern larch, American larch, takmahak, hackmatack, red larch, *Larix laricina*

BARK: Smooth and gray when young; flaky, pinkish-brown on older trees

NEEDLES: 3/4–1 in (1.9–2.5 cm) long, soft, in clusters of 10–20 from round knobs, or singly near branch tips, sprouting bright green in early May, darkening to bluish green

SEX: Tiny, round, brownish male conelets; slightly larger, bright purple female conelets; growing at round twig knobs in May

CONES: 0.5–0.8 in (1.3–2 cm) long, oval, light brown, with thin scales opening in fall, releasing seeds through winter; crops of up to 20,000 cones per tree every 3–6 years

WOOD: Yellowish-brown to reddish-brown heartwood, thin, white sapwood, rough, often spiral-grained, fairly hard, flexible, oily, rot resistant, 35 lb/cu ft (560 kg/m³)

HEAT EQUIVALENT TO 100 GALLONS OF OIL: 1.2 cords

ROOTS: Shallow, widespread

from it each spring. They are also fed by many species of fungi (some found only around tamarack), which wrap their threads around tamarack rootlets and transfer nutrients.

Moving water also provides tamarack roots with the oxygen they must have to live in soggy, acidic soils. Tamarack is often the first tree to colonize a new bog, though it's usually mixed with other species and widely spaced apart. Willowy branches allow lots of light through for other plants to grow beneath it. Its seedlings, however, must have full sunlight to grow. More shade-tolerant black spruce eventually takes over throughout much of the bog, leaving tamarack only along the open edges.

PREFERRED HABITAT: Bogs, swamps, lakeshores, or drier, rocky, open sites
COMPANION TREES: Black spruce, balsam fir, white spruce, quaking aspen, white birch
RANGE: All north woods region to northern Indiana, Ohio, West Virginia, and New Jersey; north to central Alaska and tree line in Canada
NUMBER OF U.S. LARCH SPECIES: 3
NUMBER OF LARCH SPECIES WORLDWIDE: 10
ALSO SEE: Black Spruce, Fungi, Wetlands

Strong, flexible young tamarack trunks were commonly employed, along with ironwood, for wigwam poles by the Ojibwa. Natives also made arrows, boat ribs, and dog sleds from tamarack. The rot-resistant tree was widely used for rail ties and telegraph and telephone poles before the coming of creosote preservatives and pressure-treated lumber.

WHITE CEDAR

The Tree of Life

White cedar was revered by native peoples. To many, it represented the east, one of the four sacred directional elements (north, west, and south were sweetgrass, tobacco, and sage, respectively). The sweet scent and smoke of its crackling, burning foliage was used to purify a person, place, or thing, or to make offerings of thanks to the Creator. Even today, cedar leaf oil is used in perfumes and medicines, and as a deodorizer and insect repellent.

The tree's sacred status may have sprung from its powers to heal a vast array of ailments. Among white cedar's many medicinal uses, an effective poultice was made from its fibers and placed on the eyes to cure snow blindness. Tea was also brewed from its foliage for headaches, congestion, and scurvy. Like the needles of many other evergreens, cedar contains more vitamin C than oranges. Natives saved French explorer Jacques Cartier and

AVERAGE MATURE HEIGHT: 30–50 ft (10–15 m)

AVERAGE MATURE TRUNK WIDTH: 1–1.5 ft (30–45 cm), often divided into 2 or more stems

TALLEST IN UNITED STATES: 113 ft (34 m), in Leelanau County, Michigan

LIFE SPAN: Often 300–400 years; maximum more than 1,000 years on cliffsides

ALIAS: Northern white cedar arborvitae, eastern white cedar, swamp cedar, *Thuja occidentalis*

FOLIAGE: Light, yellow-green, flat, waxy, scalelike splays, lasting up to 5 years before turning bronze and shedding

BARK: Light gray to reddish-brown, soft, in stringy, shredding vertical strips, spiraling slightly up trunk

SEX: Tiny yellowish male conelets on tips of leaves in late April and May; pinkish female conelets usually on separate branches; puberty as early as 6 years

CONES: 0.3–0.5 in (8–13 mm) long, in dense bunches at tips of branches, especially in top branches, pale green at first, turning brown as they ripen by end of summer, dropping most seeds mid-September–November, the rest through winter; big crops every 2–5 years

SEEDS: Light chestnut brown, encased in 2 wings, landing

his crew from the ravages of scurvy during their first voyage down the St. Lawrence River, in 1536, with cedar tea. Cartier brought the seedlings of the wonder tree back to France, where the king promptly named it *arbor vitae*, the "tree of life."

The tree of life is an apt name, given white cedar's tenacity, its ability to lean, bend, twist, and turn to find sunlight. Roots, similarly, snake through rocks and cliffs, wedging into the narrowest crevices and tiniest pockets of soil. Branches of uprooted cedars can shoot up to become the trunks of new trees or can burrow into soil to form roots. Fallen, mossy logs are also the most common seedbed for cedars.

Dendrochronologists—people who study tree rings—have discovered scraggly cedars that are 400 to 1,000 years old growing in extremely harsh conditions on cliff faces. Many are just a few feet tall and a couple of inches (five centimeters) thick. Some, with annual growth rings only one cell thick, are considered the slowest-growing trees in the world. Protected in their inaccessible locations from wildfire and lumberjacks, communities of the cliff-side dwarfs probably form the most ancient old-growth forests in the north woods.

Cedar lives long on steep cliffs and wetlands because it is extremely resistant to both rot and drought. One dead cliff-side cedar trunk found in Ontario is nearly 3,000 years old and bears 1,890 annual growth rings, while the stumps and logs of cedar forests flooded almost 8,000 years ago

150–200 ft (45–60 m) from parent tree
AVERAGE ANNUAL SEEDLING GROWTH RATE: 3 in (8 cm)
WOOD: Light brown, soft, weak, brittle, 19 lb/cu ft (304 kg/m³), non-resinous, aromatic; snaps, crackles, and pops when burned
HEAT EQUIVALENT TO 100 GALLONS OF OIL: 1.8 cords
ROOTS: Shallow, thick, extensive on wet and rocky ground; deep tap root formed on thicker, drier soil
PREFERRED HABITAT: Wet, organic soil or boulder-strewn areas along lakeshores and streams and in swamps with flowing water, or thin, moist, sandy loam soils around limestone cliffs and rocky slopes; up to 4,270 ft (1,300 m) in Adirondacks
COMMON NESTERS: Blackburnian, Cape May, and black-throated green warblers, ovenbirds, golden-crowned kinglets, grackles
FREQUENT VISITORS: Deer, hares, porcupines, red-backed voles, and moose browse foliage; red squirrels, mice, crossbills, and pine siskins eat seeds.
RANGE: Throughout north woods region, scattered south to northern Illinois, Ohio, southern New England, and along Appalachians to Tennessee; north in eastern Canada to James Bay and Gulf of St. Lawrence

still persist offshore in the Great Lakes. Such durability makes white cedar highly favored for hedges, decks, posts, split-rail fences, shingles, and log cabins. Having the lightest wood of any tree in the north, much less than half the density of oak, it has always been popular for canoe and boat frames.

WHITE PINE

Towering above All Others

Among the dense, towering spires that so filled with awe the first European settlers to set eyes on the vast north woods, none stood mightier than the white pine. Old-growth pine trunks commonly shot straight up 150 feet (46 meters) with barely a taper, free of branches for much their length. Some reached more than 200 feet (61 meters). High above the surrounding hardwoods, lofty pine crowns swept out in layers of long, wind-sculpted limbs. Little wonder, with its size, grace, and the many medicines it yielded, the white pine was revered by the Iroquois confederacy as the Tree of Peace. It was to become the most important tree in American history.

Seizing upon seemingly boundless forest and river resources, New England settlers built many scores of water-powered sawmills in the 1600s, at a time when they were unknown in Britain. After furs, timber quickly became the northern colonies' second-biggest export, with thousands of pine logs shipped annually. By the 1660s, one of the first coins minted in the colonies, the Boston shilling, testified to the economic importance of the trade by bearing the image of a white pine.

Its size, abundance, light weight, strength, and smooth, soft texture made white pine the favored wood for everything from shingles, window sashes, and doors to house frames, flooring, and pioneer furniture. But the great tree was most highly valued of all for masts of the great wooden

AVERAGE MATURE HEIGHT: 70–110 ft (21–33 m)

AVERAGE MATURE TRUNK WIDTH: 2–3 ft (61–91 cm)

MAXIMUM TRUNK WIDTH: 6 ft (1.8 m)

TALLEST IN UNITED STATES: 201 ft (61.3 m), in Marquette County, Michigan

GROWTH RATE: 1–1.5 ft (30–45 cm) per year for young pine; 100-year-old trees up to 80 ft (24 m) high

ANNUAL WHORLS: Each year, 5 new branches grow from the tree's top shoot, the better the growing season, the bigger the distance between each 5-branch whorl.

TREE WEIGHT: Can be more than 65 tons (59 metric tons)

LIFE SPAN: Often 200–250 years; maximum more than 450 years

ALIAS: Eastern white pine, yellow pine, Weymouth pine, majestic pine, cork pine, pattern pine, Quebec pine, *Pinus strobus*

BARK: Smooth gray-green on a young tree, turning rough, deeply furrowed, and gray-brown as it ages

NEEDLES: Soft, 2–4 in (5–10 cm) long, in clusters of 5, finely toothed edges; turn yellow and fall after 1–4 years

SEX: Small, light green male flower cones appearing in bunches near branch tips in May and disintegrating in early summer after releasing yellow pollen to the wind; puberty at 5–10 years

ships of the day. In particular, warships of the British Royal Navy required main masts 120 feet (37 meters) high and 40 inches (1 meter) thick, previously supplied by heavy, pieced-together trunks of smaller Scotch pine from Europe's Baltic region. Indeed, the Royal Navy's greed for the splendid American trees was a major factor in pushing New England into the Revolutionary War. In 1691, felling of any pine more than 2 feet (61 centimeters) in diameter on public land was reserved exclusively for His Majesty's boats. Colonists largely ignored the ban, but resentment grew as the best trees were marked by the "king's broad arrow" and authorities tried to enforce the law. The arrest of a local logger in Weare, New Hampshire, in 1772 led to the mob-beating of two lawmen and the dispatch of two British regiments to restore order in the Pine Tree Riot, one of the first acts of resistance leading up to the Revolution. Three years later, the first flag flown by American rebel forces was red with a pine tree in a white square in its upper left corner. The Stars and Stripes followed in 1777.

After the Revolution, great tracts of Maine forests were sold off to private lumber interests to help pay for the huge war debt. The relentless quest for the big pines almost brought Britain and the United States to blows again in the winter of 1839 during the abortive "Aroostook War," when troops were sent to the disputed Maine–New Brunswick border before cooler heads prevailed. Around the same time, New York was overtaking Maine as the nation's leading lumber state as loggers followed rich veins of pine into the Great Lakes region. By the 1850s, great log drives

CONES: 3–8 in (8–20 cm) long, slender, light green at first, turning woody and tan-brown as they mature over 2 summers, opening in September to release seeds, then falling off during winter; big crops every 3–5 years with up to 400 cones per tree

SEEDS: Winged, about 0.8 in (3 cm) long, averaging 70 per cone, 30,000 weighing 1 lb (450 g)

WOOD: Pale to reddish-brown heartwood, creamy-white to yellow sapwood, soft, strong, clear, with straight, even texture, 26 lb/cu ft (415 kg/m³)

ROOTS: Widespread, moderately deep

PREFERRED HABITAT: Along lakeshores and points, islands, hillcrests, moist, sandy outwash plains, in pure stands or mixed with hardwoods and other conifers

COMPANION TREES AND SHRUBS: Red pine, hemlock, sugar maple, yellow birch, white spruce, red spruce, balsam fir, aspen, beaked hazel, chokecherry

ASSOCIATED PLANTS: Canada mayflower, blueberry, wintergreen, moccasin flower, wild sarsaparilla, large-leaved aster, jack-in-the-pulpit, partridgeberry, strawberry, bracken ferns

COMMON NESTERS AND INHABITANTS: Blue jays, pine warblers, broad-winged and sharp-shinned hawks, ravens, crows, osprey, bald eagles, red squirrels, mother bears and cubs

FREQUENT VISITORS: Seeds eaten by pine and evening grosbeaks, chickadees, nuthatches, red crossbills, red-backed voles, and mice; porcupines eat twigs and bark.

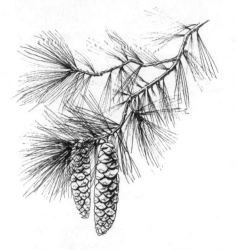

down the rivers of Michigan, Wisconsin, and Minnesota were feeding steam-powered sawmills turning out vast volumes of board and plank for the construction of the Midwest. Immense pineries came down even more quickly after the Civil War with the introduction of the large-toothed, two-man crosscut saw, doubling the cutting speed of two ax men.

This epic age of the lumberjack, and long winter nights in isolated bush camps, spawned a genre of tall tales in which storytellers each tried to outdo one another in exaggeration. Even as the age was coming to an end, the stories fused and came to create the character of Paul Bunyan, a fabled giant whose deeds were a personification of the collective industry of generations of lumberjacks transforming the countryside as they cleared the boundless forests and rearranged watersheds to flush logs downstream. Bunyan also created the Grand Canyon by dragging his pick in the ground. By 1925, he'd become a national folk hero through books and advertising. He's since been iconized by statues, paintings, cartoons, poems, and even a ballet and operetta.

Paul's feats were apparently so fantastic, there was little virgin white pine left by the early 1900s, save for in the most inaccessible high country. As loggers pushed farther into the last pine frontier in northern Minnesota, reserves were set aside that eventually led to the creation of the Boundary Waters Canoe Area Wilderness. Today, the world-famous wilderness contains the largest collection of old-growth red and white pine stands in the country, totaling 20,000 to 30,000 acres (8,100 to 12,140 hectares).

While forests have grown back in many places, the effects of human intervention remain profound. Study of the few virgin stands left has brought some biologists to counter logging industry claims that old pine forests always need catastrophic disturbances such as cutting or fire to bring in enough sunlight and prepare the soil for regeneration. Some mature pine stands have gone hundreds of years without major disturbances. Instead, new trees sprout up when an old one dies, or a small fire or windstorm opens up space in the canopy and on the forest floor. Young pines can grow in as little as 20 percent sunlight. In fact, if subject to more than 40 to 50 percent sun, the likelihood of seedlings being preyed upon by pine weevils—beetles that eat new shoots—increases significantly.

With its size, grace, and the many medicines it yielded, the white pine was revered by the Iroquois confederacy as the Tree of Peace

---

Ancient pine forests with natural gaps are very complex, with greater biological diversity than even-aged forests. The gaps provide a varied habitat for many plants and animals. Naturalists hold that modern science can never hope to fully know or re-create the immensity and minutiae of vital interrelationships that have been developed and fine-tuned over thousands of years in such a forest. There is even great genetic variety within the pines of a single stand, unlike the homogeneity of replanted trees, which are more vulnerable to the spread of disease, insects, and fire. Diversity supports ecosystem stability with an intricate web of interactions.

WHITE AND RED SPRUCE

Dense Boughs Shield against Winter

The dense, sweeping boughs that give spruce its beauty were long used by natives, trappers, lumberjacks, and campers as comfortable and springy wilderness bedding. The same qualities that make it a great mattress suit spruce to northern environments that few other trees could survive. Flexible curving branches bend under the weight of heavy snow, which is held by dense, thickly needled layers of twigs, insulating the trees from cold winds. Spruce and fir trees, in fact, brace for the weight of heavy snows by contracting—closing the space between their branches—when the atmospheric pressure drops. In Switzerland, cut Y-shaped fir branches are used as

AVERAGE MATURE HEIGHT: 60–80 ft (18–24 m)

AVERAGE MATURE TRUNK WIDTH: 1–2 ft (30–60 cm)

TALLEST RED SPRUCE IN UNITED STATES: 146 ft (44.5 m), in Great Smoky Mountains National Park, North Carolina

TALLEST WHITE SPRUCE IN UNITED STATES: 130 ft (39.6 m), in Koochiching County, Minnesota

LIFE SPAN: Commonly 100–250 years, up to 300 years for white spruce and more than 400 years for red spruce

WHITE SPRUCE ALIAS: Cat spruce, Canadian spruce, skunk spruce, *Picea glauca*

RED SPRUCE ALIAS: Eastern spruce, yellow spruce, he-balsam, *Picea rubens*

NAME ORIGIN OF SPRUCE: From Old English *Pruse,* meaning "Prussia"

NEEDLES: ½–¾ in (1.3–1.9 cm) long, 4-sided, often with bluish tint on white spruce (illustrated), shiny yellow-green and more curved on red spruce; on branch for 5–10 years

BARK: Scaly or flaky; light gray on white spruce; darker, reddish brown, more furrowed, on older red spruce

SEX: Male conelet flowers, almost ½ in (1.2 cm) long, red at first, turning yellow; green to red female flowers, 0.8–1 in (2–2.5 cm) long,

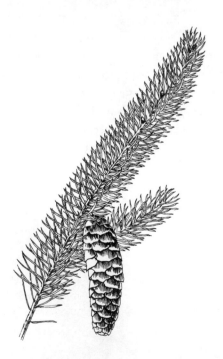

barometers, the two ends drawing close before rain or snow.

White spruce (illustrated) grows throughout most of the north woods region but is outnumbered in the east by red spruce. Both species are very similar, with the red variety having the distinction of often cutting a pagoda-like profile, with more widely spaced branches turning distinctly upward at their tips. Up close, red spruce also sports finer, more slender twigs and slightly smaller, more curved needles than its close relative.

Most often sprouting beneath the shade of other trees, both spruces can bide their time for 100 to 200 years in the understory and then accelerate growth when a space opens in the canopy. A four- to five-foot spruce in the forest shadows can be 40 to 50 years old. Red spruce saplings are especially shade-tolerant, persisting in as little as 10 percent of full sunlight, while white spruce need more than 15 percent to survive.

New England's first colonists found the thick spruce forests of the Northland virtually impenetrable when they arrived. Logging, however, has since made both red and white spruce less common across the north woods region, often replaced by aspen, paper birch, and fir. As the pine forests fell to the ax, lumberjacks were already turning to the next best thing that floated (in log drives), in New England and upstate New York by the 1830s. Spruce, with its tall, thick trunk and strong, durable wood, was soon a mainstay of the sawmills feeding the great building boom across America.

The discovery of efficient techniques for making paper from wood fiber in the 1860s greatly boosted the economic value

high on trees; appear mid-May; wind-pollinated; puberty as early as 4 years old, but usually not very productive until 30–50 years

CONES: About 2 in (5 cm) long, with thin, light brown scales on white spruce; 1.25–2 in (3–5 cm) long, more oval, with stiff, thicker, reddish-brown scales on red spruce; both dropping most of seeds September to October, but continuing winter and spring; big crops every 2–6 years for white spruce and 3–8 years for red spruce, with 8,000–12,000 cones per tree

SEEDS: About $\frac{1}{3}$ in (2 mm) long, winged, 30–130 per cone

WOOD: White or yellowish, soft, smooth, straight-grained, durable; white spruce 26 lb/cu ft (415 kg/m³), red spruce 28 lb/cu ft (450 kg/m³)

HEAT EQUIVALENT TO 100 GALLONS OF OIL: Red 1.5 cords, white 1.8 cords

SPECIAL QUALITIES: Resonance makes wood favored for pianos, guitars, and violins; used for food containers because of lack of taste and odor.

ROOTS: Usually shallow, widespread, but white spruce can put down deep taproots in well-drained soils

PREFERRED HABITAT: Cool, moist, commonly rocky soils, along shores and on uplands, with red spruce usually growing above white on mid- and upper mountain slopes up to 4,500 ft (1,370 m)

COMPANION TREES AND SHRUBS: Balsam fir, quaking aspen, paper birch, black spruce, pine

ASSOCIATED PLANTS: Feathermoss, bunchberry, twinflower, raspberry, wood sorrel, violets, bracken fern

of spruce. Paper, invented by the Chinese 2,000 years ago, was previously made from straw or rags. Spruce, even spindly black spruce, was ideal for the new process because its wood is long-fibered, light-colored, and less resinous than other conifers. As supplies of prime lumber trees, a foot (thirty centimeters) or more in diameter, dwindled in the late 1800s, the lumber barons of Maine and the Adirondacks gradually gave way to the new pulp and paper companies, which thrived on smaller trees. As logging moved west, the pattern repeated itself in Michigan, Wisconsin, and Minnesota, pine cutting giving way to the quest for spruce lumber and then pulp and paper.

Large tracts of forest are also eaten up each year by tiny brown caterpillars called spruce budworms. Forest-industry efforts to poison them with pesticides may ultimately be counterproductive. Budworms actually prefer balsam fir to spruce needles, but the pulp mills and sawmills favor spruce. Fir, being the most shade-tolerant, tends to grow faster and crowd out young spruce in the forest understory. With prolonged budworm outbreaks—which can last seven to ten years—fir dominance in the understory can be drastically cut. The budworms, by providing nutrients to spruce seedlings in their droppings and decaying fir trees, act as intermediaries in a massive energy transfer from fir to spruce. Another infamous nibbler, the forest tent caterpillar, also ultimately benefits spruce, as well as fir, by defoliating aspens and other broadleaf trees, providing more light and nutrients for understory evergreens.

COMMON NESTERS: Red squirrels, yellow-rumped, blackburnian, Cape May, bay-breasted, and black-throated green warblers

FREQUENT VISITORS: Chipmunks, mice, voles, red-breasted nuthatches, chickadees, white-winged crossbills, kinglets, and pine siskins all eat seeds; spruce grouse eat needles. Deer, moose, and hares take shelter under spruce in winter.

COMMON NIBBLERS AND AILMENTS: Spruce budworms, spruce beetles, bark beetles, yellow-headed spruce sawflies, European spruce needle miners, Warren's collar weevils, spruce cone maggots, fir coneworms, spruce seed caterpillars, cone, needle, bud, and witches' broom rusts

AVERAGE NATURAL FIRE FREQUENCY IN SPRUCE FORESTS: 60–200 years

WHITE SPRUCE RANGE: Throughout north woods region, except western Adirondacks and parts of central Michigan; across Canada and Alaska to tree line; scattered in Rockies of Montana and Black Hills

RED SPRUCE RANGE: Maine to central New York, south to New Jersey and along Appalachians to North Carolina, north to southeastern Canada

YELLOW BIRCH

Big, Tough, and Animated

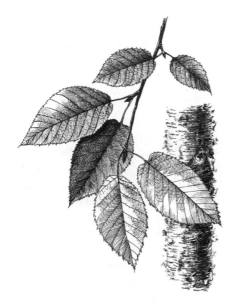

AVERAGE MATURE HEIGHT: 60–75 ft (18–23 m)

AVERAGE MATURE TRUNK WIDTH: 2–3 ft (60–90 cm)

TALLEST IN UNITED STATES: 114 ft (34.7 m), near Gould City, Michigan

LIFE SPAN: Commonly 150–300 years; up to 366 years

ALIAS: Sweet birch, gray birch, silver birch, gold birch, black birch, red birch, curly birch, hard birch, *Betula alleghaniensis*

BARK: Shiny bronze or yellowish-silver with numerous horizontal lines; smooth, soft, and paperlike, usually shredding, curling, and hanging in fringes. Trunks of old trees develop rough, gray irregular plates. Shiny, dark purple-red on saplings.

LEAVES: Oval with a pointed tip and serrated edges, 3–5 in (7–13 cm) long, dark green on top, lighter on bottom, turning yellow in fall

SEX: Dark male catkins stand 0.8 in (2 cm) long in fall and winter, opening before leaves in early spring to hang from twig tips like yellow caterpillars, 3–4 in (7.5–10 cm) long; green female catkins, 0.6–0.8 in (1.5–2 cm) long, stand erect farther back on twigs. Puberty at about 40 years.

SEEDS: Tiny, with wing flakes, start

Bronzed, shaggy yellow birch trunks add color and animate beauty to the dark reaches of the forest interior. The trees' thick, flexing roots clutch the ground, stumps, and boulders like giant birds' claws, making the birches look as if they're picking up and moving through the woods. Whole trunks may also bend and contort around rock outcrops or similarly snaking cedars. Though often toppled by the wind, yellow birches refuse to die, with upturned branches growing to become new trunks.

A great many yellow birches, though, go completely unrecognized by passersby at their feet. Unlike paper birch, they can live a very long time, with the smooth, papery bark of their youth graying and cracking into deep fissures separating large, rough plates. They take their place among the mature maples, beech, and hemlocks to become thick-bodied, towering monarchs.

Yellow birch has to be long-lived to keep its place in the mixed and hardwood forest. Opportunities for its seeds to get a start are few and far between, so year after year the tree must keep producing them. Although much more shade-tolerant than paper birch, it still needs small openings in the forest to grow. And when they germinate in spring, its tiny, thin seeds—commonly blown far and wide over the snow surface in winter—cannot produce root sprouts strong enough to break through the leaf litter to reach mineral soil. Slope erosion or light autumn brushfires that burn away the duff layer create good conditions for yellow birch seeds over a wide area. They also survive where the wind has taken down one or more trees, settling in either soil exposed by an uprooted trunk or in the decaying wood of an old stump or log. In later years, those that have grown out of stumps are often on stiltlike roots left after the rotted wood disintegrated beneath them.

Once established, yellow birch sprouts are adept at filling the gap in the canopy. Many saplings, however, meet an early end in areas with lots of deer, who love the sweet, wintergreen flavor of the tree's buds and twigs. Broken twigs give off the aromatic bubblegum scent.

The shiny bark of younger trees burns almost as well as paper birch bark, but tends to be shed in only narrow shreds from the trunk, rather than large, loose sheets. It is extremely durable, sometimes holding together the rotted wood of dead trees for many years.

falling from upright, oval cones, 1–1.5 in (2.5–4 cm) long, in late August, but most drop in October into winter. Big crops, every 1–4 years, may produce up to 36 million seeds per acre (0.4 ha).

WOOD: Reddish-tinted, golden-brown heartwood and light yellow or white sapwood, hard, strong, with fine and often wavy grain, 42 lb/cu ft (670 kg/m³)

ROOTS: Thick, strong, extensive, usually shallow, sometimes more than 5 ft (1.5 m) deep

PREFERRED HABITAT: Deciduous and mixed forests on moist, rich soil, especially on the lower slopes of hills; common in mountains up to 2,300 ft (700 m), rare above 3,000 ft (914 m)

COMPANION TREES AND SHRUBS: Sugar maple, beech, hemlock, white pine, basswood, white cedar, red pine, spruce

CAVITY DWELLERS: Heart-rot in large old trees commonly provides homes for yellow-bellied sapsuckers, porcupines, raccoons, and fishers.

FREQUENT VISITORS: Moose, deer, beavers, porcupines, and hares browse leaves, buds, or bark; red squirrels, chipmunks, grouse, chickadees, goldfinches, pine siskins, and redpolls eat seeds; yellow-bellied sapsuckers commonly tap tree.

RANGE: Throughout north woods region south to Iowa, Kentucky, and New Jersey and along Appalachians to northern Georgia; north into southeastern Canada

THE HEAVENS

THE HEAVENS

DAY SKY

Malls, offices, cars, and subways have all but made weather irrelevant to city living. But in the outdoors, weather is everything. It regulates the ebb and flow of life, from the sex lives of animals to the date of the local lake festival.

After a while, those living outdoors become, like animals and plants, attuned to every change in the day sky: shifting wind, falling or rising temperature, varying cloud cover that announces the arrival of a new weather system. A fun game is to try to guess the time by the position of the sun. It doesn't take very long to become good at it.

Like the starry night sky, the day sky is a repository of human myths and legends. Sun gods, thunder gods, and wind gods all made their home in the sky. As the habitat of such seemingly supernatural forces, the sky is an obvious place for heaven.

In a way, though, we have hell to thank for heaven. Ancient volcanoes spewed gases from deep inside the hot planet to form the early atmosphere. Later, plant life provided the oxygen necessary for life as we know it.

The weather does its thing at night as well as during the day, of course. But for simplicity, we've grouped all the weather-related topics in this section.

CLOUDS

Exploring the Skyscape

Hamlet. Do you see yonder cloud that's almost in shape of a camel?
Polonius. By the mass, and 'tis like a camel indeed.
Hamlet. Methinks it is like a weasel.
Polonius. It is backed like a weasel.
Hamlet. Or like a whale.
Polonius. Very like a whale.

—Hamlet, *III, 2*

C loud watching is an old pastime that even Shakespeare obviously enjoyed. While his Hamlet took up the activity as a device to feign madness, cloud watching can't be beaten as a salve for modern stress. Up north, the ideal viewing perch for cloud watching is a warm slab of rock jutting into a lake.

The main attraction on summer days is cumulus clouds, the familiar giant cotton balls with the flat bases that metamorphose into camels and weasels and whales. Cumulus, Latin for "heap," is one of ten main cloud types first described in 1803 by English pharmacist Luke Howard, a part-time naturalist who spent many hours flat on his back looking at the sky. Before his time, there was no specific system for classifying cloud types. So he came up with one, and it remains in use today. The German poet Goethe was so impressed with Howard's system that he wrote four poems to the man.

Clouds are airborne reservoirs of water. All air carries water in an invisible form

CLOUD: The Old English word *clud* also meant rocky mass or hill. It was first used to mean "clouds" in the thirteenth century. An earlier Old English word for cloud, *weolcen*, still exists as *welkin* in English and *Wolke* in German.

AMOUNT OF WATER IN A CLOUD: A cloud the size of a typical two-story house may contain up to half a sinkful of water.

FAMOUS CUMULONIMBUS CLOUD: God appeared as a "pillar of cloud" to lead the Israelites out of Egypt and across the Red Sea.

ALSO SEE: Woodchuck; Mist, Dew, and Fog; Rain and Snow; Thunder and Lightning; Wind and Weather Systems

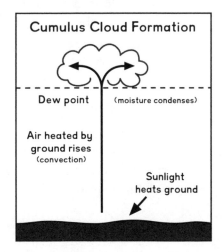

Cumulus Cloud Formation

Dew point (moisture condenses)

Air heated by ground rises (convection)

Sunlight heats ground

called water vapor. For a cloud to form, there must be enough water in the air, and the air must cool past a certain relative temperature, called the dew

HOWARD CLOUD CHART

Cloud Name	Description	Average Height
Cirrus	Wispy, feathery. May look like furrows. Very high.	8–12 km
Cirrocumulus	Blotchy cirrus clouds. May be rippled.	8–11 km
Cirrostratus	Thin veil. Doesn't block out sun. May cause halo.	7–9 km
Altostratus	Thicker than cirrostratus. Midlevel. Partially blocks sun.	2–6 km
Altocumulus	Puffy midlevel clouds. Small puffs.	2–6 km
Cumulonimbus	Giant cumulus clouds. Thunderheads, maybe anvil tops.	450 m–15 km
Stratocumulus	Expansive, puffy clouds.	150 m–2 km
Cumulus	Low puffy clouds, detached, flat bases.	450 m–2 km
Nimbostratus	Gray layer of solid or almost-solid cloud. Rain.	1–2 km
Stratus	Low-lying dull clouds. May drizzle.	0–450 m

point. At this point, tiny water droplets condense around bits of dust in the air. Billions upon billions of these droplets form visible clouds.

Cumulus clouds are created when air, heated by the ground, rises and then cools again at higher altitudes. Moisture-laden air blown over mountains also cools as it rises, and clouds may result. Large cloud banks occur along weather fronts, where a parcel of warm air meets a parcel of cold air. Exhaling on a cold day produces a minicloud as warm, moist breath heated by the lungs hits the cold air outside. Contrails from high-flying jet aircraft are artificial cirrus clouds. As hot, moisture-laden exhaust from the jet engines cools, the water vapor condenses into ice crystals.

The presence of certain cloud types in the sky is useful for predicting weather. Wispy cirrus clouds, including the type known as "mare's tails," often precede a storm front by a day or so. Veil-like cirrostratus clouds also usually mean poor weather is on the way. When these clouds obscure the sun or the moon, they may produce faint halos around the heavenly bodies, leading to the old saying "A ring around the sun or moon brings rain or snow upon you soon." Sky-covering altostratus clouds are another sign of rainy weather.

The most depressing clouds are unbroken, low-lying nimbostratus clouds. When they roll in, it usually means a day or two of rain and dreariness. Cloud watching, then, is an exercise in hope.

MIST, DEW, AND FOG

Variations on a Theme

It's early morning. Down by the lake, the air is still. Golden sunlight bathes the scene in a bright, purifying glow. A lone duck disappears into the soft white mist that lingers peacefully over the mirror-smooth water.

There's a good reason why mist is associated with such tranquil moments: It usually appears when the weather is calm and clear. The process begins at night, when the darkened Earth cools. As night swimmers know, the air cools faster than the water. When water vapor from the warm lake rises into the cool air, it soon condenses into tiny water droplets, forming the mist that hangs just above the surface. Mist vanishes when the morning sun heats the air and vaporizes the water again. If it's overcast at night, mist will usually not occur, because the air doesn't cool enough. Similarly, wind turbulence disrupts the steady cooling process.

MIST: The ancient Indo-European word *migh* or *meigh*, meaning "mist," has evolved into our modern English word. Similar in other Indo-European languages, including *migla* in Lithuanian and Latvian, *mgla* in Russian, *omíkhlé* in Greek, and, like the English, *mist* in Dutch and Swedish.

DEW: Also Indo-European roots, from *dheu*

FROST: Old English word, from the root *freusan*, for "freeze"

FOG: No clear origin for the English word, but may come from the Danish *fog*, for "spray" or "shower"

WATER VAPOR: Air is composed of up to 4% invisible water vapor at any given time. Warm air can contain more vapor. When air cools, excess water vapor condenses into visible water droplets.

ALSO SEE: Clouds, Rain and Snow

Fog is the same thing as mist, although meteorologists define fog as any bank of mist that reduces visibility to less than 3,100 feet (1 kilometer). Fog that rolls in off large lakes or the sea is created in a slightly different manner than mist over small lakes. In summer, water vapor in the warm air over land tends to condense as it hits cooler air over water. A fog bank appears. In winter, water vapor in warm sea air condenses when it moves across the cool land.

Dew is simply water vapor that condenses along surfaces that cool overnight. Because dew, like mist, occurs when the weather is good, the following old saying is fairly accurate:

When the dew is on the grass,
Rain will never come to pass.

RAIN AND SNOW

Step on a Spider and It Will Rain

Like home remedies that scientists later discover have a basis in fact, some rhymes and sayings about short-term weather—especially rain—have good reason to be true. The Roman poet Virgil noted that "when swallows fly low, there will soon be rain," or Latin words to that effect. This happens to be the case, because certain insects hang low just before a storm. One of the characteristics of a storm front is that air is more humid higher up. Water vapor tends to condense on the little bugs, making them less airworthy. So the swallow food flies closer to the ground.

Many other animals and plants react to subtle atmospheric changes before rain falls. Ants may be more active just before it rains because the relatively warmer temperature of a low-pressure rain system heats up their blood. Pinecones, as they absorb the moisture of an oncoming rain front, close up and become more supple. And the leaves of

RAIN: From Old English and Old Norse *regn*; Old High German, *Regen*

SNOW: From Old English *snaw*

MAXIMUM FALLING SPEED OF SNOW: 18 mph (30 km/h). Air friction prevents faster velocities.

RAINDROP SIZE: 1/32 in–1/5 in (0.5–5 mm) in diameter; average 1/12 in (2 mm)

CLOUD DROPLET SIZE: About 1/1000 in (0.01 mm)

NUMBER OF DROPLETS TO MAKE A RAINDROP: Estimated 30,000 to 1 million

SNOW-TO-RAIN RATIO: As a rule of thumb, 10 inches of snow is the equivalent of 1 inch of rain. Heavy, wet snow contains more water than light, powdery snow, however, so that 5 inches of wet snow equals about 1 inch of rain.

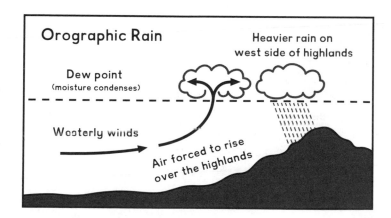

Orographic Rain

Heavier rain on west side of highlands

Dew point (moisture condenses)

Westerly winds

Air forced to rise over the highlands

some deciduous trees, such as poplar, often turn bottom side up just before rain. Moisture-laden air softens the stems, and strong updrafts associated with thunderstorms rustle the leaves. "When the leaves show their undersides, be very certain that rain betides," as one saying goes.

Most rain betides when heated air rises and then cools at higher altitudes. Water vapor in the air condenses into microscopic water droplets around dust, soot, and organic particles always present in the sky. As these droplets are tossed about in the cloud, they may collide and grow bigger. Eventually, the raindrop becomes heavy enough to fall to the ground.

Often temperatures inside a cloud are cold enough for the water droplets to freeze into six-sided ice crystals, even in summer. These form the nuclei of snowflakes, which grow as other water droplets condense along their sides. If the air beneath the cloud is warm, the snowflakes will melt and fall as rain. If it's Buffalo, they'll fall as snow.

Precipitation patterns vary across the north woods, depending on proximity to the Great Lakes, elevation, and other factors. The west side of uplands generally receive more rainfall than the east side, as prevailing westerlies rise over the land, cool the air, and drop rain as water vapor condenses. This is called "orographic precipitation," from the Greek root *oros*, or "mountain" (orography is the study of mountains). Lake-effect squalls also contribute to local winter snowfalls. As dry arctic air crosses the Great Lakes in winter, it picks up moisture that gets dumped as snow when the air crosses land and cools. The Tug Hill Plateau, in northern New York south of Lake Ontario, gets the most snow of any area in the United States east of the Rockies, up to 175 inches (444 centimeters) or more each winter.

AMOUNT OF U.S. PRECIPITATION THAT RETURNS TO THE ATMOSPHERE THROUGH EVAPORATION: About 70%
AMOUNT OF U.S. PRECIPITATION THAT ENDS UP IN STREAMS, LAKES, AQUIFERS: About 30%
ALSO SEE: Clouds; Lakes; Mist, Dew, and Fog; Thunder and Lightning; Wind and Weather Systems

Normal annual precipitation (in inches) for selected cities (total includes liquid equivalent of snowfall), from National Climatic Data Center, 1971–2000:

International Falls, Minn.	23.93
Duluth, Minn.	31.00
Green Bay, Wisc.	29.19
Marquette, Mich.	36.31
Sault Sainte Marie, Mich.	34.67
Alpena, Mich.	28.40
Houghton Lake, Mich.	28.43
Buffalo, N.Y.	40.54
Syracuse, N.Y.	40.05
Albany, N.Y.	38.60
Burlington, Vt.	36.05
Concord, N.H.	37.60
Mount Washington, N.H.	101.91
Portland, Me.	45.83
Caribou, Me.	37.44

RAINBOWS

Covenant with Humanity

If the Milky Way is the nighttime path of souls traveling from Earth to the heavens, rainbows serve the same function in daytime. To the Babylonians, the rainbow was a bridge formed by the necklace of the goddess Ishtar, linking heaven and Earth. Similar descriptions exist in Norse, Persian, and Japanese mythologies, and in Buddhist scriptures. In Turkic languages, the word for rainbow is the same word for bridge.

The rainbow is rich in other meanings for humans. One of the most famous rainbows appeared to Noah after the Great Flood had cleansed the world of sin—and pretty well everything else. God, who was feeling kind of sorry for what he had done, sent the rainbow as a promise that "never again will the waters become a flood to destroy all creation."

In a Cree Indian story, rainbows were said to be made of flowers. A young girl who loved rainbows was carried up to one by a thunderbird, and she sent some of the flowers back to Earth to beautify the land. In Ireland, leprechauns liked to bury their pots of gold at the end of a rainbow, probably because it is impossible for a mortal to get there. The ancient Greeks were among the few to look upon rainbows with trepidation. Iris, the rainbow goddess, was a messenger of the gods, but she was usually dispatched when the news was bad: impending war or perhaps the death of a loved one.

Though rainbows don't lead to gold, they usually signify improved fortunes, at least as far as the weather is concerned. A rainbow needs two ingredients, sunlight and raindrops. The sun must be located low in the sky and behind the rainbow watcher. The raindrops must be in the air in front of the observer. Late-afternoon rainbows may foretell good weather because it

> **RAINBOW:** From Old English *regnboga*. In French, *arc-en-ciel* (sky arch). In Spanish, *arco iris*
>
> **IRIS:** The name for the colored circular ring around the pupil of an eye comes from the Greek word for rainbow. Iris was also the Greek rainbow goddess.
>
> **WHY RAINBOWS APPEAR ONLY IN LATE AFTERNOON OR EARLY MORNING:** Sunlight reflects off each raindrop at angles between 42° (red) and 40° (violet). When the sun is higher than 42° in the sky, the reflected colors from a rainbow pass over an observer's head and are not visible. Generally, rainbows appear in a 3-hour period before sunset or after sunrise.
>
> **MOON BOWS:** The light from a full moon can sometimes produce a dim rainbow, if the same conditions that create a normal rainbow are in place.
>
> **SEE ALSO:** Clouds, Rain and Snow

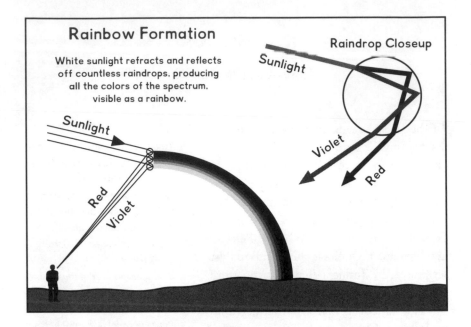

Rainbow Formation

White sunlight refracts and reflects off countless raindrops, producing all the colors of the spectrum, visible as a rainbow.

Raindrop Closeup

Sunlight

Sunlight

Violet

Red

Red

Violet

means the sun is unobstructed in the west. Since weather systems generally come from the west, clear skies are probably on the way. And since the rain in the east is moving away, the bad weather has probably passed. For the same reasons, the opposite is true of an early-morning rainbow. The clear skies have already passed to the east, and the rain in the west is bearing down upon the observer, to dampen the day.

Rainbows are created by sunlight penetrating billions of falling raindrops. Most of the sunlight passes straight through the drop; however, a small amount of light is bent as it enters the drop, and refracts into the seven main colors that make up the visible spectrum: red, orange, yellow, green, blue, indigo, and violet. The back of the raindrop acts like a mirror to reflect these colors out the front of the drop, toward the observer.

A rainbow watcher sees only one color from each raindrop. But because the sunlight is refracting and reflecting off countless raindrops, the full spectrum is visible in the beautiful arc of a rainbow. Red is always the outside color, and violet the inside. Because each observer is positioned at a different angle to the raindrops, each sees his or her own rainbow.

SKY

Thank Goodness for Algae

The sky is a security blanket that protects all life from the deadly vacuum of space. But it's a fragile blanket. For one thing, it's not very thick. If Earth were the size of a beach ball, our sustaining layer of air would be about as thick as a paper towel. Breathable air ends about six miles (10 kilometers) above sea level—or 1.2 miles (2 kilometers) below the cruising height of an airliner.

The sky's composition is also precarious. The ozone layer is thinning and permitting dangerous ultraviolet radiation to strike the Earth's surface. Also, increasing amounts of carbon dioxide pumped into the atmosphere by industrialized nations are blamed for the greenhouse effect, a gradual warming caused by heat trapped underneath a thickening layer of the gas.

It seems almost inconceivable that the sky could change so much that it would endanger our lives. But there was a time when the sky wouldn't have supported human life at all. In ancient times, it was composed mostly of carbon dioxide, water vapor, and ammonia spewed out of volcanoes. Only in the last 40 percent of the history of the planet has the atmosphere been oxygenated. For this, we must thank blue-green algae and other primitive plants, which converted the carbon

COMPOSITION OF ATMOSPHERE: 79% nitrogen; 20% oxygen; 1% other gases, including carbon dioxide, ozone, hydrogen, methane, and helium

WHY THE SKY IS BLUE: Air is transparent, which is why we can see the stars at night. The daytime color comes from the complex interaction of sunlight striking gas molecules and particles of dust and moisture. White sunlight is actually composed of the seven main colors of the spectrum—the same colors in a rainbow. During the day, all these colors except blue travel directly to the Earth's surface. The blue light is scattered by gas molecules throughout the sky. The sun, which is white when viewed from outer space, appears yellow from the surface—all the colors of the spectrum minus blue.

ALSO SEE: Clouds; Draco; Woodchuck; Mist, Dew, and Fog; Sun

There was a time when the sky wouldn't have supported human life at all

Approximate length (in hours and minutes) of "astronomical" evening twilight, the time between sunset and total sky darkness, for north woods region:

Early January	1:45
Mid-January	1:42
Early February	1:39
Mid-February	1:36
Early March	1:35
Mid-March	1:39
Early April	1:44
Mid-April	1:47
Early May	2:00
Mid-May	2:10
Early June	2:25
Mid-June	2:27
Early July	2:21
Mid-July	2:12
Early August	1:56
Mid-August	1:57
Early September	1:43
Mid-September	1:37
Early October	1:34
Mid-October	1:38
Early November	1:39
Mid-November	1:39
Early December	1:44
Mid-December	1:44

Clarke Belt
36,000 km
communication
satellites

— 500

— 400 - - - - - - -

Visible
satellites

Aurore

— 300

— 200 - - - - - - -

Shuttle and
space station

— 100

Meteors

— 20 km - - - - - - - - -

dioxide into oxygen through photosynthesis. They also provided ozone, a type of oxygen that absorbs the sun's deadly ultraviolet radiation. Our modern atmosphere remains relatively stable because of the ongoing exchange of oxygen and carbon dioxide via photosynthesis. But the sky is increasingly at peril from human activity.

Long before the age of TV forecasts, our ancestors watched the sky for clues to tomorrow's weather. The behavior of plants and animals also helped them predict the weather. Memorable ditties or sayings that pertained to long-range forecasts were more superstition than science, but short-range predictions were often quite accurate, for sound reasons:

- "Red sky at night, sailors delight.
  Red sky in the morning, sailors take warning."

  If the sun is shining in the west at sunset, this means it is not obscured by clouds. Since weather systems generally move from west to east in North America, it's a good bet that the following day will be clear. If the sun is shining in the morning, that means the good weather is far to the east. It may not be long before bad weather arrives.
- "If the maple sap runs faster, it is going to rain."

  Low pressure enables the sap to run more freely. Low pressure means bad weather.

SUN

The 0.7 Percent Solution

The source of all life on Earth begins with a slim surplus of mass deep inside the sun. Under pressure 250 billion times greater than that exerted on the surface of the Earth, and in 27 million°F (15 million°C) heat, four hydrogen atoms fuse into one helium atom. But the helium does not equal the mass of the hydrogen parents; a tiny amount, 0.7 percent, is left over. This excess mass is converted into energy that ultimately becomes the heat and light that bathes our planet and all the other worlds in the Solar System.

Science has uncovered many of the secrets of nuclear fusion, as this process is called. But most ancient cultures understood that the sun was the giver of life, and had a sun deity or being who played a prominent role in their mythology. Shamash was the sun god of Babylonia; he was responsible for justice. The Egyptians' Ra was also the great creator and defender

HISTORIC EXPEDITION: In 1768, the English dispatched astronomer Charles Green and Captain James Cook to Tahiti to record the transit of Venus across the face of the sun. The measurements were to be used to determine the distance of the sun from Earth. On his way back from Tahiti, in 1770, Cook became the first European to encounter eastern Australia. His ship sailed into Botany Bay and changed the history of that continent forever.

PERIOD OF ROTATION (THE SUN'S "DAY"): 25 Earth days at the equator
DIAMETER: 840,000 miles (1,400,000 km), or 109 times Earth's diameter
MASS: 333,000 times Earth's
TEMPERATURE: 27,000,000°F (15,000,000°C) at core, 9,900°F

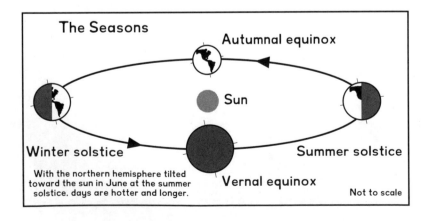

The Seasons

Autumnal equinox

Sun

Winter solstice

Summer solstice

With the northern hemisphere tilted toward the sun in June at the summer solstice. days are hotter and longer.

Vernal equinox

Not to scale

of goodness. Helios of ancient Greece rode his sun-chariot across the sky and lived in a magnificent palace where darkness never fell. Apollo was also identified as a Greek sun god, although more properly he was the god of light and truth. The sun in Ojibwa stories was a symbol of the Great Spirit, or Kitche Manitou; sometimes it was referred to as the Great Spirit's wigwam. An Inuit fable describes the sun and the moon as brother and sister who committed incest while they were humans. In the sky, they were to be forever parted. Nearly all cultures identify the sun with the masculine, perhaps because Earth and the moon are so closely associated with the feminine, and sunlight is the agent that fertilizes life.

Great festivals, such as the rowdy Roman Saturnalia, often marked significant solar events. Saturnalia was held around the winter solstice in December. At that time, the North Pole is tilted away from the sun because of Earth's 23.5-degree axial tilt to its orbital plane around the sun. At the summer solstice in June, after the Earth has traveled halfway around its orbit, the North Pole is tilted toward the sun. The Northern Hemisphere thus receives the sun's warming rays at a more direct angle in summer. In December, when shadows are longest because the sun is low, the Northern Hemisphere receives the rays at an oblique angle. In other words, the same amount of sunlight has to heat a far greater area of land in the winter than it does in the summer. The seasons are reversed in the Southern Hemisphere.

On the summer solstice, the sun rises at its most northerly point along the northeastern horizon and traces its highest arc of the year across the sky. It is the longest day of the year. The opposite

(5,500°C) at surface
AGE: 4.6 billion years
COMPOSITION BY NUMBER OF ATOMS: 92% hydrogen, almost 8% helium, heavier elements the remainder
MAGNITUDE: −27
CLOSEST DISTANCE BETWEEN EARTH AND SUN: 88 million mi (147 million km) at perihelion, in early January
FARTHEST DISTANCE: 91 million mi (152 million km) at aphelion, in early July
VERNAL (SPRING) EQUINOX: March 20–22 (exact date changes from year to year)
SUMMER SOLSTICE: June 20–22
AUTUMNAL EQUINOX: September 21–23
WINTER SOLSTICE: December 20–22
TIME IT TAKES FOR SUNLIGHT TO REACH EARTH: 8.3 minutes
SPEED OF LIGHT: 186,282 miles (299,792 km) per second
SOLAR RADIATION REACHING EARTH THAT IS ABSORBED INTO THE GROUND AND CONVERTED INTO HEAT: About 50%. Half the radiation reflects off clouds and the Earth, or is absorbed by the atmosphere.
SUN: From ancient Indo-European *sau* or *su*. Some groups of sun-related words adopted an *l* suffix or ending, including *sol* in Spanish, *soleil* in French, *solar* in English, and *helios* in Greek. Others adopted an *n* suffix or ending, including *sun, sonne* in German, and *zon* in Dutch.
ALSO SEE: Milky Way, Moon, Northern Lights, Planets and Comets, Zodiac and Ecliptic

APPROXIMATE SUNRISE AND SUNSET TIMES FOR ELY. NORTHERN MINNESOTA. 91.9°W LONGITUDE:

Date*	Sunrise	Sunset
January 1	7:57 A.M. CST	4:24 P.M. CST
February 1	7:35	5:06
March 1	6:49	5:50
April 1	5:47	6:36
May 1	5:50 A.M. DST	8:18 P.M. DST
June 1	5:13	8:57
July 1	5:12	9:10
August 1	5:43	8:44
September 1	6:24	7:50
October 1	7:05	6:48
November 1	6:51 A.M. CST	4:50 P.M. CST
December 1	7:35	4:17

APPROXIMATE SUNRISE AND SUNSET TIMES FOR BURLINGTON. VERMONT. 73.2°W LONGITUDE (SEE NOTE):

Date*	Sunrise	Sunset
January 1	7:29 A.M. EST	4:22 P.M. EST
February 1	7:12	5:00
March 1	6:31	5:39
April 1	5:34	6:18
May 1	5:44 A.M. DST	7:55 P.M. DST
June 1	5:11	8:29
July 1	5:40	8:58
August 1	5:38	8:19
September 1	6:14	7:31
October 1	6:49	6:35
November 1	6:29 A.M. EST	4:43 P.M. EST
December 1	7:08	4:14

*For dates between the chart dates, take an average. For other locations, add 4 minutes for each degree of longitude west of the closest city in the chart. Subtract 4 minutes for each degree of longitude east of the closest city. Daylight savings time starts on the first Sunday in April and ends on the last Sunday in October. This chart has been adjusted to account for DST.

ULTRAVIOLET INDEX

INDEX	RISK	APPROXIMATE MINUTES TO SKIN DAMAGE*
10+	Very high	6–20 minutes
7–9	High	8–28 minutes
5–6	Moderate	12–40 minutes
3–4	Low	17–65 minutes
1–2	Minimal	35–120 minutes

*Skin damage for someone who burns easily. Times are longer for people who burn sometimes or rarely.

occurs on the winter solstice, when the sun rises in the southeast and loops low across the southern sky. On the vernal and autumnal equinoxes, the sun rises and sets midway between the points demarcated by the solstices. This happens to be due east and due west. On the equinoxes, the hours of the day are split into roughly equal amounts of day and night, hence the name.

Our sun is in comfortable middle age. Now and then the photosphere, the sun's roiling surface, erupts with violent flares and enormous gas prominences, but this is normal for a Class G2 V nuclear-fusion reactor, as astronomers categorize our star. The flares are associated with sunspots, which are cooler areas of the photosphere caused by fluctuations in the sun's powerful magnetic field. These fluctuations have an eleven-year cycle, so every eleven years solar flares seem more pronounced.

But like all living things, the sun's time will come. In another five billion years or so, the engine of our Solar System will be running on empty. Shortly afterward, the sun will swell into a "red giant" that will engulf Mercury, Venus, and Earth. Immense gravitational forces will then cause the sun's matter to contract into a small, dense star called a white dwarf. The stored-up heat from its previous processes will radiate away, and our sun will die.

THUNDER AND LIGHTNING

Flashes Hotter Than the Sun

Anyone who has experienced the full fury of a thunderstorm, especially from inside a tent, has an idea of how our ancestors must have felt during one of nature's most awesome shows. The howling winds, the crashing thunder, and the alien lightning bolts seem like a backdrop to the end of time. Perhaps that's why the thunder gods of many ancient civilizations were the supreme beings, even more powerful than sun deities. Zeus of Olympus and Thor of Valhalla hurled thunderbolts with impunity. Marduk, the supernatural hero of ancient Babylon, was also a thunder god. One of the manifestations of the Semitic god Baal was a storm god with an arsenal of thunderbolts. Maybe they're all the same god—one story passed down and altered through the millennia.

Native peoples of North America also respected thunderstorms. To the Ojibwa and many other tribes, mythic thunderbirds, or *pinesi*, brought thunderstorms. When storms were raging, the thunderbirds were said to be hunting. Thunder was the flap of their wings; lightning the flash of their eyes. Although *pinesi* had no definite shape, they were generally associated with hawks, undoubtedly based on the observation that hawks and thunderstorms first appear about the same time each year, in April, and fade away at the same time, in October.

The classic thunderstorm occurs on hot, humid summer afternoons, when massive

TEMPERATURE OF A LIGHTNING BOLT: 18,000–72,000°F (10,000–40,000°C)

TEMPERATURE OF THE SUN'S SURFACE: About 9,900°F (5,500°C)

AVERAGE CURRENT OF A LIGHTNING BOLT: 20,000 amperes

TYPICAL HOUSEHOLD ELECTRICAL CURRENT: 20 amperes

TYPICAL WIDTH OF A LIGHTNING BOLT: 0.75 in (2 cm) at point of strongest current

MAXIMUM HEIGHT OF A THUNDERCLOUD: 12 miles (20 km)

HEIGHT OF MOUNT EVEREST: 5.3 miles (8.8 km)

HEIGHT OF MOUNT WASHINGTON, VERMONT, HIGHEST POINT IN THE NORTH WOODS: 6,288 ft (1,917 m)

SPEED OF SOUND: 1,085 ft (0.332 km) per second

HOW FAR AWAY THE LIGHTNING IS: Determine the distance to a lightning bolt by counting the number of seconds between a lightning flash and its resulting thunder. Each second is about 1,000 ft (300 m). A count of 5 means the storm is about a mile away.

ESTIMATED NUMBER OF THUNDERSTORMS OCCURRING AT THIS MOMENT: 1,800

ESTIMATED NUMBER OF LIGHTNING BOLTS STRIKING THE GROUND EVERY SECOND: 100

AVERAGE NUMBER OF TIMES THE EMPIRE STATE BUILDING GETS HIT

amounts of heated air rise to form huge cumulonimbus clouds. Within the thunderheads, powerful downdrafts ionize the air by stripping molecules of electrons, similar to the way rubbing a balloon gives it an electrical charge. The top of a thunderhead is thus positively charged, while the base is negatively charged. The ground immediately below a thunderhead is positively charged, too. Nature seeks to correct the electrical imbalance by transferring electrons from the positive ground or cloud top to the negative cloud base. Most lightning occurs within a cloud or between clouds. Only 20 percent is cloud-to-ground lightning.

Lightning forms along a route called a tunnel or channel. In cloud-to-ground lightning, one end starts at the cloud base and moves downward, while the other starts on the ground—generally from a tall point such as a tower or tree—and moves upward. The two meet, usually at a spot close to the ground, and the circuit is completed. The visible lightning bolt emanates from this point, moving up and down the tunnel in about one ten-thousandth of a second. The explosive bolt heats the air instantly, up to seven times the temperature of the surface of the sun, and the resulting air expansion vibrates as thunder. Sheet lightning is not another form of lightning but simply the glow of lightning bolts that occur within a cloud. Contrary to popular belief, lightning often hits the same place twice, especially tall towers.

Buildings and hardtop cars are the safest places to wait out thunderstorms. Appliances should be unplugged because electrical charges can sometimes surge down power lines. Standing under tall trees, or in the middle of open fields or atop hills or ridges, is dangerous. Swimmers and boaters should head for shore as soon as they hear thunder. Woods are relatively safe, but don't set up a tent underneath the

EVERY YEAR: 23

NUMBER OF DEATHS PER YEAR BY LIGHTNING IN THE UNITED STATES AND CANADA: About 100

NUMBER OF LIGHTNING-STRIKE SURVIVORS PER YEAR IN THE UNITED STATES AND CANADA: about 300

BEN FRANKLIN'S KITE: In 1752 in Philadelphia, Benjamin Franklin flew a silk kite during a thunderstorm to prove that lightning was caused by electricity. Sparks leaped from a key on the string to his hand. His invention of lightning rods made him famous around the world.

TENNYSON'S DESCRIPTION OF LIGHTNING: "Flying flame"

HENRY DAVID THOREAU'S 1857 STORM: "We listened to some of the grandest thunder which I ever heard— rapid peals, round and plump, bang, bang, bang, in succession, like artillery from some fortress in the sky," he wrote of a storm experienced on his third canoe trip in Maine.

SPEED OF FALLING HAIL: 96 mph (160 km/h)

PERCENTAGE OF FOREST FIRES CAUSED BY LIGHTNING: About 35%

PERCENTAGE OF FOREST FIRES CAUSED BY HUMAN ACTIVITY: About 65%

MAXIMUM LENGTH OF A THUNDERSTORM: About 2 hours

ALSO SEE: Clouds, Rain and Snow, Red Oak, Yellow-Bellied Sapsucker

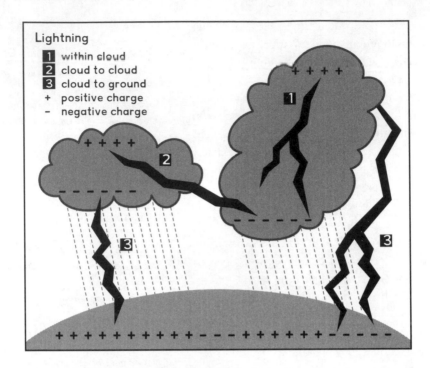

Lightning
1 within cloud
2 cloud to cloud
3 cloud to ground
+ positive charge
- negative charge

tallest tree. Place extra insulation, such as life jackets (without any metal snaps or zippers), under your sleeping bags. If you're caught in the open, the "golfer's crouch" can prevent serious injury or death: Kneel on the ground with hands on knees and bend forward. If a lightning bolt strikes nearby, the charge should pass under you without striking vital organs. Don't lie flat. Lightning strikes are lethal about 20 to 30 percent of the time, when the charge passes through the heart or spinal cord.

Tornadoes may also accompany the biggest thunderstorms and are usually preceded by heavy hail. Tornado winds can reach 300 mph (500 km/h), about twice as fast as the worst hurricane winds. Waterspouts are similar to tornadoes but not as violent, with winds approaching 48 mph (80 km/h). Both are rare in the north woods, though not unknown. North-central Minnesota and Wisconsin, and the northern Lower Peninsula of Michigan, are rated for one tornado per year per 10,000 square miles by the Oklahoma Climatological Survey. Central Oklahoma has the highest rating in the country, at nine per year per 10,000 square miles. But it doesn't take a tornado to inflict heavy damage in the north woods. Some muscular thunderstorms can unleash winds up to 100 mph (160 km/h), causing "blowdowns" that knock over hundred-year-old pines as if they were toothpicks. A big July 1999 blowdown in Minnesota's Boundary Waters Canoe Area Wilderness uprooted or snapped off an estimated twenty to twenty-five million trees.

WIND AND WEATHER SYSTEMS

A Blow-by-Blow Account

Wind is essential for life on Earth. Trees and plants owe their existence to winds that carry pollen and distribute seeds. Wind transports moisture around the world, bringing life-sustaining rains. Tailwinds and vertical air currents called thermals enable birds to migrate thousands of miles. Worldwide wind patterns distribute heat more evenly across the planet. The profound importance of wind was not lost on the ancients: Wind is one of the four elements of antiquity, along with fire, water, and earth.

The science of wind is complex. Many questions about its behavior still stump researchers, not to mention novice sailboarders. But the basics are well understood. Put simply, wind occurs when air rushes from a high-pressure zone to a low-pressure zone, answering nature's call for equilibrium. A vacuum cleaner uses the same principle. In the machine, a powerful fan creates an artificial low-pressure zone. Air outside the vacuum cleaner, now suddenly under higher pressure, swooshes up the nozzle toward the low-pressure area, carrying dust, dirt, and lost dimes along with it. The greater the difference in pressure, the faster the wind. Hurricanes and tornadoes are like enormous vacuum cleaners: Both are extremely low pressure systems, sucking deadly winds toward their centers and picking up everything in their paths.

Typical low-pressure systems aren't as violent, but they generally bring bad

FAMOUS WINDS: God blew an east wind all night long to divide the Red Sea, allowing Moses and the Israelites to escape from Egypt. In 1281, a typhoon destroyed the huge Mongolian fleet that was attacking Japan. The Japanese word for typhoon is *kamikaze*, meaning "divine wind." *Typhoon* comes from the Chinese *tai*, "big," and *feng*, "wind." Storm winds also helped the English destroy the Spanish Armada in 1588.
WIND: From the Indo-European base *we*, meaning "blow." Related words include the Latin *ventus*, the root of *vent* and *ventilate* in English; *vent* (wind) in French; and *viento* (wind) in Spanish. *We* is also the root of the Greek *aetes*, "wind," and *aer*, "air."
WEATHER: Also from the Indo-European *we*. Weather is *Wetter* in German, *weer* in Dutch, *vejr* in Danish, and *väder* in Swedish.
KING OF THE WINDS: In Greek mythology, Aeolus ruled the four winds (*aeolian* means "pertaining to the winds"). North wind: Boreas. West wind: Zephyr. South wind: Notus. East wind: Eurus.
WHY WIND FEELS COOL OR COLD AGAINST THE SKIN: Wind evaporates moisture in the skin, a process that removes heat energy. Thus, in the summer, a gentle breeze cools

BEAUFORT WIND SCALE
(NAMED AFTER FRANCIS BEAUFORT, A BRITISH ADMIRAL, WHO INVENTED THE SCALE IN 1805)

Number	Wind Speed (km/h)	Designation	Characteristic
0	up to 1	Calm	Smoke rises vertically.
1	1–5	Light air	Smoke drifts; leaves rustle.
2	6–11	Light breeze	Wind on face, small wavelets
3	12–19	Gentle breeze	Flags flutter.
4	20–29	Moderate breeze	Dust blows; branches move.
5	30–38	Fresh breeze	Flags are stretched; trees sway.
6	39–50	Strong breeze	Wires hum; wind whistles.
7	51–61	Moderate gale	Walking impeded
8	62–74	Fresh gale	Twigs break off, high waves.
9	75–86	Strong gale	Branches break; tiles are blown.
10	87–101	Whole gale	Trees uprooted, damage
11	102–120	Storm	Widespread damage
12	over 120	Hurricane	Major destruction

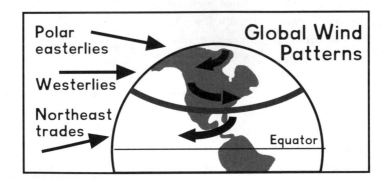

Global Wind Patterns

Polar easterlies

Westerlies

Northeast trades

Equator

weather. In a low, the inward-rushing air is warm and moves upward as it converges toward the center. As the warm, moisture-laden air ascends, it cools. Water vapor condenses into cloud banks, and it often rains.

High-pressure zones are characterized by heavy, cooler air that sinks as it moves outward. Cool air contains less moisture; therefore, the air is sometimes cloudless. A high-pressure system in the winter brings cold, clear air. In the summer, the air in a high-pressure system doesn't seem so cool because it heats up during the day as intense sunlight warms the ground. Both high-pressure and low-pressure systems generally move westward across the continent because of prevailing westerly winds.

us down. In the winter, a breeze freezes, reminding us of our northern latitudes.

ALSO SEE: Broad-Winged Hawk; Clouds; Mist, Dew, and Fog; Mosquitoes; Rain and Snow; Sky; Thunder and Lightning

---

Hurricanes and tornadoes are like enormous vacuum cleaners: Both are extremely low pressure systems, sucking deadly winds toward their centers and picking up everything in their paths

---

In the summer, gentle winds die down at night because their creator—the sun—disappears. During the day, the sun heats the ground, which then warms the air. As the warm air rises, other air rushes in to take its place, creating wind. Once the sun is gone, the process stops.

NIGHT SKY

If the grandeur of a planetary world in which the earth, as a grain of sand, is scarcely perceived, fills the understanding with wonder; with what astonishment are we transported when we behold the infinite multitude of worlds and systems which fill the extension of the Milky Way!

—*German philosopher and part-time astronomer Immanuel Kant, 1755 (translated by W. Hastie)*

I n Kant's time, before the invention of streetlights, the experience of beholding the night sky must have been more regular and intense than it is today. Now, most people are transported with astonishment only during forays to the north woods, where the sky is crisp and clear and studded with thousands of stars.

Gazing at the universe is an ancient pastime. Some scholars believe that civilization itself was born when humans acquired time-factoring skills through observations of the heavens. The invention of Western philosophy is said to stem from the ponderings of the Greek astronomer Thales in the sixth century B.C. No doubt he asked the question of every stargazer, "What is the meaning of life?"

If not the answer to the meaning of life, the stars contain the stories of cultures around the world. Myths and legends are played out every night as the constellations, planets, and moon parade across the celestial dome. This section of *The Wild Woods Guide* contains several of those stories, as well as star maps to aid the novice stargazer. We've focused on summertime constellations, since that's when most amateur stargazing takes place.

BIG DIPPER

Symbol of Freedom on the Underground Railroad

Through the millennia, people in the Northern Hemisphere have gazed into the night sky and connected the same starry dots to form what we now call the Big Dipper. It's the constellation we learn first because it's easy to pick out, it's prominent in the sky on warm summer nights, and two of its stars conveniently point to the North Star, Polaris.

In fact, long before the Golden Arches came to exist, the Big Dipper was one thing many civilizations had in common. A surprising number of myths from Europe, Asia, and North America refer to the Big Dipper as a bear. It's thought the bear story comes from prehistoric Asia and traveled both eastward and westward with various human migrations.

The native peoples of northern New England and the Maritime Provinces in Canada have just such a story, in which the four stars making up the cup of the Big Dipper represent a bear. The three stars of the handle, plus other nearby stars, represent birds. From high in the sky, the birds chased the bear closer to Earth. In autumn, the lead bird, Robin, shot an arrow at the bear. Blood splashed Robin, giving the bird its red breast. Blood also dripped onto the leaves below, giving them autumn color. The hunt's cycle is repeated every year, with the position of the constellation serving as a calendar to record the seasons. The motion of the bear through the sky during the night also serves as a clock.

LATIN AND GREEK NAMES: Ursus is the Latin word for "bear," evident in such modern words as *ursine,* meaning "bearlike." The Greek word for bear, *arkitos,* is the root for Arcas, son of Callisto; Arcturus, the bright star in the constellation Boötes; and even King Arthur, who was sometimes called Arturus. Because the stars associated with the bear stories lie in the northern sky, things relating to the north often contain the *arkitos* root—e.g., "arctic."

CLOSEST STAR IN BIG DIPPER TO EARTH: Mizar, 78 light-years away. One light-year is approximately 6 trillion miles: the distance light travels in one year

TRAVEL TIME TO MIZAR IN OUR FASTEST SPACECRAFT: 2.6 million years

FARTHEST STAR IN BIG DIPPER: Dubhe, 124 light-years away

BRIGHTEST STARS IN BIG DIPPER: Alioth and Dubhe, both magnitude 1.8

MAGNITUDE: System of ranking the brightness of stars, invented by ancient Greek astronomer Hipparchus. In his six-level system, the brightest stars were ranked 1 and the dimmest ranked 6. The modern magnitude system rests on this foundation; some very bright stars now have negative

The Greeks, as always, saw in the Dipper constellations a star opera of love and jealousy. In one version of the legend, Zeus seduces the nymph Callisto. Zeus's betrayed wife, Hera, retaliates by turning Callisto into a bear. Out of compassion, Zeus turns Callisto's son, Arcas, into a bear, too, to keep her company, placing both of them in the heavens to protect them from hunters. There they are known by their Latin names Ursa Major, the greater bear, and Ursa Minor, the lesser bear. Zeus's manner of delivering both bears to the heavens—a cosmic heave—explains their stretched tails.

Cultures around the world saw unique shapes in the Dipper configuration. The Saxons called it a wagon, as did the Babylonians. In Britain, it is still sometimes called the Plough. Ancient Egyptians looked up in the sky and saw a bull's thigh. Back in the United States, slaves called it a "drinking gourd," because it resembled the

values, while stars invisible to the naked eye but apparent in telescopes have values greater than 6.

DOUBLE-STAR NAMES: Mizar (larger star) and Alcor. This pair is called an optical double, because they are close to each other only by virtue of our line of sight from Earth. They are not gravitationally linked to each other like a true double-star system. Telescopic observations show that many stars are actually double stars, also called binaries. Mizar appears as a double star in telescopes.

ALASKA STATE FLAG: The Big Dipper and the North Star are depicted on the state's flag. Minnesota, of course, is the "North Star State."

ALSO SEE: Black Bear, Boötes, Corona Borealis, North Star and Little Dipper

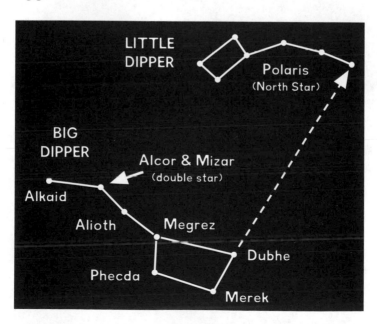

shape of gourds they hollowed out for drinking cups. The celestial drinking gourd became a navigational beacon pointing northward as slaves fled under the cover of night along the Underground Railroad in the mid-1800s. Popular folk songs contained coded lyrics with instructions for getting north to Canada and other safe areas.

The celestial drinking gourd became a navigational beacon pointing northward as slaves fled under the cover of night along the Underground Railroad in the mid-1800s

The official constellation Ursa Major, as defined by the International Astronomical Union, actually includes many more stars than just those in the Big Dipper. For this reason, the Big Dipper portion is technically called an asterism. It includes some notable astronomical features. The star at the crook of the Big Dipper's handle appears as a double star, for example. It is barely perceptible with the naked eye, which is why it was used as an eye test by many peoples, including native North Americans, before wall charts were invented.

BOÖTES

Ice Cream Cone in the Sky

The constellation Boötes contains the brightest star of the summer sky, Arcturus. This giant nuclear furnace is about 120 times more luminous than our own sun and 25 times wider. It's also relatively close to Earth, a little more than half the distance of the Big Dipper's nearest star to Earth. The only star to outshine Arcturus in the Northern Hemisphere is brilliant Sirius, the "dog star" of winter that burns low in the southern sky.

Arcturus has great significance for northern peoples. It is the harbinger of spring, a signal to start thinking about planting crops or opening up camp. Arcturus climbs over the horizon into the early evening sky around the time of the spring equinox in late March.

Arcturus means "guardian of the bear" in Greek. The star was thought to herd Ursa Major, the Great Bear or Big Dipper, around the North Star. At some point in history, this notion was extended to include the entire constellation of Boötes, which means "plowman" or "herdsman."

To find Arcturus and Boötes (pronounced bow-OW-tays), follow the curve of the handle of the Big Dipper to the bright star—the famous "arc to Arcturus." Boötes extends out from Arcturus in the shape of a giant ice cream cone; some people prefer to think of it as a kite. Continue the arc down from Arcturus to find another bright star, Spica. As summer progresses, Arcturus moves high across the night sky. It is almost directly overhead as darkness descends over the north woods in late June and early July.

How Arcturus Lit up Chicago: At the 1933 world's fair in Chicago, organizers used the star's light to turn on the fair's floodlights. The star beam was focused through a telescope onto a photoelectric cell, which generated the voltage to flip the switch. The starlight hitting the cell would have begun its journey to Earth in 1896, since Arcturus is 37 light-years away.

Brightest star in Boötes: Arcturus, magnitude –0.05

Closest stars in Boötes to Earth: Arcturus and Mufrid, both 37 light-years away

Farthest star in Boötes: Nekkar, 219 light-years away

Also see: Big Dipper, North Star and Little Dipper, Star Charts

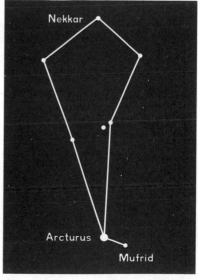

353

CASSIOPEIA

Stairway to Heaven

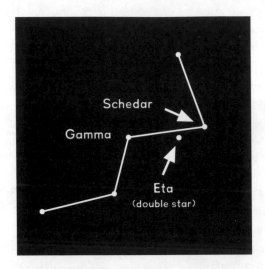

Cassiopeia, the Queen of Aethiopia in Greek mythology, easily calls attention to herself from her heavenly perch. For many stargazers Cassiopeia is the second constellation they learn after the Big Dipper. Like the Big Dipper, it is circumpolar, revolving around Polaris and never setting below the horizon at north woods latitudes.

Cassiopeia was strapped to a chair and placed in the heavens as punishment for her boastfulness

---

Northern cultures gave various meanings to Cassiopeia's distinctive shape. When it is low in the sky, it looks like a giant W. As it moves higher, it turns upside down to become an M. To the Inuit people of the Arctic, this outline reflected the pattern of stairs cut in snow, an astral stairway connecting Earth to the sky country. The ancient Egyptians called it the Leg; to the Chinese, it was the charioteer Wang Liang.

But it is the Greco-Roman tale that gives us the name Cassiopeia. The Queen of Aethiopia, married to King Cepheus, was by reputation an unpleasant woman. She bragged that she was more beautiful than the sea nymphs—not a smart move, since the nymphs were the offspring of the mighty sea god Poseidon. The enraged god dispatched the monster Cetus to attack Aethiopia's coast. An oracle advised Cepheus that the only way to save his citizens was to sacrifice his daughter Andromeda to the briny beast. This he reluctantly did, although Andromeda was rescued by Perseus before Cetus could get his flippers on her. Cassiopeia was strapped to a chair and placed in the heavens as punishment for her boastfulness. The other characters in this myth, including Cepheus, Andromeda, Cetus, and Perseus, have nearby constellations named after them.

CORONA BOREALIS

A Love Message to Ariadne

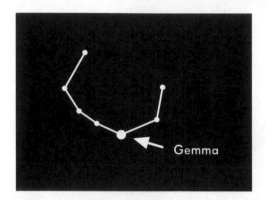

Gemma

C orona Borealis is one of those constellations that actually looks like the thing it is named after. The delicate Northern Crown, from the Latin, is a small string of stars lying between Boötes and Hercules. Not bright enough to compete with city lights, it glitters conspicuously in the night sky of wilderness areas.

Its Greek origins are traced to the story of Ariadne, the daughter of King Minos of Crete. In return for a promise of marriage, the love-struck Ariadne helped the Athenian prince Theseus to enter the Labyrinth safely and kill its evil tenant, the Minotaur. Ariadne slipped Theseus a ball of thread, which he deployed as he searched for the grotesque half man, half bull. Theseus slew the Minotaur and followed the thread back to safety. Ariadne was supposed to return to Athens with her new husband, but the boat stopped first in Naxos, where it seems Theseus dumped her. But the god Dionysus came upon the heartbroken Ariadne and fell in love with her. As a show of affection, Dionysus placed his crown in the heavens in her name.

In the mythology of several North American native groups, including the Ojibwa in Minnesota, the stars of Corona Borealis were dancing maidens.

ARIADNE, *THE OPERA:* In 1912, the German composer Richard Strauss wrote *Ariadne auf Naxos.* It was an opera-within-an-opera that told the story of lovesick Ariadne on the Greek island of Naxos.

THESEUS'S OTHER WIVES: After Ariadne, Theseus married the Amazon queen Hippolyta (also named Antiope) and after her death, Phaedra, Ariadne's sister. The hero of Athens became unpopular in his old age and was eventually murdered.

GEMMA: The name of the brightest star in Corona Borealis is Latin for "jewel" and the root of the word *gem.* The star is also sometimes called Alphekka or Alphecca.

DO-SI-DO: Gemma is an eclipsing double star or eclipsing binary. The two stars orbit each other every 17 years, and from our line of sight, one star eclipses the other as they pirouette about the sky. The system is too far away to discern with a backyard telescope.

ALSO SEE: Big Dipper, Star Charts

DRACO

Dragon of the Cosmos

Draco, according to American astronomy writer and lecturer Mark Chartrand, "has stood for all the dragons of mythology." The word *Draco* comes from the Greek *drakon*, meaning "snake." But its origins slither back long before the Greeks. Draco is a direct link to creation.

In many cosmogonies, creation is the moment of "separation" in the primitive chaos, whether it be night and day ("Let there be light") or heaven and Earth. In Babylonian mythology, the genesis story is told in *Enuma Elish*, an ancient composition dating to about 1500 B.C. In this story, the sea is called Tiamat, one of the elements of the watery chaos, and is identified with the female. Apsu is another element, representing the fresh waters, and is identified with the male. Together they begat other gods, including Enki, the Earth. Scholars link the story to the observation that earth in Mesopotamia is literally formed from the alluvial action of the Tigris and Euphrates Rivers (Apsu, the fresh waters) depositing silt in the Persian Gulf (Tiamat).

Once the basic components of the universe were created, they had to be organized. This part of the story began when the children/gods of Tiamat and Apsu rebelled against their parents. In defense, Tiamat raised a powerful army of fire-breathing dragons, and herself assumed the shape of a serpent. The younger gods crowned Marduk as their king and champion, and he led them into battle. Marduk captured Tiamat and, since he was a storm god, blew a fierce wind down her gullet. Tiamat split in two, and Marduk lifted up half her body to form the sky, represented by Draco. The moment of Marduk's victory—action over chaos—signified the moment of creation.

Similar elements of the story are contained in the Greek chronicle of the Titans versus the young gods of Olympus. Zeus, like Marduk, was a storm

DRACONIAN: Meaning "harsh measures," the word descends from Draco of Athens, a seventh century B.C. legislator. His legal code was famous for its severity, including the death penalty for many crimes.

DISTANCE OF THUBAN FROM EARTH: 309 light-years

THUBAN: The Arabic word for "snake"

MESOPOTAMIA: From the Greek, meaning "between the streams," the land between the Tigris and the Euphrates

COSMOGONY: A theory about the creation of the universe

ALSO SEE: Boötes, North Star and Little Dipper, Planets and Comets, Star Charts

DRACO

(Double star in binoculars)

LITTLE
DIPPER

Thuban
(old north star)

Polaris

god, for example. In one battle against the Titans, the goddess Athena hurled an attacking serpent into the heavens, where it wrapped around the celestial north pole. Five thousand years ago, the star Thuban in Draco was the pole star. (Because Earth wobbles on its axis while the stars stay fixed, the pole star changes over the millennia.)

There are three other dragons or serpents in the night sky: Cetus, Hydra, and Serpens. Cetus appears low in the southern sky in autumn; it is the monster in the myth of Andromeda. Hydra, the many-headed serpent slain by Hercules, is the largest constellation in the heavens and skims the southern horizon in spring. Serpens is a dim but important constellation lying south of Hercules in the summer. It is the only constellation found in two parts: Serpens Caput, the head, and Serpens Cauda, the tail. They are joined by the constellation Ophiuchus, the Serpent Bearer. The legend goes that Ophiuchus killed a snake and watched in amazement as another snake came along to revive its companion with herbs. This led to the medicinal use of plants and Ophiuchus's future as a healer. He was placed in the sky, with a serpent, in honor of his achievements. The modern symbol of medicine, the caduceus, depicting snakes wrapped around a staff, has its origins in this story.

The squarish head of Draco lies near the feet of Hercules, and its long body winds between the Big and Little Dippers. Urban lights obscure the dim stars of Draco, but in the darkness of wilderness the constellation writhes to life.

FALLING STARS

Anything to Worry About?

A paddle dips languidly into the ink-black water. A loon laughs. The night sky is a treasure chest of sparkling stars, reflected on the still lake. Every few minutes, high overhead, blue-green light streaks across the heavens. Sometimes there is a trail of sparks, like fireworks.

In mid-August, lying back in a canoe in the middle of a dark north woods lake, the Perseid meteor shower entertains like no other show on Earth.

Meteors are reminders that the space between the stars and planets is not empty. "Falling stars" are caused when rocky particles called meteoroids enter Earth's atmosphere. Nearly all meteoroids are the size of a grain of sand or smaller. But every once in a while a big sucker gets through. Imagine how surprised the grazing dinosaurs of ancient Mexico must have been when a boulder thought to be about twelve miles (twenty kilometers) wide came out of nowhere and wiped out the neighborhood. The collision, which scientists believe occurred sixty-five million years ago in the Yucatán Peninsula (then under a shallow sea), would have thrown up an enormous cloud of dust, blocking out sunlight for years. It seems certain this killed off the dinosaurs. Chicken Little has run scared ever since.

In fact, the fate of the dinosaurs has led scientists, leaders, and Hollywood directors to wonder if a giant asteroid has the name *Homo sapiens* written on it. In 1989, an

FAVORITE TARGET OF METEORITES: Wethersfield, Connecticut. Two meteorites smashed into homes in this town, one in 1971 and another in 1982.

CLOSE CALLS: An Alaskan woman suffered injuries to her arm when a meteorite slammed through the roof of her house in 1954. In 1991, a meteorite crashed into Arthur Pettifor's garden in England. He was quietly planting onions about 60 feet away.

BULL'S-EYE: A dog in Egypt was struck dead by a meteorite in 1912.

METEOR: From the Greek *meta,* meaning "beyond," and *eora,* meaning "suspension"

ESTIMATED NUMBER OF METEORITES HEAVIER THAN 3.5 OZ. (100 G) LANDING ON EARTH'S LANDMASS EACH YEAR: 5,800

ESTIMATED WEIGHT OF SPACE DUST THAT FLOATS TO EARTH EACH DAY: About 110 tons (100 metric tons)

NUMBER OF METEORITE CRATERS ON EARTH: More than 160, without about 5 new ones identified every year

NUMBER OF CRATERS IN UNITED STATES: 24

NUMBER IN CANADA: 29

NORTH WOODS CRATERS: There are no identified craters in the U.S. north woods area covered by this

asteroid about half a mile wide crossed a spot in Earth's orbit about six hours before the planet was there. Astronomers have also determined that a 0.6-mile- (1-kilometer-) wide asteroid dubbed 1950 DA has a 1 in 300 chance of slamming into Earth on March 16, 2880. These odds are considered risky enough to keep a close eye on that particular flying mountain: The force of the impact would be greater than the simultaneous detonation of every nuclear weapon on Earth. Congress has ordered NASA to track 90 percent of all large "near-Earth objects" by 2010. The idea of blasting a threatening asteroid to smithereens is generally frowned upon, because it would turn the asteroid into space buckshot that could pepper the planet. Instead, scientists are focusing on schemes to divert the asteroid just enough to change its course away from doing harm.

Meteors are reminders that the space between the stars and planets is not empty

Fortunately, large impacts are rare, at least by the standard of a human life span. But meteors arrive every day. The term *meteor* refers to the actual flare in the sky. The meteoroid vaporizes in about a second, 40 to 100 miles (65 to 160 kilometers) above the surface. A meteorite is a meteoroid large enough to survive the scorching descent to Earth. Anything bigger than an apple will make it to the ground, although a meteoroid's survival also depends on the speed it hits the atmosphere, the angle of

book. However, there is an impact crater al Glover Bluff In south-central Wisconsin, and also a buried impact site in southwestern Michigan called the Calvin Crater. There are several craters in the Canadian north woods, including the Brent Crater in Ontario's Algonquin Park. It is a circular depression 2.4 mi (4 kilometers) wide that now contains Lakes Gilmour and Tecumseh. The crater was gouged out of the Canadian shield 450 million years ago by a meteorite about 492 ft (150 meters) in diameter. The mineral-rich Sudbury Basin is also thought to be the legacy of a meteorite that hit Precambrian Ontario 1.7 billion years ago.

FORCE OF METEORITE THAT CREATED THE BRENT CRATER: Estimated 250 megatons

LARGEST NUCLEAR EXPLOSION EVER SET OFF: 60 megatons

WHY THE MOON HAS MORE IMPACT CRATERS: The moon has no atmosphere to burn up incoming meteoroids. Also, geophysical forces on Earth erode crater features. No such forces exist on the moon.

AGE OF METEORITES: About 4.6 billion years

AGE OF OUR SOLAR SYSTEM: About 4.6 billion years

"GO AND CATCH A FALLING STAR": The famous first line of John Donne's poem "Song," published in 1633, in which he suggests that fantastic feats, such as catching a falling star, are all easier than finding "a woman true, and fair"

1998 DISASTER-MOVIE PLOTS: Earthlings prepared for two comet strikes by building underground

entry, and the integrity of its structure. Bright "fireballs" are large meteors that may hit the surface, setting off hunts for space rock. Some fireballs are space junk reentering the atmosphere, often through a controlled descent.

Where does all the space gravel come from? Some of it is debris that has wandered from the asteroid belt between Mars and Jupiter, destined to evaporate in a blaze of glory. Meteorites that hit Mars and the moon blow fragments into space that may also head our way—a meteoroid domino effect. Stray meteors appear at a visible rate of about three to twelve an hour and cannot be predicted. But look for them after midnight, because by then spaceship *Earth* has spun so that we are looking "forward" into our orbit. The planet is now motoring into the path of any nearby meteoroids, so more meteors occur. Astronomers often compare this effect to a car traveling through a snowstorm: It collects more snow on the front windshield than the rear.

bunkers for one million people in the movie *Deep Impact*, starring Robert Duvall. In *Armageddon*, a team of astronauts led by the Bruce Willis character flies shuttles to an asteroid streaking toward Earth. They attempt to bury a nuclear bomb in the asteroid to blow it up before it hits the planet.

IMPACT WATCH: NASA tracks real "near Earth objects" at neo.jpl.nasa.gov.

FIREBALL ALERTS: The American Meteor Society accepts fireball sightings at www.amsmeteors.org.

ALSO SEE: Fireflies, Planets and Comets, Sky

Regular meteor showers are a different phenomenon. Most occur when Earth intersects the path of a comet that has gone by. As a comet rushes

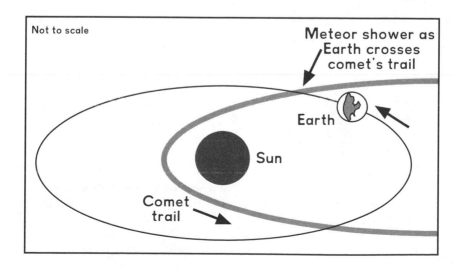

Not to scale

Meteor shower as Earth crosses comet's trail

Earth

Sun

Comet trail

toward the sun, it slowly disintegrates, leaving behind a concentrated trail of dust and dirt. Because the trail is located along a specific line in space, a meteor shower occurs each time Earth crosses it; in other words, at the same time each year. The trail of the comet Swift-Tuttle causes the Perseid meteor shower. The rate of observable meteors may vary from year to year, sometimes wildly. Most years, the Leonids in November produce about fifteen meteors per hour under the best conditions. But every thirty-three years or so, a spectacular Leonid shower may occur, with thousands of meteors falling each hour. The last good Leonid blast occurred in 2001; the next is expected in about 2034.

Keeners will note that each meteor in a shower emanates from approximately the same point in space, called the radiant. Meteor showers are named after the constellation in which the radiant is located, the radiant of the Perseids being the constellation Perseus, for example. The Perseids is one of the best showers to enjoy because of the high intensity—about fifty an hour—and the fact it's not below freezing outside.

MAJOR METEOR SHOWERS

SHOWER	DATE (PEAK)	RADIANT	RATE/ HOUR*	SPEED HITTING EARTH
Quadrantids	January 4	Draco	40	41 km/s
Lyrids	April 21	Lyra	15	48
Eta Aquarids	May 4	Aquarius	20	65
S. Delta Aquarids	July 28	Aquarius	20	41
N. Aquarids	August 12	Aquarius	20	42
Perseids	August 12	Perseus	50	60
Orionids	October 21	Orion	25	66
S. Taurids	November 2 or 3	Taurus	15	28
Leonids	November 17 or 16	Leo	15	71
Geminids	December 13	Gemini	50	35
Ursids	December 22	Ursa Minor	15	34

*Single observer under exceptional conditions. Most observers will see far fewer. Shower rates also vary from year to year, depending on recent comet passes. Meteor shower dates may move by one day depending on the year.

In the old days, people concocted all sorts of explanations for meteors. In Islamic folklore, meteors were missiles hurled by angels at evil spirits lurking around the gates of heaven. English peasants in the Middle Ages believed a falling star was a soul passing from heaven to Earth at the birth or conception of a new person—the reason they were wished upon. An Ojibwa story describes meteors as demons sent to Earth by an idle sky spirit, who wished to perplex the people living in the meteor's target zone. Pliny the Elder, a Roman philosopher and naturalist, thought a falling star marked someone's death, because every person had his or her own star in the sky. That raises the question: Did a meteor appear the day Pliny died? There should have been thousands, because the poor man went to Pompeii to study the eruptions of Mount Vesuvius in 79 A.D. and got caught in the most famous eruption ever. There were no reports of unusual meteor showers at the time.

MILKY WAY

The Path of Souls

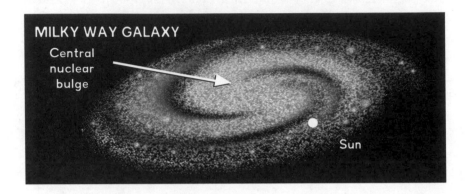

MILKY WAY GALAXY

Central
nuclear
bulge

Sun

The Milky Way, obliterated by city lights, glows to life in the dark night sky of the countryside and wilderness. Its horizon-to-horizon span suggests a pathway to the stars, a notion that captivated ancient cultures. In many mythologies, humans and their spirits ascended this path to the heavens, or gods and sky creatures descended it to join mortals on the ground. The Ojibwa called the Milky Way the Path of Souls. As part of the Ojibwa burial ritual, a campfire was lit by the death-post marking a grave. The fire was kept burning for four days to light the way for the soul-spirit, which must travel the Path of Souls to reach the Land of Souls.

In classical Greek mythology, the whitish band is said to represent a stream of milk from Rhea's breast as she suckled her son Zeus. Another story says the milk came from Hera, Zeus's wife. (The word *galaxy* comes from the Greek word for "milk," *gala* or *galaktos*.)

DIAMETER: About 100,000 light-years

THICKNESS: About 13,000 light-years

TRAVEL TIME TO LEAVE THE MILKY WAY GALAXY IN OUR FASTEST SPACECRAFT: About 570 million years

AGE: Uncertain, but probably 10 to 15 billion years

NUMBER OF STARS: Uncertain, possibly 200 billion

CLOSEST LARGE NEIGHBOR: Andromeda Galaxy, 2.2 million light-years away

NUMBER OF GALAXIES IN THE UNIVERSE: Uncertain, possibly up to 100 billion

TIME IT TAKES FOR OUR SOLAR SYSTEM TO ORBIT THE MILKY WAY: About 220 million years

SPEED OF OUR SOLAR SYSTEM AS IT ORBITS THE MILKY WAY: 150 mi/sec (250 km/sec)

OTHER NAMES FOR THE MILKY WAY: Many peoples from India to

For people of the Northern Hemisphere, the Milky Way is more prominent in summer than winter. This is due to the solar system's position about two-thirds out from the center of the galaxy. On summer nights (winter in the Southern Hemisphere), the Earth is positioned so that we look into the dense middle of the galactic disk. In winter, all we see is the final one-third of the galaxy and the dark, deep space beyond. The vast swath of the Milky Way arcs across the celestial dome from north to south on early-summer evenings. It twists in the sky as the summer progresses, until in mid-November it reaches from the eastern to western horizon.

The spout of the famous "teapot" constellation, Sagittarius, which appears low over the southern horizon in the summer, points to the hub of the Milky Way. This is where the Milky Way is at its widest and most luminous. But the galaxy's central nuclear bulge, a region where older stars are densely packed, is not clearly visible. Vast clouds of interstellar dust and gas block the view.

Several constellations are located along the Milky Way, including Cassiopeia, Cepheus, Cygnus, and Aquila. Both Cygnus the swan and Aquila the eagle fly in the direction of the astral belt. Ornithologists speculate, and natives traditionally believe, that migrating birds use the glimmer of the Milky Way as a navigational aid—making it truly a path in the heavens.

Scandinavia thought of the Milky Way as milk from the moon-cow goddess. Worlds and creatures were created from the curdled milk, including a moon of green cheese. Celts called the Milky Way *Bothar-Bo-Finne, or* Track of the White Cow—the source of the story about the cow jumping over the moon. The Egyptians called it the Nile of the Sky, which flowed from the udder of the moon-cow Hathor-Isis. Other names include Irmin's Way, Anglo-Saxon; *Hiddagal,* or River of the Divine Lady, Akkadian; *Umm al Sama,* or Mother of the Sky, Arabic; *Manavegr,* or Moon Way, Norse; Silver Stream of Heaven, Chinese.

GALILEO: Florentine astronomer and physicist, 1564–1642. Proved the glow of the Milky Way came from a multitude of stars. Condemned by the Roman Inquisition for his support of Copernican theories, which placed the sun, not the Earth, at the center of the solar system. The Vatican acknowledged its error 359 years later, in 1992.

ALSO SEE: Moon, Pegasus and Andromeda, Star Charts, Summer Triangle, Yellow-Rumped Warbler

MOON

The Original Timepiece

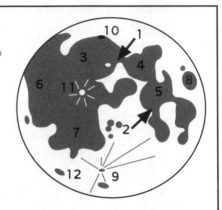

Selected Moon Landmarks

Human Sites
1. Luna 2, first on moon (September 13, 1959)
2. Apollo 11 (July 20, 1969)

Seas (Mares)
3. Sea of Rains
4. Sea of Serenity
5. Sea of Tranquility
6. Ocean of Storms
7. Sea of Clouds
8. Sea of Crises

Craters
9. Tycho (rayed crater)
10. Plato
11. Copernicus
12. Schickard

I f the sun stands for permanence, the moon is transience. Our nighttime companion transforms itself every evening; it appears and disappears, dies and is resurrected. For this reason, the moon is powerfully connected with the rhythms and mysteries of life and the passage of time.

The first calendars were based on the phases of the moon. There is evidence that cave dwellers in France recorded the lunar cycle with notches in animal bones and antlers 25,000 years before the first writing in Mesopotamia. It would have taken a few years, but eventually cavemen or cavewomen must have figured out that the seasons repeated themselves every twelve full moons or so.

In Europe, the year was based on a lunar calendar until 46 B.C.—an imperfect system because 12 lunar months do not add up to a solar year of 365 days. Julius Caesar, with the help of an Egyptian astronomer,

NUMBER OF ONE-WAY TRIPS BETWEEN NEW YORK CITY AND ADIRONDACK PARK (TOWN OF SARANAC LAKE) IT WOULD TAKE TO TRAVEL THE MEAN DISTANCE BETWEEN EARTH AND THE MOON: 746
DISTANCE FROM EARTH: 213,900 miles (356,500 km) at closest point (perigee); 243,900 miles (406,500 km) at farthest point (apogee)
DIAMETER: 2,085 miles (3,476 km)
MOON GRAVITY: About one-sixth Earth's gravity
AGE: 4.6 billion years
FIRST LUNAR PROBE TO LAND ON THE SURFACE: The Soviet's *Luna 2*, crashed September 13, 1959
FIRST MAN ON THE MOON: Neil Armstrong, *Apollo 11*, July 20, 1969
LAST MAN ON THE MOON: Eugene Cernan, *Apollo 17*, December 11, 1972
MAGNITUDE: –12.7 at full moon
WHY WE SEE ONLY ONE SIDE OF THE

resolved the problem when he ditched the idea of lunar months and divided the year into 12 independent calendar months, with a leap year every 4 years. The month of July is named after him. Later, in 1582, Pope Gregory XIII refined the Julian calendar because it was coming up short 1 day every 128 years. Gregory artificially shortened October that year—October 4 to 15, 1582, do not exist in history—and made other changes, so that the calendar is now accurate to within 1 day every 3,200 years.

Although the Julian/Gregorian calendar has been adopted almost worldwide, some cultures retain the lunar calendar for religious, festive, and day-to-day use. Moslem countries use a lunar calendar that began the day Mohammad was chased out of Mecca by unruly citizens enraged by his preachings (on July 16, 622, by the Gregorian calendar). The Moslem year of twelve lunar months makes no provision for the solar year. Every year, the seasons begin earlier, until, in thirty-two and a half years, the cycle starts repeating. The Jewish calendar is also based on the lunar month, beginning with the biblical moment of creation (3761 B.C. Gregorian time). It is adjusted for the solar year, however, with the addition of a thirteenth month every three to four years. Another lunar calendar, the Chinese, has been abandoned for civil use, but important Buddhist and Taoist festivals are still held around new and full moons. In Christian societies, Easter is still timed to the lunar and solar calendars: the Sunday after the first full moon after the spring equinox.

The lunar cycle was of great importance to native peoples in the north woods, who also used it as a calendar. Full moons

MOON: Just as the moon causes tides on Earth, the Earth's gravity causes "tides" on the moon. There is no sea, of course, but the landmass does shift. Over time, friction caused by the shifting land has slowed down the moon, so that the period of rotation on its axis—its "day"—exactly matches the 27.3 days it takes to orbit Earth. In other words, Earth's gravity has locked onto the moon so that only one side ever presents itself to us. Tides on Earth are also slowing down our planet. The day is getting longer by one second every 60,000 years. When Earth was first formed, the day used to be 22 hours.

TIDES ON LAKES: Even a cup of tea is affected by the moon's gravity. But lake tides are imperceptible to all but the most sophisticated equipment.

MOONRISE: The moon rises in the east about 53 minutes later each day on average. At full moon, the moon rises in the east at dusk, just as the sun sets in the west. At new moon, the moon rises in the east at dawn, at the same time as the sun, and is not visible.

ECLIPSES: When the moon passes exactly in front of the sun at new moon, a solar eclipse occurs. But because the moon's orbit is tilted 5° to the plane of Earth's orbit around the sun (called the ecliptic), most times there is no eclipse at new moon; the moon's shadow shoots out into space instead of falling on our planet. Similarly, a lunar eclipse occurs only at full moon, when Earth's shadow falls on the moon as our planet passes

were often named after natural events occurring around the same time, and were sometimes associated with human activities such as hunting, fishing, and food-gathering. The Ojibwa called the full moon in May the Sucker Moon. That is the month suckers spawn up north woods streams. June was the Blooming Moon, July the Berry Moon, August the Grain Moon, and September the Leaves Turning Moon.

The rhythms of the moon are also deeply linked to fertility. The twenty-nine-and-a-half-day period between full moons closely matches the average female menstrual cycle. The word *menstruation* comes from the Latin word for "monthly." Charles Darwin suggested that since humans ultimately evolved from the sea, it followed that menstrual periods were a distant echo of the tides. Whether the female and lunar cycles have a rational connection is a matter of debate. The menstrual cycles of other mammals, for example, do not match the average twenty-eight-day human one. But the fact that the lunar and human periods do coincide may have had a profound impact on the development of civilization. Some feminist scholars believe the earliest timekeeping evolved through the need of women to know the season of birth of their children, which would have required a knowledge of the link between menstrual and moon phases, and the nine-month or nine-moon gestation period. This could have led to the first calendars, perhaps those same cave calendars of France.

Symbolically, the fact the moon is "reborn" each month has led to its deep association with women since ancient times. Many mythologies and religions have moon goddesses; the most famous is

directly in front of the sun. But usually that 5° tilt causes Earth's shadow to miss the moon's disk.

"ONCE IN A BLUE MOON": There are two explanations for this expression. The second full moon in a month with 2 full moons (it happens twice every 5 years or so) is said to be a blue moon. Also, the full moon sometimes appears blue due to atmospheric conditions created by high dust content after volcanic eruptions or large forest fires. Huge fires in Canada in September 1950 created stunning blue moons.

HARVEST MOON: The full moon closest to the autumnal equinox, occuring either in September or October. Owing to the alignment of Earth, moon, and sun at this time of year, the bright moon before, after, and during the harvest moon stays in the night sky longer than other times of the year—ideal for farmers harvesting their crops at night.

WHY THE MOON SEEMS BIGGER WHEN IT'S CLOSE TO THE HORIZON: The best explanation for this illusion is that the full moon seems large when it is near the horizon because the eye can easily compare its size with other objects, such as buildings. To check the illusion, hold a round aspirin tablet at arm's length and place it over the moon. It covers the moon whether it's near the horizon or higher up.

MOON GODDESSES: Artemis, the Greek goddess of hunting; Selene, a Greek Titan sometimes associated with Artemis (selenology is the study of the moon); Hecate, the Greek goddess of the new moon (and thus darkness); Diana, the

probably Artemis, the Greek goddess of hunting, whose Roman equivalent is Diana. The Ojibwa thought of the moon as Grandmother Moon, the first mother in the creation myth who still keeps watch over her offspring. Sioux Indians called it the Old Woman Who Never Dies.

The moon is related to another aspect of the human condition: madness. Lunacy, from the Latin *luna*, or "moon," has been attributed to a mysterious connection between the full moon and our mental state. It is traditionally thought that lunar gravity—the same force that causes the tides and probably earthquakes and volcanic eruptions—somehow pulls our psyches out of kilter, perhaps in the same way it starts the menstrual flow. There is little proof for this, although there is no doubting the fact that 200 years ago, inmates in English lunatic asylums were flogged just before the full moon to deter violent behavior. Who was actually mad in this case is another question.

Roman goddess of hunting; Mama Qilla, the Inca moon goddess; Isis, the mother of Egypt; Galata, the Celtic moon goddess; Hina, of Polynesia

HOW TO TELL IF THE MOON IS WAXING OR WANING: If the right-hand side of the moon is illuminated, the moon is waxing—heading toward full moon. If the left-hand side is illuminated, it is waning—past full moon and heading into new moon.

SEE ALSO: Milky Way, Planets and Comets, Sun

In Christian societies, Easter is still timed to the lunar and solar calendars: the Sunday after the first full moon after the spring equinox

---

One moon mystery remains unsolved even after visits to the silvery orb by several well-educated middle-aged American men: How was it that Earth came to have a companion in the first place? Scientists have a few theories. The moon may have formed close to Earth at the same time Earth condensed out of the cloud of dust and gas that became our solar system. Alternatively, the moon may have formed elsewhere in the solar system but was somehow captured by Earth's gravitational field. The most popular theory proposes that a huge asteroid, possibly as large as Mars, smashed into Earth early in the planet's evolution and threw up debris that eventually coalesced into the moon. No one knows for sure.

NORTHERN LIGHTS

Ghostly Illuminations from Solar Wind

Poet Robert Frost likened them to "tingling nerves." The Inuit of Alaska and northern Canada called them the Dance of the Dead. Astronomers describe them as ionospheric gaseous luminations triggered by precipitating energetic particles. But to most people, they are the northern lights, among nature's most stunning creations.

The northern lights are usually seen as a shimmering white or greenish glow just above the northern horizon. At first, they may be mistaken for the haze of city lights, or even the glow of a gibbous moon before it rises over the horizon. But dark-adjusted eyes soon detect the telltale pulses of vertical shafts of light, which intensify and then fade seconds later in a wavy, ethereal curtain. Sometimes a ray will shoot high into the sky, then dissolve into the blackness. In an intense display, the curtain rises higher until it appears directly overhead like a surreal tunnel of light reaching to the zenith. This is called the aurora's corona. Magnificent streams of light cascade up and down the crown, accompanied by eerie pulses of white light. It's like a scene from a sci-fi movie, except it's real.

The northern lights are the result of solar wind entering Earth's magnetic field. Solar wind comprises millions of tons of electrons and protons emitted by the sun every minute. When these atomic particles enter the magnetic field surrounding Earth, they are separated, creating a vast store of electrical potential high above the surface.

AURORA BOREALIS: From *aurora*, the Latin word for "dawn" (Aurora was the Roman goddess of dawn), and *boreas*, Greek for "north wind"

SPEED OF SOLAR WIND: 1 million–2.2 million mph (1.8 million–3.6 million km/h)

NEXT PEAK OF THE 11-YEAR SOLAR CYCLE: 2011–2012

GEOMAGNETIC UPDATES: Space weather updates are posted on the Internet by the Space Environment Center at www.sec.noaa.gov. Radio station WWV in Boulder, Colorado, runs a 24-hour service that reports geomagnetic conditions. Aurora activity may be inferred from the information but isn't guaranteed. Call 303-497-3235.

JUPITER'S NORTHERN LIGHTS: Telescopes have spotted aurorae above Jupiter. But unlike Earth's displays, which are generated by solar wind, Jupiter's aurorae appear to be caused by charged particles spewed by volcanoes on one of the Jovian moons, Io.

WAUSSNODAE, OJIBWA NORTHERN LIGHTS: The Ojibwa believed the northern lights were torches lit by grandfathers to illuminate the Path of Souls for soul-spirits ascending to their final home. The Path of Souls was the Milky Way.

BEST PLACE IN THE WORLD TO OBSERVE NORTHERN LIGHTS: Northern Canada, because the north magnetic pole is

The magnetic field, in effect, becomes a 20,000- to 150,000-volt battery of static electricity. For reasons not yet fully understood, an occasional disturbance will send a burst of this energy along the lines of Earth's magnetic field, toward the north or south magnetic pole. The energy excites oxygen and nitrogen molecules, at altitudes of 60 to 600 miles (100 to 960 kilometers), into a gaseous glow: the northern lights, or aurora borealis.

located in Canada's Arctic archipelago. Some locations get northern lights about 100 nights a year, attracting aurora-starved tourists from around the world.

BEST VIEWING TIME: Between 11 P.M. and 2 A.M.

AURORA AUSTRALIS: The southern lights are rarely seen except by penguins. Of the populated continents, only the tip of South America extends far enough south into the prime viewing zone.

ALSO SEE: Sky, Sun

Although it's almost impossible to predict exactly when the northern lights will occur, or their intensity, some things are known about their behavior. In years when the solar wind blows stronger, the northern lights are more intense. "Gusts" of solar wind are caused by sunspots and solar flares, which intensify approximately every eleven years. The northern lights thus tend to put on greater displays every eleven years or so, according to this solar cycle. The peak may last for two or three years. On March 13, 1989, at the beginning of one peak period, a spectacular and rare display of red northern lights was seen as far south as the Caribbean. The energy storm was so powerful, it knocked out the Hydro-Québec power grid, putting six million people in the dark. According to Minnesota Power, transformers in the northeastern United States fail 60 percent more often than elsewhere in the country as a result of "solar storms" affecting the region. Many satellites have also been disrupted by energetic solar wind.

Some people claim they hear the northern lights as a soft crackling. Skeptical scientists tend to discount this possibility because the aurora occurs so far above Earth in the thin atmosphere. But so many people have reported hearing the murmurings of the spirits that the jury is still out.

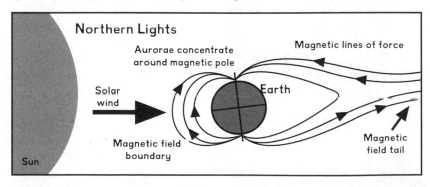

Northern Lights

Aurorae concentrate around magnetic pole

Magnetic lines of force

Solar wind

Earth

Magnetic field boundary

Magnetic field tail

Sun

NORTH STAR AND LITTLE DIPPER

The Peg That Fastens the Universe

The North Star, Polaris, is the most important star in all the heavens. It is not the brightest star in the night sky, but by dint of its fixed location almost exactly over Earth's north pole, it has assumed a prominent role in civilization. It was the star by which early mariners navigated their way about the treacherous seas. It was central to the cosmology of many cultures. It remains a powerful metaphor for the constant; the truth. As Hitler was consolidating his forces and war broke out in Spain, Illinois-born poet Archibald MacLeish wrote in his poem, "Pole Star for This Year,"

> We too turn now to that star:
> We too in whose trustless hearts
> All truth alters and the lights
> Of earth are out now turn to that star.

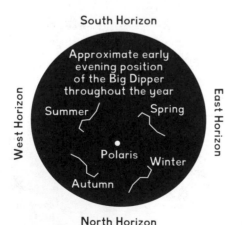

South Horizon

West Horizon

East Horizon

Approximate early evening position of the Big Dipper throughout the year

Summer

Spring

Polaris

Winter

Autumn

North Horizon

NORTH STAR STATE: Minnesota's official state motto is *"L' Etoile du Nord,"* meaning "Star of the North." The motto and a star made up of smaller stars appear on the state flag.

CYNOSURE: The Greeks also called Polaris the Dog's Tail, or *Kynosoura.* This is the root of the word *cynosure,* meaning "center of attraction."

DISTANCE OF POLARIS FROM EARTH: 431 light-years

HOW TO DETERMINE LATITUDE: At the North Pole, Polaris is directly overhead, or 90° straight up. The star is at a 45° angle to a viewer at 45° latitude, and so on. A sextant measures the angle. Early navigators who sailed below the equator got lost because Polaris disappeared over the horizon.

PRECESSION: Gravitational forces of the moon and sun affect the spinning of the Earth, causing our planet to wobble on its axis like the wobbling of a spinning top as it slows down. Called precession, this wobble has a cycle of about 26,000 years. Because of precession, the star marking the celestial north pole changes over the millennia. The Babylonians observed the phenomenon 5,000 years ago; the Greek astronomer Hipparchus recorded this effect in the second century B.C. Hipparchus also

Because of the rotation of the Earth, all the northern constellations appear to revolve counterclockwise around Polaris. The observation of this movement, as well as the cycles of the moon, sun, and planets, gave the ancients their sense of time. People of many old cultures believed the appearance of specific stars at certain times of the year actually caused events, such as the flooding of the Nile. This is the origin of astrology.

invented the system of magnitude for classifying the brightness of stars.

IS THERE A SOUTH POLE STAR? No. The spot in the sky marking the celestial south pole is not occupied by a convenient star.

ALSO SEE: Big Dipper, Draco, Star Charts, Zodiac and Ecliptic

The North Star appears in all mythologies. Its apparent immobility in the whirling procession of the stars must have been observed by the earliest cave dwellers. The Moguls called it the Golden Peg that fastened the universe together. In Scandinavia's violent mythology, it was the World Spike, the *Veralder Nagli*. (The Norse gods constructed their sky out of the chopped-up bits of adversaries; the nail in the center of the universe finished off the job.) In an Arab myth, the Big Dipper was a coffin that held the body of a great warrior killed by the evil North Star. The stars that revolve around the North Star, including the Big Dipper, formed a funeral procession. Chinese stories about the North Star relate it to Tai Chi, the great Absolute or Unity; it was the perfect union of the yin and yang principles. The North Star was also a symbol for the emperor, representing permanence in a transient world.

The pole star has actually changed over the millennia because the Earth wobbles slightly on its axis, a phenomenon known as precession. Four thousand years ago, the pole star was Thuban, in the constellation Draco. Archaeologists have discovered that Egyptian pyramids were built to align with Thuban. Polaris will be nearest the spot that is the true celestial north in the year 2100. Astronomers predict the bright star Vega will become the pole star 12,000 years from now.

In modern astronomy, Polaris is placed at the end of the constellation Ursa Minor, the lesser bear, commonly called the Little Dipper. Ursa Minor is a dim constellation, several of whose stars are at the limits of naked-eye visibility. Polaris is usually the only star visible from a city. Ursa Minor is, of course, related to Ursa Major, the great bear hauled into the heavens by Zeus in the Greek myth. One way to remember the arrangement of the two Dippers in the night sky is to think of them pouring their contents into each other.

PEGASUS AND ANDROMEDA

The Steed and the Princess

Late-night campfire gatherings are ideal occasions to watch the grand procession of constellations across the night sky. One of the greatest sights is the flight of the legendary winged horse, Pegasus. In mid-July, this majestic constellation soars above the eastern horizon at about 10 P.M. and by 4 A.M. it is high in the southern sky. (The later in the year, the earlier it rises; add about one hour for every two weeks.) Pegasus's most famous feature, the Great Square, is like a huge window into the inky depths of the universe.

The ancient Mesopotamians first construed these stars as a heavenly horse. Its form, like the constellation Hercules, is upside down: The head and neck are the suite of stars along the bottom, while the two prongs coming from the top right of the Great Square are the horse's forequarters. The hindquarters are missing; one theory is that the nearby constellation Aries was formed with stars that may have been, in ancient times, Pegasus's rear end.

Greek poets wrote various episodes in the story of Pegasus. He was born when drops of blood from the head of the Gorgon Medusa fell into the sea foam. Medusa had been decapitated by Perseus, who used the head as a novel wedding present for his mother and her lover. The sea foam accounts for Pegasus's whiteness.

Another story concerns Bellerophon, a young man whose greatest desire was to tame and ride Pegasus. As a pair, their most famous

PLOT OF 1971 B-MOVIE ANDROMEDA STRAIN: A lethal virus from deep space arrives in the United States. Scientists race against time to save the world.

NUMBER OF STARS IN ANDROMEDA GALAXY: Uncertain, perhaps 300 billion to 500 billion

DISTANCE OF ALPHERATZ, THE SHARED STAR IN ANDROMEDA AND PEGASUS, FROM EARTH: 97 light-years

MEDUSA: The only mortal Gorgon, three mythical monsters with hair of serpents. Medusa's countenance was so horrible to behold that viewers were immediately turned to stone. Perseus, in killing Medusa, avoided this fate by using his bronze shield as a mirror. Shortly afterward, he used Medusa's head to help save Andromeda from Cetus. Perseus waved the head in front of Cetus, and the sea monster fossilized instantly.

CHIMERA (PRONOUNCED KUH-MIR-AH): This monster's name entered the English language with several related meanings. Chimera is an absurd creation of the imagination, or any grotesque, fantastical creature; it is a hybrid organism with mixed characteristics; it is the genus of fishes that includes sharks and rays.

HOMER: Scholars aren't sure whether a person named Homer actually existed, but the *Iliad* and

adventure was the slaying of the Chimera, a ferocious monster with the head of a lion, the body of a goat, and the tail of a serpent. Astride Pegasus, Bellerophon was invincible.

Almost. Success went to his head, and Bellerophon decided to ride up to Olympus to join the gods. Pegasus thought better of the idea and threw Bellerophon to the ground below. (In another version, Zeus sent a horsefly to sting Pegasus, causing the steed to buck his rider.) Pegasus ascended with the permission of the gods, to become a member of the Olympian stalls—and a constellation in the heavens.

the *Odyssey* are traditionally attributed to him. Part of Pegasus's story is contained in the *Iliad*. Homer, if he lived, probably wrote in the ninth century B.C.

HESIOD: Greek poet of the eighth century B.C. who told the story of the Chimera

SEE ALSO: Cassiopeia, Deerflies and Horseflies, Star Charts

Alpheratz, the top-left star in the Great Square, is officially a member of the constellation Andromeda. The two constellations are connected in mythology as well as in form. It was during his journey home after slaying Medusa that Perseus spotted Andromeda chained to rocks in the sea off ancient Aethiopia. Perseus rescued Andromeda before she was assaulted by the sea monster Cetus, and later the two were married. Perseus also lies next to Andromeda in the night sky.

The famous Andromeda Galaxy is so named because it is found in the vicinity of the constellation. The galaxy is the farthest object from Earth detectable with the naked eye, 2.2 million light-years away. The light we see today left the Andromeda Galaxy just as our species was evolving in Africa. On a dark night, the galaxy is visible as an oval smudge.

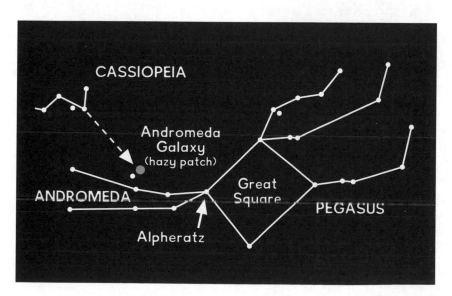

PLANETS AND COMETS

Wanderers of the Night Sky

Four and a half billion years ago, in this particular corner of the universe, there was no sun, no Earth, no solar system at all. But there was matter—a vast, churning cloud of gas and dust. Gravity caused this cloud to begin contracting, until internal heat from the great inward pressure ignited a powerful nuclear-fusion reaction in the center of the nebula. The sun was born.

Leftover material was blown away from the solar furnace but remained trapped in the sun's gravitational grasp. Over aeons, this rotating matter coalesced into asteroids and comets, and eventually into the nine planets that today make up our cosmic neighborhood.

As the planets move along their orbits around the sun, they appear in different positions against our night sky. Hence, the word *planet* comes from *planetes*, Greek for "wanderer." All the planets rotate around the sun in the same direction and on a rough plane called the ecliptic.

MERCURY: THE MESSENGER

The naked eye can detect Mercury, Venus, Mars, Jupiter, and Saturn, the planets (plus Earth) known to the ancients. Mercury is the most difficult to observe, because of its small size and its orbit close to the sun. It can be seen skimming the western horizon at dusk or the eastern horizon at dawn at certain times of the year. It is named after the Roman god Mercury, the messenger with winged sandals, a winged hat, and a

PLANETARY AND NIGHT SKY UPDATES: The Rose Center for Earth and Space, part of the American Museum of Natural History in New York, maintains a regularly updated space watch; call 212-769-5917 for a voice recording, or visit www.amnh.org/rose/

ALSO SEE: Falling Stars, Milky Way, Moon, Northern Lights, Sun, Zodiac and Ecliptic, Appalachians

Mercury ☿
DISTANCE FROM SUN: 35 million mi (58 million km)
DIAMETER: 2,928 mi (4,880 km)
DAY: 59 Earth days
YEAR: 88 Earth days
SURFACE TEMPERATURE: 806°F (430°C) dayside, −292°F (−180°C) nightside
MOONS: 0
SUCCESSFUL PROBES: Mariner 10, 1974
DAY OF THE WEEK: Wednesday, from Woden, the supreme god in Scandinavian mythology (also called Odin); mercredi in French; Miércoles in Spanish
NOTABLE: Craters on Mercury are named after men and women of the arts, including Rubens, Dickens, and Beethoven. Mercury has a highly elliptical orbit.

winged magic wand, who faithfully delivered Jupiter's memos.

VENUS: THE GODDESS OF LOVE AND BEAUTY

Venus, in contrast with Mercury, is the easiest planet to observe. After the sun and the moon, it is the brightest object in the sky, a radiant jewel in the early evening or early-morning darkness. It is observable for about six months out of every eighteen and travels closer to Earth than any other planet. Venus shines brilliantly because three-quarters of the sunlight hitting the sphere reflects off the dense, white, carbon dioxide atmosphere that enshrouds the planet. Lovely from a distance, Venus is in fact a greenhouse hell, with a surface temperature of 896°F (480°C). Had they known the astronomical truth about this nightmarish world, the Romans might have been disappointed. Venus, after all, was their goddess of love and beauty.

MOTHER EARTH

Nearly Venus's twin in size, but in all other respects completely different, is our own world. Earth is the only planet to support life, thanks to miraculous circumstances such as its distance from the sun and the 23.5-degree tilt that produces the seasons. These conditions give Earth its ability to produce and hold water, which covers 70 percent of the planet.

The Earth's surface is divided into six or seven major crustal plates and many smaller plates that move about on the slippery mantle. Plate movement is caused when convection currents formed deep within the planet rise to the surface along midocean ridges. This upwelling of hot magma pushes the

---

Venus ♀

DISTANCE FROM SUN: 65 million mi (108 million km)

DIAMETER: 7,260 mi (12,100 km)

DAY: 243 Earth days

YEAR: 225 Earth days

SURFACE TEMPERATURE: 896°F (480°C)

MOONS: 0

SUCCESSFUL PROBES: *Mariner 2,* 1962; *Venera 7* (landed), 1970; *Venera 9* (landed), 1975; *Magellan,* 1990–92

DAY OF THE WEEK: Friday, from Old English *Frigg* or Norse *Freya,* translation of Latin *Venus; vendredi* in French; *Viernes* in Spanish

NOTABLE: The Venusian day is longer than its year. The planet spins in the opposite direction from Earth and most other planets. Venereal diseases are "diseases of Venus." Surface features are named after famous women, both real and fictional.

Earth ⊕

DISTANCE FROM SUN: 90 million mi (150 million km)

DIAMETER: 7,654 mi (12,756 km)

DAY: 23.9 hours

YEAR: 365.2 days

SPINNING SPEED: 23,040 mph (38,400 km/h)

ORBITAL SPEED: 63,360 mph (105,600 km/h)

SURFACE TEMPERATURE: 59°F (15°C)

MOONS: 1

ATMOSPHERE: 77% nitrogen, 21% oxygen; traces of carbon dioxide, methane, neon, and other gases

NOTABLE: Earth was the center of the universe until 1543, when

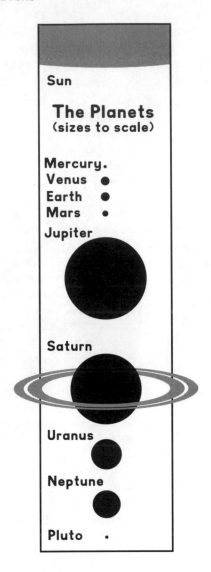

Sun

The Planets
(sizes to scale)

Mercury.
Venus ●
Earth ●
Mars ·
Jupiter

Saturn

Uranus

Neptune

Pluto ·

Polish astronomer Nicholas Copernicus pointed out that we circle
the sun, not vice versa. (Some
early Greek astronomers also
thought this, but like Copernicus,
they had a hard time convincing
people.) Earth is considered a
double planet, like Pluto, because
of its relatively large single satellite. Its name comes from the Old
English *oerthe*, meaning "dry
land." It is the only planet with a
name not derived from Greco-
Roman mythology.
MOST NUMEROUS ANIMAL LIFE-FORM:
Possibly springtails. One repre-
sentative species, called
snowfleas, is abundant in the
north woods.

Mars ♂
DISTANCE FROM SUN: 137 million mi
(228 million km)
DIAMETER: 4,072 mi (6,787 km)
DAY: 24.6 hours
YEAR: 687 Earth days
SURFACE TEMPERATURE: −58°F
(−50°C)
MOONS: 2, Phobos ("Fear") and
Deimos ("Panic"), Mars's dogs in
Roman mythology
SUCCESSFUL PROBES: Mariner 4,
1965; *Mariners 6* and *7*, 1969;
Vikings 1 and *2* (landed), 1976;
Mars Observer, 1993; *Path-
finder* (first roving vehicle on
another planet), 1997; *Mars
Global Surveyor*, 1999;
Odyssey, 2001
DAY OF THE WEEK: Tuesday, from
Old English *Tiw*, equated with
the Latin *Mars; mardi* in French;
Martes in Spanish

ridges apart, creating new crust and shoving the plates outward; Europe and North America are moving about one inch (2.5 centimeters) farther apart each year. At the other edge of the plates, such as in Califor-nia, old crust descends back into the interior under overlapping fault lines. Earthquakes and volcanoes occur along midocean ridges and faults. Mountain ranges may be formed where continents collide; the Himalayas are the result of the Indian subcontinent crashing into Asia.

This idea of moving plates was first considered when Europeans noticed that the shapes of the two sides of the Atlantic seemed to fit together. At the time, Europeans thought earth was only 6,000 years old, according to biblical reckoning. Recent scientific inquiry, dating only from the 1960s, proved the theory of plate tectonics. Plates have been moving about on the surface of the Earth for at least 2.5 billion years, and as little as 200 million years ago all the continents were attached in a supercontinent called Pangaea.

MARS: THE GOD OF WAR

Until recently, hopeful (or fearful) humans thought there was intelligent life on Mars, our closest neighbor after Venus. Evidence was supposedly found in 1877, when Italian astronomer Giovanni Schiaparelli reported seeing natural channels on the planet's surface, and others mistook this as to mean artificial canals were present. Reputable scientists dreamed up various schemes for communicating with Martians, including a giant mirror to engrave words on the Martian desert with the focused rays of the sun. In 1976, two *Viking* landers failed to meet any welcoming committees, but the idea of some kind of life on Mars has been gaining ground in recent years. In 1996, headlines around the world proclaimed the possibility of life on Mars after scientists examined a chunk of rock blown off Mars that subsequently landed on Earth as a meteorite. Many scientists came to the conclusion that unusual microsopic patterns on the meteorite were fossilized evidence of bacteria-like organisms. Recent close-up

NOTABLE: Mars has polar caps like Earth, but they are composed of frozen carbon dioxide and water. They advance and recede with the planet's long seasons.

Jupiter ♃
DISTANCE FROM SUN: 467 million mi (778 million km)
DIAMETER: 85,680 mi (142,800 km)
DAY: 9.9 hours
YEAR: 11.9 Earth years
TEMPERATURE AT CLOUD TOPS: −202°F (−130°C)
MOONS: 39; largest Ganymede
MAGNITUDE: −2.1 to −2.3
SUCCESSFUL PROBES: Pioneer 10, 1973; *Pioneer 11,* 1974; *Voyagers 1 and 2,* 1979; *Galileo* (with atmospheric probe), 1995; *Cassini,* 2001
DAY OF THE WEEK: Thursday, from the Norse god Thor, equated with the Latin *Jupiter; jeudi* in French; *Jueves* in Spanish
NOTABLE: The surface area of the Great Red Spot is larger than Earth's. The Chinese studied Jupiter at least as far back as 1000 B.C., when the 12-year orbit was observed.

Saturn ♄
DISTANCE FROM SUN: 856 million mi (1,427 million km)
DIAMETER: 72,360 mi (120,600 km)
DAY: 10.7 hours
YEAR: 29.5 earth years
TEMPERATURE AT CLOUD TOPS: −300°F (−185°C)
MOONS: 30 (maybe more); largest Titan
SUCCESSFUL PROBES: Pioneer 11, 1979; *Voyager 1,* 1980; *Voyager 2,* 1981; *Cassini-Huygens,* 2005

photos of Mars by space probes reveal topographic features that strongly suggest water once sloshed on the surface.

While primitive life may have once existed on the planet, Mars today is sterile. The surface is covered in red, iron-oxide dust that is sometimes blown into huge dust storms. The red dust accounts for Mars's appearance from Earth. Mars's bloodlike color explains how the planet got its name. Mars was revered as the Roman god of war. The Greeks called him Ares. The red star Antares in the constellation Scorpius looks a lot like Mars. *Antares* is Arabic for "rival of Mars."

ASTEROIDS:
THE MINOR PLANETS

There is a vast gap in space between Mars and the next planet, Jupiter. In 1800, a German astronomer, Johann Schröter, formed a group called the Celestial Police to find what was thought to be a missing planet in this gap. The group, along with other astronomers, soon found instead the asteriod belt. There are more than 3,000 identified asteroids in the belt, but millions more smaller ones, down to the size of a pebble. Pieces dislodged in asteroid collisions occasionally fall to Earth as stray meteors. Other asteroids have large elliptical orbits that take them away from the main belt, crossing the orbits of other planets, including that of Earth. But why didn't Schröter and his gang find a major planet in the asteroid belt? Astronomers theorize that the disruptive gravitational forces of nearby Jupiter prevent the space gravel from agglomerating into a planet.

(scheduled descent into Titan's atmosphere)
DAY OF THE WEEK: Saturday
NOTABLE: Saturn's moon Titan is bigger than Mercury and Pluto and has a dense nitrogen atmosphere. It can be seen with a backyard telescope.

Uranus ♅
DISTANCE FROM SUN: 1,722 million mi (2,870 million km)
DIAMETER: 30,780 miles (51,300 km)
DAY: 17.2 hours
YEAR: 84 Earth years
TEMPERATURE AT CLOUD TOPS: −328°F (−200°C)
MOONS: 21; largest Titania
SUCCESSFUL PROBES: *Voyager 2*, 1986
NOTABLE: Uranus spins "horizontally" on a 98° tilt, while all other planets spin more or less "upright." Scientists speculate that a gigantic passing object may have knocked Uranus on its side.

Neptune ♆
DISTANCE FROM SUN: 2,698 million mi (4,497 million km)
DIAMETER: 29,460 mi (49,100 km)
DAY: 16.1 hours
YEAR: 165 Earth years
TEMPERATURE AT CLOUD TOPS: −328°F (−200°C)
MOONS: 8; largest Triton
SUCCESSFUL PROBES: *Voyager 2*, 1989
NOTABLE: Neptune's moon Triton has nitrogen geysers and revolves around the planet in the "wrong" direction. *Voyager 2* passed only 3,000 mi (4,900 km) above Neptune's north pole, a cosmic pool shot of unbelievable accuracy.

JUPITER:
THE KING

Jupiter is immense. It contains 70 percent of the mass of the entire solar system, excluding the sun. Though not as brilliant from Earth as Venus (because of its great distance), through binoculars Jupiter appears as a distinct white disk against the starry dots in the blackness. Some of those dots are Jupiter's moons. Four of its thirty-nine satellites—Io, Europa, Ganymede, and Callisto—are easily visible through a small telescope or binoculars mounted on a tripod. The sight of Jupiter and its moons is one of the most thrilling nighttime views for a novice stargazer. Each night, the moons are in a different position.

As befitting its size, Jupiter was named after Rome's supreme god, who was fashioned after Zeus, the chief Olympian in ancient Greece.

SATURN:
THE GOD OF AGRICULTURE

Astronomers have detected faint rings around Jupiter, Uranus, and Neptune. But they are nothing like the great rings of Saturn. The first sight of Saturn's rings through a backyard telescope is unforgettable. Suddenly, the solar system seems tangible.

The rings themselves are composed of billions upon billions of icy particles, ranging in size from dust flakes to garages. There are thousands of separate rings. The whole system, estimated to be only about 660 feet (200 meters) thick, revolves precisely around Saturn's equator. No one knows why Saturn alone has rings so pronounced.

Pluto ♇

DISTANCE FROM SUN: 3,540 million mi (5,900 million km)

DIAMETER: 1,380 miles (2,300 km)

DAY: 6.4 Earth days

YEAR: 248 Earth years

SURFACE TEMPERATURE: −382°F (−230°C)

MOONS: 1; Charon

SUCCESSFUL PROBES: None sent

NOTABLE: Pluto has an exaggerated elliptical orbit. From 1979 to 1999, it was actually closer to the sun than Neptune was.

Kuiper Belt

DISTANCE FROM SUN: Just beyond the orbits of Pluto and Neptune, about 3,600 million mi (6,000 million km)

ESTIMATED NUMBER OF ICE/ROCK BODIES IN BELT: Tens of thousands

TYPICAL SIZE OF OBSERVED BODIES: 60 to 240 mi (100 to 400 km) in diameter

NAMED FOR: Dutch-American astronomer Gerard P. Kuiper. In 1951, he championed the notion that a zone of small celestial objects existed beyond the planets.

Oort Cloud

DISTANCE FROM SUN: 6–12 trillion mi (9.6–18.8 trillion km), or 1–2 light-years

ESTIMATED NUMBER OF ICE/ROCK BODIES IN CLOUD: Billions

NAMED FOR: Dutch astronomer Jan Oort. He proposed in 1950 that comets were born in a distant sphere of primordial matter.

PROBES: Voyager 2 should pass through the Oort Cloud around the year 60,000. On board is Chuck Berry's tune "Johnny B. Goode," among other artifacts of human achievement.

Orbits
of the
Planets
(distances
to scale)

•SUN
•MERCURY
•VENUS
•EARTH
•MARS

•JUPITER

•SATURN

•URANUS

For Pluto,
double the
distance
from the
sun to
Uranus

•NEPTUNE

Saturn was the Roman god of agriculture, and every December a great festival called the Saturnalia was held to mark the winter solstice. Businesses and public institutions were closed, citizens exchanged presents, wars were interrupted, and slaves were freed. In other words, the people partied.

URANUS, NEPTUNE, PLUTO:
THE DISTANT PLANETS

Of the final three planets in the solar system, only Uranus can be seen with the unaided eye. But it is extremely dim, and an observer needs to know its exact location in order to spot it. The planet was discovered in 1781 by English astronomer William Herschel, and was named Uranus after the Greek father of heaven, king of the Titans.

Neptune, the last of the gas giants, was mathematically predicted before it was finally seen from the Berlin Observatory in 1845. It was named after Jupiter's brother, the god of the sea. To the Greeks, he was Poseidon.

Distant Pluto, first seen in 1930 by Clyde Tombaugh at the Lowell Observatory, is the last planet in the solar system. It is smaller than the moon and is actually considered a double planet because its own moon,

Charon, is about half Pluto's size. Pluto is thought to be an old comet, or perhaps an escaped moon from Neptune. Pluto was the Roman god of the underworld who rarely left his dark kingdom. Charon was the boatman who ferried the dead across the river Styx.

KUIPER BELT AND OORT CLOUD:
COMET NURSERIES

Beyond the orbits of the planets lie two zones that astronomers believe are holding tanks for icy, rocky chunks of space debris—comets in waiting—left over from the birth of the solar system. The Kuiper Belt, the closer of these zones, is akin to the asteroid belt between Mars and Jupiter but is located on the other side of Pluto's orbit. The Oort Cloud is a much more massive and distant zone. It forms a spherical casing around the solar system, with an outer edge perhaps 2 light-years, or about 18.8 trillion kilometers, away from the sun.

The average comet is composed of a rocky nucleus about 3,300 to 6,600 feet (a kilometer or two) in diameter. An icy layer around the nucleus is warmed as the comet approaches the sun. The ice vaporizes into a cloud called the coma. Solar radiation blows some of the material away from the cloud, creating a tail that can be hundreds of thousands of miles long. The tail gets bigger as the comet approaches the sun (the word *comet* comes from the Greek *kometes*, "long haired").

Some comets have such huge orbits that they are seen once and never again; these "long-period" comets are believed to originate from the distant Oort Cloud. "Short-period" comets, or those with orbits of less than 200 years, appear to come from the closer Kuiper Belt. They develop orbits within the inner solar system and return regularly, such as Comet Encke every three years and Comet Halley every seventy-six years. Comet Halley is named after English astronomer Edmond Halley, who in 1682 noticed the comet's regular return. It was last seen in 1985–86 and will reappear in 2061. The Chinese have records of Comet Halley dating back before the birth of Christ.

SATELLITES

Smile—They're Taking Pictures!

Iridium

The world entered a new era on October 4, 1957. On that date, the Soviet Union launched *Sputnik*, the first successful spacecraft. Now nearly every industrialized country has satellites orbiting the planet.

It's usually possible to spot a satellite within minutes of gazing into the early-evening sky. Although the sky appears black, sunlight is still streaming high overhead for a few hours after sunset (and a few hours before dawn). Satellites soaring through space as they orbit Earth reflect these sunbeams.

The artificial stars travel in all directions. They don't blink like aircraft, but some satellites seem to pulsate slowly. This is caused by a satellite's spin: As it revolves, it may present more surface area—such as the large solar "wings" that generate electrical power—toward the sun. A satellite "disappears" when it enters Earth's shadow. Visible satellites orbit Earth at altitudes between 120 and 300 miles (200 and 500 kilometers). Space shuttles fly about 120 miles (200 kilometers) high; the International Space Station orbits Earth at an average altitude of 220 miles (354 kilometers).

PIECES OF MAN-MADE SPACE JUNK ORBITING EARTH: More than a million, but 7,200 pieces larger than 4 in (10 cm) in diameter are tracked by Earth stations

FIRST U.S. SATELLITE: Explorer 1, launched January 31, 1958. Canada was the third country in space with the launch of the *Alouette* satellite on September 29, 1962.

SATELLITE SIZES: Sputnik was about the size of a basketball. The cargo bay of the space shuttle is large enough to hold a bus. When completed in 2005, the interior of the International Space Station will be about the size of two 747 jumbo-jet passenger cabins.

IRIDIUM FLASH: The 66 satellites in the Iridium global telephone service have added a new sight in the night sky. An "Iridium flash" is a very bright, 10- to 30-second flash of light caused by sunlight glinting off the satellite's main mission antenna.

SEE ALSO: Falling Stars, Northern Lights, Sky

STAR CHARTS

Seasonal Road Maps to the Heavens

The first printed star map was produced by German painter and engraver Albrecht Dürer in 1515, a few decades after the invention of the printing press. But humans had been charting the night sky for millennia before that, bringing order to the heavenly confusion by grouping stars into constellations. The star patterns provided a home to mythological characters and served as navigational aids.

The modern constellations are descended from the *Almagest*, a star catalog hand-produced by the famous Alexandrian astronomer Claudius Ptolemy around 150 A.D. Most of his constellations, in turn, were derived from ancient tradition going back to at least 2000 B.C. Until modern times, most star maps were works of art, depicting heroes, heroines, villains, and other mythological figures in their places in the sky. Modern star charts showing just the stars and other main astronomical features are, however, easier to use.

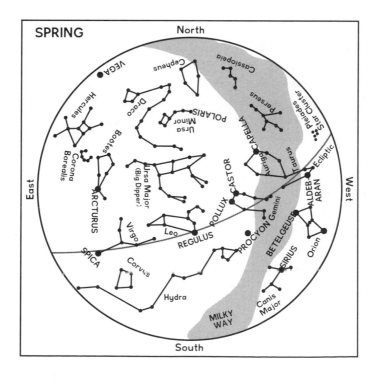

385

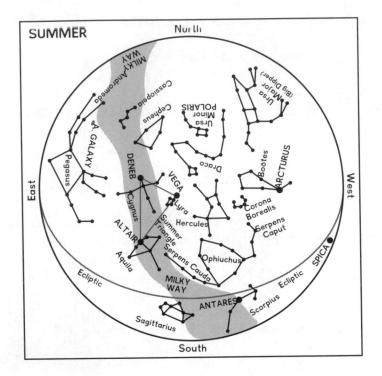

Many bright stars have their own names that have been handed down over the centuries. Most are Arabic, because Arabs preserved and translated the classic works of Greco-Roman civilization while the barbarians cast Europe into the Dark Ages. In 1603, the German astronomer Johan Bayer took a scientific approach to naming stars. He named the brightest star of each constellation alpha, after the first letter of the Greek alphabet. The second-brightest star was named beta, and so on. (There are a few exceptions to this scheme.) Thus, astronomers refer to the brightest star in Lyra as Alpha Lyrae, although it also has an ancient Arabic name, Vega.

The rotation of the Earth makes it appear as if all the stars are circling Polaris, the North Star, in a counterclockwise direction. Because of this motion, the star charts included here are not exact for every time of night, every night of the year, or every location in the Northern Hemisphere. But they are good guides to the heavens shortly after nightfall in the middle of each season in the northern continental United States.

To use a chart, hold this book over your head and face south. The position of the constellations in the night sky should roughly match those in the chart. Find the most prominent features first—the Big Dipper, Summer

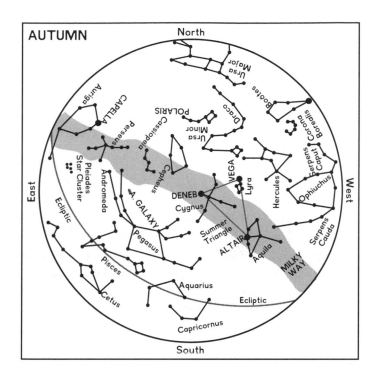

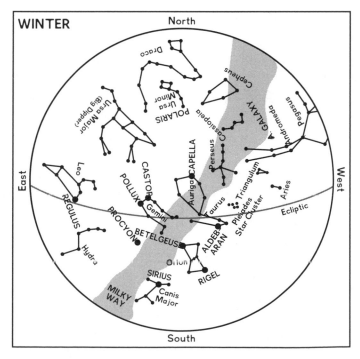

Triangle, or Orion in winter—and use them as guideposts to the other constellations. Star names are printed in UPPER CASE, while constellations are printed in Upper and Lower Case.

Most star names are Arabic, because Arabs preserved and translated the classic works of Greco-Roman civilization while the barbarians cast Europe into the Dark Ages

---

To find planets, look for what appear to be bright stars along the ecliptic. Planets travel along this imaginary line in space.

Most of the summer constellations have their own entries and star maps in this book. Some have interesting astronomical features, such as double stars and star clusters. A good pair of binoculars is an excellent viewing aid.

Use a flashlight with red cloth or red paper wrapped around the light as you use the charts to navigate your way through the night sky. The red light will help your eyes adjust to the dark.

After a while, you will become familiar with the night sky and will be able to follow the march of the seasons by simply gazing into the starry depths—repeating a habit formed by our earliest ancestors.

SUMMER TRIANGLE

The Swan, the Eagle, and the Vulture

Three brilliant stars dominate the heavens from June to September. They are Vega, Deneb, and Altair, and together they form the unmistakable Summer Triangle. Over the course of a summer night, the triangle flies high across the sky like an enormous celestial kite, passing almost directly overhead. The formation is called an asterism because it is not an official constellation. But its prominence makes it one of the first groupings of stars introduced to novice stargazers.

Vega, Deneb, and Altair are, however, members of their own constellations. Vega, the brightest of the three, is the lucida of the constellation Lyra. It is named after the lyre the Greek musician Orpheus used to enchant listeners during his various adventures. The most famous story concerns his attempt to rescue his wife, Eurydice, from the underworld of Hades. Orpheus took his lyre and entered the gates of hell to bring her back to life. His beautiful music so charmed Hades that the god granted Orpheus's wish, but with one condition: He must not look back as his wife followed him to the land of the living. Orpheus obeyed until, just as he stepped out into the sun, he could resist no longer and glanced back. It was too soon, and Eurydice disappeared. Orpheus was later reunited in death with his wife, and Zeus placed the lyre in the heavens to commemorate the musician's sweet melodies.

Vega is an Arabic word meaning "the

Scan zone: The Summer Triangle is one of the best areas of the sky to scan with binoculars. The Milky Way runs thick through this part of the sky dome, and hundreds of stars invisible to the naked eye materialize.

What to look for: The stars Delta and Epsilon Lyrae are double stars in binoculars. Epsilon Lyrae is actually a double-double, visible through telescopes. Beta Lyrae is an eclipsing double star: 2 orbiting stars that eclipse each other from our vantage point, producing what seems to be a star of variable brightness. Its luminosity changes over a period of about 13 days. The 2 stars in Beta Lyrae are so close to each other that astronomers believe superheated gas is flowing between them at 1 million mph (1.6 million km/h)

Distance of Vega from Earth: 25 light-years

Distance of Altair from Earth: 17 light-years

Distance of Deneb from Earth: 1,467 light-years

Magnitude of Vega: 0.0

Magnitude of Altair: 0.8

Magnitude of Deneb: 1.3

Lucida: The brightest star in a constellation, from which we get the word *lucid*

Also see: Milky Way, Star Charts

389

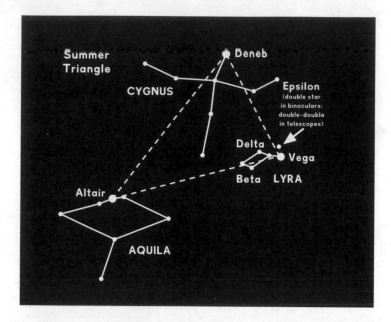

stooping one," or "vulture"—the ancient conception of the constellation before the Greeks. The other two constellations of the Summer Triangle, Cygnus and Aquila, represent birds to this day. Cygnus looks much like its namesake, the swan. It is easy to imagine the outline of the great white swan as it flies along the shimmering path of the Milky Way. Deneb marks the tail of Cygnus; the word is Arabic for "tail of the hen." Early Christians also gave their own name, the Northern Cross, to Cygnus.

One of the Greek myths for Cygnus is said to explain the origin of the term *swan song*. Phaeton, the young man who created the Milky Way during a wild ride in his dad's sun chariot, had a close friend named Cycnus. When Zeus struck Phaeton dead with a thunderbolt, the mortal fell into a river. Cycnus tried several times to retrieve the body of his friend for burial, but his dives were unsuccessful. As he sang songs of grief along the riverbank, the gods took pity on him and placed him in the heavens as a swan. Thus was born, supposedly, the superstition that swans sing sad songs before they die.

Aquila, the constellation that includes Altair, was another bird of Greek mythology—the eagle that transported Zeus's thunderbolts. *Aquila* is Latin for "eagle," and the modern word *aquiline* means of or like an eagle.

A comparison of Deneb and Vega gives a good idea of how difficult it is to judge the size of stars and their distance from Earth. To the naked eye, Vega is slightly brighter than Deneb. Yet Deneb is, by astronomical reckoning, almost 60,000 times more luminous than Vega. The explanation, of course, is distance. Vega is only about 25 light-years from Earth, while Deneb, a colossal star 60 times wider than our sun, is about 1,500 light-years away.

ZODIAC AND ECLIPTIC

Highway in the Sky

Pico della Mirandola was one of the first to scoff at the science of astrology. The Renaissance scholar declared in 1487 that the positions of the sun, moon, and planets, in relation to the background constellations, had diddly-squat to do with human behavior, contrary to what the ancients believed. Today, astrology has more implications for the science of newspaper publishing than anything else.

But the zodiac remains a vital feature of the sky. First conceived by the Mesopotamians about 5,000 years ago, the constellations of the zodiac lie along an imaginary line in the heavens called the ecliptic. Think of it as a highway in the sky. The sun, moon, and planets all travel along this highway, more or less, as they cross the starry expanse. When astronomers say, "Saturn is in Sagittarius," they mean Saturn, from our point of view on Earth, is positioned along the ecliptic somewhere within the boundaries of the zodiacal constellation Sagittarius. It's a convenient way to describe the location of the wandering spheres.

Because the Earth wobbles slightly on its axis, the zodiac has actually shifted two signs since its invention

HOROSCOPE: From the Greek *horoskopos,* meaning "observer of the hour of nativity." From *hora,* "hour," and *skopos,* "watcher."

ECLIPTIC: The plane defined by Earth's orbit around the sun. The orbits of other planets are also roughly along this plane. To an observer positioned on the north side or "above" the ecliptic, all the planets would orbit the sun in a counterclockwise direction. The plane is called the ecliptic because when the moon crosses it, eclipses occur. If the moon is between Earth and the sun, there is a solar eclipse. If Earth is between the sun and the moon, there is a lunar eclipse.

TIME SPAN FOR ZODIAC TO SHIFT ONE FULL SIGN AT EQUINOX, DUE TO EARTH'S "WOBBLE": 2,160 years

TIME SPAN FOR ZODIAC TO SHIFT FULL 360°: 25,920 years. This is called the Platonic Year.

RETROGRADING: Planets move eastward, night after night, against the backdrop of stars. But occasionally they change direction. This phenomenon is called "retrograding." It's exactly the same effect one notices when passing a car on the highway. For a moment, it looks as if the other car is moving backward. Of course, it is only moving slower. The visible outer

The first full-time astrologers were priests who nightly scrutinized the night sky to keep track of the stars, moon, and planets. The position of the celestial spheres became associated with certain events, such as the annual flooding of rivers. It was an easy leap for the ancient Mesopotamian mind to believe that the stars actually caused events when they reappeared. What other explanation was

planets—Mars, Jupiter, and Saturn—retrograde when Earth overtakes them. Mercury and Venus, the inner planets, retrograde when they overtake Earth.

ALSO SEE: Moon; North Star and Little Dipper; Planets and Comets; Star Charts; Sun

there? Astronomer-priests thus commanded the people when to hold seasonal festivals or when to plant. Astrology was part of everyday life.

The ecliptic was divided into twelve constellations, and the signs of the zodiac were named after them. The word *zodiac* is Greek for "circle of animals." Some constellations are bigger than others, but the zodiacal circle was divided into twelve equal sections of 30 degrees each to equal 360 degrees. The astrologers probably chose twelve divisions because it takes Jupiter—well known to the ancients because of its brightness—twelve years to complete one journey around the ecliptic.

Each zodiac sign was associated with the time of year the sun was located

THE ZODIAC

CONSTELLATION/ SIGN	REPRESENTATION	ASTROLOGICAL PERIOD	SAID BY THE ANCIENTS TO RULE THE:
Aries	Ram	March 21–April 19	Head and face
Taurus	Bull	April 20–May 20	Neck
Gemini	The Twins	May 21–June 20	Breast
Cancer	Crab	June 21–July 22	Arms
Leo	Lion	July 23–August 22	Heart
Virgo	Maiden (Virgin)	August 23–September 22	Bowels
Libra	Scales	September 23–October 22	Reins (wrist)
Scorpio	Scorpion	October 23–November 21	Secrets (genitals)
Sagittarius	Archer	November 22–December 21	Thighs
Capricorn	Goat or Sea Goat	December 22–January 19	Knees
Aquarius	The Water Carrier	January 20–February 18	Legs (shins)
Pisces	Fish	February 19–March 20	Feet

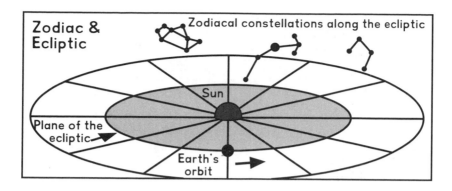

"in" it. The sun was in Libra, for instance, around the time of the autumnal equinox (the background stars couldn't be seen during the day, of course, but astronomer-priests could figure out the sun's location based on their knowledge of the ecliptic). But because the Earth wobbles slightly on its axis, an effect called precession, the zodiac has actually shifted two signs since its invention. Thus, the sun is no longer in Libra when the astrological period called Libra begins on September 23. The astrological signs no longer match astronomical facts.

Libra, the Scales, is the only sign that doesn't represent a real or imaginary creature. It was an appropriate choice for the equinox, when day and night are almost perfectly balanced. Libra was once considered the claws of nearby Scorpius, but the Romans altered the sky map and put these stars in a constellation representing justice.

Most of the signs have Greek or Roman stories attached to them. Scorpius, which appears low in the south during the summer, is said to be the scorpion that Hera sent to kill the great hunter Orion. The unfortunate woodsman claimed that no animal was his match. Hera despised such hubris. To keep Orion and Scorpius safe from each other in the heavens, the gods placed them at opposite ends of the sky. By the time Scorpius appears, Orion is gone. The famous bright red star Antares is the "heart" of Scorpius.

MOTHER EARTH

MOTHER EARTH

This is the most beautiful lake country on the continent. We can afford to cherish and protect it. In the end, we turn to nature in a frenzied, chaotic world—there to find silence, oneness, wholeness, spiritual release.

—Sigurd F. Olson, Minnesota conservationist, writer, and teacher

The great north woods drape across several distinct geological zones; this section of the book looks at four of them. The Adirondack Mountains of northeastern New York are part of the vast Canadian Shield. To the east and south, the complex Appalachian Province, which comprises the Appalachian Mountains and surrounding areas, underlies the forests of Vermont, New Hampshire, Maine, and the Maritime Provinces of Canada. The Michigan Basin forms the southern and central parts of that Great Lakes state. Finally, Sigurd Olson's beloved Superior Uplands of northern Minnesota, Wisconsin, and Michigan also belong to the Canadian Shield.

Soil, humus, wetlands, lakes, and glacial rubble cover the north woods bedrock, and are also covered here in "Mother Earth." Together with climate, these are the elements that create the rich north woods ecosystems.

ADIRONDACKS

The Canadian Shield Wilderness of New York

Though just a cannon shot from Vermont's Green Mountains and a short drive from the Catskills of south-central New York, the fabled Adirondack Mountains are actually kin to the Superior Uplands of Minnesota and Wisconsin, half a continent away. Both the uplands and the Adirondacks belong to the Canadian Shield, the ancient rock that forms the nucleus of the North American continent. The shield extends a finger south from Ontario across the St. Lawrence River, forming the Thousands Islands, then continues into upstate New York to form the Adirondacks.

The rocks of the Adirondacks were born 1.1 billion years ago, when single-cell bacteria and algae slime ruled the world. It was a period of great mountain building in what was to become eastern North America. During this so-called Grenville Orogeny, geologists believe ancient continents collided, squeezing the rock in the collision zone. Some rock was forced down, as much as eighteen miles (thirty kilometers) below the surface. Other rock went up, forming a mountain range that may have rivaled the Himalayas. The geological zone today called the Grenville Province of the shield includes the Adirondacks, the Algonquin Park and Georgian Bay regions of Ontario, and the Laurentian Mountains of Quebec.

Over millions of years, the mountain range was eroded, and in fact the Adiron-

HIGHEST ADIRONDACK PEAK: Mount Marcy, 5,344 ft (1,629 m), named after New York governor William Learned Marcy by Ebenezer Emmons, a state surveyor who led the first known expedition to the top in 1837.

NAME ORIGIN: Different stories explain the origin and definition of *Adirondack*. Ebenezer Emmons said the word came from the name of a native tribe that hunted the area. Another story—possibly related—suggests *Adirondack* means bark-eaters, and was an Iroquois insult aimed at their Algonquian-speaking enemies, who supposedly hunted in the area but were so incompetent, they had to resort to eating trees. Another theory says *Adirondack* derived from a native expression meaning "They of the Great Rocks." A native name for the area, Couchsachraga, means the dismal wilderness or habitation of winter.

OROGENY: A geological period of mountain building. From the Greek *oros*, meaning "mountain," and the Latin *genus*, meaning "birth." Orography is the study of mountains.

ADIRONDACK OLYMPICS: 1932 and 1980, both at Lake Placid. In the 1980 Games, the underdog U.S.

dack region was inundated by an ancient sea. Sedimentary rock laid down by the sea built up over the basement rock, which became highly metamorphosed due to the tremendous pressure and heat encountered eighteen miles (30 kilometers) below the surface.

Now, incredibly, that basement rock is at the surface. Virtually all the sedimentary rock has been scoured away. This process was enhanced by the mysterious uplifting of the Adirondack dome, which geologists reckon began sometime within the last sixty-five million years (exit dinosaurs). The uplift continues to this day, at a rate of about two to three millimeters (0.08 to 0.12 inches) per year. As the harder basement rock rose, it was stripped of its sedimentary clothing by water and glacial erosion.

Adirondack rock is highly deformed by folding and faulting, the geological wrinkles of old age. The bedrock is mostly gneiss (pronounced "nice"), a metamorphic rock made from earlier granites and sedimentaries.

The rocks of the Adirondacks were born when single-cell bacteria and algae slime ruled the world

The light to dark gray anorthosite rock of the High Peaks region of the Adirondacks is a different sort. This is an intrusive igneous rock, meaning rock formed by magma migrating upward into folds or cracks in the crust that then cools into a

hockey team beat the favored Soviet Union team, and Wisconsinite Eric Heiden won 5 gold medals in speed skating.

MURRAY'S FOOLS : In 1869, Reverend William H. H. Murray of Boston published *Adventures in the Wilderness; or, Camp-Life in the Adirondacks.* The book became hugely popular in the post–Civil War era, but soon newspapers were mocking "Murray's Fools," the pleasure-seeking urbanites who flocked to the Adirondacks only to complain of bugs and other discomforts.

MAD DASH TO THE PRESIDENCY: In September 1901, President McKinley lay dying after being shot in Buffalo by an assassin. Notified of the president's dire predicament, Vice President Theodore Roosevelt, hiking the Adirondacks at the time, made a celebrated mad dash to the presidency out of the park, taking the oath of office along the way in North Creek.

BIG STATE PARK: Adirondack State Park is about the size of Vermont, and is larger than Yellowstone, Olympic, and Yosemite National Parks combined.

PERCENTAGE OF LAND IN ADIRONDACK STATE PARK THAT'S PRIVATELY OWNED: 51.7%

PERCENTAGE OWNED BY NEW YORK STATE: 42.5%

PERCENTAGE COVERED BY WATER: 5.8%

PERCENTAGE OF NEW YORK STATE COVERED BY ADIRONDACK PARK: 17%

ESTIMATED TEMPERATURE AT WHICH ADIRONDACK BEDROCK WAS METAMORPHOSED DURING ITS DEEP-EARTH DAYS: 1,110–1,470°F (600–800°C)

solid. Mountain building invites such intrusions. Anorthosite is composed primarily of a mineral called plagioclase feldspar. *Feldspar* comes from Germanic roots for "fieldstone," and comprises Earth's most abundant minerals, primarily aluminum and silicon. Anorthosite is uncommon on Earth's surface, but it is the same rock that forms the highlands of the moon.

Most recently, the glaciers of the last ice age deposited tons of rubble throughout the region. Lake Placid and other lakes are the children of the glaciers, which retreated about 11,000 years ago.

The Adirondacks were extensively logged in the 1800s, with many tall, straight white pines forming the masts of Civil War ships. Iron was also mined in the area until the great Mesabi finds in Minnesota made the New York operations uneconomical.

TEMPERATURE OF BLAST FURNACE IN STEEL MILL: 1,800°F (1,000°C)
ESTIMATED TEMPERATURE OF EARTH'S LIQUID CORE: 8,130°F (4,500°C)
ESTIMATED UPWARD SPEED OF MOLTEN ROCK IN A BATHOLITH (INTRUSION OF HOT MAGMA): 6 ft (2 m) per year
PROPORTION OF EARTH'S CRUST MADE OF SILICON, OXYGEN, AND ALUMINUM: 82%
ESTIMATED PORTION OF CANADIAN SHIELD MADE UP OF GNEISS: Up to 80%
GNEISS: From the Slavic word for "rotted" or "decomposed"
METAMORPHIC: From the Greek *meta*, "beyond," and *morphe*, "form"
ALSO SEE: Appalachians, Superior Uplands, Humus and Soil

But the greatest resource in the Adirondacks is the wilderness. The American conservation movement got its start in the Adirondacks, aided partly by the invention of photography, which recorded the devastation left by the logging industry. Writers, artists, and pleasure-seekers flocked to the area, lured by its beauty, and their passion also fueled early battles to preserve the Adirondacks as a wild place. Theodore Roosevelt was introduced to the

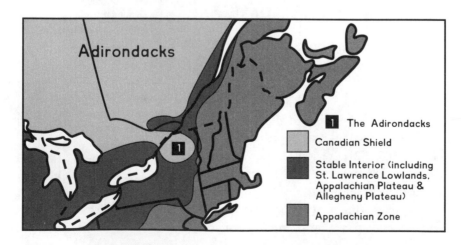

Adirondacks

1 The Adirondacks
Canadian Shield
Stable Interior (including St. Lawrence Lowlands, Appalachian Plateau & Allegheny Plateau)
Appalachian Zone

Adirondacks in the 1870s, and his first publication as a nature writer was "Summer Birds of the Adirondacks in Franklin County, N.Y."

The cry to save the Adirondacks from development culminated in the historic 1885 declaration of the Adirondack Forest Preserve by the New York state legislature. The law stipulated that the lands now or hereafter constituting the forest preserve shall be forever kept as wild forest lands. In 1892, the Adirondack State Park was created, encompassing the forest preserve lands and private lands. The forest preserve is now 2.5 million acres, owned by the state, within the 6-million-acre Adirondack State Park. It is the largest park in the nation outside Alaska.

APPALACHIANS

The Complex Geology of New England

The Appalachian Mountains, stretching from Alabama north to Newfoundland and crossing through New England's north woods, are North America's crumpled front fender. The ridges, ranges, peaks, and plateaus that make up the broken Appalachian chain testify to the barely imaginable collision of two ancient continents beginning 505 million years ago and lasting 225 million years, ending just before the dinosaur age. The geological zone called the Appalachian Province includes New England and refers to a broader area than just the famed mountains, but the underlying rock structures are related.

According to the widely accepted theory of plate tectonics, Earth's continents have repeatedly conjoined and split apart over the aeons, like rafts coming together on an ocean and then drifting apart. The Appalachian Orogeny is one such episode in the ongoing rearrangement of our planet's real estate. Geologists may differ on some details, but they have a good picture of what happened during this period, because the evidence is fresher compared to much older physiographic provinces, such as the Canadian Shield. There, billions of years of erosion and other natural forces have blurred the facts.

The Appalachian story is a three-act play, with a prologue and an epilogue. The prologue picks up after the end of an earlier mountain-building period, called the

FACIES: A geological term referring to the characteristics of a particular rock type, including composition and origin. From the Latin, meaning "form" or "face."

APPALACHIAN COAL FIELDS: Huge swamps packed with plant life were a feature of the ancient supercontinent Pangaea. As plants died, the organic matter accumulated underwater, arresting decomposition. Later, inorganic sediments in the water covered the compacted plant matter, building up until the plant layer was compacted to become coal.

FIRST COMMERCIAL COAL MINE IN UNITED STATES: Near Richmond, Virginia, opened in 1730

PERCENTAGE OF U.S. COAL MINED IN APPALACHIAN REGION: About 40%

BIGGEST COAL-MINING STATE TODAY: Wyoming

PERCENTAGE OF MINED U.S. COAL USED FOR GENERATING ELECTRICITY: About 90%

PANGAEA: From the Greek for "all land"

ACADIA NATIONAL PARK: The complex geology of the famed park on the northeastern Maine coast testifies to the colossal tectonic forces that shaped the Appalachian region. Sedimentary, igneous, and metamorphic rock all lie within the park, which has also been shaped by glaciers.

Formation of the Appalachians

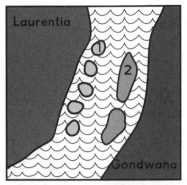

Ancient supercontinent splits into two
continents with volcanic island chain (1)
and Avalonia subcontinent (2) in new
ocean. About 800 million years ago.

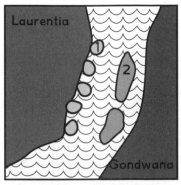

Laurentia collides with island chain.
forming Taconic Mountains.
About 480 to 440 million years ago.

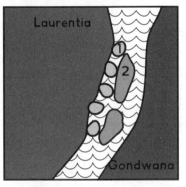

Laurentia next docks with Avalonia.
About 380 to 310 million years ago.

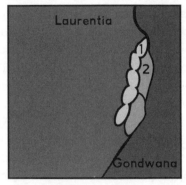

Docking complete. Appalachians and
new supercontinent of Pangaea formed.
About 300 to 250 million years ago.
Pangaea will later rift to form new
ocean. the Atlantic.

Grenville Orogeny, during which the rocks of the Adirondacks were formed. At this time, about one billion years ago, geologists theorize Earth had one giant supercontinent. About 800 million years ago, this supercontinent began to rift, or break apart, creating two giant continents with a new ocean between them. (Other continents were formed elsewhere on the globe, with their own cycles of rifting and reattaching.) In this ocean, volcanoes formed new island chains and a subcontinent called Avalonia.

The first act begins with our two giant continents making moves to reunite. The new island chains collide with the continent on the west, named Laurentia, in an episode called the Taconic Orogeny, the first of three orogenies that together make up the Appalachian Orogeny. The Taconic Mountains of western Vermont and southeastern New York date from this time, about 480 to 440 million years ago.

In the second act, the subcontinent Avalonia follows the island chain and also crashes into Laurentia. This scene is called the Acadian Orogeny and dates from 380 to 310 million years ago. The majority of bedrock in New England derives from this period, including the Manhattan Schist in Central Park, most of Massachusetts and Maine, and all of New Hampshire and eastern Vermont. Most of New Brunswick, Nova Scotia, and Newfoundland and all of Prince Edward Island also fall in the Acadian zone.

With the islands and Avalonia now part of Laurentia, there is only one collision remaining. The eastern continent, called Gondwana, slams into Laurentia in the third act. The dividing ocean disappears and dry land is again conglomerated into one supercontinent, now named Pangaea. This final collision, or the Alleghenian Orogeny of about 300 to 250 million years ago, has a greater effect in the Appalachian Province south of New England than it does in the north.

The epilogue hints at the sequel. Pangaea breaks up and another new ocean, the Atlantic, emerges. Sections of old Avalonia remain in what is now North America, along parts of Nova Scotia and Newfoundland, the northeastern coast of Maine, eastern Massachusetts (including Cape Cod), Rhode Island, and eastern Connecticut. Other bits of Avalonia are torn off and can be found in north Africa, Europe, England, and Ireland. The mid-Atlantic rift continues to enlarge the ocean to this day, while the Pacific is shrinking. Presumably, perhaps in a hundred million years or so, the continents will again

CATSKILL MOUNTAINS: Geologically part of North America's stable interior, the sedimentary rock of the Catskills was uplifted during the Acadian Orogeny and subsequently eroded to form the current landscape of hills, scarps, and valleys. Catskill comes from the Dutch *kaaterskill,* meaning "wildcat creek."

GRANITE STATE: New Hampshire's official nickname. Large granitic intrusions, including the southern portion of the White Mountains, appear to have formed when Pangaea broke up about 200 million years ago, inviting magma toward the surface in this part of what became New Hampshire. Older intrusions from earlier mountain-building episodes are also common. One such Devonian-era intrusion, approximately 400 million years old, forms the famous Barre quarries of northeastern Vermont, the largest granite quarries in the United States.

GREEN MOUNTAIN STATE: Vermont's official nickname. *Vermont* is French for "green mountain" (*monts verts.*) The Green Mountains date from the Taconic Orogeny, the first mountain-building period that began forming the modern Appalachian region, about 500 million years ago.

GREEN MOUNTAIN BOYS: Led by Ethan Allen, this armed group fought in 1770–71 against New York claims to lands then held by the colony of New Hampshire. The Green Mountain Boys later supported the colonies in the War of Independence against the British, helping

dock together to form one new supercontinent. Maybe our successors will be able to take Amtrak to Shanghai.

Appalachian rocks are three main types. The sedimentary rocks are the same as those that extend underneath the Great Plains, forming North America's stable interior. But, of course, the Appalachian rocks have been smashed by the continental crashes, leaving them folded, tilted, and cracked along faults. What's more, the collisions put the rocks under enormous pressure and brought some deeper into the crust's hot zone, heating and squeezing the constituent minerals to create newer metamorphic rocks. Mountain building and faulting also permits magma from the inner crust to seep upward into pockets and cracks. These intrusions may break the surface, forming lava-spewing volcanoes, or they may cool under the surface into hard granite, which is later exposed by erosion. Thus, Maine's Mount Katahdin, the northern terminus of the Appalachian Trail, is an exposed granite dome, while New Hampshire's Mount Washington, the highest peak in the Appalachians, is largely composed of metamorphosed sedimentary and volcanic rock.

While continental collisions formed the basic underlying geology of the Appalachian Province, the last ice age authored the current topography of the New England north woods. The glaciers gouged valleys and plowed rubble into vast moraines, and left behind glacial lakes, eskers, boulders, and till as they retreated about 11,000 years ago. A granite boulder found on a sedimentary bed, miles from any other granite, is further evidence of the ongoing geological drama.

Benedict Arnold (then on the side of the revolutionaries) to capture strategic Fort Ticonderoga in 1775. Vermont later became an independent republic but joined the Union in 1791 as the fourteenth state.

HIGHEST PEAK IN VERMONT: Mount Mansfield, 4,393 ft. (1,318 m)

HIGHEST PEAK IN NEW HAMPSHIRE: Mount Washington, 6,288 ft (1,886 m), the highest peak in the U.S. northeast, in the Presidential Range of the White Mountains

HIGHEST PEAK IN MAINE: Mount Katahdin (Baxter Peak), 5,268 ft (1,580 m)

FRANCONIA NOTCH: Glaciers gouged the famous notch through the granite of New Hampshire's White Mountains about 15,000 years ago, leaving behind lakes, gorges, and potholes.

OLD MAN OF THE MOUNTAINS: A ledge of granite 40 ft (12 m) high that takes the shape of a man's face when viewed from the right angle, on Profile Mountain in the Franconia Notch. The face has become the state symbol of New Hampshire.

LENGTH OF THE APPALACHIAN TRAIL: 2,160 mi (3,456 km)

SOUTHERN TERMINUS: Springer Mountain, Georgia

NORTHERN TERMINUS: Mount Katahdin, Maine

FOUNDER: Benton MacKaye, U.S. Labor Department functionary and trail visionary. Washington lawyer Myron Avery also played a major role in finishing the trail.

FORMALLY COMPLETED: 1937

ALSO SEE: Adirondacks; Eskers, Moraines, and Other Glacial Features

ESKERS, MORAINES, AND OTHER GLACIAL FEATURES

Landscaping on a Grand Scale

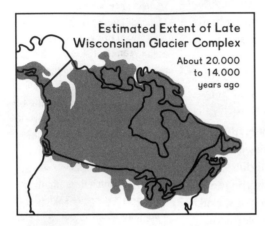

Estimated Extent of Late Wisconsinan Glacier Complex

About 20,000 to 14,000 years ago

W inters today can get pretty cold up north, but they're nothing compared to 14,000 years ago. At that time, the northern United States was frozen solid all year round. The land that would become the north woods sat under a gigantic ice sheet up to two miles thick.

But over the next four thousand years, the world warmed up, the ice receded, plant and animal life began to flourish, and humans moved into the area from the warmer south. The glaciers, as they melted, left behind vast lakes, millions of tons of rubble, and exposed bedrock that forms the modern north woods landscape.

The rubble, or glacial till, is composed of clay, sand, gravel, and boulders, and is found in several types of formations across the north woods and adjacent areas. Eskers are sinuous ridges typically a few miles long and 33 to 150 feet (10 to 45 meters) high.

CURRENT EXTENT OF GLACIAL COVERAGE OVER WORLD'S LAND SURFACE: 10%, mostly in Antarctica and Greenland

MAXIMUM EXTENT OF GLACIAL COVERAGE OVER ENTIRE PLANET AT HEIGHT OF ICE AGE: 30%

MAXIMUM EXTENT OF GLACIAL COVERAGE OVER THE CONTINENTAL UNITED STATES, INCLUDING ALASKA: 25%

MAXIMUM EXTENT OF GLACIAL COVERAGE OVER CANADA: 97%

RECENT ICE AGES: Began up to 2.5 million years ago. Four main glaciations are recorded, called (from oldest to most recent) the Nebraskan, Kansan, Illinoian, and Wisconsinan. Each glaciation lasted about 100,000 years, with warm periods in between. Many scientists believe we are currently experiencing an interglacial period.

WHAT CAUSES ICE AGES? The exact sequence of events is unknown, but Earth's 26,000-year wobble on its axis, volcanic activity, and other factors are believed to interact to cause ice ages. Volcanic ash spewed into the atmosphere can dramatically cool the planet in a relatively short period of time.

LAST REMNANT OF ICE AGE IN NORTH AMERICA: Barnes Ice Cap, Baffin Island, Canada, 3,720 sq mi (9,300 km²)

They are the deposits left by ancient glacial streams. These meltwater streams either ran along the tops of glaciers, in crevasses, or through tunnels in the middle or underneath the ice. The streams usually ran in the same direction the ice flowed.

Moraines are much larger formations, some hundreds of miles long and up to 825 feet (250 meters) high. A moraine contains massive amounts of till, released from a glacier as it melted, or bulldozed by the front or side walls of a glacier as it plowed forward. A terminal moraine marks the farthest advance of a glacier. Martha's Vineyard and Nantucket Islands are the exposed tops of a terminal moraine that stretches into the Atlantic and continues onto Long Island. Michigan's Lower Peninsula is crisscrossed by moraines that provide today's ski hills, and the Ice Age Trail in Wisconsin is a series of trails along the many terminal moraines in the state. The most recent ice sheet covering northern North America is called the Wisconsinan because of the superb examples of glacial till found in that state.

> *SPEED OF ADVANCING ICE FLOW:* Varies greatly, depending on climatic conditions and terrain. Mountain glaciers in cold climates may move as slowly as 3.2–13 ft (1–4 m) a year. Warmer climates speed up this rate to about 984 ft (300 m) a year. But some outlet glaciers may temporarily surge at rates up to 4.3 mi (7 km) a year.
>
> *BOUNCE:* Geologists estimate the Earth's crust in the north woods region was depressed by as much as 330 ft (100 m) by the crushing weight of the last ice age glaciers. The land has been rebounding since the glaciers peaked in size about 15,000 years ago.
>
> *ESKER:* From the Irish *eiscir,* meaning "ridge"
>
> *ALSO SEE:* Adirondacks, Appalachians, Michigan Basin, Lakes, Superior Uplands, Wetlands

Far from being pristine white or snowy, glaciers consist of dirty ice packed full of debris. The embedded debris causes glaciers to act like enormous sheets of sandpaper scraping the underlying rock. Evidence for this is seen in scratches across polished rock faces, or in smoothly gouged or furrowed rocks.

Other glacial features include drumlins, kames, kettles, and erratics. Drumlins are humpy hills sometimes called whalebacks and they tend to occur in groups. The steeper side of a drumlin faces the direction from which the glacier advanced, while the gentler slope points in the direction of the advance. Cone-shaped kames mark the bases of old waterfalls. They are made of debris carried over the edge of a glacier, or a crevasse in the ice, by a meltwater stream. Kettles are small, round depressions usually occupied by a lake or bog. They are formed when a block of ice is trapped underneath till and later melts. Erratics are boulders moved far from their place of origin by the Herculean forces of the ice sheet, carried as far as 600 miles (1,000 kilometers), though usually no more than 60 miles (100 kilometers), and randomly deposited as the ice melted. Sometimes erratics assume bizarre perches atop smaller rocks.

HUMUS AND SOIL

The Skin of the Earth

People of almost every culture, from native North Americans to ancient Egyptians and Chinese, conceived of the earth, the soil, as the primal womb of life, Mother Earth. Their observation of the endless cycles of decay and regeneration probably inspired early beliefs in reincarnation. The more that soil is understood in modern times, the more the original concept of it as a living layer, the water-moistened skin of the planet, seems to ring true.

Growing and thickening with the weathering of rock and with each year's dead vegetation in the humus layer, soil reclaims and recycles the materials of life via a vast network of roots and fungal threads that run through it. Soil teems with unimaginable quantities of living things. Echoing the ageless attachment people and nations have had to their soil, one forester astutely described it as the most fundamental form of wealth.

Atop the soil proper lies humus. Virtually every living thing eventually ends up in the organic humus layer—the return of dust to dust. Plant-eating animals capture and pass on through the food chain only a small fraction of the ecosystem's energy and nutrients. But underfoot, on the forest floor, lies a seething mass of fungi, bacteria, insects, and other agents of decomposition that dine on 90 percent of all plant matter. Humus also acts like a giant sponge, absorbing up to five times its weight in

NUMBER OF ROUNDWORMS PER CUBIC YARD (METER) OF SOIL: Up to 20 million

POSSIBLE ORGANISMS FOUND IN 1 CUBIC YARD (METER) OF SOIL: More than 1,000 species, including tens of millions of springtails, mites, protozoa, roundworms, and bacteria, with most living in the top inch (2.5 cm). Earthworms, ants, and other insects also aid plants and the soil by burrowing channels for air, water, and nutrients, as well as by acting as a check on fungi and other organisms harmful to plants.

DECOMPOSER ORGANISMS IN SOIL: Fungi, bacteria, springtails, earthworms, snails, slugs, potworms, roundworms, mites, fly larvae, beetles and their larvae, millipedes, protozoa

PODZOL: Acidic soil with low nutrients. From the Russian word for "wood ashes," used to describe gray podzol.

POSSIBLE HAZARDS TO THE SOIL OF CLEAR-CUTTING FORESTS: Soil compaction by large tree-cutting vehicles and bulldozers, erosion, flooding or drying out, loss of nutrients from removal or vaporizing of slash in too-intensive burnings, loss of beneficial fungi

AMOUNT OF LEAVES AND BRANCHES THAT FALLS ON THE FLOORS OF HARDWOOD FORESTS ANNUALLY: 1.1–2.2 tons/acre (2.5–5 metric tons/ha)

water, allowing rain and meltwater to percolate into the soil for plant use, rather than run off quickly and cause erosion.

Minuscule springtails, mites, and insects are the shock troops of decomposition. They chew holes into leaves, conifer needles, and other dead plant parts falling on the forest litter. By breaking through the waxy outer layers, the tiny animals drain a plant's defensive chemicals and start the breakdown of tough cellulose and lignin structures. Bacteria and fungal threads can then invade and feed on the plant's tender innards, capturing 80 to 90 percent of the energy in dead plant matter. Hordes of bacteria and other microorganisms cover dead leaves and turn them black and slimy by the time they reach the bottom of the litter layer. Deeper still, decaying vegetation falls apart into small bits of moist humus.

Dead twigs, branches, and tree trunks also eventually contribute to the humus layer, though more slowly. Bark- and wood-boring beetles, mites, and other animals eat

PORTION OF CARBON RETURNED TO THE ATMOSPHERE ANNUALLY THAT IS EXPIRED BY DECOMPOSER ORGANISMS: 80%
RATIO OF CARBON TO NITROGEN IN SUGAR MAPLE LEAVES: 20 to 1
RATIO OF CARBON TO NITROGEN IN PINE NEEDLES: 66 to 1
RATIO OF CARBON TO NITROGEN IN ANIMAL FLESH: Between 3 and 5 to 1
TIME IT TAKES SUGAR MAPLE AND ALDER LEAVES TO DECOMPOSE: 1–1.5 years
TIME IT TAKES PINE NEEDLES TO DECOMPOSE: 3–9 years
TIME IT TAKES AN ANIMAL CARCASS TO DECOMPOSE: A few weeks
LIGNIN (THE HARDEST MATERIAL IN WOOD TO BREAK DOWN) CONTENT OF VEGETATION: 10–30%
LIGNIN CONTENT OF HUMUS: 30–60%
ALSO SEE: Spiders, Fungi, Lichens, Thunder and Lightning, Appalachians, Adirondacks, Superior Uplands

tunnels into the wood, allowing other insects, fungal strands, and the roots of living plants to follow. The wood is processed and fertilized by the droppings and bodies of the animals eating into it. There is so much activity by decomposers that a dead tree contains more living cells than a living one. As it rots, it also soaks up water, acting as a reservoir for roots and soil animals. A fallen giant pine or hemlock can take hundreds of years to decay, ultimately influencing its surroundings far longer than the duration of its life.

Chemical compounds from the humus layer leach into and mix with the mineral soil, eventually to be reabsorbed and incorporated into new life by tree and plant roots. Soil contains sixteen basic chemical elements needed for life. The proportions of those elements occurring in the soil, together with precipitation, dictate the types of life in each ecosystem. Calcium, potassium, sodium, phosphorus, iron, and magnesium, among the most important, react with water at varying temperatures to give soil its color. Most Canadian Shield topsoils are red, from the leaching of iron and aluminum oxides from decomposing vegetation in the humus layer above. Shield subsoils are naturally gray.

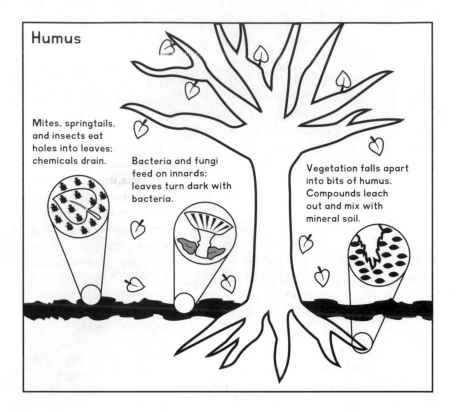

Humus

Mites. springtails. and insects eat holes into leaves; chemicals drain.

Bacteria and fungi feed on innards; leaves turn dark with bacteria.

Vegetation falls apart into bits of humus. Compounds leach out and mix with mineral soil.

The shield's predominantly podzolic soils, found in the Superior Uplands and the Adirondacks, are high in potassium, aluminum, and iron, derived from granite and similar bedrock. But they are low in the calcium and magnesium common to the deeper, limestone-based soils of the Michigan Basin or the Appalachians. Because silicates, the primary material of granite and quartz, are acidic materials, granitic soils are not very fertile.

Sand grains are the largest particles in soil, followed by microscopic bits of clay and silt. Fertile loam soils contain a mixture of all three, which make up about half the volume of richer soils, such as those found on the Great Plains. About a quarter of the space is filled with films of water around the particles, and another quarter is larger air-filled spaces, providing oxygen for roots and soil animals. Trees and plants themselves send 50 to 80 percent of their energy into their roots, which, along with fungal fibers, break up rocks and hold the soil down. Some kinds of fungi and microbes also produce extracellular polysaccharids, which glue soil particles into clumps that are not dissolved by water.

LAKES

A Fragile Habitat

Across the face of the north woods, deep, rugged depressions in the Earth's bedrock crust have been filled with cool, fresh, clear, dark water. Rock and water, together with climate, determine the nature of all life in the ecosystem. Even humans, consisting of about 70 percent water, become part of whatever lake they drink.

More than 600 lakes and streams in the Adirondacks are unable to support aquatic life because of acid rain

Most of the lakes puddling the north woods were formed by huge blocks of glacial ice that as they melted filled up the pockmarks and gouges in the eroded surface. Because there are so many lakes, especially in headwater areas such as the Adirondacks and northern Minnesota and Wisconsin, many have small drainage basins around them, with short, fast-running streams. The abundance of lakes and connecting rivers has long provided ideal transportation routes, with relatively short portages, for the first peoples of the north woods, and the European explorers, trappers, and modern canoe campers who followed.

APPROXIMATE NUMBER OF LAKES IN THE NORTH WOODS STATES: Minnesota, the land of 10,000 lakes, actually has 15,291 greater than 10 acres (4 ha); Wisconsin, 15,057 (6,040 named); Michigan, 11,000; New York, 7,500 lakes and ponds; Vermont, 825 lakes and ponds; New Hampshire, 800 lakes and ponds; Maine, 2,500.

APPROXIMATE NUMBER OF LAKES IN THE PROVINCE OF ONTARIO: 250,000

AVERAGE TIME TAKEN BY WATER FLOWING INTO UPPER LAKE SUPERIOR TO REACH THE ST. LAWRENCE RIVER: 329 years

TIME IT TAKES FOR LAKE SUPERIOR TO TURN OVER (REPLACE ITS ENTIRE VOLUME): 191 years

NUMBER OF OTHER GREAT LAKES THAT COULD FIT INTO LAKE SUPERIOR, BY VOLUME OF WATER: All 4

MAXIMUM DEPTH OF LAKE SUPERIOR: 1,323 ft (410 m)

DEPTH OF LAKE SUPERIOR'S DEEPEST POINT COMPARED TO SEA LEVEL: Actually 700 ft (215 m) below sea level

MAXIMUM DEPTH OF LAKE HURON: 750 ft (229 m)

MAXIMUM DEPTH OF LAKE MICHIGAN: 923 ft (282 m)

MAXIMUM DEPTH OF LAKE ERIE: 211 ft (65 m)

MAXIMUM DEPTH OF LAKE ONTARIO: 778 ft (237 m)

With their often-small watersheds of thin soil and hard, acidic rock, most lakes on the Canadian Shield areas of the north woods do not receive nearly as many nutrients as those farther south. Much of the plant debris that does wash into them sinks to the cold, deep bottom, where bacterial decay is very slow and circulation is limited to spring and fall, locking up their nutrients for much of the year. Low nutrient levels curtail algae growth, the base of the aquatic food chain.

Circulation within lakes is limited because cold water is heavier than warm water. During the summer, a warm layer, ten to twenty feet (three to six meters) deep, floats on top of a much colder transition zone of several feet. After that, all the way to the bottom, the lake is about 41 to 43°F (5 to 6°C) all summer and never mixes with the top layer. In autumn, however, the upper layer cools until it reaches the same temperature as the lower, cold zone, eliminating the barrier and allowing water, oxygen, and nutrients to circulate through the entire lake body. Though vital to the health of the aqueous system, the fall

LARGEST FRESHWATER LAKE (BY SURFACE AREA) IN THE WORLD: Lake Superior

pH (POTENTIAL HYDROGEN) OF DISTILLED WATER: 7

pH OF RAIN UNAFFECTED BY POLLUTION: 5.6

TYPICAL pH OF RAIN FALLING ON THE NORTH WOODS: 4.4–5.0

NATURAL pH OF A CANADIAN SHIELD LAKE: 6.2–6.5

pH OF HIGHLY ACIDIC LAKES (30–40% ABOVE NORMAL): 4.7

pH OF LEMON JUICE: 2

PEOPLE WHO STUDY LAKES, PONDS, AND STREAMS: Limnologists

ALSO SEE: Brook Trout, Adirondacks, Michigan Basin, Humus and Soil, Superior Uplands

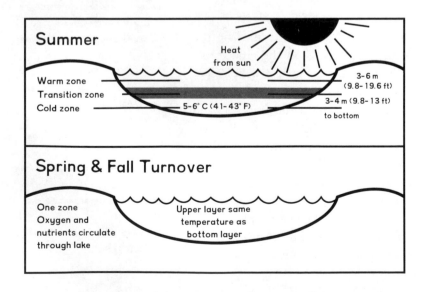

Summer

Heat from sun

Warm zone
Transition zone
Cold zone — 5-6° C (41-43° F)

3-6 m (9.8-19.6 ft)

3-4 m (9.8-13 ft) to bottom

Spring & Fall Turnover

One zone
Oxygen and nutrients circulate through lake

Upper layer same temperature as bottom layer

turnover, as well as that of early spring, can be a dangerous time to canoe, since the free flow of water allows winds to stir the whole lake, not just the top fifteen feet (five meters), creating much bigger waves.

Ice in winter cuts the entire lake off from its oxygen supply, which is captured from the air by wave action. With spring breakup, the whole reservoir again circulates until the upper layer warms and reestablishes the temperature barrier, first in the shallows, then radiating to the center of the lake.

Unfortunately, with the oxygen and nutrients that come in the spring, lakes can also receive an acid shock from the runoff of melting snow. Precipitation is naturally more acidic than lake or ground water because it reacts with nitrogen in the air. Rain or snow contaminated with sulfur dioxide and nitrogen oxides from industrial emissions is 4 to 400 times more acidic than normal precipitation. Lakes in north woods regions with granite-based soils and coniferous forests are especially vulnerable because they are already more acidic than southern lakes, and they have few nutrients to neutralize acid rain. Lakes in New York, Vermont, New Hampshire, and Maine have another disadvantage, compared to lakes in the Superior Uplands: They are downwind of major industrial areas. More than 600 lakes and streams in the Adirondacks are unable to support aquatic life because of acid rain.

Massive acid loading in spring runoff can push many organisms over the edge, especially those near the base of the aquatic food chain such as freshwater shrimp and stone fly larvae. It can also strike early-spawning fish, including pike, pickerel, minnows, and white suckers, that congregate near inlets, where the acid infusion is greatest. In highly acidic conditions, some die in twenty-four to thirty-six hours. The eggs of fish and amphibians, especially spring peepers and salamanders, can also be severely affected. Compounding the damage, acidic runoff may leach natural toxic metals such as mercury, zinc, and aluminum out of the soil.

MICHIGAN BASIN

Once Upon a Time, a Tropical Sea

The pine forests and clear waters of northern Michigan, where a young Ernest Hemingway learned to fish and hunt, belong to a geological region called the Michigan Basin. About 600 million years ago, the basin was the broad bay of a shallow, warm, tropical saltwater sea lapping at the southern shores of the ancient continent of Laurentia, today's Canadian Shield. There was no life on dry land. The first multicellular marine organisms were just beginning to appear. It was the start of the Paleozoic era, when life blossomed on Earth after four billion years of Precambrian preamble.

Over the next 300 million years, layers of sand, mud, algae, coral, and primitive marine life-forms accumulated in the Michigan Basin, up to 7.2 miles (12,000 meters) thick at its center, which is in the middle of lower Michigan near present-day Six Lakes. Each layer became a distinct bed of sedimentary rock. Gradually, as the sediments collected, the center of the basin began to sink, creating a saucer shape. Then, over the next 200 million years, deep-Earth forces pushed the entire basin upward out of the water, like a raised bowl, until the rim finally broke free of the surrounding land.

Erosion, nature's belt-sander, flattened the upward-folded edges of the bowl, so that the oldest sedimentary layers are closest to the surface at the outer edge of the basin. Geological maps show roughly concentric

SALTY: The Michigan Basin is home to about 20% of the nation's salt supply. Because the ancient Niagara Escarpment and other reef formations acted like a barrier around the basin, preventing natural drainage, much of the salt water evaporated, leaving formations of salt and gypsum as sedimentary layers. Salt rock is called halite.

PETOSKEY STONES: Fossilized remnants of the basin's ancient coral reefs can be found on northern Michigan beaches as Petoskey stones. Coral, an animal that feeds on plankton in tropical waters, manifests in the stones as striking hexagonal patterns, sometimes with a dark spot marking the coral's tentacles. Some stones have been polished by wave action; others found inland are rougher. Named after the city of Petoskey near Little Traverse Bay, where the stones can be found, the Petoskey stone has been adopted as Michigan's state stone.

PALEOZOIC: The geological era following the Precambrian, dating from 600 million to about 250 million years ago. From the Greek *palios*, meaning "old" or "ancient," and *zoe*, for "life." Followed by the Mesozoic era, the age of the dinosaurs.

rings of rock becoming progressively younger toward the center of the basin.

Most of the sedimentary layers are relatively soft limestones, shales, and sandstones. But one layer is harder Silurian dolomite, about 425 million years old. Dolomite (also called dolostone) is a type of magnesium-enriched limestone formed from the basin's ancient coral reefs. The belt-sander had a tougher go with this rock, which now tops the striking 1,400-mile- (2,240-kilometer) long Niagara Escarpment. The escarpment's horseshoe shape stretches from Door County Peninsula in Wisconsin, north to the Garden Peninsula in Michigan's Upper Peninsula, through Drummond Island and Ontario's Manitoulin Island, down Ontario's Bruce Peninsula, cutting through southwestern Ontario and onward to near Rochester, New York. Newlyweds and foreign tourists are drawn to the escarpment's star attraction, Niagara Falls, at the point where the Niagara River leaps over the edge toward the Maid of the Mist.

Although dolomite resists erosion better than other sedimentary rock, the Niagara Escarpment is not unaffected by erosion. In fact, the escarpment is retreating toward the basin's center as softer shales and sandstones underlying the dolomite erode and the heavy caprock collapses after losing its support. This movement can be seen clearly at Niagara Falls and other sites on the escarpment, where huge piles of fallen rock called talus lie at the foot of the cliff. Since the retreat of the last glaciers 10,000 years ago, when the Niagara River was formed, the falls have actually moved upstream almost seven miles (11 kilometers) from near Lewiston, New York, to their current location. This

MICHIGAN: Algonquian for "large" (*michi*) and "lake" (*gami*)

NIAGARA: Meaning "thunder of water," a word of the Iroquoian Neutral natives who lived in the area. Some scholars say *Niagara* is the last remaining word of the Neutral dialect.

HEIGHT OF THE NIAGARA ESCARPMENT: The Horseshoe Falls at Niagara Falls drop 167 ft (50 m), but some points on the Niagara Escarpment are as high as 1,000 ft (300 m) above the level of Lake Huron.

GEOLOGICAL BEAUTIFICATION PROJECT: U.S. engineers stopped the flow of water over the American Falls in 1969 to study the possibility of removing eroded rocks from the bottom of the cliff, to tidy up the falls' appearance for the benefit of Niagara tourists. The scheme was abandoned because of the massive cost.

HEMINGWAY'S STOMPING GROUNDS: Many of Hemingway's Nick Adams short stories were based in northern Michigan. The author spent summers with his family there until 1917. *The Big Two-Hearted River* is a famous fishing story. It's also a meditation on the First World War. It was set in the Paleozoic geology of the Upper Peninsula. "Up in Michigan" is decidedly not a fishing story. But it is set in the hamlet of Horton Bay on Lake Charlevoix. The Hemingway family cottage on nearby Walloon Lake is a National Historic Site. The Michigan Hemingway Society meets every October in Petoskey.

action left behind the Niagara Gorge. With the falls retreating about three feet (one meter) per year, tourist operators will have to relocate to Buffalo in 28,000 years, when the thundering waters will reach the mouth of Lake Erie.

Hiking trails follow the top of the escarpment at many locations, and it's easy to imagine—to sometimes actually see—the shape of the Michigan Basin. On one side of the escarpment is the precipice, but on the other, the land slopes gently toward central Michigan, the center of the bowl, about 240 miles (380 kilometers) away.

Except for the escarpment and shoreline outcrops, the ancient Paleozoic rocks of the Michigan Basin are actually hidden. Glaciers of the last ice age advancing from Canada bulldozed unimaginable tons of till and rubble over the entire Michigan Basin. The uplands of the Lower Peninsula are on moraines, long ridges of till formed at the

> **PICTURED ROCKS NATIONAL LAKESHORE:** On the southern shore of Lake Superior along the Upper Peninsula, the 600-million-year-old Cambrian sandstone has been eroded by waves and ice, creating cliffs, caves, and columns.
>
> **SLEEPING BEAR DUNES NATIONAL LAKESHORE:** The spectacular dunes of this park west of Traverse City were deposited about 4,000 years ago by ancient Lake Nipissing, one of many precursors of today's modern Great Lakes. The highest dunes rise 460 ft (139 m) above Lake Michigan, although they are not solid sand; the dunes lie on glacial till.
>
> **ALSO SEE:** Superior Uplands; Eskers, Moraines, and other Glacial Features; Jack Pine

leading edge of a glacier. The ski runs of Michigan's resorts lie on the slopes of hills formed 22,000 to 9,500 years ago, as the last glaciers advanced and retreated from the region. The sandy soils support Hemingway's beloved jack and white pine forests.

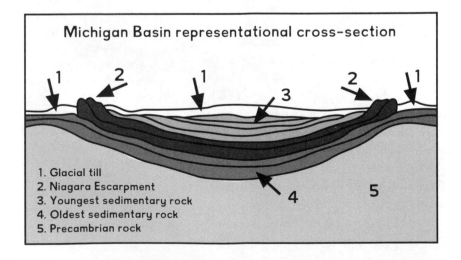

Michigan Basin representational cross-section

1. Glacial till
2. Niagara Escarpment
3. Youngest sedimentary rock
4. Oldest sedimentary rock
5. Precambrian rock

SUPERIOR UPLANDS

The Old Wilderness of the Midwest

The north woods of the New England states sit atop bedrock that is millions of years old. But in the Superior Uplands of Minnesota, Wisconsin, and northern Michigan, the north woods blanket the ancient Canadian Shield, where exposed rock can be billions of years old. Sigurd Olson, the famed conservationist and writer largely responsible for establishing the Boundary Waters Canoe Area Wilderness in northeastern Minnesota, called this beloved region the old wilderness. He and others who have felt a deep attachment to this land of lakes, rivers, bogs, and pungent northern woods often describe it as sacred, and sheer age has something to do with it.

The Canadian Shield is the foundation of the North American continent. It covers a vast area of Canada, from the Arctic tundra of the Northwest Territories, south around Hudson Bay, to almost all of Quebec and Labrador. In the United States, it extends into northern Minnesota, Wisconsin, and Michigan's Upper Peninsula, with another lobe forming the Adirondack Mountains in New York.

Though the shield is a distinct zone, it is by no means homogeneous. Since its creation four billion years ago—when Earth had no life, no atmosphere, no e-mail—the shield has been crumpled, torn, submerged, uplifted, eroded, heated, cooled, poked through with volcanoes, pierced underground by superhot magma, and gouged by glaciers, over and over again, and not

CANADIAN SHIELD ALIAS: Precambrian Shield, Laurentian Shield, Laurentian Highlands, Laurentian Plateau, Laurentia

TOTAL AREA OF CANADIAN SHIELD: 1.86 million sq mi (4.8 million km²)

TOTAL AREA OF SHIELD IN UNITED STATES: 90,000 sq mi (78,000 in the Superior Uplands, 12,000 in the Adirondacks)

AGE OF OLDEST SHIELD ROCKS: 3.96 billion years, Acasta gneiss from Northwest Territories, Canada. The oldest shield rocks in the United States are found near Ely, Minnesota, the jump-off town for the Boundary Waters Canoe Area Wilderness. The so-called Ely Formation is about 3 billion years old, and includes outcrops in the town. These rocks are metamorphosed basaltic lava from ancient volcanoes and are called greenstone because of their color, a by-product of metamorphism.

AGE OF EARTH: 4.6 billion years

SHIELD: Austrian geologist Eduard Suess first used the word *shield* in 1892 to describe the bedrock that seemed to form the foundation of each continent. The shields of other continents are mostly buried under younger rock.

PRECAMBRIAN: Cambria was the Roman word for Wales. Sedimentary rock from the area, about 600 million years old, seemed to

necessarily in that order. Originally composed of igneous rock, the relentless forces of a kinetic planet have often altered that rock, so metamorphic and sedimentary rocks are part of the shield, too. Yet shield rock remains a testament to the early life of the planet and is so old, in fact, that a chunk of shield granite around a north woods campfire may be older than many of the stars in the seemingly ageless night sky.

Two shield subregions, called provinces, are found in the Superior Uplands. The Superior Province stretches into north-central Minnesota, including Voyageur National Park, Chippewa National Forest, and parts of Superior National Forest. The Superior Province generally contains the oldest shield rocks, between 2.5 and 3.9 billion years old. (By comparison, astronomers reckon the Big Dipper stars are mere infants at only 200 million years old or so.) The Southern Province, younger than the Superior Province, includes the North Shore of Lake Superior, northern Wisconsin, and the western half of Michigan's Upper Peninsula. Another shield province, the Grenville, includes the Adirondacks.

contain the oldest-known fossils. Older rock didn't appear to have fossils and thus was called Precambrian. Precambrian fossils were found later.

VALUABLE METALS FOUND ON SHIELD: Gold, silver, nickel, zinc, uranium, copper, iron, platinum, selenium, cobalt, lead

IGNEOUS ROCK: Molten rock called magma, residing underneath the Earth's crust, forces its way to the surface along cracks and weak points. Some escapes to the surface as lava. Some, such as granite, hardens before it reaches the surface. Both are called igneous rock, from the Latin word for "fire," *ignis.*

SEDIMENTARY ROCK: Composed of particles of eroded rock, and chemicals from the skeletal remains of marine animals and the remains of plant matter; laid down at the bottom of seas in distinctive horizontal layers, which are often later folded by geological forces

METAMORPHIC ROCK: Originally igneous or sedimentary rock that has been altered by heat and

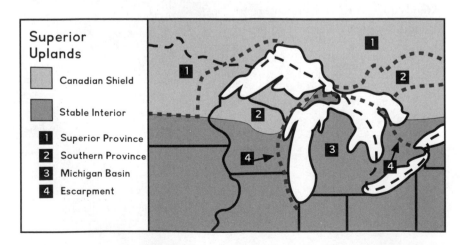

Superior Uplands

- Canadian Shield
- Stable Interior
- 1 Superior Province
- 2 Southern Province
- 3 Michigan Basin
- 4 Escarpment

About one billion years ago, the Superior Uplands witnessed an event that threatened to rip apart the proto–North American continent along a line from the middle of present-day Lake Superior to northern Kansas. Stark evidence of this midcontinent rift zone, as it is called today, can be seen along Highway 61 as it traces the North Shore of Lake Superior in Minnesota. As tectonic forces yanked this zone in opposite directions, the Earth's crust ruptured, allowing hot lava underneath to erupt and flow over the surface. Many Highway 61 rock cuts, and the waterfalls of rivers cascading into Lake Superior, show exposed basalt and rhyolite, the two main types of rock formed by hardened lava. Sometimes the lava can clearly be seen sitting atop older rock. This rifting episode was an early chapter in the history of what would become the Lake Superior Basin, formed when the unimaginable weight of the newly hardened lava and the loss of magma underneath caused the crust to sink.

The Canadian Shield is a miner's paradise, but two minerals in particular are associated with the Superior Uplands: iron and copper. The great Mesabi Iron Range of Minnesota, which at one time produced one-third of the world's iron ore and peaked in production during World War II, lies in the state's northeast; other iron ranges include the Vermilion and Cuyuna in Minnesota, Gogebic in Wisconsin, and Marquette and Menominee in Michigan. Iron comprises about 5 percent of all the elements in the Earth's crust, and it's believed to have entered ancient seas through volcanism or leaching. The iron precipitated out of the water and was laid

pressure. Gneiss, a metamorphic rock, comprises a large portion of the shield.

FIRST APPEARANCE OF HUMANS IN SHIELD COUNTRY: About 10,000 years ago, as the last glacier retreated

INVENTION OF BIRCH-BARK CANOE FOR TRAVERSING SHIELD LAKES: At least 7,000 years ago

ANCIENT SHIELD LIFE: Woolly mammoths, mastodons, and giant beavers weighing 440 lb (200 kg) once roamed shield country. They all died out by the end of the last ice age, about 10,000 years ago. Changing climate and, in the case of woolly mammoths, human predation sealed their fate.

ARROWHEAD COUNTRY: The northeastern region of Minnesota that sits on the shield, named for its triangular shape. It includes the million-acre Boundary Waters Canoe Area Wilderness, nestled against the Canadian border. Established after many conservation battles and given its official name in 1958, the BWCAW is the largest wilderness area in the United States outside Alaska, and the largest roadless area in the eastern United States.

IRON: Fourth-most-plentiful element in Earth's crust, after oxygen, silicon, and aluminum. Found in many ores, including goethite (named after German writer Goethe, who had an interest in minerals) and hematite (from the Greek *haimatites*, or "bloodlike," describing its red color). A low-grade ore, taconite, is still mined in Minnesota; its name derives from the Taconic mountain-building period

down in sedimentary rock in various types of iron ore. Geological processes brought the ore toward the surface, where it was mined in underground mines or, later, huge open-pit mines such as the Hull-Rust-Mahoning Mine near Hibbing, Minnesota, the largest open-pit iron ore mine in the world.

The famous copper deposits of Michigan's Keweenaw Peninsula formed during the great rifting episode 1.1 billion years ago. When the lava cooled on the surface, gaseous bubbles were often trapped in the rock. Over time, the gas escaped. Minerals such as copper, dissolved in groundwater and steam, leached into the bubbles as well as cracks in the rock. When the water evaporated, copper and other minerals remained. These copper deposits have been worked since about 5000 B.C., first by the Copper Indians and most recently by modern industry in the nineteenth and twentieth centuries.

Since the rifting episode, the Canadian Shield has been reasonably stable. Ancient seas invaded and retreated over parts of the shield; sedimentary rock was laid down atop the older Precambrian rock; erosion continued nonstop, and the dinosaur age

of about 500 million years ago, when the Taconic Mountains of New York and Vermont were formed.

IRON LEGEND: Iron was said to have been discovered in Minnesota's Mesabi Range when prospector Frank Hibbing, freezing in a tent in January, declared: "I believe there is iron under me. My bones feel rusty and chilly." He obtained the first lease to mine iron in the area in 1891; the city of Hibbing (hometown to Bob Dylan) is named after him.

SIZE OF HULL-RUST-MAHONING IRON MINE: 2,291 acres (916 ha), the world's biggest open-pit iron mine

SIZE OF NEW YORK'S CENTRAL PARK: 840 acres (336 ha)

EXTENT OF NATIVE COPPER TRADE: Copper traded by the Old Copper Culture Indians of Michigan (3000 to 1000 B.C.) has been found in Labrador, Florida, and Alabama

ALSO SEE: Paper Birch; Adirondacks; Eskers, Moraines, and Other Glacial Features; Falling Stars; Lakes; Painted Turtle; Planets and Comets

came and went. The most recent major geological act concluded only 11,000 years ago. Ice sheets up to two miles (3.2 kilometers) thick bulldozed away any softer sedimentary rock, exposing the shield in the contours we see today. When the glaciers retreated, they left behind the broken-up rock rubble found on many north woods trails. Where the glaciers didn't reach, such as in southern Michigan and the driftless area of Wisconsin, the shield remains hidden. It extends underneath most of North America, lying at the bottom of the Grand Canyon in Arizona. The Colorado River has cut through the sedimentary rock there just as the glaciers cut through to the Precambrian basement in the Superior Uplands.

WETLANDS

Mother Nature's Kidneys

The vapors and gases that sometimes rise from swamps and other still bodies of water were once believed to be the cause of many of the contagions that long plagued humanity. Even after the discovery of microbial pathogens in the past century, the popular bias against wetlands generally held sway. Only now are wetlands coming to be recognized by the public for the vital roles they play, including actually purifying water and providing hatcheries, food, and habitat for a vast array of species.

The wetlands of the north woods can be divided into four main categories: swamps, marshes, bogs, and fens.

Swamps, often located along the edges of rivers, are wetlands specifically featuring trees. Usually sitting on top of clay or other nonporous material, swamps are flooded or wet all year long, though standing water sometimes dries up in summer. Because swamps are undefined collecting basins, their water levels may fluctuate significantly. They slow down the flow of water, helping prevent flooding and erosion. During dry spells, they are reservoirs, their soaked soils keeping the water table close to the surface, while releasing water slowly into outflowing streams. The abundant dead trees in swamps are mined by woodpeckers, which in turn provide cavities for many songbirds. The relative inaccessibility of swamps also makes them favored locations for heron rookeries and wolf dens.

PORTION OF UNITED STATES COVERED BY WETLANDS: About 5%

PERCENTAGE OF ENDANGERED OR THREATENED ANIMAL SPECIES THAT DEPEND ON WETLAND HABITATS: About 50%

PERCENTAGE OF ENDANGERED OR THREATENED PLANT SPECIES THAT DEPEND ON WETLAND HABITATS: About 33%

ESTIMATED LOSS OF U.S. WETLANDS SINCE EUROPEAN SETTLEMENT: More than 50% of total surface area

MAIN USE FOR DRAINED WETLANDS: Agriculture

ONE OF THE WORLD'S LARGEST PEAT BOGS: Northern Minnesota's Red Lake bog, known as the Big Bog, 50 miles long by 12 miles wide (80 by 19 kilometers). Red Lake is a remnant of ancient Lake Agassiz, a huge lake left behind by melting glaciers. Its cousins include Lake of the Woods on the U.S.-Canada border and 250-mile- (400-kilometer) long Lake Winnipeg in Manitoba

NUMBER OF YEARS REQUIRED TO FORM 0.4 IN (1 CM) OF PEAT: 20

SURVIVAL STRATEGY FOR PLANTS IN NUTRIENT-POOR PEAT LANDS: Meat-eating sundew and pitcher plants trap unlucky insects looking for nectar in all the wrong places.

COMMON SWAMP VEGETATION: Red maple, white cedar, black ash, silver maple, white elm, speckled alder, black spruce, fir, dogwood,

In more open areas near the mouths of rivers, in shallow bays, and around ponds, marshes form. Marshes are the richest of all habitats, forming where silty, organic sediments collect in calm water. They teem with life. The still water, filled with insects, pollen, algae, and bits of organic matter, allows cattails and other water plants to sink roots and take advantage of the superconcentration of nutrients in the muck. Fast-growing marsh plants are far more efficient than most others at capturing nutrients and quickly turning them into living tissue. The rich plant life in turn supports high densities of insects, snails, fish, frogs, birds, and mammals.

With their absorbent plants, marshes effectively filter silt and other contaminants. They have been dubbed Mother Nature's kidneys. Creating marshes, which use less land than municipal water-treatment lagoons, has been suggested as the best means of cleaning up water pollutants, including sewage.

At the opposite end of the scale, bogs are the most nutrient-poor wetlands. With no drainage outlets, their water becomes stagnant. Many were formed 10,000 years ago by chunks of glacial ice that left depressions when they melted. Bogs maintain cold microhabitats because cold air settles in low pockets of land in summer. Dead vegetation tends to accumulate in bogs rather than decompose, because the cold, acidic, low-oxygen conditions are inhospitable to bacteria and most fungi. Sphagnum moss, which thrives in bogs, intensifies the condition by drawing atoms of calcium, magnesium, and other mineral nutrients from the water in exchange for hydrogen ions, making the bog even more acidic.

naked mitrewort, bitter cress, duckweed, enchanter's nightshade, raspberry, jewelweed, northern green orchid

SWAMP DWELLERS: Swamp sparrows, barred owls, great blue herons, turkey vultures, woodpeckers, wood ducks, hooded mergansers, Canada warblers, northern waterthrushes, deer, wolves, mink, pike, turtles, frogs

A SWAMP WITH MAINLY SHRUBS: Carr

MARSH VEGETATION: Cattails, water lilies, horsetail, water arum, water shield, wild iris, grasses, rushes, pickerelweed, sedges

MARSH DWELLERS: Red-winged blackbirds, swamp sparrows, marsh wrens, herons, bitterns, ducks, rails, osprey, muskrat, water snakes, snapping turtles, painted turtles, frogs, minnows, large-mouthed bass

BOG VEGETATION: Sphagnum moss, black spruce, tamarack, sundew, pitcher plants, orchids, Labrador tea, bog laurel, leatherleaf, crowberry, cranberry, bog rosemary

BOG DWELLERS: White-throated sparrows, Wilson's warblers, hawks, foxes, weasels, lynx, bobcats, red-backed voles, southern bog lemmings, pickerel frogs

FEN VEGETATION: Sedges, grasses, reeds, shrubs, tamarack, cedar

ALSO SEE: Black Ash, Beaver, Cattail, Black Spruce, Tamarack, Red Maple, Moss

Bog formation in a kettle lake

Retreating glacier leaves
an ice block covered by
glacial till.

Ice block melts, forming a kettle
lake with no natural outlet.

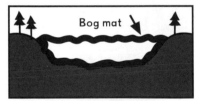

Over time, sedges, sphagnum
moss, and other plants form a
bog mat across the still water,
with peat accumulating on the
bottom and possibly filling the
entire kettle lake. Trees invade
from the edges.

*With their absorbent
plants, marshes have
been dubbed Mother
Nature's kidneys*

Compressed, unrotted vegetation piled up over the centuries in bogs, called peat, can be used as a long-burning fuel. The species succession of plant life after the retreat of the glaciers can be traced and dated from well-preserved pollen grains extracted from peat-bog layers. Intact prehistoric animals and 3,000-year-old human bodies have been unearthed from bogs in various parts of the world. Over millions of years, the peat will turn into coal.

Fens are somewhat like bogs, though they are not as acidic and are dominated by sedges—grasslike plants with unjointed, three-sided stems. Peat builds up at the bottom of fens, also.

Recommended Reading

Appetite whetted? We recommend the following books and magazines to further enhance your knowledge and enjoyment of the great north woods:

The Birds of North America Series (The American Ornithologists' Union) comprises detailed authoritative accounts on several hundred North American birds written by leading experts on each species.

The Boundary Waters Wilderness Ecosystem (University of Minnesota Press), by Miron Heinselman, is an in-depth and fascinating text on the role of wildfires, natural development, and wildlife inhabitants in one of America's premier forest regions.

A Field Guide to Geology: Eastern North America (Peterson Field Guides, Houghton Mifflin), by David C. Roberts, is a very good introductory guide to the region's geology, with geological histories and information about geological formations along many highway routes.

Guide to the Adirondack Trails (Adirondack Mountain Club) is an essential eight-volume set for hikers in the Adirondacks, with trail information as well as historical tidbits.

National Geographic Society Field Guide to the Birds of North America is often cited as the best of the bird field guides. A new edition, the fourth, was published in November 2002 with updated information such as new range maps.

A Natural History of Trees (Houghton Mifflin), by Donald Peattie, though written in 1950, is one of the most informative and beautifully written books about North American trees.

New England Wildlife (University Press of New England), by Richard DeGraaf and Mariko Yanasaki, takes in a comprehensive sweep of mammals, birds, amphibians, and reptiles, with illustrations, regional range maps, and information on habitat and abundance.

Nightwatch: A Practical Guide to Viewing the Universe (Firefly Books), by Terence Dickinson, is an excellent guide to observing the night sky, particularly from north woods latitudes. It contains everything from superb star maps to advice on how to take pictures of the heavens.

North Woods (Appalachian Mountain Club), by Peter Marchand, explains the many factors that shape the ecology and natural succession of the New England and Adirondack regions' mountain forests.

Northwoods Wildlife (Key Porter Books), by Janine Benyus, closely examines the characteristics of the varied habitats of the north woods and the birds, mammals, amphibians, and reptiles found in each.

Observer's Handbook, an annual publication of the Royal Astronomical Society of Canada, has become a North American reference favorite, with contributions from Canadian and American astronomers. It contains a huge amount of useful astronomical information, much of which is accessible to the average reader.

Peterson's Field Guide to Eastern Forests (Houghton Mifflin), by John Kricher, is an excellent text that explains the interrelationships among the many aspects of woodland habitats. The Peterson series also includes excellent field guides, with detailed color illustrations and range maps, for birds, wildflowers, trees, mammals, insects, reptiles, and amphibians.

Rock Picker's Guide to Lake Superior's North Shore (Kollath-Stensaas Publishing), by Mark Sparky Stensaas and Rick Kollath, is a slim but compelling and useful book about the geology and minerals of this popular area of the north woods.

Stokes Guide to Amphibians and Reptiles (Little, Brown), by Thomas Tyning, like the other books on birds, insects, and wildflowers in the Stokes series, offers fairly detailed accounts of most major north woods species, along with black-and-white illustrations and range maps.

Tracking and the Art of Seeing (HarperResource), by Paul Rezendes, is the guide that will help you identify the tracks you've seen in mud or snow, as well as inform you about other signs of animal life in the woods.

Trailside Botany (Pfeifer-Hamilton), by John Bates, is a handy guide with accounts and black-and-white illustrations of 101 north woods plants.

In addition to books, many magazines and journals focus on areas of the great north woods, including *Boundary Waters Journal* (for paddling Minnesota and Ontario); *Lake Superior Magazine; Wisconsin Trails; Adirondack Magazine; Adirondack Life; Vermont Life; Natural New England;* and *Down East* (Maine).

Index

Page numbers in *italics* refer to illustrations.